U.S. Fish & Wildlife Service

Guam National Wildlife Refuge

Comprehensive Conservation Plan

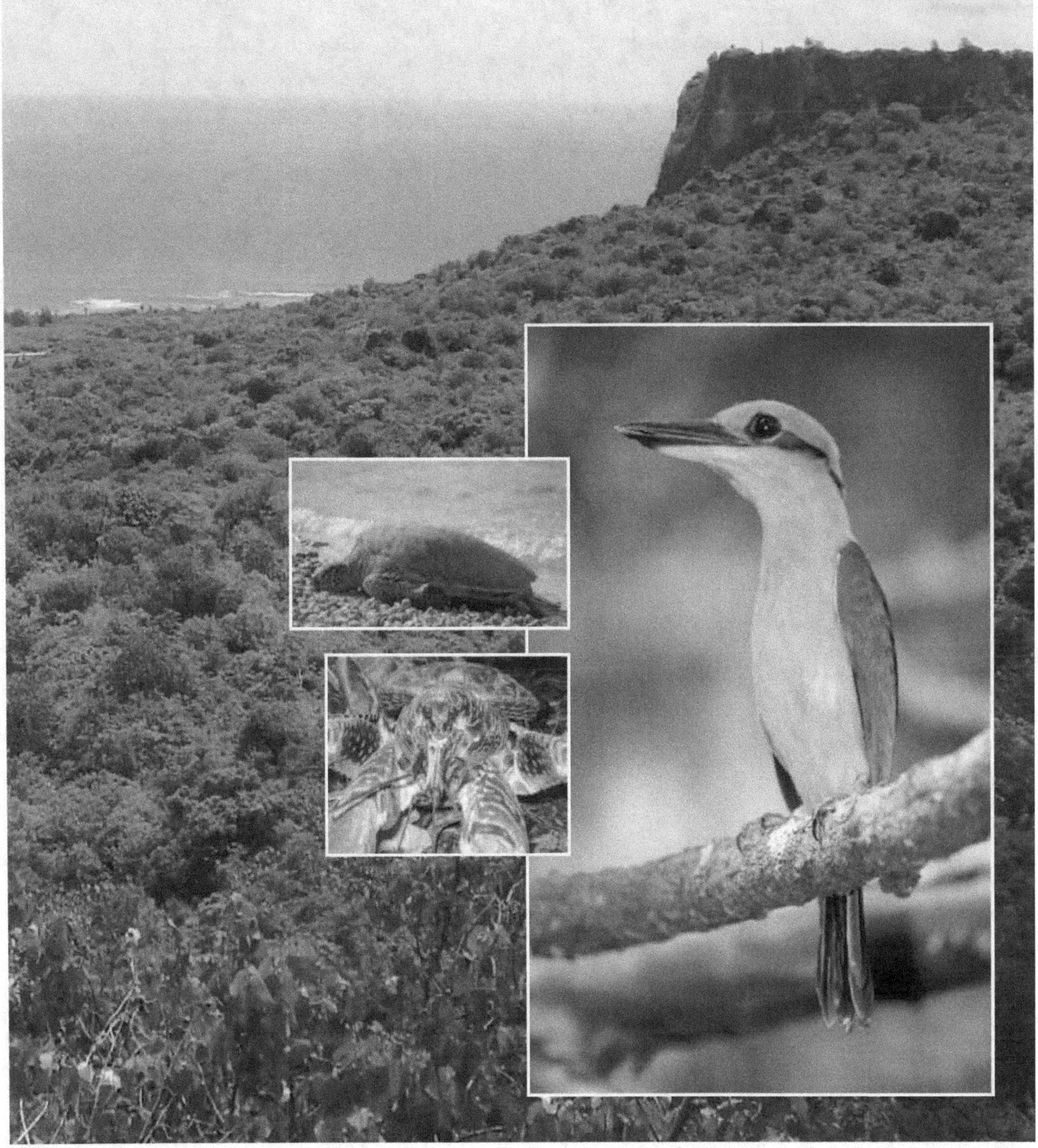

Guam National Wildlife Refuge
Vision Statement

Guam National Wildlife Refuge hosts a unique and fragile blend of native plants and animals found nowhere else in the world. It stands as a special place and source of pride for all. Here at Guam National Wildlife Refuge, the U.S. Fish and Wildlife Service works with others to conserve and restore the precious resources of both land and sea. Guam's native wildlife flourish in the native limestone and coastal forests and sea creatures are bountiful in the tropical blue waters. Visitors seek out the beauty and tranquility provided and enjoy seeing and learning about wildlife. The refuge is a vital link between Guam's cultural and natural heritage, a vibrant reminder of the place nature holds in all of our lives and a treasure for future generations.

CCPs provide long-term guidance for management decisions and set forth goals, objectives and strategies needed to accomplish refuge purposes and identify the Service's best estimate of future needs. These plans detail program planning levels that are sometimes substantially above current budget allocations and, as such, are primarily for Service strategic planning and program prioritization purposes. The plans do not constitute a commitment for staffing increases, operational and maintenance increases or funding for future land acquisition.

Photo: Hermit crab. ©Isaac Chellman

Guam National Wildlife Refuge
Comprehensive Conservation Plan

Prepared by:

Guam National Wildlife Refuge
Route 3A, Spur Road
Yigo, Guam 96929

and

U.S. Fish and Wildlife Service
300 Ala Moana Blvd., Room 5-231
Honolulu, Hawaii 96850

September 2009

Approved: _David J. Wesley_   _9/30/09_
Acting Regional Director, Region 1   Date
Portland, Oregon

U.S. Fish and Wildlife Service
Guam National Wildlife Refuge
Comprehensive Conservation Plan
Approval Submission

In accordance with the National Wildlife Refuge System Administration Act, as amended, the U.S. Fish and Wildlife Service completed a Comprehensive Conservation Plan (CCP) for Guam National Wildlife Refuge (Refuge). The purpose of this CCP is to specify a management direction for the Refuge for the next 15 years. The goals, objectives, and strategies for improving Refuge conditions—including the types of habitat we will provide, partnership opportunities, and management actions needed to achieve desired future conditions—are described in the CCP. The Service's preferred alternative for managing the Refuge is described in this CCP and the effects on the human environment were described in the Draft CCP and Environmental Assessment.

This CCP is submitted for the Regional Director's approval by:

_____   9/25/09
Joseph Schwegerl, Project Leader   Date
Guam National Wildlife Refuge

Concur: _____   9/25/09
Barry Stieglitz   Date
Hawaiian and Pacific Islands
National Wildlife Refuge Complex

Concur: _____   9/29/09
Carolyn Bohan   Date
Regional Chief, National Wildlife Refuge System

Finding of No Significant Impact
for the
Guam National Wildlife Refuge
Comprehensive Conservation Plan
Unincorporated U.S. Territory of Guam

The U.S. Fish and Wildlife Service (Service) has completed the Comprehensive Conservation Plan (CCP) and Environmental Assessment (EA) for Guam National Wildlife Refuge (Refuge), located on the Island of Guam, an unincorporated U.S. Territory. The CCP will guide management of the Refuge for the next 15 years. The CCP and EA describe the Service's proposals for managing the Refuge and their effects on the human environment under two alternatives, including the no action alternative.

Decision
- Following comprehensive review and analysis, the Service selected Alternative B for implementation because it is the alternative that best meets the following criteria:
- Achieves the mission of the National Wildlife Refuge System.
- Achieves the purposes of the Refuge.
- Will be able to achieve the vision and goals for the Refuge.
- Maintains and restores the ecological integrity of the habitats and populations on the Refuge.
- Addresses the important issues identified during the scoping process.
- Addresses the legal mandates of the Service and the Refuge.
- Is consistent with the scientific principles of sound wildlife management and endangered species recovery.
- Facilitates priority public uses compatible with the Refuge's purposes and the Refuge System mission.

Based upon comments received and additional consideration by Refuge staff, the preferred alternative as described in detail in the CCP and EA has been modified such that the Uranao right-of-way will remain in its existing location. Implementing this modified alternative will have no significant impacts on any of the environmental resources identified in the CCP and EA.

Public Review
The planning process incorporated a variety of public involvement techniques in developing and reviewing the CCP. This included two public open houses, planning updates, numerous meetings with partners, elected officials, and neighbors, and public review and comment on the planning documents. The details of the Service's public involvement program are described in the CCP.

Conclusions
Based on review and evaluation of the information contained in the supporting references, I have determined that implementing Alternative B as described in the Draft CCP/EA, including modifications listed above, for management of Guam National Wildlife Refuge is not a major Federal action that would significantly affect the quality of the human environment within the

This Finding of No Significant Impact and supporting references are on file at the Guam National Wildlife Refuge - USFWS, P.O. Box 8134, MOU-3, Dededo, Guam 96912 and U.S. Fish and Wildlife Service, Division of Planning and Visitor Services, 911 NE 11th Avenue, Portland, Oregon, 97232. These documents can also be found on the Internet at http://www.fws.gov/pacific/planning/main/docs/HI-PI/docsguam.htm. These documents are available for public inspection. Interested and affected parties are being notified of our decision.

Supporting References

U.S. Fish and Wildlife Service. 2009. *Guam National Wildlife Refuge Draft Comprehensive Conservation Plan and Environmental Assessment.*

U.S. Fish and Wildlife Service. 2009. *Guam National Wildlife Refuge Comprehensive Conservation Plan.*

_____
Acting Regional Director

_____
9/30/09
Date

Table of Contents

Appendices

Figures

Tables

Chapter 1. Introduction

1.1 Introduction

The unincorporated U.S. territory of Guahan (Guam) is the largest and southernmost island in the Mariana Archipelago, a chain of volcanic islands in Micronesia (GDAWR 2006a). It is located at latitude 13°28' N and longitude 144°45' E. Guahan Island is situated in the western Pacific Ocean, approximately 3,800 miles west of Honolulu, HI, and 1,500 miles south of Tokyo, Japan. The island is approximately 212 square miles. The Guam National Wildlife Refuge (Refuge or NWR) is comprised of three units: the Andersen Air Force Base Overlay Unit (Air Force Overlay Unit), the Navy Overlay Unit, and the Ritidian Unit. The Ritidian Unit, known to the Native Chamorro people as Puntan Litekyan, is located on the northern tip of Guam and encompasses 1,217 acres, including 385 terrestrial acres and 832 acres of submerged areas offshore (Figures 1 and 2).

Guam Refuge was established in 1993, in response to the 1984 listing of six species as endangered pursuant to the Endangered Species Act of 1966 (ESA). In 2004, the U.S. Fish and Wildlife Service (Service) designated critical habitat for three of these species: the Mariana fruit bat (*Pteropus mariannus mariannus*) or "fanihi" in the Chamorro language of Guam; the Guam Micronesian Kingfisher or "sihek" (*Halcyon cinnamomina cinnamomina*); and Mariana crow or "å'ga" (*Corvus kubaryi*). The 385 terrestrial acres of the Ritidian Unit are the only designated critical habitat on Guam for these species. The human-related impacts of development, agriculture, and introduced pest species have negatively impacted Guam's native wildlife and habitats. The absence of many tropical bird species is the most obvious, attributed in large part to the introduction of the brown treesnake (hereinafter BTS) (*Boiga irregularis*) or "kulepbla" in the Chamorro language of Guam.

The U.S. Fish and Wildlife Service (Service) has prepared this Comprehensive Conservation Plan (CCP) for Guam Refuge in compliance with the National Wildlife Refuge System Administration Act of 1966 (Administration Act) as amended (16 U.S.C 668dd-668ee), and the National Environmental Policy Act (NEPA), as amended (42 U.S.C. 4321-4347), which mandates the Service to address "...significant problems that may adversely affect the populations and habitats of fish, wildlife and plants and the actions necessary to correct or mitigate such problems." Once an Alternative is selected and approved for implementation by the Service's Regional Director, the CCP will guide resource management on the Refuge's Ritidian Unit for 15 years.

In separate efforts, the U.S. Air Force (Air Force) and the U.S. Navy (Navy) are currently drafting Integrated Natural Resource Management Plans (INRMPs) to address resource management for the Air Force and Navy Overlay Units. The Service will be a signatory to the INRMPs. The focus of the CCP is the Ritidian Unit, the only fee-title land the Service owns in Guam. Guam Refuge's CCP and the INRMPs for the Air Force and Navy Overlay Units will serve to fulfill the CCP requirements for all units of Guam National Wildlife Refuge when they are completed.

1.2 Agency Background

The U.S. Fish and Wildlife Service

Guam National Wildlife Refuge is managed by the U.S. Fish and Wildlife Service (Service), within the U.S. Department of the Interior. The Service is the primary Federal entity responsible for conserving and enhancing the Nation's fish and wildlife populations and their habitats. Although the Service shares this responsibility with other Federal, State, tribal, local, and private entities, the Service has specific trust resource responsibilities for migratory birds, threatened and endangered species, certain anadromous fish, certain marine mammals, coral reef ecosystems, wetlands, and other special aquatic habitats. The Service also has similar trust responsibilities for the lands and waters it administers to support the conservation and enhancement of all fish and wildlife and their associated habitats.

The mission of the Service is "working with others to conserve, protect and enhance fish, wildlife, plants and their habitats for the continuing benefit of the American people." National natural resources entrusted to the Service for conservation and protection include migratory birds, endangered and threatened species, inter-jurisdictional fish, wetlands, and certain marine mammals. The Service also manages national fish hatcheries, enforces federal wildlife laws and international treaties on importing and exporting wildlife, assists with state fish and wildlife programs, and helps other countries develop wildlife conservation programs.

National Wildlife Refuge System

The National Wildlife Refuge System (NWRS or Refuge System) is the world's largest network of public lands and waters set aside specifically for conserving wildlife and protecting ecosystems. From its inception in 1903, the Refuge System has grown to encompass 550 national wildlife refuges in all 50 states, and waterfowl production areas in 10 states, covering more than 150 million acres of public lands. More than 36 million visitors annually fish, hunt, observe and photograph wildlife, or participate in environmental education and interpretive activities on national wildlife refuges.

National Wildlife Refuge System Mission and Goals

The mission of the Refuge System is:
"to administer a national network of lands and waters for the conservation, management, and where appropriate, restoration of the fish, wildlife, and plant resources and their habitats within the United States for the benefit of present and future generations of Americans" (Administration Act).

Wildlife conservation is the fundamental mission of the Refuge System. The goals of the Refuge System, as articulated in the Mission, Goals, and Purposes Policy (601 FW1), follow:

- Conserve a diversity of fish, wildlife, and plants and their habitats, including species that are endangered or threatened with becoming endangered.

Figure 1.

Guam NWR

The back sides of pages with maps are blank to facilitate map readability.

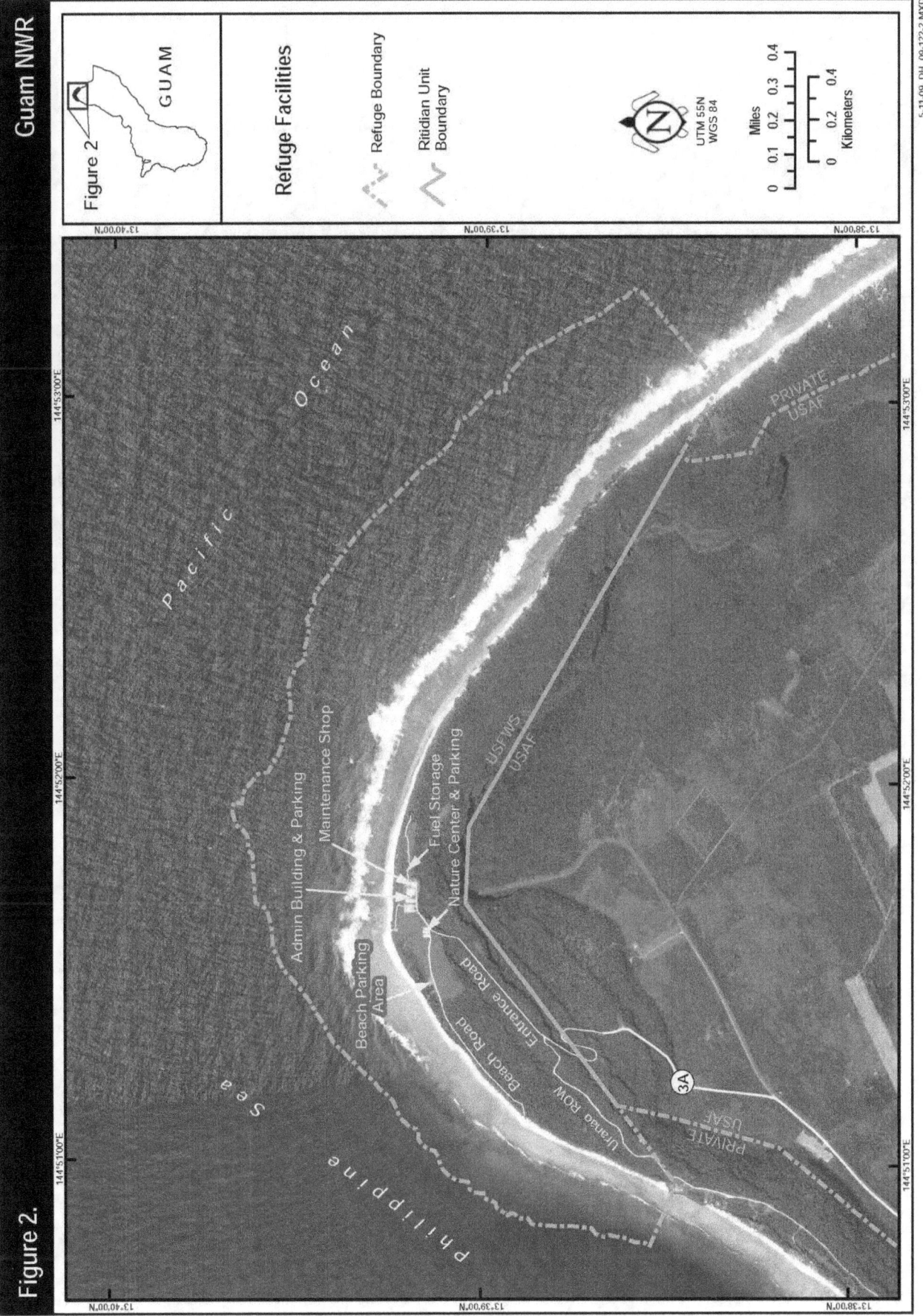

Figure 2.

Guam NWR

Figure 2

GUAM

Refuge Facilities

- - - Refuge Boundary

Riidian Unit Boundary

UTM 55N
WGS 84

Miles
0   0.1   0.2   0.3   0.4

0   0.2   0.4
Kilometers

Pacific Ocean

Philippine Sea

Admin Building & Parking

Maintenance Shop

Beach Parking Area

Fuel Storage

Nature Center & Parking

Beach Road

Entrance Road

Uranao ROW

USFWS
USAF

PRIVATE
USAF

PRIVATE
USAF

3A

5-11-09, DH, 09-122-2.MXD

The back sides of pages with maps are blank to facilitate map readability.

- Develop and maintain a network of habitats for migratory birds, anadromous and inter-jurisdictional fish, and pinniped populations that is strategically distributed and carefully managed to meet important life history needs of these species across their ranges.

- Conserve those ecosystems, plant communities, wetlands of national or international significance, and landscapes and seascapes that are unique, rare, declining, or underrepresented in existing protection efforts.

- Provide and enhance opportunities to participate in compatible wildlife-dependent recreation (hunting, fishing, wildlife observation and photography, and environmental education and interpretation).

- Foster understanding and instill appreciation of the diversity and interconnectedness of fish, wildlife and plants and their habitats.

National Wildlife Refuge System Administration Act

Of all the laws governing activities on national wildlife refuges, the Administration Act undoubtedly exerts the greatest influence. The Administration Act was amended by the National Wildlife Refuge System Improvement Act of 1997 (Act). The Act included a unifying mission for all national wildlife refuges, a new process for determining compatible uses on refuges, and a requirement that each refuge will be managed under a CCP developed in an open public process.

The Act states that the Secretary of the Interior shall provide for the conservation of fish, wildlife, plants, and their habitats within the Refuge System, and ensure that the biological integrity, diversity, and environmental health of the Refuge System are maintained. House Report 105–106 accompanying the Act states "...the fundamental mission of our System is wildlife conservation: wildlife and wildlife conservation must come first." Biological integrity, diversity, and environmental health are critical components of wildlife conservation. As later made clear in the Biological Integrity, Diversity, and Environmental Health Policy, "the highest measure of biological integrity, diversity, and environmental health is viewed as those intact and self-sustaining habitats and wildlife populations that existed during historic conditions."

Under the Act, each refuge must be managed to fulfill the Refuge System mission as well as the specific purposes for which it was established. The Act requires the Service to monitor the status and trends of fish, wildlife, and plants on every refuge. Additionally, the Act identifies six priority wildlife-dependent recreational uses. These uses are hunting, fishing, wildlife observation and photography, and environmental education and interpretation. Under the Act, the Service is to grant these six wildlife-dependent public uses special consideration in the planning, management, establishment, and expansion of units of the Refuge System. The overarching goal is to enhance wildlife-dependent recreation opportunities and access to quality visitor experiences on refuges, while managing refuges to conserve fish, wildlife, plants, and their habitats.

New and ongoing recreational uses should help visitors focus on wildlife and other natural resources. These uses should provide an opportunity to make visitors aware of resource issues, management plans, and how the refuge contributes to the Refuge System and Service missions. When determined compatible on a refuge-specific basis, these six uses assume priority status among all uses of the refuge in question. The Service is directed to make extra efforts to facilitate priority wildlife-dependent public use opportunities.

When preparing a CCP, refuge managers must re-evaluate all general public, recreational, and economic uses (even those occurring to further refuge habitat management goals) proposed or occurring on a refuge for appropriateness and compatibility. No refuge use may be allowed or continued unless it is determined to be appropriate and compatible. Generally, an appropriate use is one that contributes to fulfilling refuge purpose(s), the Refuge System mission, or goals and objectives described in a refuge management plan. A compatible use is defined as a use that, in the sound professional judgment of the refuge manager, will not materially interfere with or detract from the fulfillment of the mission of the Refuge System or the purposes of the refuge. Updated Appropriateness Findings and Compatibility Determinations for existing and proposed uses for Guam Refuge are in Appendix B of this CCP/EA.

The Act also requires that, in addition to formally established guidance, the CCP must be developed with the participation of the public. Public comments play a role in identifying issues, guiding alternatives considered during development of the CCP, and selecting a preferred alternative. It is Service policy to develop CCPs in an open public process; the agency is committed to securing public input throughout the process.

1.3 Refuge Establishment and Refuge Purposes

Refuge Establishment

Guam Refuge was established in 1993. At the time of establishment, Service policy did not require a notice to be posted in the Federal Register. The best record regarding Refuge establishment is the Final Environmental Assessment for the Proposed Guam National Wildlife Refuge and associated Finding of No Significant Impact (USFWS 1993). The Refuge's authorizing authorities most relevant to the four principle reasons Guam Refuge was established are the ESA, Fish and Wildlife Act, Migratory Bird Conservation Act, and Refuge Recreation Act.

Refuge Purposes

The purpose for which a refuge was established or acquired is of key importance in refuge planning. Purposes must form the foundation for planning and management decisions. The purposes of a refuge are specified in or derived from the law, proclamation, executive order, agreement, public land order, donation document, or administrative memorandum establishing, authorizing, or expanding a refuge, refuge unit, or refuge subunit.

Unless the establishing law, order, or other document indicates otherwise, purposes dealing with the conservation, management, and restoration of fish, wildlife, and plants, and the habitats on which they depend take precedence over other purposes in the management and administration of any refuge unit. Where a refuge has multiple purposes related to fish, wildlife, and plant conservation, the more specific purpose will take precedence in instances of conflict. When an additional unit is acquired for a different purpose than the original unit, the additional unit maintains the purpose for which it was acquired and gains the purpose(s) of the original unit, but the original unit does not take on the purpose(s) of the newer addition.

By law, refuges are to be managed to achieve their purposes. When a conflict exists between the Refuge System mission and the purpose of an individual refuge, the refuge purpose may supersede the Refuge System mission. Refuge purposes are also the driving force in the development of the refuge vision statements, goals, objectives, and strategies in the CCP, and are critical to determining the compatibility of all existing and proposed refuge uses.

Guam Refuge purpose(s) ensure that the Refuge will be managed to fulfill the Refuge System mission and the specific purposes for which the Refuge was established. The Refuge purpose is used to prioritize Refuge activities and to ensure secondary uses do not detract from the purpose of the Refuge (see Appendix F. Refuge Purposes Research).

Ritidian Unit Purposes

The Refuge purposes for the Ritidian Unit of Guam Refuge are as follows:

"...to conserve (A) fish or wildlife which are listed as endangered species or threatened species...or (B) plants..." 16 U.S.C. 1534 (Endangered Species Act of 1973).

"...for the development, advancement, management, conservation, and protection of fish and wildlife resources..." 16 U.S.C. 742f(a)(4), (Fish and Wildlife Act of 1956).

"...for use as an inviolate sanctuary, or for any other management purpose, for migratory birds" 16 U.S.C. 715d (Migratory Bird Conservation Act).

"...suitable for (1) incidental fish and wildlife-oriented recreational development, (2) the protection of natural resources, (3) the conservation of endangered species or threatened species..." 16 U.S.C. 460k-1 (Refuge Recreation Act (16 U.S.C. § 460k-460k-4), as amended).

Purposes of the U.S. Navy and U.S. Air Force Overlay Units

The purposes of the Refuge's Navy and Air Force Overlay Units are separate from the purposes of the Ritidian Unit (USFWS memo dated March 25, 1994). The following purposes for the Overlay Units are specified in Cooperative Agreements with the Navy and Air Force, dated March 4, 1994, and March 10, 1994, respectively.

A. "...to conserve (A) fish or wildlife which are listed as endangered species or threatened species...or (B) plants...(C) the ecosystems upon which endangered species and threatened species depend..." (Endangered Species Act of 1973, 16 U.S.C. 1534);

B. "...shall be administered by him [Secretary of the Interior] directly or in accordance with cooperative agreements...and in accordance with such rules and regulations for the conservation, maintenance, and management of wildlife, resources thereof, and its habitat thereon..." (Fish and Wildlife Coordination Act, 16 U.S.C. 664);

C. "...for the development, advancement, management, conservation, and protection of fish and wildlife resources" (Fish and Wildlife Act of 1956, 16 U.S.C. 742f(a)(4));

D. "...for the benefit of the United States Fish and Wildlife Service, in performing its activities and services. Such acceptance may be subject to the terms of any restrictive or affirmative covenant, or condition of servitude, if such terms are deemed by the Secretary to be in accordance with law and compatible with the purposes for which acceptance is sought." (Fish and Wildlife Act of 1956, 16 U.S.C. 742f(b)(1));

E. "...(1) incidental fish and wildlife-oriented recreational development, (2) the protection of natural resources, (3) the conservation of endangered species and threatened species" (Refuge Recreation Act, 16 U.S.C. 460k-l);

F. "...the Secretary...may accept and use...donations of...real...property. Such acceptance may be accomplished under the terms and conditions of restrictive covenants imposed by the donors..." (Refuge Recreation Act, 16 U.S.C. 460k-2); and

G. "To ensure that [Air Force and Navy] lands within the Guam National Wildlife Refuge remain available for the use of the [Air Force and Navy] to carry out its responsibilities to organize, supply, equip, train, service, mobilize, demobilize, administer, and maintain forces" (10 U.S.C. 8013).

1.4 Relationship to Regional, Ecosystem, and Species Recovery Plans

When developing a CCP, the Service considers the goals and objectives of existing national, regional, and ecosystem plans; state or territorial fish and wildlife conservation plans; and other landscape-scale plans developed for the same watershed or ecosystem in which the refuge is located. To the extent possible, the CCP is expected to be consistent with these existing plans and assist in meeting their conservation goals and objectives (Part 602 FW 3.3). This section summarizes some of the key plans that were reviewed by members of the planning team during CCP development.

Guam Conservation Plans

Guam Comprehensive Wildlife Conservation Strategy, 2006. With passage of the Commerce, Justice, and State Appropriations Act of 2001, Congress mandated each state and territory to develop its own comprehensive strategy. The strategy is required to have eight elements, including a description of the status of species determined to be of greatest conservation need, important habitats and their condition, conservation actions, monitoring of these species, and gauging conservation success. A good faith effort to include the public during plan development was important.

Guam's Comprehensive Wildlife Conservation Strategies (GCWCS) identified 65 species including 31 terrestrial (2 mammals, 13 birds, 5 lizards, 3 snails, 2 insects and 6 plants); 7 freshwater (4 fish, 1 eel, 2 plants), and 27 marine organisms (14 marine mammals, 2 fish, 4 clams, 1 gastropod, 1 spiny lobster, 2 sea turtle, 3 marine plants). A conservation table is devoted to each of the species summarizing their status, goals, objectives, and action plans (Elements 1, 3, and 4). Besides identifying actions necessary for each species, other conservation actions that affect general groups of species were identified, and included the development of Memorandas of Understanding, rehabilitation of habitats, public education, and law enforcement.

U.S. Navy (COMNAVMAR) INRMP and Andersen Air Force Base INRMP. The purpose of the INRMPs for Navy and Air Force lands in Guam is to inform Navy and Air Force planners and implementers of mission activities and to provide natural resource managers with sufficient biological background and management guidance to ensure Navy and Air Force mission goals are met without compromising natural resources present on lands under their control. In accordance with the Sikes Act of 1960, as amended, the Department of Defense (DOD) shall maintain a multi-purpose, sustainable, natural resources management program. The Sikes Act also requires that all DOD conservation programs ensure the continued access to land, air, and water resources for realistic military training and testing while ensuring that the natural and cultural resources are sustained in a healthy condition for future generations.

The Navy and Air Force will work with the Service to help ensure that installation activities, including site cleanup, will protect fish and wildlife to the maximum extent practicable. Where feasible, habitat rehabilitation measures will be factored into remedial actions to enhance fish and wildlife resources on Navy and Air Force lands. The INRMPs cover all of the DOD overlay lands for Guam Refuge. The Service will be a signatory to the INRMPs, which will serve as the CCP for the overlay lands.

Endangered Species Recovery Plans

Vanikoro swiftlet[1] "Guam Swiftlet or Yayaguak" (*Aerodramus vanikorensis*), 1991. Current Status: The Guam swiftlet is on the Federal list of endangered species. Eleven colonies are known on Guam, Aguijan, and Saipan. Population estimates were 400 individuals in one colony on Guam, 970 in five colonies on Aguijan, and 3,160 in five colonies on Saipan. Guam swiftlets nest and roost in limestone caves with entrances typically 6.5 feet (2 meters) high or higher, and cave chambers with dark zones where the birds nest. Swiftlets leave the cave to feed and drink, and although they may forage over a wide variety of terrain and vegetation, they seem to favor ridge crests and open grassy areas where they capture small insects while flying.

Current information documents the decline of swiftlet populations on the islands of Guam, Rota, and possibly Saipan; however, there is no direct evidence of factors causing the recent decline. This species is believed to be threatened by various activities, including guano mining and vandalism that result in disturbance of caves and by brown treesnake (BTS) predation. The recovery objective is downlisting to threatened. The recovery criteria include protecting and managing the existing 11 colonies and their habitats, and establishing an additional 9 colonies on Guam and Rota. The total population numbers then must be increased by about 50 percent and sustained over 3 consecutive years. To achieve downlisting the following actions are identified:
- Permanently secure and manage the 11 known active swiftlet caves, one formerly active cave on Rota, and the immediately surrounding "buffer" habitat;
- Survey for, secure, and manage additional swiftlet colonies and potentially usable caves;
- Conduct specific research on population biology and suspected limiting factors;
- Control BTS at selected caves on Guam;

---

[1] Recent taxonomic revision has raised the formerly named Mariana gray swiftlet—subspecies of the Vanikoro swiftlet (*Aerodramus vanikorensis bartschi*)—to a full species, called the Guam Swiftlet (*Aerodramus vanikorensis*), and separated it from the gray swiftlet of the south Pacific (AOU 1995).

- Expand remote population into suitable historical habitat; develop and implement techniques for reintroduction of swiftlets into suitable habitat, as needed; and
- Monitor populations and develop criteria for delisting.

Native Forest Birds of Guam and Rota of the Commonwealth of Northern Mariana Islands, 1990. Of the five species of native forest birds listed as endangered, the Guam broadbill and the Bridled white-eye are probably extinct. The Guam rail exists only in captive breeding populations on the island of Guam and in mainland zoos. The Guam Micronesian kingfisher numbered fewer than 50 individuals in the wild in 1984, and has declined drastically since then. It exists mainly as captive breeding populations in stateside zoos. The Mariana crow is the only native Guam forest bird with populations still existing in the wild. In 1985 there were probably less than 100 crows left in the wild on Guam, however, the Rota population was estimated to be 1,318 birds and was found throughout the island of Rota. The five listed birds inhabit the various forest types on Guam including limestone forest, broken forest, coconut forest, scrub forest, beach scrub, and agriforest. The Guam rail has the widest ecological distribution and was found over much of Guam in all habitats, including open fields, except for wetlands.

The major cause of extirpation or extinction for the Guam native forest birds has been predation by the introduced BTS. The recovery objective for each species is downlisting. The recovery criteria include controlling and/or eradicating the BTS on Guam and reestablishing wild population levels as follows:
- Guam rail: 2,000 birds (1,000 in Northern Guam and 1,000 in Southern Guam);
- Guam Micronesian kingfisher: 1,500 birds (1,000 in Northern Guam and 500 in Southern Guam);
- Mariana crow: 700 birds on Rota and 700 birds on Guam (500 in Northern Guam and 200 in Southern Guam).

No recovery objectives have been set for the Guam broadbill and Bridled white-eye, other than capturing donor stock to establish captive breeding populations if possible; these two species are thought to be extinct. The actions identified for increasing the populations of native forest birds include:
- Establish captive breeding populations for the crow, kingfisher, and rail; control BTS and other exotic predators and exotic diseases;
- Reintroduce the crow and captive-bred rail and kingfisher to Guam;
- Conduct research needed to manage forest habitat for birds; and
- Conduct necessary management activities at existing locations on Guam.

There is a population of Guam rail on Rota that is in the process of becoming established and is supplemented with additional re-introductions of individuals.

Mariana crow "Å'ga" (*Corvus kubaryi*), 2005. Current Species Status: The Mariana crow is on the Federal list of endangered species. Historically, it was found on the islands of Guam and Rota in the Mariana archipelago. The last known native Mariana crow is believed to have disappeared from Guam sometime in 2002 or 2003. Ten Mariana crows survive in the wild on Guam today, all individuals originating from Rota. Current estimates for Rota indicate that approximately 85 pairs of Mariana crow persist on the island, but that this population may be experiencing a serious decline. The species utilizes a wide variety of forested habitats including limestone, strand, ravine, agricultural forests, and secondary forests. However, all evidence suggests Mariana crows are most abundant in native limestone forests. On both Guam and Rota, nests have been found exclusively in native tree species; native trees also serve as the crow's primary foraging source. Habitat loss, nutritional deficiencies, human persecution, contaminants, and introduced species such as disease organisms, cats (*Felis catus*), rats (*Rattus spp.*), black drongos (*Dicrurus macrocercus*), monitor lizards (*Varanus indicus*), and BTS, have all been suggested as factors in the decline of this species. However, the BTS is believed to be the overriding factor in the extirpation of the Mariana crow from Guam. Habitat loss, human persecution, and possibly rat predation on nests are believed to be major factors in the decline on Rota. Therefore, the majority of the recovery actions address the BTS threat, habitat loss, and human persecution.

The recovery objective is to conserve and recover the species to the point where we can downlist it to threatened status and then delist it (remove it from the list of endangered and threatened species). The recovery criterion for downlisting includes meeting the following conditions:

- Mariana crows occur in two populations: one on Rota consisting of a minimum of 75 territorial pairs, and one in northern Guam consisting of a minimum of 75 territorial pairs;
- Both populations are stable or increasing based on quantitative surveys or demographic monitoring that demonstrates an average intrinsic growth rate not less than 1.0 over a period of at least 10 consecutive years;
- Sufficient Mariana crow habitat, based on quantitative estimates of territory and home range size, is protected and managed to achieve the first two criteria;
- BTS and other introduced predators found to be a threat to the Mariana crow are controlled at levels sufficient to achieve the first two criteria;
- BTS interdiction efforts are in place to prevent the establishment of BTS on Rota; and
- Efforts to resolve Mariana crow and landowner conflicts have been implemented.

To prevent the extinction of the Mariana crow, three categories of recovery actions are highest priority. Especially important in this respect is development of means to reduce BTS over wide areas on Guam, reducing BTS at ports and cargo areas, and detecting BTS on Rota and elsewhere where potential incipient populations are likely to be small. Important Mariana crow habitat on Rota and Guam must be protected. This includes protecting current reserves on Guam and Rota as well as areas of high crow density and habitat quality on Rota. Essential research into the species population status and its viability on Rota must be reestablished and led by an experienced scientist. This includes detailed research into the relative importance of presumed important limiting factors (rats and human persecution) to the survival and reproduction of the Mariana crow on Rota, surveying and monitoring of the Rota population, and development of a data center. Accomplishment of these recovery actions will do much to assist the restoration of Mariana crows. However, recovery in the complex human sociopolitical environment that characterizes the region is critically dependent on the trust and cooperation of the people of Guam and Rota. All participants in the recovery effort must work to earn this trust and cooperation as they carry out stipulated recovery actions.

Guam Micronesian kingfisher "Sihek" (*Halcyon cinnamomina cinnamomina*), 2004. The Guam Micronesian kingfisher was listed as an endangered subspecies in 1984 (USFWS 1984). By 1988 it was extirpated from the wild, and this subspecies is now found only in captivity. As of May 2008 the population consisted of 60 males, 36 females, and 4 unsexed chicks distributed among 17 captive propagation institutions in the mainland United States and Guam. The sihek has a recovery priority number of 6 on a scale of 1 (highest) to 18 (lowest), reflecting a high degree of threat, relatively low prospects for recovery, and its taxonomic status as a subspecies. Recovery actions focus on increasing the size of the captive population, controlling BTS, protecting and enhancing habitat for reintroduction, and reintroducing the sihek into the wild on Guam.

Mariana fruit bat "Fanihi" (*Pteropus mariannus mariannus*) and Little Mariana fruit bat "Fanihi" (*Pteropus tokudae*), 1990. Both the Mariana fruit bat and Little Mariana fruit bat are listed as endangered. By 1948 biologists found the Mariana fruit bat to be uncommon in northern Guam and by 1984 it was estimated that there were 425 to 500 Mariana fruit bats left. The Little Mariana fruit bat may be extinct. Mariana fruit bats forage and roost in mature, native limestone forest and ravine forest. Illegal colony hunting and predation of young by the BTS are the most serious threats. The objective of the Mariana fruit bat recovery plan is downlisting. There are no set objectives for the Little Mariana fruit bat. The recovery criteria include increasing the Mariana fruit bat population to at least 2,500, with a minimum of three permanent colonies each supporting at least 400 bats. The actions needed to achieve the recovery criteria are eliminating illegal hunting, controlling BTS and other exotic predators, researching the biology of the species, conducting necessary management activities at existing locations, reintroducing the bats, and verifying recovery objectives.

Micronesian megapode "Sasangat" (*Megapodius laperouse laperouse*) 1998. The Micronesian megapode, a pigeon-sized bird, is listed on the federal list of endangered species. Small remnant populations are known to exist on the southern Mariana Islands of Aguiguan, Tinian, Saipan, and Farallon de Medinilla, while larger populations persist on the northern uninhabited Mariana Islands of Anatahan, Guguan, Sarigan, Alamagan, Pagan, Ascuncion, Maug, and possibly Agrihan. The total number of individuals throughout the Mariana archipelago is estimated to be 1,440 to 1,975 birds. Micronesian megapodes are generally dependent on native limestone forest, but may occasionally use native and nonnative secondary forest adjacent to limestone forest. Megapodes primarily select nest sites in sun-warmed cinder fields or areas warmed by geothermal heat, but secondarily will nest in the roots of rotting trees, logs, and in patches of rotting sword grass.

Historically, megapodes and their eggs may have been over exploited by native human populations, but this activity has not been documented recently. Current threats to megapodes include habitat degradation by feral ungulates and commercial/residential development; competition with introduced galliformes; and predation by introduced monitor lizards, cats, rats, pigs, and dogs. Megapode populations may also be threatened by stochastic natural phenomenon such as volcanism, drought, and typhoons. However, the greatest potential threat to megapode populations is the establishment of BTS on the islands north of Guam. The ultimate objective of the recovery plan is to delist the Micronesian megapode. Criteria for downlisting were established in the recovery plan as well. The following steps must be accomplished for downlisting:
  - There must be a BTS interdiction and control plan in place, and implementation in effect, for all of the Mariana Islands;
  - Current threats to all extant megapode populations must be assessed and controlled; and
  - The comparatively large populations on Anatahan, Sarigan, Guguan, Pagan, and Maug must remain at their current population levels or be increasing for a period of 5 consecutive years.

For delisting, the total number of megapodes in the Marianas should be at least 2,650 birds distributed over 10 islands, including at least 2 populations of 600 birds or greater, 3 populations of 300 or greater, 2 populations of 200 or greater, and 3 populations of 50 or greater. All populations must be stable or increasing for five consecutive years after achieving these levels. The following actions are identified as necessary: survey for, protect, and manage existing populations; conduct essential research on the ecology and biology of Micronesian megapodes; promote expansion of megapodes into suitable habitat; monitor megapode populations; and establish a BTS interdiction and control plan.

Hayun lagu or Trongkon guafi (*Serianthes nelsonii*) 1994. The tree species *Serianthes nelsonii* is federally listed as endangered. Two populations are known from Rota and Guam in the southern Mariana Islands. These populations consist of 121 mature trees on Rota and 1 mature tree on Guam. All remaining *Serianthes nelsonii* occur in native limestone forest on soils derived from limestone substrates, with most trees growing on or near steep hillsides or cliffs. The species formerly inhabited sites with volcanic soils in southern Guam. Current information suggests that a number of factors are involved in the decline of the species, with overbrowsing by introduced ungulates, especially Philippine deer, and predation on seeds and seedlings by insects thought to be the two major problems. These have resulted in nearly complete lack of regeneration for a number of years, producing a population highly skewed toward mature individuals.

The recovery objective is to downlist the species to threatened. The recovery criteria include protecting and managing the existing 122 trees and their habitats. Populations on both islands must be expanded so that each contains at least two subpopulations, each with enough reproductive plants to effectively maintain the populations through the production of seeds, seedlings, and mature plants. The actions needed to meet these criteria include securing the habitat of current populations and managing threats, conducting research on limiting factors, augmenting existing populations, excluding ungulates, reestablishing the species in its former range, and validating recovery objectives.

Green Turtle *(Chelonia mydas)* 1998. The green turtle is listed as threatened under the Endangered Species Act (ESA) throughout its Pacific Range, except for the endangered population nesting on the Pacific coast of Mexico which is covered under the Recovery Plan for the East Pacific green turtle. In reviewing this species' current status, the Recovery Team found that, outside of Hawaii, the green turtle populations have seriously declined and should probably be classified as endangered. By far, the most serious threat to these stocks is from direct take of turtles and eggs, both within U.S. jurisdiction and on shared stocks that are killed when they migrate out of U.S. jurisdiction (e.g., nesting turtles from American Samoa migrate to Fiji and French Polynesia to feed). Another serious threat to green turtle populations throughout the Pacific is associated with increasing human populations and development. In particular, human development is having an increasingly serious impact on nesting beaches. The recovery goal is to delist the species. To consider delisting, all of the following criteria must be met: all regional stocks that use U.S. waters have been identified to source beaches based on reasonable geographic parameters; each stock must average 5,000 (or a biologically reasonable estimate based on the goal of maintaining a stable population in perpetuity) females estimated to nest annually (FENA) over six years; nesting populations at "source beaches" are either stable or increasing over a 25-year monitoring period; existing foraging areas are maintained as healthy environments; foraging populations are exhibiting statistically significant increases at several key foraging grounds within each stock region; a management plan to maintain sustained populations of turtles is in place, and international agreements are in place to protect shared stocks.

Eight major actions are needed to achieve recovery (seven of which are applicable to conservation efforts in Guam): stop the direct harvest of green turtles and eggs through education and law enforcement actions; reduce incidental mortalities by commercial and artisanal fisheries; determine population size, status, and trends through long-term regular nesting beach and in-water censuses; identify stock home ranges using DNA analysis; support conservation and biologically-viable management of green turtle populations in countries that share U.S. green turtle stocks; identify and protect primary nesting and foraging areas for the species; eliminate adverse effects of development on nesting and foraging habitats; and control nonnative predators of eggs and hatchlings (e.g., mongoose, feral cats, and pigs) in the Hawaiian population.

Hawksbill Turtle *(Eretmochelys imbricata)* **1998.** The hawksbill turtle is listed as endangered throughout its range. In the Pacific, this species is rapidly approaching extinction due to a number of factors, but the intentional harvest of the species for meat, eggs, and the tortoiseshell and stuffed curio trade is of greatest impact. Increasing human populations and the concurrent destruction of the habitat are also of major concern for the Pacific hawksbill populations. In a review of the status of the species, the Recovery Team (which is made up of biologists with extensive experience in the insular Pacific) noted how seriously depleted hawksbill populations had become in the Pacific. The status of this species is clearly of a highest concern for the Pacific and it is recommended that immediate actions be taken to prevent its extinction. The recovery goal is to delist the species. To consider delisting, all of the following criteria must be met:
- All regional stocks that use U.S. waters have been identified to source beaches based on reasonable geographic parameters;
- Each stock must average 1,000 females FENA (or a biologically reasonable estimate based on the goal of maintaining a stable population in perpetuity) over six years;
- All FENA at "source beaches" are either stable or increasing for 25 years; existing foraging areas are maintained as healthy environments;
- Foraging populations are exhibiting statistically significant increases at several key foraging grounds within each stock region;
- A management plan designed to maintain sustained populations of turtles is in place;
- Formal cooperative relationships with regional sea turtle management programs (South Pacific Regional Environment Program [SPREP]) are in place; and
- International agreements are in place to protect shared stocks.

The major recovery actions for the Hawksbill Turtle are the same as those outlined in the Green Turtle Recovery Plan. They are outlined above.

Brown Treesnake Control Plan

The BTS is a native species of Indonesia, New Guinea, the Solomon Islands, and Australia. Its introduction to Guam has resulted in a biological invasion that is unprecedented in its scope, and it has been primarily responsible for the extirpation of most of Guam's native terrestrial vertebrates, including fruit bats, lizards, and virtually all of the Island's forest birds. In addition, BTS has caused more than 1,000 power outages; preyed on poultry, damaging agricultural interests; killed pets; and inflicted numerous children with venomous snake bites. A large number of governmental agencies and private entities have been working to prevent similar ecological disasters on other Pacific islands, since the threat of BTS dispersing to other islands and continents is significant. The BTS is a major threat to the biodiversity of the Pacific region and other areas at risk. High densities of snakes occur in many urban areas on Guam where cargo is loaded for transport by air and sea to other Pacific islands, and dispersal has occurred on islands in Hawaii, the Commonwealth of the Northern Mariana Islands, other islands in the Pacific and Indian Ocean, and even on the continental United States.

In recognition of the BTS dispersal threat, the U.S. Congress authorized a cooperative program to control BTS outside of its historic range. The Brown Tree Snake Technical Working Group is charged with an integrated pest management approach that would:
- Reduce existing BTS populations over large geographic areas on Guam;
- Prevent the spread of BTS to other Pacific islands and mainland areas;
- Eradicate or contain new populations as soon as detected;
- Develop effective and environmentally sound control and/or eradication strategies and methods;
- Protect endangered species and other wildlife from BTS predation;
- Assist organizations and individuals on Guam with managing and controlling BTS populations to reduce disruptions of electrical supplies and human-snake encounters resulting in emotional trauma and bites; and
- Develop adequate information on the biology, dispersal dynamics, and control of BTS to support Federal, State, Territorial, and Commonwealth needs.

To meet these objectives, the BTS Technical Working Group proposed the following tasks:
- Reduce BTS populations over large geographic areas on Guam;
- Eliminate BTS from the transportation network; eradicate snakes in recently established populations;
- Control snakes to reduce predation on endangered species and other native animals;
- Control snakes to reduce human contacts resulting in snakebites and emotional trauma;
- Control snakes to reduce electrical outages and damage to equipment;
- Provide information and educational materials to the public, government agencies, and commerce to reduce risks of ecological and economic damages due to the establishment of this exotic pest; and
- Provide for the prompt and continuous evaluation of the effectiveness and viability of control actions, including both operational and research facets of the program, as well as a periodic review and updating of the Brown Tree Snake Control Plan. A draft of the current update is included as Appendix K.

These tasks are interrelated and, as such, are not listed in any order of priority; all are essential parts of both a short- and long-term strategy needed to control BTS outside its native habitat.

Migratory Bird Plans

Though migratory birds utilize the Ritidian Unit, Guam is not in the majority of U.S. national and regional migratory bird plans. Guam is in the East Asian-Australasian Flyway. The Pacific Region Seabird Conservation Plan includes Guam Refuge. The Service's priorities for seabird management, monitoring, research, outreach, planning, and coordination are identified in the Pacific Region Seabird Conservation Plan. The plan serves as a guide to coordinate Service activities for seabird conservation at the regional scale. The plan includes a review of seabird resources and habitats; a description of issues and threats; and a summary of current management, monitoring, and outreach efforts. All species are prioritized by conservation concern at the regional scale and recommendations for conservation actions are identified and prioritized.

1.5 Refuge Vision

The refuge vision statement is a broad general statement that describes what the Refuge staff perceives as Guams Refuge's fundamental attributes and contributions to a healthy world environment. This statement will guide management activities for the lifespan of this plan, as well as into the near future. The vision statement for Guam Refuge is as follows:

Guam National Wildlife Refuge hosts a unique and fragile blend of native plants and animals found nowhere else in the world. It stands as a special place and source of pride for all. Here at Guam National Wildlife Refuge, the U.S. Fish and Wildlife Service works with others to conserve and restore the precious resources of both land and sea. Guam's native wildlife flourishes in the native limestone and coastal forests, and sea creatures are bountiful in the tropical blue waters. Visitors seek out the beauty and tranquility provided and enjoy seeing and learning about wildlife. The Refuge is a vital link between Guam's cultural and natural heritage, a vibrant reminder of the place nature holds in all of our lives, and a treasure for future generations.

1.6 Refuge Goals

Goals and objectives are the unifying elements of successful refuge management. They identify and focus management priorities, resolve issues, and link to refuge purposes, Service policy, and the Refuge System mission.

A CCP describes management actions that help bring a refuge closer to its vision. A vision broadly reflects refuge purposes, Refuge System mission and goals, other statutory requirements, and larger-scale plans as appropriate. Public use and wildlife/habitat management goals then define general targets in support of the vision, followed by objectives that direct efforts into incremental and measurable steps toward achieving those goals. Finally, strategies identify specific tools and actions to accomplish objectives. The following goal order does not imply any priority in this CCP.

Goal 1: Restore, protect, and maintain native limestone forest representative of historic Guam and other Mariana Islands.

Goal 2: Restore, protect, and maintain the shoreline habitat community representative of historic Guam and other Mariana Islands.

Goal 3: Conserve, protect, and maintain the native halophytic-xerophytic plant community representative of historic Guam and other Mariana Islands.

Goal 4: Conserve, protect, and maintain limestone cave habitat to meet the life-history needs of endemic, cave-dwelling species characteristic of historic Guam and other Mariana Islands.

Goal 5: Restore, protect, and maintain native marine communities representative of historic Guam and other Mariana Islands.

Goal 6: Protect and promote the recovery of extirpated and/or federally listed threatened and endangered species that are endemic to Guam, along with benefits to locally listed species and species of greatest conservation need.

Goal 7: Gather scientific information (research, inventory, and monitoring) to contribute to our knowledge and understanding of Refuge resources, and the threats and impacts to Pacific Island ecosystems in support of management decisions associated with Goals 1-6.

Goal 8: Teach students and teachers the value of the Refuge's ecology and the management practices necessary to recover and protect the Refuge's natural and cultural resources.

Goal 9: Provide opportunities for residents and visitors to enjoy, value, and support the Refuge.

Goal 10: Protect, preserve, evaluate, and when appropriate, interpret the Refuge's Chamorro cultural resources and associated practices.

Chapter 2. Planning Purpose, Need, and Issues

2.1 Planning Process

The CCP development process follows applicable policies contained within the Service's Fish and Wildlife Manual (Part 602 FW2.1, November 1996; Part 601 FW1, Part 603 FW1, and Part 605 FW1, June 2006), and the Wilderness Act of 1964 with respect to wilderness study and review. This CCP was completed in association with an EA and is intended to meet the dual requirements of compliance with the NWRS Administration Act, as amended (Act), and NEPA. Both the Act and NEPA require the Service to actively seek public involvement in the preparation and adoption of environmental and conservation documents and policies. Furthermore, NEPA also requires the Service to consider a reasonable range of alternatives including its Preferred Alternative and the "No Action" alternative; the latter defined as continuation of current management practices.

2.2 Purpose and Need for the CCP

The purpose of the CCP is to provide the Refuge System, the Service, partners, and citizens with a management plan for improving fish and wildlife habitat conditions and infrastructure for wildlife, staff, and Refuge visitors for 15 years. An approved CCP will help ensure that the Service manages Guam Refuge to achieve its purposes, vision, goals, and objectives, and to help fulfill the System mission.

Another purpose of the CCP is to provide reasonable, scientifically grounded guidance for improving the Refuge's forest, subterranean, coastal, and marine habitats for the long-term conservation of native plants, animals, and migratory birds. The CCP will identify appropriate actions for protecting and sustaining the cultural and biological features of forest and coastal communities; endangered species populations and habitats; migratory shorebirds; and threatened, endangered, or rare species. A final purpose of the CCP is to provide guidance and evaluate priority wildlife-dependent recreation programs on the Refuge which may include hunting, fishing, wildlife observation, photography, environmental education, and interpretation.

The CCP is needed for a variety of reasons. Primary among these is the need to establish improved habitat conditions in the Refuge's forest, subterranean, coastal, and marine environments that are being degraded by pest plants and animals, most notably BTS and feral ungulates. There is a need to address Guam Refuge's contributions to aid in the recovery of listed species, and assess and possibly mitigate potential impacts of global climate change. There is also a need to effectively work with current partners such as the Guam Division of Aquatic and Wildlife Resources (GDAWR), U.S. Geological Survey's Biological Resources Division, U.S. Navy, U.S. Air Force, National Oceanic and Atmospheric Administration (NOAA), National Park Service, other divisions within the Service, and seek new partnerships to restore habitats, improve environmental education and interpretive opportunities and volunteer program, and recover endangered species populations.

There is a need to evaluate the existing visitor service program to determine which wildlife-dependent public uses are compatible and to what extent improvements or alterations should be made to the program.

2.3 Planning and Management Guidance

The Service, an agency within the Department of the Interior (DOI), is the principal Federal agency responsible for conserving, protecting and enhancing fish, wildlife and plants and their habitats for the continuing benefit of the American people. The Service manages the Refuge System, which encompasses more than 150 million acres, 550 national wildlife refuges and other units, and 37 wetland management districts.

Refuges are guided by various federal laws and executive orders, Service policies, and international treaties. Fundamental are the mission and goals of the Refuge System and the designated purposes of the Refuge as described in establishing legislation, executive orders, or other documents establishing, authorizing, or expanding a refuge.

Key concepts and guidance of the Refuge System derive from the Administration Act; the Refuge Recreation Act of 1962 (16 U.S.C. 460k-460k-4), as amended; Title 50 of the Code of Federal Regulations; and the Fish and Wildlife Service Manual. The Administration Act is implemented through regulations covering the Refuge System, published in Title 50, subchapter C of the Code of Federal Regulations. These regulations govern general administration of units of the Refuge System. This CCP and the previously released EA are intended to comply with both the Administration Act and NEPA.

2.4 Planning and Issue Identification

Issues to be addressed in the CCP

The following issues are within the scope of the CCP/EA and are being addressed in the planning process.

Habitat and Species Management: Habitat conditions should be restored on Guam Refuge's limestone forest, cave, coastal strand, and marine habitats, some of which are highly degraded by invasive plants and animals. Additional management activities can occur to aid in the control of BTS, rats (as BTS is controlled), and feral ungulates. Endangered species and other species are of management concern (e.g., land snails, marine fishes).

Wildlife-Dependent Uses: As defined by the Improvement Act, wildlife-dependent public uses are hunting, fishing, wildlife observation, wildlife photography, environmental interpretation, and environmental education. Some wildlife-dependent public uses should be offered at the Refuge and improvements to these programs can be provided to enhance public enjoyment and increase the knowledge and awareness that exemplifies a quality experience for Refuge visitors. Should the Refuge participate in a fee collection program to offset visitor service costs? Do fishing, scuba diving, and snorkeling activities harm the coral reefs and should these activities continue to be permissible? These questions and others will be answered through Compatibility Determinations and Appropriate Use Findings.

Non-Wildlife-Dependent Uses: Shall Guam Refuge continue to offer various non-wildlife-dependent recreational opportunities such as barbequing and beach use? Is swimming safe and should it continue at locations currently deemed to be safe? What facilities and program support should be offered?

Cultural Resources: What steps should be taken to better protect and interpret cultural resources? What cultural practices historically occurred on the Refuge and what requirements will continue to allow these practices? How do we continue to incorporate the Chamorro culture, through their stories and language, into the appropriate visitor experience? What actions should we undertake to develop a visitor services program that highlights the Refuge's commitment to preservation of the Chamorro language, culture, and traditions through protection, interpretation, and conservation of Guam's natural and cultural resources?

Global Climate Change: How will global climate change affect the coral reefs and coastal environments of the Ritidian Unit? What other species and habitats might be affected? How can the visitor services program interpret this in an empowering and hopeful, yet accurate, manner?

Coral Reef: There were also suggestions regarding the development of response protocols for the numerous stressors affecting coral reef resources, including vessel groundings, chemical or oil spills, coral bleaching, and coral disease. The Refuge was encouraged to increase its participation with local, Federal, and nongovernmental organizations whose efforts are directed toward the preservation and restoration of the coral reef habitat.

Interagency Coordination and Cooperation: Does the relationship between Guam Refuge, the Navy, and the Air Force need improvement, and if so, how can this be accomplished? Can the Refuge better participate in endangered species recovery plans, Guam's Wildlife Conservation Strategy, and other conservation initiatives? The CCP should incorporate and complement the strategies developed within current recovery plans including the Service's threatened and endangered species recovery plans and Guam's Comprehensive Wildlife Conservation Strategy.

Issues Outside the Scope of the CCP/EA

In general, the CCP will incorporate Navy and Air Force management information from their respective INRMPs. While the Navy and Air Force have the lead on natural resources management issues on each of their lands, we have requested that Refuge habitat management priorities be incorporated into the INRMPs as they are developed. The DOD provides administrative oversight, staffing, and funding for projects that conserve, enhance, and restore high quality habitats on the Navy and Air Force Bases. The DOD works cooperatively with the Service on natural resources conservation and management in accordance with the Cooperative Agreements for the Overlay Refuges. The Navy and Air Force also work cooperatively with the DAWR and other on-island experts. The Navy and Air Force are currently revising their respective INRMPs, which are incorporated by reference in this Draft CCP/EA.

The Service does not manage visitor services on the Overlay Units; the Navy and Air Force manage visitor services on their lands. The Navy and Air Forces Bases are closed to the public unless access is granted. There is a public hunting program at Andersen Air Force Base for feral deer and pigs, and limited access for collection of medicinal plants and coconut crabs under permit.

A preliminary wilderness evaluation has been completed for the Ritidian Unit (see Appendix D) and a preliminary determination was made that the unit does not appear to meet the minimum requirements for recommending wilderness designation. The Service will not conduct a wilderness evaluation for the Overlay Units because the DOD is the responsible agency.

Chapter 3. Management Direction

3.1 Overview

In developing the management direction for the CCP, the Service reviewed and considered a variety of resource, social, economic, and organizational aspects important for managing the Refuge. These background conditions are described more fully in Chapters 4, 5, and 6. As is appropriate for a national wildlife refuge, resource considerations were fundamental in designing alternatives. House Report 105-106 accompanying the Improvement Act states "...the fundamental mission of our System is wildlife conservation: wildlife and wildlife conservation must come first." The planning team reviewed scientific reports and studies to better understand ecosystem trends and the latest scientific recommendations for species and habitats. The Service met with staff from local, territorial, and Federal agencies, and elected officials to ascertain priorities and problems as perceived by others.

Our management direction has a number of components. In addition to the specific strategies outlined in the following section, there are a number of assumptions and programs that apply to most or multiple goals and objectives. The following list is intended to describe some of these cross-goal strategies.

- Implementation Subject to Funding Availability: Actions as described will be implemented over a perioed of 15 years as funding becomes available. Projects are listed in Appendix C.

- Refuge Revenue Sharing Payment: Annual payments to the Government of Guam under the Refuge Revenue Sharing Program will continue according to the established formula and subject to payments authorized by Congress.

- Refuge facilities that are available in support of Refuge management are depicted in Figure 2. No additional administrative facilities are planned or included in the CCP.

- The Refuge has a pack-it-in, pack-it-out policy. Trash that is left by visitors is picked up by Refuge staff as it is encountered.

- Take of humphead wrasse and bumphead parrotfish will be discontinued based on evaluations and information provided by NOAA. We will work to change the Code of Federal Regulations for fishing at Guam Refuge to implement this change.

- Marine debris is removed from beach and marine environments when it is encountered. Anchoring marine vessels in Refuge waters is strictly prohibited to protect coral communities.

- Sea turtles and seabirds are known to be attracted to artificial lights at night. Seabirds will fly into street or building lights leading to injury and often death. Young sea turtles can become disoriented after hatching and crawl toward artificial lights instead of heading to the ocean. All unnatural nighttime lighting on the Refuge has been eliminated from the Refuge's administrative site to protect turtles and nocturnal seabirds. There will be no new unnatural lighting in the future.

- Participation in Planning and Review of Regional Development Activities: The Service will actively participate in planning and studies for ongoing and future industrial and urban development, contamination, and other potential concerns that may adversely affect the Refuge's wildlife resources and habitats. The Service will cultivate working relationships with pertinent Territorial and Federal agencies to stay abreast of current and potential developments, and will utilize effective outreach tools and technologies and environmental education and interpretation as needed to raise awareness of the Refuge's resources.

- The Service will continue to uphold Federal laws protecting cultural resources, including the National Historic Preservation Act (NHPA) and the Archaeological Resources Protection Act (ARPA). These laws also mandate consultation with the State Historic Preservation Office (SHPO) and other preservation partners. The NHPA mandates that all projects using Federal funding, permitting, or licensing be reviewed by a cultural resource professional to determine if there is the potential to affect cultural resources. An inventory will be conducted as necessary and appropriate actions to mitigate effects will be identified prior to implementation of the project. A project-specific determination will be conducted for all undertakings as defined by NHPA, including habitat maintenance and restoration projects, and new or expanded trails, roads, facilities, and public use areas.

Integrated Pest Management

In accordance with 517 DM 1 and 7 RM 14, an integrated pest management (IPM) approach would be utilized, where practicable, to eradicate, control, or contain pest and invasive species (herein collectively referred to as pests) on the Refuge. IPM involves using methods based upon effectiveness, cost, and minimal ecological disruption, and considers minimum potential effects to non-target species and the Refuge environment. Pesticides may be used where physical, cultural, and biological methods, or combinations thereof, are impractical or incapable of providing adequate control, eradication, or containment. If a pesticide would be needed on the Refuge, the most specific (selective) chemical available for the target species would be used unless considerations of persistence or other environmental and/or biotic hazards would preclude it. In accordance with 517 DM 1, pesticide usage would be further restricted because only pesticides registered with the U.S. Environmental Protection Agency (EPA) in full compliance with the Federal Insecticide, Fungicide, and Rodenticide Act (FIFRA) and as provided in regulations, orders, or permits issued by EPA may be applied on lands and waters under Refuge jurisdiction.

Environmental harm by pest species refers to a biologically substantial decrease in environmental quality as indicated by a variety of potential factors, including declines in native species populations or communities, degraded habitat quality or long-term habitat loss, and/or altered ecological processes. Environmental harm may be a result of direct effects of pests on native species, including preying and feeding on them; causing or vectoring diseases; preventing them from reproducing or killing their young; out-competing them for food, nutrients, light, nest sites or other vital resources; or hybridizing with them so frequently that within a few generations, few if any truly native individuals remain. In contrast, environmental harm can be the result of an indirect effect of pest species. For example, decreased waterfowl use may result from invasive plant infestations reducing the availability and/or abundance of native wetland plants that provide forage during the winter.

Environmental harm may also include detrimental changes in ecological processes. For example, cheatgrass infestations in shrub steppe habitat can alter fire return intervals, displacing native species and communities of bunch grasses, forbs, and shrubs. Environmental harm may also cause or be associated with economic losses and damage to human, plant, and animal health. For example, invasions by fire-promoting grasses that alter entire plant and animal communities, eliminating or sharply reducing populations of many native plant and animal species, can also greatly increase fire-fighting costs.

See Appendix J for the Refuge's IPM program documentation for managing pests for this CCP. Along with a more detailed discussion of IPM techniques, this documentation describes the selective use of pesticides for pest management on the Refuge, where necessary. Throughout the life of the CCP or HMP, most proposed pesticide uses on the Refuge would be evaluated for potential effects to the Refuge's biological resources and environmental quality. These potential effects would be documented in "Chemical Profiles" (see example in Appendix J). Pesticide uses with appropriate and practical best management practices (BMPs) for habitat management as well as cropland/facilities maintenance would be approved for use on the Refuge where there likely would be only minor, temporary, and localized effects to species and environmental quality based upon non-exceedance of threshold values in Chemical Profiles. However, pesticides may be used on a refuge where substantial effects to species and the environment are possible (exceed threshold values) in order to protect human health and safety (e.g., mosquito-borne disease).

3.2 Description of Management Direction

We intend to install a multi-species barrier "wall" along the Ritidian Unit boundary on the east end to the cliff, and on the west end to tie into the Air Force's ungulate fence proposed for the Air Force Overlay Unit. A concrete barrier is necessary to withstand a typhoon. The barrier would be ungulate, rodent, and snake proof, and if implemented, could result in a nearly pest-free Refuge. Management efforts would involve an initial investment in the cost and effort of constructing a physical barricade. Once completed, pest species from within the confines of the pest barricade would be removed. The USGS has developed this type of snake and rodent barrier.

The efforts necessary to keep pest species from repopulating the area are hoped to be a minimal maintenance level. The barrier itself needs to be coordinated between Andersen AFB and the Service. The combination of Service and AFB fencing would serve to encompass landholdings from both agencies. The current proposed AFB fencing project includes three separate fenced units and is proposed as an ungulate-excluding fence only. Refuge staff will coordinate with AFB and Service Ecological Services staff to determine whether or not there are opportunities to partner in a way that would be most advantageous to Guam's native wildlife. Initial discussions between some of the parties regarding type of fence and final locations have taken place. It is possible that the Refuge staff would change the material that is used for the fencing project or the specific location. Either of these changes would not change the nature or scale of the impacts that are described in the Guam Refuge CCP/EA. The enclosed area will be large enough to accommodate the spatial needs of native crabs and lizards.

Ungulate control will increase with the use of snares, and will be more effective with a wall in place (eliminating ingress). Pest plants will be controlled with the use of pesticides and manual removal. Native plant propagation and out-planting will be conducted following the removal of ungulates. Survival of young plants will increase dramatically without ungulates eating and trampling them. BTS removal will be increased through trapping, baiting, and hand removal. Snakes will be kept out of the Refuge with a snake/pest barrier surrounding the Ritidian Unit as well as a portion of the Air Force Overlay Unit.

Habitat management activities currently include the collection of native seeds from Refuge lands, germinating the seeds and raising seedlings in a plant nursery provided by the Guam Department of Agriculture (DOA), then out-planting of seedlings both on- and off-Refuge. *Serianthes nelsonii* seeds have been collected on Rota. These seeds have been germinated and raised in one of DOA's nurseries. Out-planting has been delayed because plants that are out-planted need constant protection from invasive species, such as white fly, scale, ungulates, and mile-a-minute vine. Small areas, approximately 10 acres in size, are currently fenced to exclude ungulates for these restoration efforts.

Research and monitoring programs are designed to evaluate pest species impacts on native plants and animals, and evaluate habitat for potential restoration of endangered species. Specifically, researchers are investigating control methods for the scale insect, which is impacting native cycads; monitoring the spread of the invasive rhinoceros beetle which impacts coconut trees; and evaluating potential forage and roost sites of bats and wildlife use of caves. Some archaeological research occurs within limestone caves and other habitats on the Refuge. Zoo-archaeologists are looking at non-fossilized prehistoric bone deposits to determine past cave use and presence of swiflets and other species. A marine habitat study has recently been concluded.

Some caves on the Ritidian Unit are considered significant under the Federal Cave Resources Protection Act of 1988. Section 4 of the Federal Cave Resources Protection Act of 1988 (102 Stat. 4546; 16 U.S.C. 4301) authorizes the Secretary to issue regulations providing for the identification of significant caves. Section 5 authorizes the Secretary to withhold information concerning the location of significant caves under certain circumstances. "Significant cave" means a cave located on Federal land that has been determined to meet the criteria in S 37.11(c). Within the limestone cave habitat, Refuge staff will locate all of the caves on the Refuge. Once the caves are located, they will be mapped using global positioning and geographic information systems (GPS and GIS). These caves will also be surveyed for species composition. Invasive species such as moths, rodents, and snakes will be removed or controlled so native species can re-colonize their original habitat. With the exception of one cave on the self-guided walk, access to the limestone caves is not permitted in order to limit unintentional damage caused by visitors. All visitors to the Ritidian Cave must be accompanied by Refuge staff.

Introduced mud dauber wasps use the limestone caves for nest building. The wasps build mud nests that are attached to the walls and ceilings of the caves. Sometimes these nests are built on walls that contain Chamorro pictographs, impacting some pictographs with mud. Plastic netting has been placed over the main pictograph cave entrances to protect the pictographs from wasp nests. This netting, along with existing fencing, is also intended to protect the caves from human and feral animal disturbance. Some areas within the Refuge are closed to the public due to the high number of ancient Chamorro artifacts. The University of Guam's Micronesia Area Research Center performs field work for training archaeologists on the Refuge. All construction projects disturbing earth on the coastal strand must have an archaeological resource monitor. Human remains and cultural artifacts are frequently found on the Refuge.

We will conduct the following actions to manage native marine communities:
- Surveys to identify marine species and conservation needs;
- Surveys for potentially extirpated species such as the giant clam;
- Creel surveys to identify the number and species of fish being harvested within Refuge boundaries;
- Coral surveys to identify coral damage from human uses; and
- Dive surveys to encompass areas beyond the reef crest to a depth of 100 feet, the official boundary of the Refuge.

Opportunistic removal of pest species will be done on all surveys. With a pest barrier in place there could be less trespass by poachers who enter the Refuge to illegally harvest fish and in doing so, often damage or kill corals.

Actions related to managing federally listed threatened and endangered species endemic to Guam include efforts to restore populations of all native bat and bird species, except for the Mariana common moorhen (*Gallinula chloropus guami*), which does not naturally occur in the Ritidian Unit. Surveys will be conducted to evaluate habitat for the Bridled white-eye, Guam rail, and Micronesian kingfisher, along with any other species that could potentially be repatriated.

The Refuge will also participate in captive breeding programs and establish a captive rearing facility on the Refuge. A soft release site will be established, so that animals being repatriated at the Refuge can gradually acclimatize themselves to the wild. Roost sites for bats, crows, and other birds will be identified and protected for future use by any repatriated species, or for species that are released by the captive breeding program. The Refuge has been exploring options for repatriating endangered species to the Refuge, although no release activities have occurred.

Refuge and GDAWR staff are currently evaluating caves for the possibility of repatriating swiftlets. While there have been no releases for the sihek (kingfisher), Guam Refuge would accept surplus animals from GDAWR's captive rearing program to be released on the Refuge grounds. There have also been initial discussions about releasing Koko (rails) within the Refuge. Repatriation will be delayed until BTS populations are controlled. In addition, Refuge staff and volunteers will continue monitoring the beaches for green and hawksbill turtle nests during the nesting season. Volunteers are assisting with nest identification and tagging turtles with satellite tags as a part of the Haggan Watch Program. Refuge staff members currently provide instructions for the Haggan Watch Program.

The Haggan Watch Program is a partnership with GDAWR to have trained volunteers walking the beaches of Guam looking for signs of sea turtle nests and crawls on a regular schedule. Little is currently known about turtle nesting behavior on Guam and this program is designed to give biologists a better understanding of when nesting turtles are on-island, while at the same time increasing public awareness of the status of these threatened and endangered animals. In addition to discussing sea turtle nest and crawl identification tools, volunteers are given information about the current threats to the sea turtle populations, including illegal poaching. Haggan is considered a delicacy by many on Guam, and was traditionally served at weddings and other large family gatherings and celebrations. Haggan Watch Program volunteers continue to monitor Guam's beaches, including those on the Refuge. Since the program began, several nest sites (both on and off the Refuge) have been discovered which would have likely been unknown without the efforts of the dedicated volunteers.

We will increase monitoring and research activity to gather scientific information and increase our knowledge and understanding of the Refuge's resources and the threats and impacts to Pacific island ecosystems, in support of management decisions. Surveys will be conducted with an emphasis on key species such as snails, ironwood tree, and endangered species. Surveys will also be conducted for migratory birds using this area as a flyway.

Much of the Refuge, including most of the marine reef system, is not open to public access. Self-guided visitor service activities consist primarily of a self-guided interpretive trail; access points to beach habitat for fishing, snorkeling, barbecuing, picnicking, and sunbathing; and a nature center. Figure 3 illustrates existing and planned visitor facilities and trails. The nature center contains natural and cultural history exhibits and a bookstore. Only one limestone cave is open to the public without staff escort using a self-guided trail. Localized closures of beach and beach strand habitat occur when turtle nest sites are found. Restrictions on the use of amplified sound are enforced on the Ritidian Unit. Other activities that are currently being conducted at the Refuge are environmental education, limited bird watching, scuba diving, kayaking, photography, offshore fishing from boats, and hiking. Refuge staff members are currently in the process of developing a self-guided nature trail near the Nature Center, which will include a kiosk and interpretive signs along a boardwalk that is handicap accessible.

Refuge staff who are trained to present visitor service programs conduct presentations both on and off the Refuge on various Refuge topics, depending upon the teacher's needs. Schools come to the Refuge to visit the nature center and participate in guided interpretive cave walks.

To share and involve the public in the resources and management practices necessary to recover and preserve the Refuge's natural and cultural recourses, the Refuge will increase its visitor service program to include both on- and off-site efforts. Schools with budgets large enough to transport students to the Refuge will make up the primary student audience on-site. For schools unable to bring students to the Refuge, we will offer an off-site environmental education program. Refuge staff will focus on developing partnerships through schoolyard habitat programs.

Visitor opportunities will be expanded to include an additional self-guided interpretive trail. Existing activities such as access points to beach habitat for fishing, snorkeling, barbecuing, and sunbathing, and staffing the nature center, will continue. A trail that includes opportunities to visit a limestone cave will remain open as a self-guided interpretive opportunity. Localized closures of beach and beach strand habitat occur when turtle nest sites are located. Restrictions on the use of amplified sound will continue. Other activities that will continue at the Refuge are limited bird watching, scuba diving, kayaking, fishing, photography, offshore fishing from boats, and hiking. The trail nearest the nature center would consist of a kiosk, interpretive signs, and a boardwalk that is handicap accessible.

All interpretive materials in English and Chamorro will be translated into Japanese and Korean. A new accessible self-guided trail will continue to be constructed. Information via brochures and exhibits about conservation of natural resources and habitat restoration will be shared with visitors to enhance awareness and reduce the impact visitors have on the Refuge.

The fishing program will be reevaluated based on information obtained during creel and reef surveys. A wildlife observation and photography clinic will be implemented. A display area will be created for local wildlife photographs to be exhibited.

Traditional cultural practices are allowed on Refuge lands. These practices include medicinal plant collection and food plant collection; Special Use Permits (SUPs) are issued for the collection of medicinal plants, breadfruit, and coconuts. Firewood collection is permitted after storms and when available from construction projects.

The Refuge has rich cultural aspects that date back to pre-European settlement. To preserve and protect Guam's tangible cultural resources and Guam's native heritage practices, protection of cultural resources will continue to be enforced. Sites such as caves, latte stones, and middens (see Appendix I) will be cataloged and mapped, but not published. Increased historical research of cultural materials, pictographs, latte stones, and middens will be necessary to identify the history and age of these items, and accurately interpret and document archaeological resources. With a pest wall in place, trespass will likely be reduced thus minimizing vandalism to and poaching of ancient cultural items such as pictographs and pottery pieces.

Figure 3.

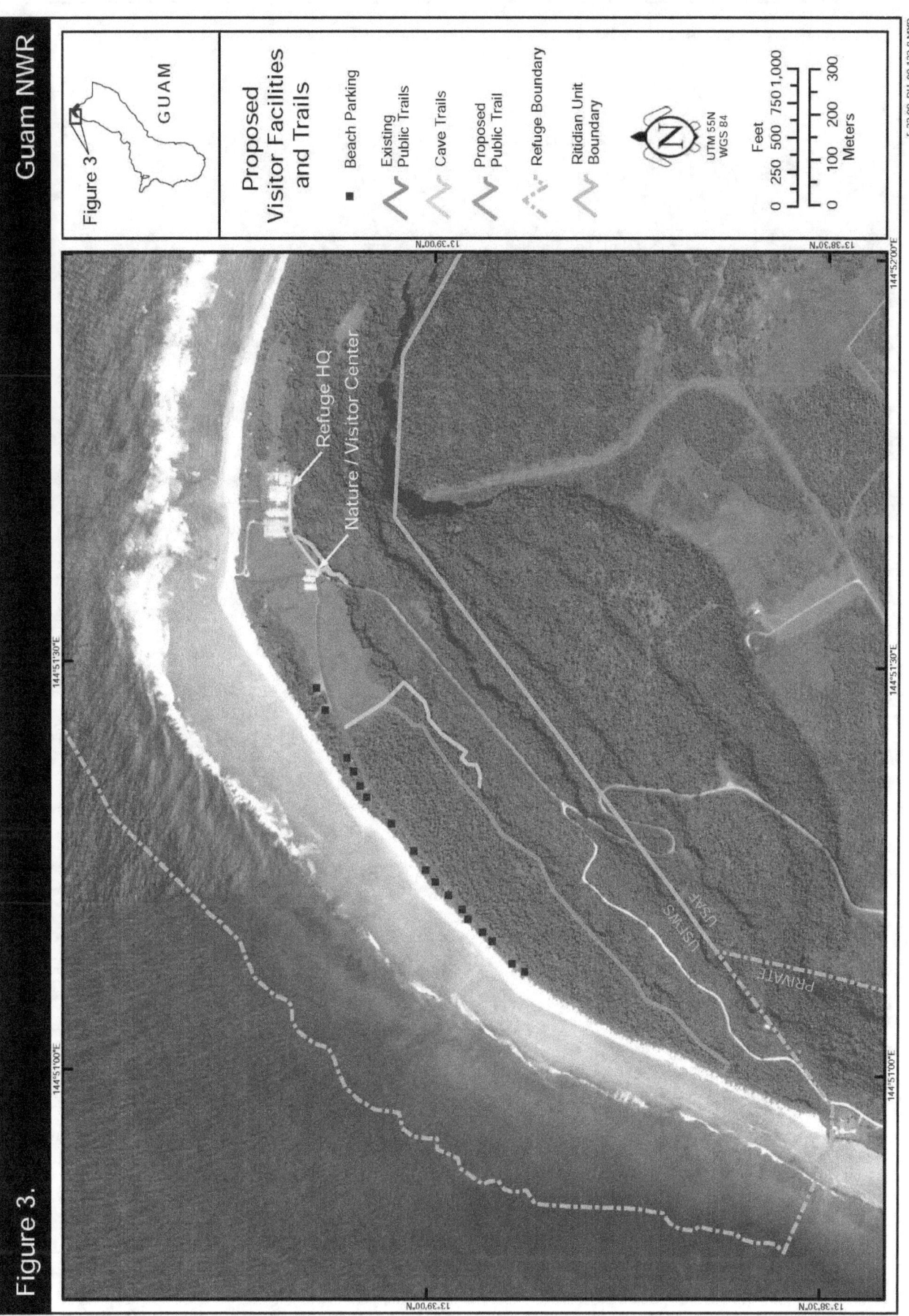

Guam NWR

Figure 3

GUAM

Proposed Visitor Facilities and Trails

■ Beach Parking

Existing Public Trails

Cave Trails

Proposed Public Trail

Refuge Boundary

Ritidian Unit Boundary

UTM 55N
WGS 84

Feet
0   250   500   750   1,000

Meters
0   100   200   300

5-22-09, DH, 09-122-8.MXD

Refuge HQ

Nature / Visitor Center

USFWS
USAF

PRIVATE

The back sides of pages with maps are blank to facilitate map readability.

3.3 Goals, Objectives, Strategies, and Rationale

Goals and objectives are the unifying elements of successful refuge management. They identify and focus management priorities, resolve issues, and link to refuge purposes, Service policy, and the Refuge System mission.

A CCP describes management actions that help bring a refuge closer to its vision. A vision broadly reflects a refuge's purposes, Refuge System mission and goals, other statutory requirements, and larger-scale plans as appropriate. Goals then define general targets in support of the vision, followed by objectives that direct effort into incremental and measurable steps toward achieving those goals. Finally, strategies identify specific tools and actions to accomplish objectives. Unless specifically stated, all objectives are applicable throughout the life of this plan.

Goals for the Guam Refuge for the next 15 years are presented on the following pages. Each goal is followed by the objectives that pertain to that goal. The goal order does not imply any priority in this CCP. Some objectives pertain to multiple goals and have simply been placed in the most reasonable spot. Similarly, some strategies pertain to multiple objectives. Following the goals, objectives, and strategies is a brief rationale intended to provide further background information pertaining to the importance of an objective relative to legal mandates for managing units of the System including refuge purpose, trust resource responsibilities (federally listed threatened and endangered species and migratory birds), and maintaining/restoring biological integrity, diversity, and environmental health.

Goals and Objectives for the U.S. Air Force and U.S. Navy Overlay Units

The Air Force and Navy Overlay Units are undergoing separate INRMP planning processes that will involve Service personnel. Because the habitat types found on the Overlay Units are also found on the Ritidian Unit, we urge our DOD partners to integrate the goals, objectives, and strategies in this CCP into the management of the Overlay Units. Cohesive management of adjacent and nearby lands would offer distinct advantages in terms of habitat and species benefits.

Goal 1. Restore, protect, and maintain native limestone forest representative of historic Guam and other Mariana Islands.

Objective 1a: Protect, restore and maintain native limestone forest.
Protect, restore, and maintain the 220 acres of native limestone forest habitat on the Ritidian Unit of the Guam Refuge to promote the recovery of threatened and endangered plants and animals, as well as benefit other migratory birds and native forest-dependent species (e.g., land snails, lizards, coconut crabs). Native limestone forest habitat has the following characteristics: <ul><li>Dominant, tall tree species consisting of *Aglaia mariannensis*, *Guamia mariannae*, and *Ficus prolixa*. (Quinata 1994).</li><li>Understory species include the above as well as *Morinda citrifolia*, *Cycas micronesica* and *Wikstroemia elliptica*.</li><li>Rare plant species found in native limestone forest include *Heritieria longipetiolata*, *Serianthes nelsonii*, *Solanum guamense*, *Canavalia sericea*, and Cycads free of</li></ul>

mortality causing pests.
- Minimal reptilian and rodent species (e.g., BTS, monitor lizard, rats,).
- Natural systems govern seed survival.
- Minimal ungulate species (feral pig, Philippine deer).
- Reduced pest plant species (*Leucaena leucocephala*).
- Minimal human disturbance.

Strategies
Repatriate and/or out-plant native plants.
Build and maintain a multi-species barrier to exclude ungulate, reptilian, and rodent pest species.
Control pest plant species using appropriate IPM techniques including: • pesticide applications; • mowing; • brush cutting; • approved bio-controls; • hand removal/hand pulling.
Restrict public access to limit the spread of pest species.
Remove ungulates from within exclosure through appropriate IPM techniques, including shooting, trapping, and snaring.
Remove reptilian and rodent pests from within exclosure through appropriate IPM techniques including trapping, baiting, and shooting.

Rationale
The Ritidian Unit is a politically distinct unit of continuous terrain containing several habitat types, including limestone forest. Limestone forest is one of the forest community types that comprise the primary constituent elements listed in the critical habitat determination for the Mariana fruit bat, Mariana crow, and Micronesian kingfisher. Several threats exist to the natural regeneration of plants within this community, including the loss of pollinators and seed dispersers, insect and mammal seed predators, and feral ungulate trampling and grazing. Ungulate fencing or a multi-species barrier is key to habitat protection and management. Native overstory and understory trees are important to the biological integrity, diversity, and environmental health of the limestone forest community. In addition, native trees provide opportunities for foraging, loafing, and nesting of threatened and endangered species. Pest species can be defined as invasive exotic or native species which are not ecologically balanced with the existing environment and pose a threat to biological integrity, diversity, and environmental health. Pest plant species of concern which impact the diversity and abundance of native plant species includes Tangan tangan, mile-a-minute vine, and many grasses.

Objective 1b: Cooperate with and provide management guidance to the Navy and Air Force for native limestone forest habitat on the Overlay Units through close coordination and development of the respective INRMPs.
Refuge and Ecological Services staffs will be involved with preparing/approving the INRMPs. Service priorities for the Overlay Units include exclusionary fencing, BTS suppression, habitat restoration, pest species removal, and endangered/extirpated species releases.

Goal 2. Restore, protect, and maintain the shoreline habitat community representative of historic Guam and other Mariana Islands.

Objective 2a: Protect, restore, and maintain the shoreline habitat community.
Protect, manage, and restore 120 acres of shoreline community (sand beach, coastal strand, and coastal back strand forest habitats) to promote the recovery of threatened and endangered animals and plants, as well as benefit other native and migratory birds and native snails on the Ritidian Unit, with the following characteristics: <ul><li>Strand communities consist of well drained soils and vegetation that is adapted to salt spray from coastal waters and is occasionally inundated with saltwater during storm events.</li><li>The varying plant communities found in coastal strand often consist of an overstory made up of coconut, ironwood, and fagot, with an understory consisting of hibiscus, beach morning glory, and scaevola.</li><li>7-10% cover of native grasses (e.g., *Eragrostis spp.*) and herbaceous vegetation (e.g., *Ipomoea indica*) (natives) in coastal strand habitat.</li><li>Less than 10% cover of invasive grasses, herbaceous (*Carica papaya*) and woody (e.g., *Leucana leucocephala*) species (invasives) in coastal strand and coastal back strand forest habitat.</li><li>Dominant tall tree species consisting of *Aglai mariannensis*, *Guamia mariannae*, and *Ficus prolixa*. (Quinata 1994).</li><li>Understory species include the above as well as *Morinda citrifolia*, *Cycas micronesica* and *Wikstroemia elliptica*.</li><li>Rare plant species found in native limestone forest include *Heritieria longipetiolata*, *Serianthes nelsonii*, *Solanum guamense*, *Canavalia sericea*.</li><li>Cycads free of mortality causing pests.</li><li>Minimal reptilian and rodent species (e.g., BTS, monitor lizards, rats,).</li><li>Minimal ungulate species (feral pigs, Philippine deer).</li><li>Minimal human disturbance.</li></ul>
Strategies
Build and maintain a multi-species barrier to exclude ungulate, reptilian, and rodent pest species.
Restore 42-acre planted coconut grove near office to native habitat.
Support GDAWR (2006) to meet objectives within the Guam Comprehensive Wildlife Conservation Strategy.
Restore the 16-acre open field adjacent to the Nature Center to coastal strand habitat.
Propagate and interplant native coastal strand forest and beach strand vegetation.
The Refuge law enforcement officer will coordinate with GDAWR law enforcement to protect coastal strand.
Jointly monitor with GDAWR and NOAA for marine debris and implement measures for its removal.
Maintain no exterior lights.
Control pest plant species using appropriate IPM techniques including: <ul><li>pesticide applications;</li><li>mowing;</li><li>brush cutting;</li><li>approved bio-controls; and</li></ul>

• hand removal/hand pulling.
Remove ungulates from within exclosure through appropriate IPM techniques including shooting, trapping, and snaring.
Remove reptilian and rodent pests from within exclosure through appropriate IPM techniques including trapping, baiting, and shooting.
Close areas of coastal strand to reduce trampling of vegetation and nests, and the threat of introduction of pest plants.
Provide limited access points and picnic spots for beach access to reduce the human-use footprint in the environment.
Rationale:
Shoreline communities, by nature, are frequently disturbed by storms, tides, and flooding events. The coastal strand habitat is generally comprised of plants that are relatively widespread, easily dispersed, resistant to disturbance, and can reestablish from populations on other islands (Lobban and Schefter 1997). Coastal strand forests also are prone to disturbance. These attributes are conducive to restoration activities. Several endangered species and other species of concern rely on these habitats. These species include the Mariana fruit bat, Mariana crow, Guam rail, Micronesian kingfisher, rare plants, and land snails. Shoreline communities may also be used in the future by repatriated Guam rail, Micronesian kingfisher, and Guam swiftlet. Green turtles, and possibly hawksbill turtles, nest, feed, and loaf in this community as well. These areas are also utilized by foraging shorebirds and nesting seabirds.

Objective 2b: Cooperate with and provide management guidance to Navy and Air Force cooperators to restore, conserve, protect, and maintain the shoreline habitat community on Overlay Units through close coordination and development of the respective INRMPs.
The Service's Refuge and Ecological Services staff will be involved with preparation and approval of the INRMPs. Service priorities for the Overlay Units include exclusionary fencing, BTS suppression, habitat restoration, pest species removal, and endangered/extirpated species releases.

Goal 3. Conserve, protect, and maintain the native halophytic-xerophytic plant community representative of historic Guam and the other Mariana Islands.

Objective 3a: Conserve, protect, and maintain the halophytic-xerophytic plant community.
Protect and maintain 45 acres of halophytic-xerophytic plant community on the Ritidian Unit to benefit native and migratory birds: Ruddy turnstone (*Arenaria interpres*), Wandering tattler (*Heteroscelus incanus*), Pacific golden-plover (*Pluvialis fulva*), Intermediate egret (*Egretta intermedia*), and Pacific reef-heron (*Egretta sacra*). Halophytic-xerophytic plant communities have the following characteristics: • Occur on terraces, cliff edges, and vertical cliffs and can be subject to extreme salt spray. • Vegetation is usually low and tangled, often in dense thickets. • Typical native species include *Sporobolus farinosus*, *Polyscias grandifolia*, *Wollastonia biflora* var. *canescens*, *Capparis cordifolia*, *Ficus spp.*, *Peperomia*, *Portulaca australis*, and *Bikkia mariannensis*.

• Minimal invasive plants or animals such as BTS, rats, and mile-a-minute vine.
Strategies
Maintain closure to public access.
Control pest species using appropriate IPM techniques including: • pesticide applications;   • approved bio-controls;   • hand removal/hand pulling;   • non-public removal of feral ungulates.
Rationale:
Halophytic-xerophytic plant communities are fragile and uniquely adapted to extreme climate and growing conditions. These may be level or cliff habitats. Salt spray, wind, sunlight exposure, and limited soils all contribute to limited but unique plant diversity. Ungulate trampling and introduction of pest plants are the two greatest threats. Climate change may become a threat. Because of the limited amount of halophytic-xerophytic habitat throughout Micronesia, it is especially important to the biological integrity, diversity, and environmental health of the Refuge. Refuge staff members plan to remove nonnative vines such as the dodder.

Objective 3b: Cooperate with and provide management guidance to Navy and Air Force cooperators to restore, conserve, protect, and maintain the halophytic-xerophytic habitat community on the Overlay Units through close coordination during development of their respective INRMPs.
The Service's Refuge and Ecological Services staff will be involved with preparation and approval of the INRMPs. Service priorities for the Overlay Units include exclusionary fencing, BTS suppression, habitat restoration, pest species removal, and endangered/extirpated species releases.

Goal 4. Conserve, protect, and maintain limestone cave habitat to meet the life-history needs of endemic, cave-dwelling species characteristic of historic Guam and other Mariana Islands.

Objective 4a: Conserve, protect, and maintain limestone cave habitat
Protect and maintain caves and cave dependant species (e.g., Guam swiftlet) throughout the year on the Ritidian Unit, with the following characteristics: • Minimal mud dauber wasps and other invasive insect species (e.g., cockroaches and ants).   • Minimal degradation (i.e., trampling, plant dispersement, excrement) by ungulates and rodents.
Strategies
Encourage/cooperate with researchers to identify IPM strategies to control wasps (see strategies under Objective 7b).
Allow human access of Ritidian Cave by a guided tour (see objective 9a).
Incorporate cave restoration as a component within an overall habitat management plan (see Objective 7a).
Control pest species using appropriate IPM techniques including pesticide applications, approved bio-controls, trapping mammals, and hand removal/hand pulling .
Rationale:

The endangered Guam swiftlet once inhabited caves on the Ritidian Unit, and are now confined to a few caves in southern Guam on the Navy Overlay Unit. The Navy, GDAWR, and the Service have discussed the need to re-establish a swiftlet colony in caves at the Ritidian Unit to decrease the potential for a catastrophic loss of the birds from their current limited range. Nonnative animals often use caves and change the nutrient cycles and atmosphere of the caves by dying and defecating in them.

Objective 4b: Cooperate with and provide management guidance to Navy and Air Force cooperators to restore, conserve, protect, and maintain the halophytic-xerophytic habitat community on the Overlay Units through close coordination and development of the respective INRMPs

The Service's Refuge and Ecological Services staffs will be involved with preparation and approval of the INRMPs. Service priorities for the Overlay Units include exclusionary fencing, BTS suppression, habitat restoration, pest species removal, and endangered/extirpated species releases.

Goal 5. Restore, protect, and maintain native marine communities representative of historic Guam and other Mariana Islands.

Objective 5a: Restore, protect, and maintain marine submerged lands and nearshore waters

Protect and maintain approximately 832 acres of marine submerged lands and the associated nearshore waters to a depth of 100 feet (30 meters) at the Ritidian Unit for the benefit of sea turtles and a diverse assemblage of other native marine life. The marine community has the following characteristics:

- Shoreline and coral reefs free of marine debris.
- Minimal presence of invasive/undesirable species (e.g., invasive algae).
- Minimal human disturbance, especially during turtle breeding season (time period).
- Highest quality, unpolluted marine waters.

Strategies

Use IPM techniques to control and, where possible, eradicate invasive marine species including hand removal, mechanical and biological controls, and pesticide applications.

Remove marine debris from coral reefs and shoreline habitats.

Remove concrete, metal, and other structural materials.

Close areas to visitor use to protect species and habitat.

Rationale:

The Ritidian Unit has high quality and unique coral assemblages when compared to other areas on Guam (Randall, R. 2000). Marine debris and trampling are threats to the coral reef ecosystem. The Refuge hopes to reduce these threats by educating and regulating visitors and responding quickly to influxes of large amounts of marine debris.

Goal 6. Protect and promote the recovery of extirpated and/or federally listed threatened and endangered species that are endemic to Guam, along with benefits to locally listed species and species of greatest conservation need.

Objective 6a: Cooperate in captive rearing and release of endangered species endemic to Guam.
Cooperate with GDAWR, Navy, and Air Force to develop a captive rearing program and soft release sites for the Mariana crow, Micronesian kingfisher, Guam rail, and Mariana fruit bat.
Strategies
Work with cooperators to implement recovery tasks, initially on the Ritidian Unit, and then on the Overlay Units.
Supervise and support Navy-funded biologist for the Navy Overlay Unit.
Participate in captive rearing program.
Develop soft release sites.
Use appropriate IPM techniques to control invasive/pest species (BTS, deer, pigs, carabao, monitor lizards, cats, dogs, feral chickens, rats, shrews, predatory flatworms, mud-dauber wasps) including: • pesticide applications; • trapping; • shooting (non-public removal); • fencing/screening; • biological controls.
Rationale:
The purpose of the Refuge and the expectation of the public on Guam are for the Refuge to restore those species impacted by BTS and other causes for future generations. The Ritidian Unit has been designated as Critical Habitat for three listed species: the threatened Mariana fruit bat and endangered Micronesian kingfisher and Mariana crow. Green turtles nest and hawksbill turtles are suspected to nest on the Ritidian Unit

Objective 6b: Promote recovery of the federally listed endangered Guam swiftlet.
Cooperate with GDAWR, Navy, and Air Force on habitat improvements for a healthy, self-sustaining, wild population of the endangered Guam swiftlet, with the following characteristics: Predator-free caves.
Strategies
Establish a colony of Guam swiftlets through transplant releases into one predator-free cave at the Ritidian Unit.
Assist Navy and Air Force cooperators with Guam swiftlet recovery tasks, initially on the Overlay Units, then on the Ritidian Unit.
Rationale:
The purpose of the Refuge and the expectation of the public on Guam are for us to restore species decimated and extirpated by BTS and other causes, for future generations. The zoo-archaeological record (bones) demonstrates that swiftlets previously occupied caves on the Ritidian Unit. Threats to the caves include BTS, mud dauber wasps, cockroaches, and disturbance by humans and feral animals.

Objective 6c: Contribute to the repatriation of extirpated species.

Within 10 years of CCP approval, contribute to the restoration of suitable, predator-free habitats on the Ritidian Unit as a basis for potential repatriation of extirpated species (e.g., Rufous fantail or "Chichirika"; Cardinal Honeyeater or "Egigi"; and Mariana Fruit-Dove or "Totot").
Strategies
Work with cooperators to document species status and appropriate restoration actions.
Develop repatriation plan.
Rationale:
The purpose of the Refuge and the expectation of the public on Guam are for us to restore those species decimated and extirpated by BTS and other causes for future generations.

Objective 6d: Minimize disturbance to nesting, loafing, and foraging sea turtles.
Minimize disturbance to nesting green and hawksbill turtles, turtle nests and eggs, and loafing and foraging sites on lands and associated waters of the Ritidian Unit.
Strategies
Nest site fencing to protect from predators.
Maintain closed area for turtle protection (boats).
Localized beach closures surrounding nest sites.
Enhance and continue supporting the Haggan Watch turtle nest monitoring program to search for nest crawls.
Rationale:
The volunteer Haggan Watch program is generating interest in the protection of sea turtles. It aids in turtle counts and successful nest location. Education and enforcement are still necessary due to traditional sea turtle consumption and turtle egg poaching. Eggs may also be dug up by feral pigs and monitor lizards.

Objective 6e: Protect and promote the recovery of the endangered *Serianthes nelsonii* tree.
Work with cooperators to establish healthy, self-sustaining populations of the endangered tree, *Serianthes nelsonii*, with the following characteristics: reduced ungulate populations in outplanting areas; and suitable soil characteristics.
Strategies
Out-plant and maintain up to 100 *Serianthes nelsonii* trees to a pest-resistant size in various areas of the Refuge within 15 years.
Rationale:
In 2006 a small project began to increase *Serianthes nelsonii* populations on Guam and Rota. Seeds were collected from Rota and seedlings were easily germinated, but were attacked by pests almost immediately. Seedlings are still in the nursery due to the need for constant care.

Goal 7. Gather scientific information (i.e., research, inventory, and monitoring) to increase our knowledge and understanding of Refuge resources, and the threats and impacts to Pacific Island ecosystems in support of management decisions associated with Goals 1-6.

Objective 7a: Promote management-related research.
Continue to promote management-related research and monitoring. Highest priority research needs are pest species control and eradication.

Strategies
Establish and develop partnerships with other agencies, organizations, and universities to pursue joint research projects.
Encourage Refuge staff to publish in peer-reviewed scientific journals, and attend professional society and agency-sponsored meetings and conferences.
Require researchers to use regionally comparable field methods where feasible and appropriate.
Identify and pursue funding opportunities for research.
Identify areas of mutual interest between partners and the Refuge, including research, monitoring, habitat restoration, and endangered species recovery.
Establish and monitor transects and perform creel surveys. Continue and expand partnerships to manage coral reef ecosystems.
Continue joint wildlife surveys, such as turtle monitoring, with GDAWR.
Research restoration of native pollinators.
Rationale:
The Refuge System encourages compatible research activities on Refuge lands. Research and monitoring projects on Refuge lands enhance scientific understanding of ecosystems and lead to better management. Disseminating research findings is a responsibility of Service staff. Presenting results and ideas helps foster understanding and respect for Refuge management actions, and also leads to conservation of natural resources through understanding and informed management decisions. Research presentations also provide a forum for research and management improvements through peer-review. Modification of databases and methods to be comparable and compatible to other research is a cost-effective way to conduct comprehensive Refuge research. Being able to compare Refuge data with other local, regional, and even global data will help guide ecosystem management priorities for Refuge resources.

Objective 7b: Conduct inventories and monitoring on terrestrial habitat, habitat use, and response to management activities.
Inventory and monitor Refuge resources (in priority order): • presence of pest species; • endangered species presence and habitat use; • vegetative species and plant communities; and • responses of habitat and wildlife to management activities such as ungulate removal, out-planting, and BTS control.
Strategies
Document presence/absence of native and nonnative species.
Conduct comprehensive inventory of plant species distribution, including use of GPS and vegetation transects.
Evaluate wasp impacts to cave habitats and assess efficacy of control methods.
Coordinate with Regional Office GIS staff to assess and/or develop remote sensing capability to map and monitor habitats.
Monitor BTS population and size trends associated with evaluating effectiveness of control methods.
Monitor cycads for presence of pests.

Develop and maintain a photographic inventory of plant responses.
Develop and implement a Refuge terrestrial and marine habitat and wildlife monitoring plan within two years of CCP approval.
Rationale:
In general, collecting baseline biological information is essential to adequately understand and manage the Refuge. Long-term monitoring efforts are extremely valuable in terms of the information provided and in adaptive management techniques.

Objective 7c: Inventory and monitor marine communities.
Monitor (in priority order): <ul><li>turtle species presence, absence, nesting and use;</li><li>coral species abundance, frequency, health, density, diversity, and distribution;</li><li>fish species presence, absence, and habitat associations;</li><li>other invertebrates;</li><li>marine plants; and</li><li>human use of marine resources.</li></ul>
Strategies
Develop partnerships with local staff of federal and territorial agencies, such as the Service's Ecological Services, National Park Service, and NOAA, and accompany on marine surveys.
Develop and implement a Refuge terrestrial and marine habitat and wildlife monitoring plan within two years of CCP approval.
Record observations of corals, fish, turtles, marine mammals, and their habitats.
Conduct Rapid Ecological Assessments (REA) on all existing survey routes to document coral, fish, and turtle density, diversity, distribution, and habitat associations.
Develop and conduct surveys of nearshore and other areas for turtle use.
Inventory marine habitats to establish a baseline on benthic structure, coral species richness and diversity, and algal abundance and diversity.
Conduct creel surveys to document fishing pressure.
Rationale:
In general, collection of baseline biological information is essential to adequately understand and manage the Refuge. Long-term monitoring efforts are extremely valuable in terms of the information provided and in adaptive management techniques.
Objective 7d: Seek partnerships to understand impacts of global climate change.
Develop partnerships to increase scientific understanding of the impacts of global climate change on tropical island ecosystems, specifically as these impacts relate to Guam Refuge.
Strategies
Develop partnerships with agencies or institutions to conduct baseline global climate change investigations.
Establish monitoring protocol which measures: <ul><li>water quality (temperature, dissolved oxygen, pH, CO_2,)</li><li>coral health (presence and distribution of coral bleaching and disease)</li><li>bacterial, nutrient, and sediment loads</li><li>sea level elevation</li></ul>
Assess global climate change impacts to Refuge resources.
Rationale:

It is increasingly important to understand the impacts that global climate change might have on Pacific Ocean islands and the wildlife resources they provide. In order to determine if management activities are necessary to offset the impacts of global climate change, Refuge staff will need a baseline from which to measure future change. Climate change and solutions to such should be incorporated in interpretive and environmental education mediums.

Goal 8. Teach students and teachers the value of the Refuge's ecology and the management practices necessary to recover and protect the Refuge's natural and cultural resources.

Objective 8a: Provide a quality environmental education program.
Provide a quality on- and off-site environmental education program with specific learning objectives and diverse opportunities with the following attributes: • Helps fulfill the Territorial standards for learning.   • Content is based on the Refuge's biological and cultural management goals and objectives and includes accurate information about climate change with obtainable solutions.   • Supports the Service's "Connecting People with Nature" priority.
Strategies
Train volunteers, interns from local colleges, AmeriCorps, or the Student Conservation Association to organize and instruct the environmental educational program.
Explore opportunities to recruit additional teacher volunteers from the local school system.
Develop curricula for the environmental education program.
Provide support and resources for a Friends group and volunteers.
Design and conduct regular needs assessments, and pre- and post-visit evaluations with teachers and students, to improve programs as needed.
Develop, train, and utilize Refuge staff to instruct more "teach the teacher" workshops.
Include teachers and students in long-term science data collection and restoration/conservation management activities as Refuge habitat work projects.
Respond to all requests and inquiries for environmental education programs in a timely manner, and advertise education programs at local schools.
Make independent environmental education study sites available.
Develop and provide site-specific materials and tools for educators' use.
Utilize and retrofit existing high quality programs, such as Navigating Change and Project Wild, to make site-specific to Guam Refuge.
Encourage non-participating local schools to participate in programs.
Rationale:
Refuge staff members have the opportunity to emphasize and expand upon meaningful hands-on connections between children and the importance of wildlife, wildlife habitats, and open space to their personal and community health and well-being. In addition, they would promote understanding and support for the Refuge. For environmental education and outreach opportunities, we would work on a long-term emphasis to help change local perception of the purpose and need for the Refuge. The number of habitats in close proximity to the Ritidian Unit provides a unique opportunity to develop a wide variety of programs for returning students and visitors. Fiscal challenges make it difficult for some schools to take advantage of Refuge opportunities.

Goal 9. Provide opportunities for residents and visitors to enjoy, value, and support the Refuge.

Objective 9a: Provide a quality interpretive and nature-related recreational program.
Provide safe, year-round, attractive, and accessible opportunities for Refuge visitors to observe, photograph, learn about, and enjoy Refuge habitats and wildlife, with the following attributes: <ul><li>Interpretive themes should address endangered species, invasive species, marine ecosystem, climate change, and the cultural heritage inherent in the Refuge's natural and cultural resources;</li><li>Facilities should be accessible to individuals with disabilities and safe for all visitors; and</li><li>Access to natural public use areas provided to Refuge visitors.</li></ul>
Strategies
Develop a roving interpretive program with trained volunteers. Docents will give guided programs or short 10 minute Beach Interpretive Talks.
Develop and maintain an accessible interpretive self-guided trail across from the nature center.
Develop an accessible interpretive self-guided trail in the coastal strand with interpretive exhibits located in kiosks.
Offer guided tours to the pictograph cave.
Develop a visitor services step-down plan that defines specific interpretive themes and how to achieve outcomes and reach specific audiences.
Develop interpretive materials (brochures, kiosk panels, species lists) with assistance from Honolulu and Regional Office staff.
Maintain guided tours to Ritidian Cave.
Maintain trails, and informational/interpretive signs to alert visitors to regulations and hazards.
Periodically monitor and evaluate the interpretive program's content by consulting with university faculty to review, update, and ground-truth cultural resource information.
Provide specific directional and interpretive/informational signage for beach and trail access, including turtle nesting closure information in cooperation with other agencies (NOAA and GDAWR).
Develop and implement a volunteer corps that supports management activities (Haggan Watch, out-planting, interpretive tours, etc.).
Evaluate an entrance fee program with annual passes.
Establish a Refuge Friends group.
Evaluate opportunities to open the Refuge during federal holidays and extended hours.
Investigate grant opportunities to strengthen outreach and environmental education partnerships
Rationale:
The Improvement Act defines environmental education and interpretation as wildlife-dependent public uses. Such uses are to receive special consideration in planning for and managing the Refuge. When determined compatible on a Refuge-specific basis, these uses are priority public uses of that national wildlife refuge. National wildlife refuges are to seek opportunities to allow these uses in an appropriate and compatible manner.   At Guam Refuge, there is a unique opportunity to reach out to non-wildlife-oriented Refuge visitors about Guam's native wildlife and cultural heritage. In addition, there is an opportunity to make connections and parallels between Guam's cultural and natural resources and heritage.

The Ritidian Unit provides an opportunity to experience multiple habitat types in close proximity.

Interpretation of cultural resources can instill a conservation ethic among the public and those who encounter or manage the resources. The aim of the cultural resource interpretive program is to:

(1) translate the results of cultural research into language and media that can be understood and appreciated by a variety of audiences; (2) relate the connection between cultural and natural resources and the role of humans in the environment; (3) foster an awareness and appreciation of native cultures; and (4) instill an ethic for the conservation of Guam's cultural heritage.

Objective 9b: Provide a quality recreational fishing program.

Provide safe, year-round, attractive, and accessible opportunities for Refuge visitors to fish (rod and reel, talaya (i.e., throw-net), spear fish (hand spears and Hawaiian slings)) and hand collect with the following attributes:

- Safe environment for visitors;
- Visitor access to public use areas;
- Visitors keep only what they need;
- Visitors understand the need for regulations; and
- Turtle nesting areas are protected.

Strategies

Publish Refuge fishing regulations as established.

Enforce the Code of Federal Regulations for Guam Refuge.

Institute a fishing resources education program.

Base program management on creel survey and other marine monitoring information.

Evaluate opportunities to open the Refuge during federal holidays and extended hours.

Rationale:

The Improvement Act defined environmental education and interpretation as wildlife-dependent public uses. Such uses are to receive special consideration in planning for and management of the refuges. When determined compatible on a refuge, these uses are priority general public uses. National wildlife refuges are to seek opportunities to allow these uses if appropriate and compatible. On Guam the local population's interest in fishing is high, thus the Refuge provides an immediate direct connection of local interest. The diverse cultural subsistence fishing practices that occur on the Refuge can have unanticipated impacts on the resources. On Guam, fishing licenses are not required, however, catch from the Refuge may not be sold or traded.

Objective 9c: Investigate and evaluate the potential for an access fee at Guam NWR.

The recreation fee program provides opportunities for resource management agencies to charge entrance fees on public lands to provide public programs that require additional facilities and/or staffing. There are a number of criteria and evaluations that must be performed to be included in the fee program. Staff will conduct the evaluations and initiate the fee program as appropriate. There will be an additional public process associated with any fee proposals.

Goal 10. Protect, preserve, evaluate, and when appropriate, interpret the Refuge's Chamorro cultural resources and associated practices.

Objective 10a: In cooperation with preservation partners (e.g., the Guam Preservation Trust and the University of Guam), evaluate, preserve, and protect the Refuge's cultural heritage and resources.
Evaluate known and potential cultural resources and historical sites on the Ritidian Unit, preserve site integrity, and protect sites from management and visitor activity as part of a cultural heritage program with the following attributes: • Complies with applicable cultural heritage laws and regulations; • Assures protection and preservation of cultural resources; and • Encourages cooperative partnerships for the study and preservation of cultural resources.
Strategies
Conduct on-site surveys to identify archaeological, cultural, and historical sites that coincide with existing and planned roads, facilities, visitor service areas, and habitat projects.
Implement the Guam Refuge Cultural Resources Overview and Management Plan (Appendix I).
Design and evaluate management activities to mitigate impacts to archaeological, cultural, and historical sites as necessary.
Ensure research programs and activities do not negatively impact cultural resources.
Rationale:
Various federal historic preservation laws and regulations require the Service to implement the kind of program described under this objective. Proactive survey, inventory, and research projects help ensure that we have the information needed to understand and protect cultural resource values and meet the requirements of the NHPA. Locations and timing of cultural resource surveys will be scheduled to minimize impacts to wildlife and habitats.

Objective 10b: Provide opportunities for cultural practitioners to participate in cultural practices on the Refuge.
Opportunities will continue for cultural practitioners to participate in cultural practice activities on the Refuge, including: • Collect medicinal plants; • Visit caves with cultural significance; and • Perform traditional ceremonies.
Strategies
Continue to provide opportunities for groups or individuals with cultural ties to collect medicinal plants.
Rationale:
The indigenous population developed medicinal remedies and practices before the islands were discovered by western civilizations. Where appropriate and compatible, Refuge staff members propose to allow for traditional uses.

Chapter 4. Physical Environment

4.1 Climate

The climate on Guam is characterized by warm temperatures and high relative humidity throughout the year, similar to other tropical islands in the Western Pacific. Annual variations in temperature, rain, wind, humidity, and storm frequency correspond to Guam's two distinct seasons: the wet season (July to November) and the dry season (December through June). The average annual temperature of Guam at sea level is 81°F, with the lowest temperatures recorded in January, the highest between June and November (Figure 6). Average humidity ranges between 65 to 80 percent during the day and 85 to 100 percent at night (Khosrowpanah and Jocson 2005). Humidity is at its highest during the wet season.

Mean island-wide rainfall on Guam is between 80 and 110 inches (in) per year (Figure 6). During the dry season, average monthly precipitation is 4.58 in. Rainfall increases during the rainy season to a mean of 11.75 in per month (http://ns.gov.gu/climate.html). In addition to seasonal variation, rainfall also depends on site location and elevation. Precipitation is not consistent throughout Guam; instead rainfall patterns follow the northeast-southwest orientation of the island. Rainfall is highest in central-northern Guam and along the western and southern mountains. The coastal lowlands typically receive less rainfall (Lander and Guard 2003). The least amount of rain falls on the areas southwest of Mount Santa Rosa, south of Ritidian Point, and along the southern coast. At Andersen AFB immediately south of the Ritidian Unit, mean monthly rainfall from 1950 to 2000 ranged between 4.1 in and 13.4 in (Lander and Guard 2003). Strong rainfall gradients are produced along the major mountain ranges and by the rain shadows of Mount Santa Rosa and Mount Barrigada (Lander and Guard 2003). Prolonged drought periods occur almost every four years during El Niño/Southern Oscillation (ENSO) events (Gingerich 2003).

Northeast trade winds are prevalent throughout the year, with an average annual wind speed between 4 and 12 miles per hour (mph) (Lander and Guard 2003). Winds tend to be stronger during the dry season, while weaker southern and southeasterly winds occur in the wet season (Neill and Rea 2004). Mean annual solar radiation from 1980 to 1990 was 4,834 watts per square meter (W/m^2) with cloud cover ranging from roughly 0 percent in the dry season to 30 percent in the wet season (Asami et al. 2004).

Wind speed and rainfall are also influenced by tropical storms, typhoons, and squalls. The Mariana Islands lie in the western Pacific typhoon trough; Guam often experiences typhoons (winds between 75 and 150 mph) and super-typhoons (winds over 150 mph) (USFWS and USAF 2002). Typhoons bring violent winds, generally heavy rain, and inundation of low-lying coastal areas and typically occur once or twice a year (USFWS 1992).

These storms can bring almost 20 in of rain in a single event (Mylroie et al. 2001). In 1976, Typhoon Pamela brought winds of 160 mph (USFWS 1992). Four super-typhoons have hit Guam over the past 10 years, causing extreme waves and winds greater than 150 mph (Guard et al. 2003). During 2002, Guam experienced the eye passage of two typhoons that produced high short-term rainfall and stream flows (Lander and Guard 2003). Although storms may occur throughout the year, the probability increases from July through September (Prasad and Manner 1994).

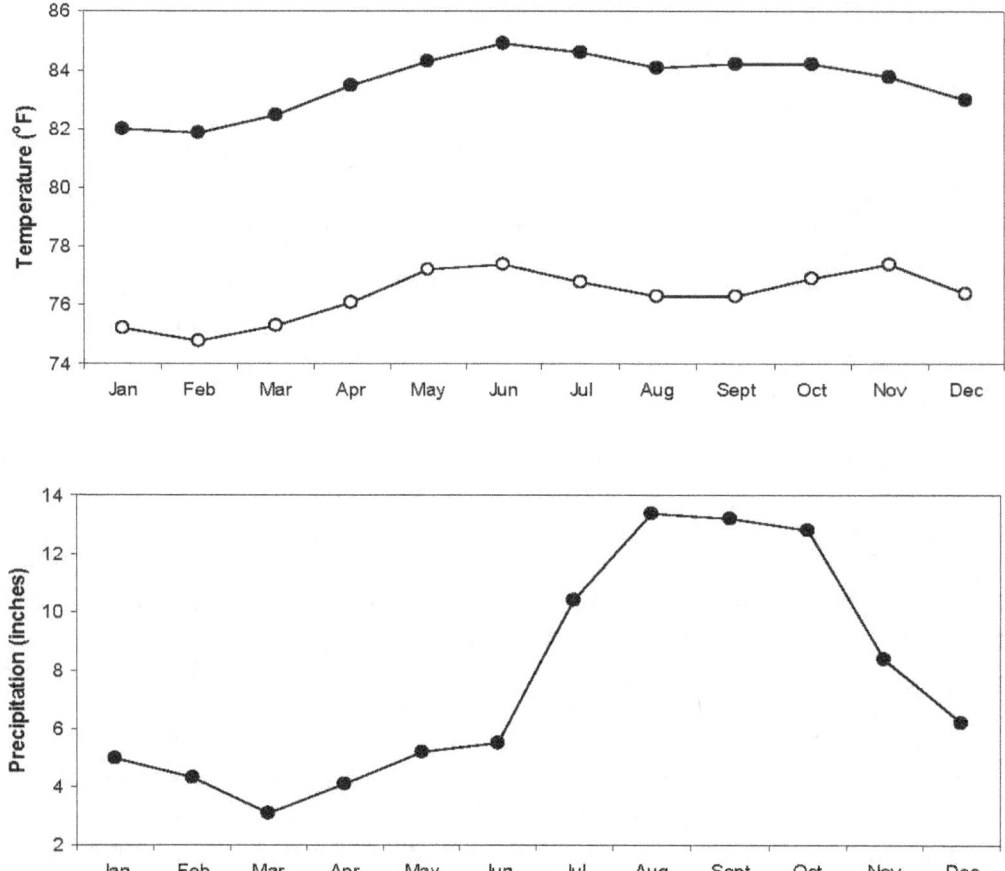

Figure 4. Average maximum and minimum temperature (°F) and total monthly precipitation for data taken at Andersen AFB, Guam, between 1953 and 2001. Source: Donnegan et al. (2004).

Prevailing ocean currents surrounding the island can further influence weather patterns by moderating the surrounding surface air temperature. Guam is situated in the north-westward-flowing North Equatorial Current. This current generates eddies in the lee of the island and is prevalent from June to December. The speed of this current varies from 4 in to 8 in per second (Wolanski et al. 2003). In addition, the Subtropical Countercurrent is associated with the northern part of the Marianas (Eldredge 1983). Sea surface temperatures surrounding Guam range from 81 to 86°F; however, water temperatures can be roughly 2° higher close to shore, in lagoons, and over reef flats (Jones et al. 1976, Paulay 2003). On the reef flat and fore reef off Ritidian Point, mean water temperature was 82.9°F, with higher records during summer months and low tides (Donaldson and Rongo 2006). The mean seawater density is approximately 25.7 percent (Eldredge 1983). There are both annual and super-annual variations in the oceanographic climate of the waters surrounding the Mariana Islands due to the influence of ENSO events where the Western Pacific Warm Pool (WPWP) migrates in response to large-scale climatic factors. During ENSO warm phase events, the easterly winds diminish and the WPWP moves eastward. In ENSO cool phases, the trades keep the warm water in a more westerly location (Asami et al. 2004).

4.2 Global Climate Change

Previous Changes in Global Climate and Future Projections

A continuously growing body of unequivocal scientific evidence has emerged supporting the theory of global climate change. During the 20th century the global environment experienced variations in average worldwide temperatures, sea levels, and chemical concentrations. Global air temperatures on the earth's surface have increased by 1.3°F since the mid 19th century (Solomon et al. 2007). Eleven of 12 years from 1995 to 2006 were the warmest on record since 1850 (IPCC 2007). Subsequently, sea levels rose approximately 1.7 mm (0.07 in) ± 0.5 mm/yr during the 20th century (Solomon et al. 2007); this rate rose dramatically to 3.1 mm (0.122 in) ± 0.7mm/yr since 1993 (IPCC 2007). While the concept of climate change is now widely accepted, the extent and impact of future changes as well as the exact source (natural or human induced) remains a debate (OPIC 2000). Emerging consensus contends that increasing quantities of greenhouse gases (GHGs) in the atmosphere, especially carbon dioxide (CO_2), are beginning to impact climate and may be the dominant force driving recent warming trends. The amount of GHGs globally has grown due to human activities since pre-industrial times, with an increase of 70% between 1970 and 2004 (IPCC 2007). The CO_2 has increased by about 80% in the same time period. The atmospheric concentrations of CO_2 and methane in 2005 were 379 ppm[3] and 1774 ppb, respectively. These amounts greatly exceed concentrations recorded in the global environment over the last 650,000 years (Solomon et al. 2007). The GHGs and other emissions from human activity have enhanced the heat trapping capability of the earth's atmosphere, causing warmer temperatures. Although the increase in carbon dioxide is largely attributed to fossil fuel use, land use changes have also increased the amount of cleared land surfaces, thereby reflecting more solar radiation (IPCC 2001, IPCC 2007, Solomon et al. 2007).

Global forecasting models offer a variety of predictions based on different emission scenarios. The Overseas Private Investment Corporation (OPIC) (2000) suggests that a further increase in GHG emissions could double atmospheric concentrations of CO_2 by 2060 and subsequently increase temperatures by as much as 2 to 6.5°F over the next century. Recent model experiments by Solomon et al. (2007) show that if GHGs and other emissions remain at 2000 levels, a further global average temperature warming of about 0.1°C per decade is expected. Sea-level rise is expected to accelerate by two to five times the current rates due to both ocean thermal expansion and the melting of glaciers and polar ice caps. Consequently, patterns of precipitation and evaporation may be altered. These changes may lead to more severe weather, shifts in ocean circulation (currents, upwelling), as well as adverse impacts to economies and human health (OPIC 2000, IPCC 2001, Buddemeier et al. 2004, IPCC 2007). Although there is considerable debate regarding the extent and the ultimate impact these changes will have on earth's environment, projected impacts that may have a significant effect on the coastal Refuge on Guam are discussed on the following pages.

Small Island Areas

The Intergovernmental Panel on Climate Change (IPCC), the international organization assessing risks of human induced climate change, recognizes that small island groups are particularly vulnerable to climate change. The following characteristics contribute to this vulnerability: small emergent land area compared to the large expanses of surrounding ocean;

limited natural resources; high susceptibility to natural disasters; and inadequate funds to mitigate impacts (IPCC 2001, IPCC 2007). The IPCC (2007) considers sea-level rise will exacerbate inundation, storm surges, erosion, and other coastal hazards, in addition to deterioration in costal conditions. Climate change is also expected to reduce water resources in small islands that could cause severe water shortages during low-rainfall periods. Higher temperatures may also increase the likelihood of invasion by nonnative species (IPCC 2007). Small islands such as Guam are considered to be under immediate threat of major environmental change due to a limited capacity to adapt to future climate changes. The Pacific Islands Regional Integrated Science and Assessment (Pacific RISA) is working to develop programs dealing with climate risk management in the Pacific region.

Coral Bleaching

Coral bleaching, the expulsion of symbiotic zooxanthellae from coral polyps and subsequent loss of photosynthetic pigments, is the result of both natural and anthropogenic stresses. Although corals may pale in response to seasonal increases in sea surface temperature, there has been a higher frequency of large scale bleaching events since the 1980s (Nicholls et al. 2007). The most severe global bleaching event ever recorded occurred in 1997-98 when over 50 countries showed signs of bleaching (Grimsditch and Salm 2005). Many species of coral currently exist in the upper limits of their specific temperature range; an increase in average sea-surface temperatures (even by 1.8 or 3.6°F) over a sustained period has been shown to cause mass bleaching, especially in shallow water habitats (Grimsditch and Salm 2005). Other variables contributing to bleaching episodes include extended periods of high temperatures, freshwater flooding, ultraviolet radiation, precipitation changes, salinity changes, light changes, sedimentation, and marine pollution.

Bleaching episodes in equatorial islands appear to be linked to the ENSO. Widespread bleaching events occurred during the El Niños of 1982-83, 1987-88, and 1997-98 (Buddemeier et al. 2004). During the warm phase of ENSO, or El Niño, sea-surface temperatures are usually warm, trade winds weak, and sea level decreases in the western Pacific (IPCC 2001, Buddemeier et al. 2004). These combined factors result in a dramatic increase in coral bleaching (Buddemeier et al. 2004). While El Niño events have increased in intensity and frequency over the past decades, some longer-term records have not found a direct link to global warming (Cobb et al. 2003) and do not predict significant changes in El Niño; however, they do suggest an evolution toward more "El Niño-like" patterns (Buddemeier et al. 2004). Most climate projections reveal that this trend is likely to increase rapidly in the next 50 years (Walther et al. 2002).

Most climate projections suggest that more intense wind speeds and precipitation amounts will accompany more frequent tropical typhoon/cyclones and increased tropical sea-surface temperatures in the next 50 years (Walther et al. 2002; Solomon et al. 2007). The third IPCC (2001) has concluded, with "moderate confidence," that the intensity of tropical cyclones is likely to increase by 10-20 percent in the Pacific region when atmospheric levels of CO_2 reach double pre-industrial levels (IPCC 2001). One model projects the frequency of 4 in per day rainfall events will double, and a 15-18 percent increase in rainfall intensity over large areas of the Pacific (IPCC 2001). Solomon et al. (2007) state it is "more likely than not" that the rise in intense tropical cyclones is due to anthropogenic activity. If coral reef ecosystems do not acclimate to projected thermal stresses, more frequent bleaching events and widespread mortality will occur. The ability of coral reef ecosystems to withstand these impacts will depend on the extent of degradation from other anthropogenic pressures and the frequency of future bleaching events (Nicholls et al. 2007).

Large-scale coral bleaching events are not common on Guam (Porter et al. 2005). Only two large scale bleaching events have been recorded on Guam and none of the reported cases have been accompanied by mass mortality. The bleaching event observed in 1994, which is not believed to be caused by increased seawater temperatures, affected roughly 68 percent of surveyed taxa. Minimal mortality was observed and interspecies response to bleaching was highly variable (Paulay and Benayahu 1999). Similarly, a 1996 bleaching event resulted in approximately half of the Acropora species showing moderate to heavy bleaching. Little mortality was seen during this event.

Preliminary information on more recent bleaching events has been documented. In June 2004, an event was recorded in Pago Bay, possibly due to the freshwater influx from Tropical Storm Tingting (Porter et al. 2005). On July 21, 2007, during a survey of the reef flat in the area of the Ritidian Unit that is closed to visitor use, coral bleaching was noticed. Further surveys to determine the extent of the bleaching have been conducted, but additional research is pending (C. Bandy, USFWS, personal communication). Scientists at the University of Guam Marine Laboratory have reported annual cases of coral bleaching on Guam that did not result in mass mortality; however, the threat of climate change-related bleaching events has increased due to rapid development and deforestation that could intensify atmospheric and sea surface temperature rises (Prasad and Manner 1994, Porter et al. 2005).

Ocean Acidification

Glacial and interglacial periods in the Earth's history, as measured from deep Antarctic ice cores, reveal cyclical fluctuations in the concentration of global CO_2. However, recent increases fall outside the range of peak prehistoric CO_2 levels. Current atmospheric CO_2 concentrations are at their highest levels in more than 160,000 years, with humans emitting 25 billion tons of CO_2 annually (Buddemeier et al. 2004). The rate of increase is also five to ten times more rapid than any of the sustained changes in the ice-core record (Vitousek 1994). The higher the concentration of CO_2 in the atmosphere, the greater the amount of CO_2 dissolved in the surface ocean. When CO_2 dissolves in seawater it forms carbonic acid (H_2CO_3), a weak acid that releases additional hydrogen ions and increases the acidity of the ocean. In order to buffer this acidity, the hydrogen ions react with carbonate (CO_3^{2-}) ions and convert them to bicarbonate ions (HCO_3^-). However, this buffering ability has diminished due to the rapidly rising CO_2 concentrations and the global seawater pH has decreased by 0.1 units since 1750, with regional variations (Royal Society 2005, IPCC 2007). Models predict that over the 21st century average surface ocean pH will continue to fall between 0.14 and 0.35 units (Solomon et al. 2007).

Increased atmospheric CO_2 and ocean acidification may impact marine organisms. As the concentration of carbonic acid and bicarbonate ions rises, the concentration of carbonate ions decreases. Many corals and marine organisms use calcium (Ca^{2+}) and carbonate ions from seawater to secrete $CaCO_3$ skeletons (Buddemeier et al. 2004, IPCC 2007). A lowered calcification rate means calcifying organisms (corals) may grow skeletons at a slower rate, lower density, and/or decreasing strength. Thus, changes in global seawater chemistry reduce the ability of corals to successfully compete for space and increase susceptibility to breakage (Grimsditch and Salm 2005). Furthermore, because coral growth rate will be inhibited, ocean chemical concentration changes may not be capable of keeping up with expected increases in sea level elevations. In addition to changes in the carbonate system, changes in ocean chemistry may affect the availability of nutrients and toxins to marine organisms.

Sea Level Rise

Climate change-induced thermal expansion of the sea is the main factor contributing to global sea level rise. Between 1961 and 2003, thermal expansion accounted for 0.016 in (0.4 mm) ± 0.1 mm sea level rise per year (Solomon et al. 2007, IPCC 2007). Melting ice-sheets, ice caps, and alpine glaciers also influence ocean levels (IPCC 2007). Near Pacific Island ecosystems, two factors may contribute to sea level rise: the rate and extent of global sea level rise and changes in episodic events, such as ENSO and storm-related conditions (Carter et al. 2001). While global sea levels are expected to increase by more than 31.5 in during the next two centuries, it is not possible to discuss uniform changes on a global scale due to localized variations (Michener et al. 1997).

Sea level change in the Pacific is highly variable due to geologic uplift (Carter et al. 2001). In contrast to the world's oceans, relative sea level near Guam is declining due to continuous tectonic uplift (Prasad and Manner 1994). Kayanne et al. (1993) determined that because tectonic uplift is abrupt, it is possible to separate this effect in order to predict sea level changes caused by climate change. When uplift is subtracted, sea level in the Mariana Islands rose 6 feet from 6,000 and 4,200 years before present and has remained stable to date (Kayanne et al. 1993). The Association of South Pacific Environmental Institutions Regional Task Team has identified Guam as one of the most vulnerable of the Pacific Islands to any sea level rise (Prasad and Manner 1994). The Ritidian Unit buildings are situated 18.6 feet above the high tide mark (C. Bandy, USFWS, personal communication). From a social and economic perspective, areas near the limestone plateau would be the least affected by sea level rise due to minimal activities on the shoreline (Prasad and Manner 1994), although damage to the submerged lands will likely occur.

Higher sea levels may inundate low-lying land areas, decreasing habitat for both marine and terrestrial species. For example, the narrow strip of nesting sea turtle habitat on Ritidian beach could be reduced as a result of coastal inundation. Fish et al. (2005) predicted that a 1.6-foot sea level rise will eliminate up to 32% of sea turtle nesting beach habitat in the Caribbean. Furthermore, sea level rises will increase the volume of water that covers reef habitats, causing some coral species to "starve" due to decreased light availability. It is possible that growth rates of most coral reefs will match predicted sea level rises (Buddemeier et al. 2004).

Cliff and shoreline erosion rates and patterns will be influenced by changes in sea level. As the ocean rises, wave activity amplifies erosion. Cliffs formed in softer lithologies are more likely to retreat (Nicholls et al. 2007). Accelerated erosion and enhanced sedimentation could further smother and stress corals (Porter et al. 2007).

Water Resources

Changes to freshwater resources as a result of variations in precipitation, evaporation, and ENSO patterns are variable depending on location and therefore difficult to predict. However, decreased salinity in both the mid- and high-latitude waters suggest that precipitation and evaporation rates are changing over the oceans (Solomon et al. 2007). Associated with the tropical Pacific and high latitude areas, recent studies demonstrate that the volume of precipitation per event is "very likely" to increase, while the number of precipitation events is "likely" to decrease in most subtropical regions (Solomon et al. 2007). Conversely, more intense and prolonged droughts have been observed in the tropics and subtropics since the 1970s (Solomon et al. 2007).

The IPCC (2007) recognizes that in the Federated States of Micronesia and the Marshall Islands rainwater is the main source of water; more frequent and intense ENSO events will further stress meager water resources. Guam's water supply is sensitive to precipitation patterns and changes in storm tracks. Lack of rain could impact lens recharge and decrease available water supplies (Prasad and Manner 1994). If the opposite effect takes place, an increase in water will result in increased flood risks and sedimentation, and impeded drainage. Furthermore, increases in sea level could alter the transition zone between the freshwater lens and underlying seawater in the northern aquifer and contaminate the water supply with seawater intrusion (Prasad and Manner 1994).

Ecological Responses

Evidence suggests that recent climatic changes have affected a broad range of individual species and populations in both the marine and terrestrial environment. Organisms have responded by changes in (1) phenology (timing of seasonal activities) and physiology; (2) range and distribution; (3) community composition and interaction; and (4) ecosystem structure and dynamics (Walther et al. 2002). The reproductive physiology and population dynamics of amphibians and reptiles are highly influenced by environmental conditions such as temperature and humidity. Sea turtle sex is determined by the temperature of the nest environment;, higher temperatures could result in a higher female-to-male ratio (Baker et al. 2006).

Warming has also caused species to shift toward the poles or higher altitudes. Furthermore, changes in climatic conditions can alter community composition. For example, increases in nitrogen availability can alter species composition by favoring those plant species that respond to nitrogen rises (Vitousek 1994). Similarly, increases in CO_2 levels can impact plant photosynthetic rates, alter plant species composition, decrease nutrient levels, and lower herbivore weights (Ehleringer et al. 2002). In the marine environment, variable atmospheric circulation has been shown to influence fish recruitment (Walther et al. 2002). Changes in the frequency or severity of tropical cyclones (hurricanes and typhoons) may impact reefs by causing coral breakage and deposition of debris, which will affect species composition and abundance (Nicholls et al. 2007). Although there is uncertainty regarding these trajectories, it is probable that there will be ecological consequences (Walther et al. 2002).

4.3 Hydrology

Guam is divided into two hydrogeological areas: the northern limestone province and the southern volcanic highlands. Northern Guam consists of six watershed sub-basins. The Ritidian Unit is split by the boundary of the Finegayan sub-basin and the Agafa Gumas sub-basin (Figure 7).

The volcanic rocks in southern Guam have a low permeability that slows infiltration and allows groundwater discharge to streams. There are 97 streams flowing in 20 watersheds in the south (Guam EPA 2006, Puglise and Kelty 2007). The watersheds and streams become increasingly steep and small toward the western southern coast (GDAWR 2006a). Approximately 46 of these rivers discharge to the ocean and 9 have estuarine regions. The rivers range in length from less than 0.62 miles to more than 3 miles (GDAWR 2006a). Heavy rainfall and runoff cause intense flooding in the basins (Gingerich 2003).

Surface water is the main source of freshwater in the south, with surface reservoirs providing an average of 9.9 million gallons per day (Gingerich 2003). The Fena Reservoir system is the primary source of domestic water for southern Guam, supplying water to both the Navy and local residents. This man-made reservoir, which was built after World War II, drains a 5.9 mi^2 area in the south (Gingerich 2003, Neill and Rea 2004, GDAWR 2006a). The reservoir provides 10-12 million gallons per day during the wet season and only 6-8 million gallons per day in the dry season (SWCA and Tom Nance Water Resource Engineering 2007). Supplemental Navy water sources to alleviate shortages during the dry season have been recently studied (SWCA and Tom Nance, Water Resource Engineering, 2007).

There are no permanent streams or lakes in the northern portion of the island due to the porous limestone substrate that allows rainwater infiltration (USFWS 1992, Gingerich 2003); however, there is a considerable amount of groundwater in this region. The Northern Guam Lens Aquifer (NGLA), the principle groundwater source for the island, is a karst aquifer comprised of uplifted limestone units (Unified Watershed Assessment 1998, Jocson et al. 2002). The aquifer is a freshwater lens that sits below the lowest water table and floats on denser seawater. A transitional or brackish zone exists between these layers and mixing occurs during tidal and pumping fluctuations. The less dense fresh and brackish water tends to move seaward from the aquifer (Mylroie et al. 2001, Jocson et al. 2002, Gingerich 2003).

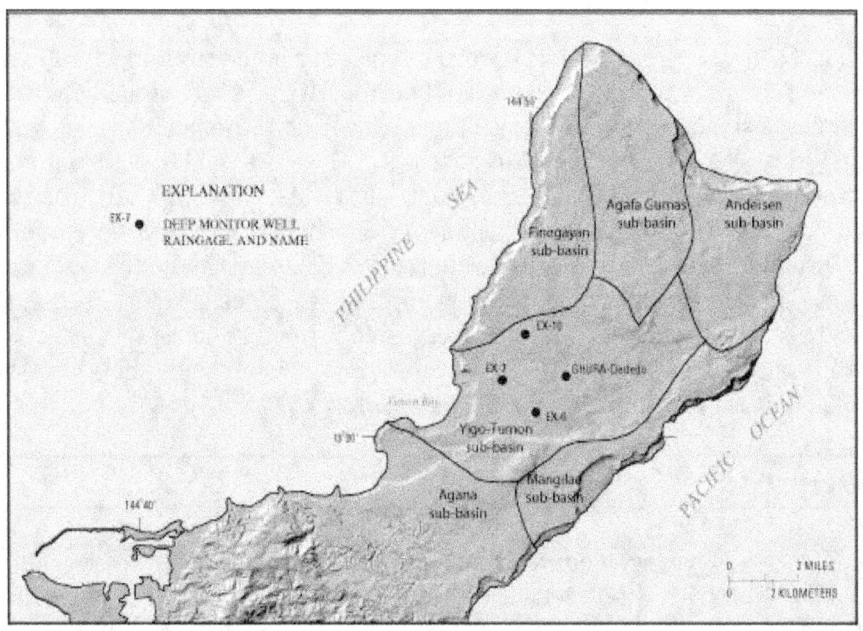

Figure 5. Watershed Sub-basins in Northern Guam. Source: USGS (2007). Available at http://hi.water.usgs.gov/studies/guamlens/index.html.

The freshwater lens system on northern Guam consists of basal and para-basal water. Basal water occurs in the permeable limestone and is relatively thin, while para-basal water extends to an unknown depth below the limestone to the underlying low permeable volcanic rocks (Gingerich 2003). The NGLA is recharged by rainfall percolation through surface soils into limestone cavities. Observation wells have shown that high water levels correspond with heavy, episodic rain events. Levels can rise within hours after heavy rainfall. However, most of the lens recharge occurs during light to moderate rainfall, as opposed to the large downpours from tropical storms and typhoons. The high volume of water created during these events cannot be captured by the freshwater lens (Khosrowpanah and Jocson 2005). Groundwater is also discharged from widened fractures or caves on cliff faces, from seeps and springs on beaches during occasional low tides, and from embayments enclosed by cliffs (Mylroie et al. 1999).

Groundwater from the Northern Guam Lens supplies about 80 percent of the island's drinking water. Roughly 180 wells tap the upper part of the freshwater lens, drawing about 35 million gallons per day (Gingerich 2003). Most of this water comes from the Yigo-Tumon sub-basin (http://hi.water.usgs.gov/studies/guamlens/index.html). The chloride concentrations of freshwater lenses are an indicator of salinity levels. The EPA considers drinking water contaminated when chloride concentrations exceed 250 mg/L. The chloride concentrations of the wells on northern Guam range from 6 to 585 mg/L (Gingerich 2003).

The proposed military build-up and the accompanying construction and service workers are expected to increase the population of Guam by 25 percent over the next 10-15 years. The responsible agencies are studying the capacity of Guam to produce enough water for all.

Rainwater collection tanks are used to provide water for Refuge uses. These tanks were installed at the Administration Building in 2003 and the Nature Center in 2004. When rainfall is low, water trucks deliver non-potable water to fill the tanks (C. Bandy, USFWS, personal communication). The water is made potable through the Refuge treatment systems.

Wetlands and other freshwater habitats on Guam comprise a small percentage of the total area. These include freshwater swamps, marshes, mangroves, streams, and rivers (GDAWR 2006a, Stephens 2007). In addition, there are several aquaculture ponds adjacent to estuaries in the south (USFWS 1992). There are no swamps, marshes, mangroves, streams, rivers, or aquaculture ponds at the Ritidian Unit.

4.4 Topography and Bathymetry

The topography of northern Guam is referred to as "karst topography" due to the abundance of sinkholes and limestone caverns (Khosrowpanah and Jocson 2005). The limestone plateau in the northern portion is relatively flat, with gentle slopes at elevations between 200 and 600 feet (Tracey et al. 1964). These elevations increase toward the northern tip (Young 1988). The volcanic summits of Mt. Santa Rosa and Mataguac Hill rise above the limestone plateau, to approximately 858 feet and 630 feet, respectively (Mylroie et al. 2001). Barrigada Hill, which is made of limestone, also rises above the limestone plateau to 665 feet (Khosrowpanah and Jocson 2005). The costal edges of the plateau adjoin steep jagged pinnacles and sheer cliffs of porous limestone. These cliffs drop to a narrow lowland terrace measuring between 300 and 900 feet from the base of the cliffs to the shore (Young 1988, USFWS and U.S. Air Force 2002). A narrow strip of sandy beach frames the shoreline. The continuous stretch of sandy shoreline from Urunao Point to Tagua Point makes up the majority of Guam's 35.9 miles of sandy beaches (Mylroie et al. 2001, Guam EPA 2006).

In contrast to the north, the topography in the south is distinguished by mountainous uplands that run north to south along the western coast. These mountains are dissected by various rivers, creating many steep slopes (Young 1988). The southern mountains rise to the highest point on

Guam, Mount Lamlam at an elevation of 1,328 feet (Puglise and Kelty 2007). The eastern slopes are steep near the ridgeline, but become more gradual as elevation decreases, terminating in broad valleys near the coastline. Offshore, wide reef flats are cut by numerous bays (USFWS 1992, Guam EPA 2006). Sea floor topography off the coast of Ritidian Point is depicted in Figure 8. The northern coast is surrounded by a shallow fringing reef up to 200 feet offshore (USFWS and U.S. Air Force 2002). The submerged portion of the Ritidian Unit extends offshore to the 100-foot depth. The backreef is a relatively flat area, 16 to 33 feet deep, which consists of hard pavement with 50 to 90 percent turf (Burdick 2005). This rises to the reef crest which is formed by terraced algal pools. The reef complex is transected at various points by spur-and-groove zones (cracks or fissures) that create shallow to slightly deeper pools in the backreef. Grooves run parallel to the shore and may merge with the reef crest to create deeper pools. Scattered sand flats are also found beyond the forereef (Burdick 2005). The ocean depth increases suddenly just off the reef (USFWS and U.S. Air Force 2002). This fringing reef offers the beach protection from heavy surf (Mylroie et al. 2001).

4.5 Geology and Soils

Guam is situated on the Mariana Ridge at the boundary of the Philippine and Pacific Plates, a tectonically active region. Interactions between these plates created the deep Mariana Trench that lies 60 to 100 miles east of Guam (Khosrowpanah and Jocson 2005). Because Guam is surrounded by tropical seas, coral reef formation is an important factor in the development and structure of the island. Guam's geology is a complex result of the tectonic movements of the plates, volcanic activity typical of island arc systems, and the production of limestone by reef growth.

The volcanics that formed the basement rocks of Guam probably emerged in the early Cenozoic Era (65 million years ago to present; Prasad and Manner 1994). The geological surface features have been classified into three major regions: the northern limestone plateau, the central volcanics, and the southern volcanics. The Alutom formation, which forms the central part of the island, contains the oldest exposed rocks. These volcanics are of Eocene (54.8 to 33.7 million years ago) to Oligocene (33.7 to 23.8 million years ago) age and were laid down by a volcano which was located to the west of the modern island (Tracey et al. 1964, Gingerich 2003). The southern half of Guam is composed mostly of the Umatac formation. These volcanics were derived from a younger, Miocene age (23.8 to 5.3 million years ago) volcano that was situated to the southwest of Guam. Neither of the volcanoes that formed these regions is above sea level today. The older volcanics contain limestone fragments and are capped by younger limestone in some locations (Mylroie et al. 2001). The northern limestone plateau was probably formed by a barrier reef lagoonal complex. The plateau is separated from the primarily volcanic terrain in the south by the northwest-southeast trending Pago-Adelup Fault (Mylroie et al. 2001). Subsequent tectonic activity has caused uplift and emergence of the barrier reef and associated lagoon limestone deposits (Randall 1979, Kurashina et al. 1990).

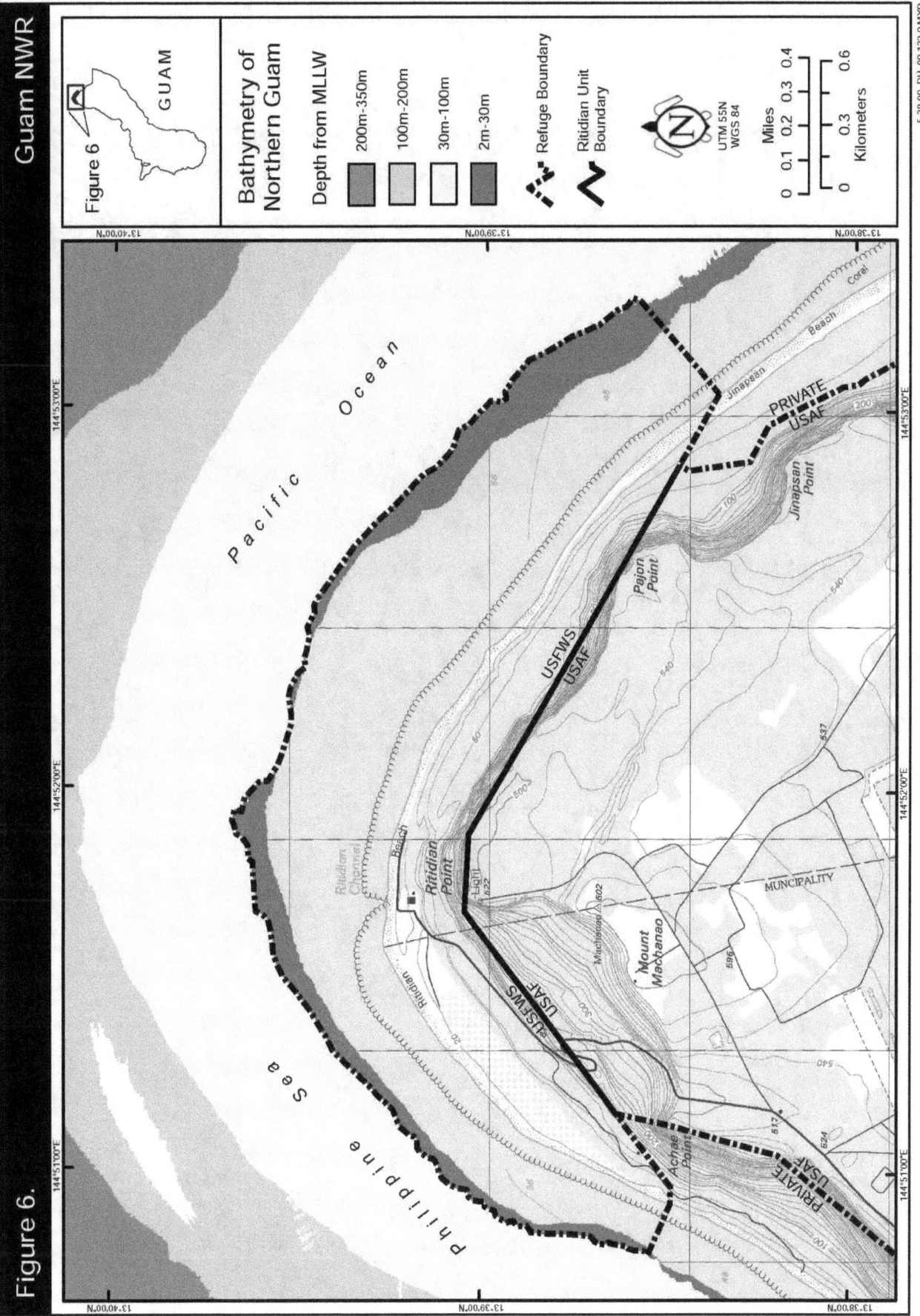

Figure 6.

The back sides of pages with maps are blank to facilitate map readability.

The most extensive surface unit on Guam is the Pliocene (5.3 to 1.8 million years) to Pleistocene (1.8 million to 10,000 years) age Mariana Limestone, which covers most of the island's northern half and dominates the perimeter of the northern plateau. This formation consists of reef and lagoonal limestone ranging from 0 to 500 feet in thickness (Tracey et al. 1964, Gingerich 2003). The late Miocene age Barrigada Limestone covers 9 percent of the island's surface, forming the bulk of the northern aquifer. This formation, which overlies the volcanic basement and comprises most of the bedrock, extends to the plateau surface in the interior of northern Guam (Tracey et al. 1964).

The limestone plateau that forms the northern physiographic province generally slopes from an elevation of about 600 feet in the north to about 200 feet in the middle of the island. At the northern margin, the plateau is bordered on the seaward edges by steep scarps of relatively unstable limestone. These seaward slopes have been subsequently modified by erosion and slumping, complicated by changing sea levels. As a result, complex terrace systems, exposed caves, and large detached limestone blocks are typical of the slopes (Kurashina et al. 1990, Mylorie et al. 2001). Seaward of these scarps is a low (0 to 79 ft) terraced band that ranges from 300 to 900 ft wide (USFWS 1992). The shore is primarily sandy beach with almost no terriginous material (Kurashina et al. 1990).

The Ritidian Unit is primarily located on the low terrace and beach zone lying seaward of the scarps at the base of the northern limestone plateau. Cliff faces in this area are cut by fractures, joints, and fissures and are covered by dense recrystallized limestone in some locations. Drip stone formations are also found here (Kurashina et al. 1990, Mylroie et al. 2001).

The complex nature of the formation of Guam is reflected in the island's soils (Figure 7). The five types of soils on the island are laterite, or volcanic; riverine mud; coral rock; coral sand; and argillaceous soils, or mixtures of coral and laterite (USFWS and U.S. Air Force 2002). While the southern portion is made up of erodible, volcanic soils (Puglise and Kelty 2007), northern Guam has little volcanic material. The terraces and benches in northern Guam, seaward of the limestone scarps, consist predominantly of reefal limestone and sand derived from corals, coralline algae, the green alga Halimeda, and foraminiferan and molluscan skeletal material (Kurashina et al. 1990). Young (1988) classified the northern coastal soils of Guam as "Ritidian-Rock outcrop." These very shallow and well drained soils lie on plateaus, mountains, and escarpments. The soils gently slope to extremely steep soils and Ritidian-Rock (Rock) outcrop. Three detailed soil units have been identified along the northern coastal tip of Guam by Young (1988) and are described below.

Shioya loamy sand, 0 to 5 percent slopes

The Shioya loamy sand is typically found on long and narrow coastal strands. The sand is "deep and very deep, excessively drained soil" that formed in water-deposited coral sand (Young 1988). The surface layer, which is often buried or removed due to high land use, is composed of dark brown loamy sand that is approximately 9.84 in thick. The substratum is very pale brown and reaches a depth of more than 5 feet. In addition, there are small areas of Inarajan sand clay loam adjacent to coastal plains and valleys and Ritidian Rock outcrop along the shoreline (Young 1988).

Ritidian-Rock outcrop complex, 3 to 15 percent slopes

The Ritidian-Rock outcrop complex, 3 to 15 percent slopes, is located on plateaus and escarpments with short or irregular slopes. It consists of 45 percent of Ritidian extremely cobbly clay loam interspersed with 35 percent Rock outcrop, and 10 percent Guam cobbly clay loam. The remaining 10 percent is composed of rock outcrop on steep escarpments, fairly level Ritidian soils, and limestone quarries (Young 1988). The small pockets of Ritidian soil, which are very shallow and well drained, consist of dark reddish brown extremely cobbly clay loam with a thickness of almost 100 mm (4 in). The rock outcrop lying under the soil is irregularly exposed areas of white, porous coralline limestone ranging between 2 and 9.8 in thick. The majority of the surface (60 to 90 percent) is covered with gravel, cobbles, and stones (Young 1988).

Ritidian-Rock outcrop complex, 15 to 60 percent slopes

The Ritidian-Rock outcrop complex continues toward the escarpment, with slope increases from 15 to 60 percent. This soil is located on dissected limestone plateaus and escarpments with long and plane slopes. It consists of 50 percent Ritidian extremely cobbly clay loam interspersed with 45 percent Rock outcrop. Additionally, portions of the unit consist of vertical limestone cliffs, small areas of less than 15 percent slopes, and patches of Guam cobbly clay loam (Young 1988).

The soils types in the three detailed soil units are mildly (pH 7.4 to 7.8) to moderately (pH 7.9 to 8.4) alkaline and highly permeable. In addition, runoff is slow and there is a slight hazard of water erosion (Young 1988).

4.6 Environmental Contaminants

The Agency for Toxic Substances and Disease Registry (ATSDR) of the U.S. Department of Health and Human Services defines a contaminant as "a substance that is either present in an environment where it does not belong or is present at levels that might cause harmful (adverse) health effects" (ATSDR 2002).

Significant contaminants have been identified on DOD lands on and adjacent to the Refuge. Prior to incorporation into the Guam Refuge, a Preliminary Assessment was conducted at the Ritidian Unit (formerly a Naval Facility compound) in 1993. This assessment identified potentially contaminated sites at the Ritidian Unit. The Navy has legal responsibility for contaminants at Ritidian Point and the formal Site and Remedial Investigations are incorporated in the Navy's Installation Restoration Program (IRP) (USFWS 1993, 1994). The IRP is being conducted in accordance with the Comprehensive Environmental Response, Compensation, and Liability Act (CERCLA) as amended by the Superfund Amendments and Reauthorization Act (SARA) and other applicable Federal, territorial, and state environmental regulations and requirements. See http://www.atsdr.cdc.gov/HAC/pha/anderson/and_toc.html#1of for IRP site locations.

Previous military activities at Andersen AFB involved the use and storage of fuels, chemicals, and pesticides. Large quantities of hazardous materials and equipment were disposed of on the installation following wartime activity (ATSDR 2002). As a result, preliminary assessments in the 1980s identified 50 hazardous sites on Andersen AFB.

Figure 7.   Guam NWR

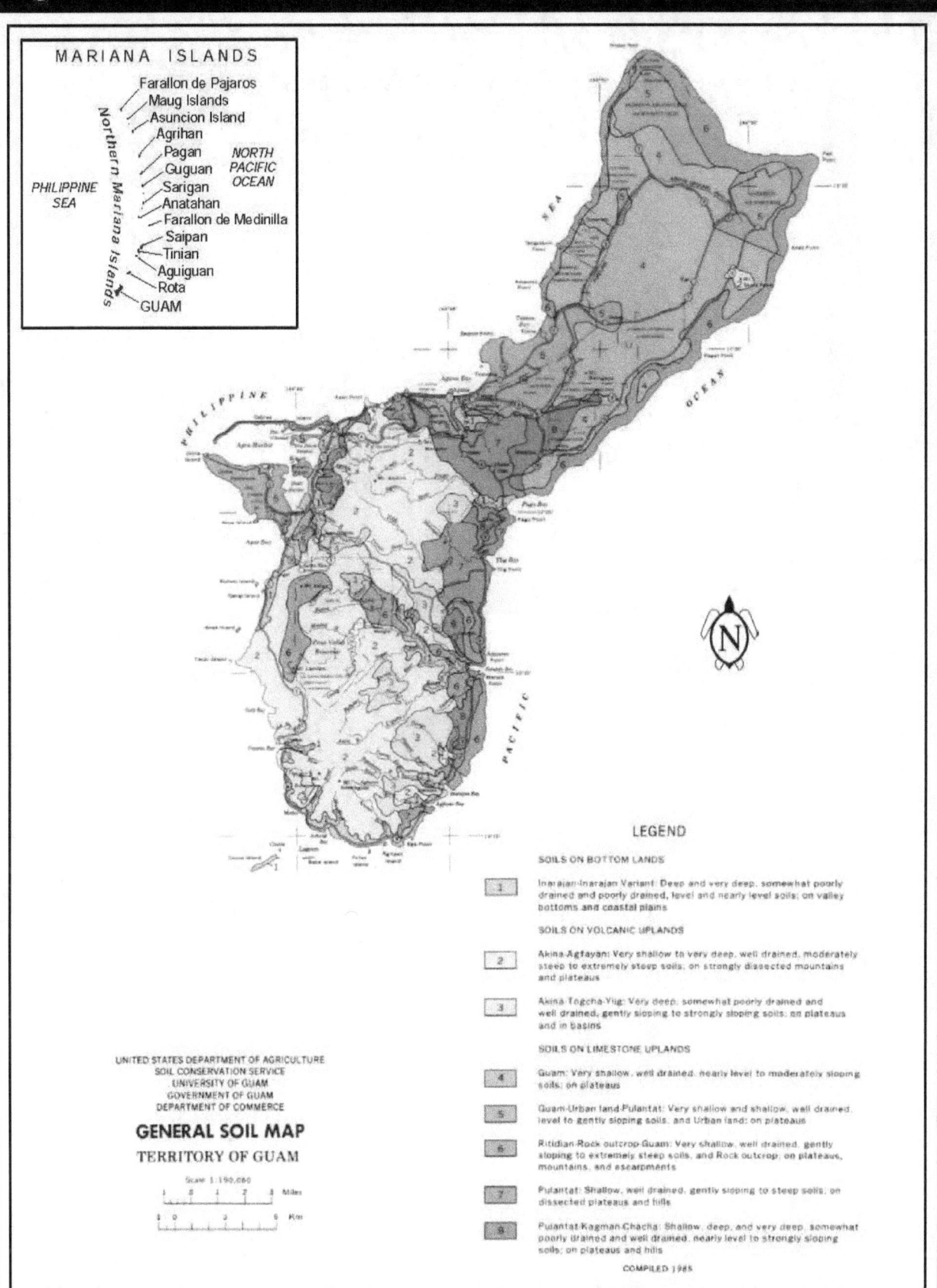

GENERAL SOIL MAP

TERRITORY OF GUAM

UNITED STATES DEPARTMENT OF AGRICULTURE
SOIL CONSERVATION SERVICE
UNIVERSITY OF GUAM
GOVERNMENT OF GUAM
DEPARTMENT OF COMMERCE

Scale 1:190,080

LEGEND

SOILS ON BOTTOM LANDS

1 Inarajan-Inarajan Variant: Deep and very deep, somewhat poorly drained and poorly drained, level and nearly level soils; on valley bottoms and coastal plains

SOILS ON VOLCANIC UPLANDS

2 Akina-Agfayan: Very shallow to very deep, well drained, moderately steep to extremely steep soils; on strongly dissected mountains and plateaus

3 Akina-Togcha-Ylig: Very deep, somewhat poorly drained and well drained, gently sloping to strongly sloping soils; on plateaus and in basins

SOILS ON LIMESTONE UPLANDS

4 Guam: Very shallow, well drained, nearly level to moderately sloping soils; on plateaus

5 Guam-Urban land-Pulantat: Very shallow and shallow, well drained, level to gently sloping soils, and Urban land; on plateaus

6 Ritidian-Rock outcrop-Guam: Very shallow, well drained, gently sloping to extremely steep soils, and Rock outcrop; on plateaus, mountains, and escarpments

7 Pulantat: Shallow, well drained, gently sloping to steep soils; on dissected plateaus and hills

8 Pulantat-Kagman-Chacha: Shallow, deep, and very deep, somewhat poorly drained and well drained, nearly level to strongly sloping soils; on plateaus and hills

COMPILED 1985

5-13-09, DH, 09-122-5.MXD

The back sides of pages with maps are blank to facilitate map readability.

In October 1992, Andersen AFB was incorporated into the EPA's National Priorities List due to groundwater contamination (USFWS 1993). The National Priorities List identifies the most serious uncontrolled or abandoned hazardous waste sites in the United States.

Contaminants and hazards found in the groundwater and soils on Andersen AFB include volatile organic compounds (VOCs), metals, asphalt, dioxins, polychlorinated biphenyl (PCBs), and unexploded ordnance (UXO) (ODUSD[I&E] 2006). In particular, groundwater underlying the base has been found to be contaminated with VOCs such as trichloroethylene and tetrachloroethylene (ATSDR 2002). Some contaminants were detected at levels above ATSDR's health-based comparison values and EPA Safe Drinking Water Standards (ATSDR 2002). Groundwater contamination is not expected to be a public health hazard for individuals drinking from the Andersen AFB due to (1) the military's remediation actions; (2) the natural groundwater flow patterns; and (3) the mixing of drinking water in the base's distribution system (ATSDR 2002). Although most of the contamination is suspected to be contained within Andersen AFB property, some chemicals may be dispersed off-base. The cities of Yigo and Dededo are located within 1 mile of military land. Water supplies that deliver water to these areas are downgradient of known contamination plumes underlying the base (ATSDR 2002).

Soil investigations at IRP sites throughout the base have found high levels of VOCs, semi-volatile organic compounds (SVOCs), total petroleum hydrocarbons, pesticides, and metals. Because access to these areas is restricted and contamination often lies in subsurface soils, ATSDR (2002) has determined that soil contamination is not an apparent public health hazard (ATSDR 2002). In addition, samples of biota (such as deer, wild pig, lizard, brown treesnake, and papaya) have showed minor evidence for arsenic and aluminum toxicity; however, ATSDR studies have concluded that the consumption of local biota poses no public health hazard (ATSDR 2002).

Although no incidents have been reported, UXO encounters are possible in the Northwest Field disposal areas. Access restrictions and educational programs have reduced this risk (ATSDR 2002). Indoor air radon levels were also found to be elevated at base housing units. The Air Force has subsequently initiated a radon monitoring and abatement program. Radon abatement was conducted on 755 homes. Recent tests have shown that only a few housing units maintain elevated levels of radon (ATSDR 2002). There is no record of the Refuge buildings being tested for radon (C. Bandy, USFWS, personal communication).

According to the Federal Facility Agreement (FFA) signed in 1993, the Air Force is responsible for remediation of existing contamination on Andersen AFB. As part of the IRP, remedial investigations and feasibility studies are being conducted and warning signs have been posted as a safety precaution. The original 50 sites were consolidated into 39 IRP sites and 4 operational units (ODUSD [I&E] 2006). The IRP sites on the Northwest Field that were contaminated during runway operation include four landfills (IRP 7/LF-9, IRP 16/LF-21, IRP 17/LF-22, and IRP 21/LF-26), a waste pile (IRP 30/WP-4), a chemical storage area (IRP 31/CS-4), and a dump site at Ritidian Point (ATSDR 2002). Later studies by the Air Force identified 53 areas of concern that did not fall under CERCLA guidelines. Only nine of these require limited remediation (ATSDR 2002).

The IRP sites are at varying stages of investigation and completion. During fiscal year 2006, the interim remedial action and remediation verification reports (RVR) were completed for the Ritidian Dump site (ODUSD [I&E] 2006). Several interim remedial actions have been completed or started for landfills and other areas of concern. A right of entry has been granted to enter the Urunao dump sites, which were added as an IRP site (ATSDR 2002). Remediation and cleanup costs at the base reached $100.4 million by fiscal year 2006 and an additional $40.5 million is estimated prior to the projected completion date of 2014 (ODUSD[I&E] 2006). Hazardous waste is now properly removed from the site, while non-hazardous waste is disposed of at the 10-acre sanitary landfill in the North Field (ATSDR 2002).

4.7 Surrounding Land Uses

Guam is made up of primarily forest and non-forested vegetation (Figure 8). The U.S. Government is the largest landowner on the island, owning approximately 39,000 acres, or 29 percent of the island (First Hawaiian Bank 2006). The Government of Guam owns approximately 25 percent and the remaining 45 percent is privately owned (OIA 2007). Local government land ownership has increased since the mid 1980s, as some Federal military land has been transferred to the Government of Guam and previous private landowners (USFWS 1992, OIA 2007).

The 1992 Draft Environmental Assessment for the Guam Refuge states that the Guam Public Land Use Plan classifies all public lands into three categories: development, agriculture, and conservation. Under the land use plan, the Ritidian Unit is classified as conservation. However, the Guam Land Use Map provided in Prasad and Manner (1994) divides the island into five land uses: military, urban, rural, agricultural, and conservation. In this map, the Ritidian Unit is classified as military, although the area has since been transferred into the Refuge System. A current land use plan is being developed for Guam and was not available prior to the completion of this CCP.

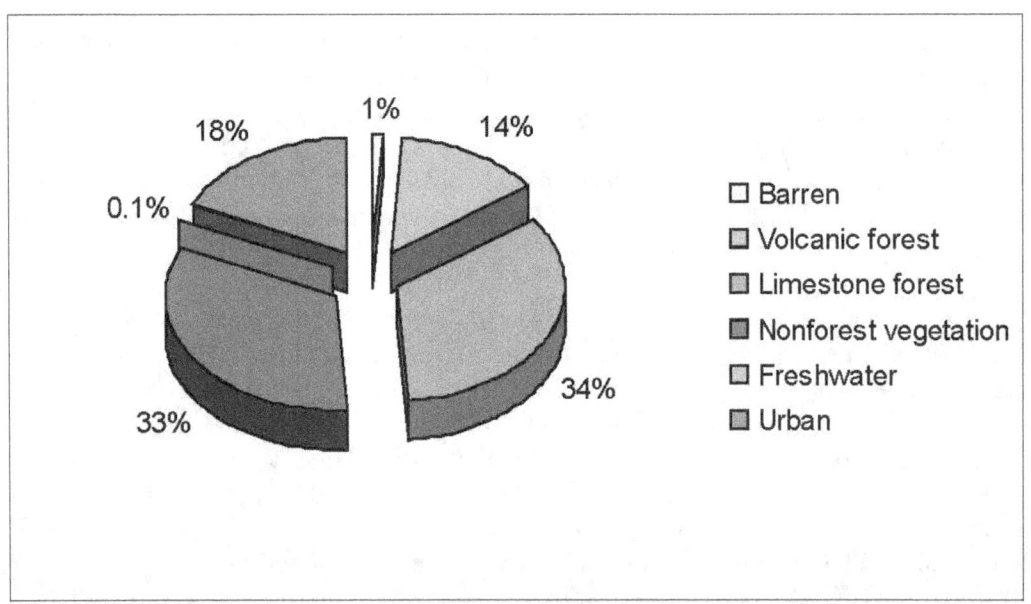

Figure 8. Land Percentage of various land cover types on Guam based upon 2002 high resolution satellite imagery. Source: Donnegan et al. (2004).

Chapter 5. Refuge Biology and Habitat

This chapter addresses the biological resources and habitats found on Guam Refuge. However, it is not an exhaustive overview of all species and habitats. The chapter begins with a discussion of biological integrity, as required under the Improvement Act. The bulk of the chapter is then focused on the presentation of pertinent background information for each of the eight conservation targets designated under the CCP. That background information includes a description, location, condition and trends associated with wildlife or habitats, key ecological attributes, and finally, stresses and sources of stress (collectively, "threats") to the target. The information presented was used as the CCP team developed goals and objectives for each of the conservation targets. In some cases, the information collected for key ecological attributes was later modified.

5.1 Biological Integrity Analysis

The first settlers of Guam are thought to have arrived about 3,500 years ago. These settlers brought with them plants and animals such as breadfruit, coconut, monitor lizards and possibly rats, all of which are now naturalized on Guam. The land now protected by Guam Refuge did not escape these introductions and fell victim to many others which all contributed to the drastic changes to native flora and fauna.

The ecosystem at Ritidian Point has hosted human inhabitants for thousands of years, but it was not until the last few hundred years that the land underwent the most drastic and destructive changes. In the late 1600s, the Spanish colonized Guam, bringing with them plants and animals such as papaya, tomato, guava, pigs, chicken, water buffalo, and Philippine deer. The introduction of ungulates, such as pigs and deer, severely impacted native forests. Ungulates eat and trample young trees and plants before they reach maturity; therefore, tree propagation has been slowed, and the understory and the amount of mature trees and vegetation have dramatically decreased.

One of the most well known introductions is the Brown treesnake (BTS). After World War II, the BTS is thought to have stowed away in military cargo coming from the Admiralty Islands, Papua, New Guinea. Soon after BTS arrived on Guam it reached unprecedented numbers. The introduction of BTS caused the extirpation or extinction of nearly all of the native forest vertebrates. The most noticeable impacts of BTS were on the avifauna. Nine of 11 species of native forest birds were extirpated from Guam. Five of these were endemic species or subspecies and are now extinct. The only native mammals found on Guam were three species of bats: the Pacific sheath-tailed bat, the Mariana fruit bat, and the little Mariana fruit bat. Out of these, only the Mariana fruit bat remains in small numbers on the island and is thought to be an occasional visitor to the Refuge. The BTS has also had severe effects on Guam's native lizards. At least one species of gecko and three species of skink are thought to have been extirpated from Guam. The remaining lizard populations are in decline.

5.2 Conservation Target Selection and Analysis

Selection

Early in the planning process, the team cooperatively identified eight priority species, groups, and communities for this Refuge, as recommended under the Service's Habitat Management Planning policy (620 FW1). These priorities, also called conservation targets, frame the CCP actions for wildlife and habitat. The conservation targets are species, species groups, or features that the Refuge will actively manage to conserve and restore over the life of the CCP. Negative features of the landscape, such as invasive plants, may demand a large part of the Refuge management effort, but are not designated as conservation targets. The three main criteria for selection of these targets included:
- inclusion of the four main natural habitat types found at the Refuge;
- reflective of the Refuge System mission and the Refuge's purposes; and
- recommended as a conservation target in the Wildlife and Habitat Management Review recommendations from October 2003.

Other criteria that were considered to some degree in the selection of the targets included:
- highly localized and restricted mobility species; and
- species groups and Refuge features of special management concern.

Table 1. Conservation targets

Habitats
Coral assemblages and reef types
Beach Strand
Coastal back strand
Limestone Forest
Caves
Native plants
Native marine vertebrates and invertebrates
Endangered animals and plants (indigenous/endemic to the Refuge)
Bats
Birds
Sea turtles
Trees
Seabirds
Migratory waterfowl and waterbirds
Shorebirds

In addition to the review of conservation targets listed above, the CCP will describe the historic native ecological system, including fish, wildlife, plants, and their habitats and major ecological forces.

Analysis

Goals and objectives were designed directly around the conservation targets. In developing objectives, the team analyzed each conservation target to determine its key ecological attributes-those aspects of the environment, such as ecological processes or patterns of biological structure and composition-that are critical to sustain the long-term viability of the target. The team developed "desired" conditions that were based partly on scientific literature review and partly on team professional judgment. These desired condition levels for specific indicators were used to help design objectives for each target, as presented in Chapter 2. The team listed and ranked stresses and sources of stress (collectively "threats") for most of the targets. A stress is the impairment or degradation of a key ecological attribute for a conservation target.

5.3 Habitats, Plants, and Wildlife

The Ritidian Unit is made up of a diversity of different habitat types ranging from fringing reef platforms, including marine species and coral, to beach strand, to coastal back strand, to limestone forest, and caves.

Habitat Types, Plants, and Marine Wildlife

Submerged lands and waters comprise over 68 percent of the Ritidian Unit, stretching from the coastline to the 100-foot depth offshore (Federal Register 2007a). This marine ecosystem includes pelagic waters, fringing reefs, reef channels, seagrass beds, limestone intertidal benches, and submarine cliffs (USFWS 1994c). Compared to the remainder of Guam, the marine resources and coral reef habitats at the Refuge are relatively pristine (Donaldson and Rongo 2006). The Ritidian Unit has a higher species diversity and coverage than much of Guam, as well as coral assemblages of *Acropora prolifera* not found elsewhere on the island (Kurashina et al. 2000).

The condition of the marine resources may be attributed to the fewer number of people and lack of rivers, as well as limited development and access in the northern region compared to the rest of the island (WPRFMC 2005). The marine waters off northern Guam are exceptionally clean because of minimal terrestrial sedimentation from the limestone plateau. Wave surge also enhances water quality by flushing contaminants or debris and circulating nutrients. The unpolluted water enhances the settlement and propagation of corals and algae

Coral Assemblages and Benthic Cover

The majority of the coral reef habitat is comprised of a 712 foot-wide fringing reef (Eldredge 1983, Kurashina et al. 1990). Patches of aggregate reef occur in combination with coral, coralline algae, or macroalgae. A spur and groove formation, which lies perpendicular to the shore, exists seaward beyond the aggregate reef. An isolated, single coral patch reef can be found on the north-west perimeter of the Refuge (Randall and Myers 1983, Burdick 2004).

The Ritidian Channel is the only cut through the reef for several miles in each direction. This channel is located on the northern tip of Ritidian Point (Kurashina et al. 1990). Marine and coral reef surveys conducted at the Ritidian Unit (e.g. Donaldson and Rongo 2006) have found a marked distinction between habitat areas to the west of the Ritidian Channel (open to public use), an area subject to greater wave energy, and areas east of the Ritidian Channel (closed to public use) which receive less exposure. This exposure to wave energy significantly influences the condition and species present in these areas. Sites protected from wave energy, including the reef flats and fore reef, have greater species richness, diversity, and benthic coverage compared to exposed sites. Kurashina et al. (1990) recorded vigorous coral growth of 72 species from 23 genera east of the Ritidian Channel, while only 7 species representing 9 genera were recorded to the west. In addition, the benthic structure differed between these areas; coral cover is greatest at the closed sites (Donaldson and Rongo 2006).

Inner and Outer Reef Flats

Reef flats are relatively flat platforms extending from the shoreline to the reef crest of the fringing reef. The inner reef flat is the portion adjacent to the shoreline, while the more elevated seaward portion of the reef flat is defined as the outer reef flat (GDAWR 2006a).

The benthic coverage estimated by Donaldson and Rongo (2006) at the various reef flat sites is listed in Table 2. Turf algae was the dominant benthic component of the reef flats, comprising between 66 and 75 percent coverage on both the inner and outer reef flats. Sand and coral were the next most abundant cover, with values differing between the inner and outer flats and the closed and open areas. More sand coverage was observed at the open sites than the closed sites. Coral coverage did not differ between the inner and outer reef flats; however, coral coverage was significantly higher at the closed sites compared to the open sites. Of the 10 coral species observed at the closed sites, the most common were *Acropora palifera*, *Pocillopora damicornis*, and *Porites lichen*. Only two coral species, *Pocillopora damicornis* and *Porites lutea*, were seen in the open sites. Rubble was recorded only at the open sites on both the inner and outer reef. Appendix L lists the coral species and families reported from the inner and outer reef flats during surveys by Donaldson and Rongo (2006).

Kurashina et al. (1990) also observed a significant difference between coral coverage east and west of the channel. Coral coverage ranged from 0.3 to 28 percent along the eastern platform of the inner reef flat from the Ritidian Channel to Pajon Point. Areas with a high percentage of substrate were covered with large thickets of *Acropora aspera*, a staghorn coral that is rare on Guam's shallow fore reefs (Paulay 2003). Coverage of *A. aspera* along the eastern inner reef ranged between 30 and 98 percent. Coral density along transects in the eastern inner reef flat ranged between 0.04 and 0.35 percent. Mean colony diameter also varied with some colonies reaching 37 in (Kurashina et al. 1990).

Table 2. Mean percent benthic coverage and coral species richness at the reef flats.
Source: Donaldson and Rongo (2006).

Cover Type	Reef Location			
	Closed inner	Open inner	Closed outer	Open outer
Turf algae	66.16	64.38	69.06	75.0
Macroalgae	5.63	1.56	5.79	1.09
Coralline algae	0	0	0.47	0
Sand	9.53	31.41	5.48	18.28
Rubble	0	1.09	0	0.47
Corals	19.53	0.94	19.2	4.53
Coral Richness	14	9	7	11

In the closed portion of the inner reef flat (from the channel to Archae Point), coral coverage was lower, ranging from 0.64 percent along more exposed regions to 9.93 percent in deeper areas. Average coral density of the closed inner reef was estimated at 0.13 percent (Kurashina et al. 1990).

A higher species diversity and density was observed by Kurashina et al. (1990) in the shallower outer reef flat than the inner reef flat. Coral density ranged from 0.03 to 1.12 colonies per m² and coverage was recorded between 0.03 to 64.82 percent (Kurashina et al. 1990). Compared to the inner reef, coral was also smaller in size on the outer reef (4.3 to 30 inches). Unlike the inner reef flat, no *A. aspera* thickets were observed in the outer reef flat; however, occasional colonies of *Stylophora mordax* were seen scattered along the outer reef. This coral is generally restricted to subtidal reef margin and fore reef habitats.

The eastern reef platform also maintains an abundant, dense, and unique community of fleshy algae. Large thalli of *Udotea geppi*, *Avrainvillea sp.* and *Microdictyon okamurai* dominate the substrate, reaching approximately 50 cm in height in some locations (Kurashina et al. 1990). High variation in the benthic coverage in the inner and outer reef flats is due to water depth differences and exposure during low tides (Kurashina et al. 1990).

Reef Crest

The reef crest is a raised algal ridge that is primarily capped by encrusting algae. Holes and tunnels are abundant throughout the crest and little sediment or sand accumulates on this portion of the reef. The crest is intertidal, with exposed peaks during low tide that do not support coral growth, but instead provide a growth substrate for the seaweed *Sargassum* (Lobban and Schefter 1997).

A total of 43 coral species from 18 genera were observed in the reef crest ridge slopes east of the channel (Kurashina et al. 1990). These coral were primarily recorded in the upper margins and walls of open surge channels and pools. Corals observed by Kurashina et al. (1990) include *Pocillopora setchelli*, *Goniastrea retiformis*, *Favia stelligera*, *Millepora platyphylla*, *Heliopora coerulea*, *Porites superfusa*, and various species of *Acropora*. In the deeper ridges, thick layers of encrusting crustose algae serve were the main benthic substrate. Shading by overhanging shelves results in lower coral coverage in the deeper areas compared to the upper margins. Although coral coverage is lower, coral communities are more diverse in these deeper areas, with approximately 37 coral species recorded (Kurashina et al. 1990).

Along the open reef crest west of the Ritidian Channel, coral coverage and distribution is scarce. On the floors of shallow channels within the crest, the following species were observed: *Pocillopora setchelli*, *Acropora digitifera*, *A. azurea*, *A. cerealis*, *A. monticulosa*, *Montastrea curta*, and *Goniastrea retiformis*. Several additional coral colonies were reported in a large pothole along the backcrest; however, the remainder of the western reef crest is devoid of coral due to periodic exposure (Kurashina et al. 1990).

Fore Reef

The area extending seaward of the reef crest to the outer ocean is defined as the reef front or fore reef. The fore reef is subject to heavy seas and strong tidal currents that directly impact the coral communities and structure in these areas. Zones that are more protected from these conditions are often covered with large stands of branching or tabular corals, while more exposed areas tend to have smaller corals (GDAWR 2006a). Donaldson and Rongo (2006) documented the general substrata and fish present at the fore reef of the Ritidian Unit; however, quantitative surveys were not conducted due to lack of visibility from heavy seas and strong currents.

The closed fore reef to the east of the channel consists mostly of flat pavement, transversed by sand channels greater than 65 feet deep. Coral abundance and diversity is poor at this site, with scattered single colonies of *Pocillopora eydouxi* (Donaldson and Rongo 2006). The open fore reef habitat to the west is characterized by sloping pavement and rubble fields. Coral coverage is mainly comprised of *Pocillopora eydouxi* or *Acropora* sp. and is less abundant than the closed sites (Donaldson and Rongo 2006).

Beach Strand

The beach strand habitat at the Ritidian Unit encompasses the open sandy area and coastal outcroppings between the vegetated land and the ocean. The shoreline width varies with the tide, reaching a thickness of 150 ft (Kurashina et al. 1990). The sand at the Refuge is biogenic, or produced when waves break up biological sources such as limestone, corals, algae, shells, and single-celled animals.

Herbaceous and shrubby strand vegetation in beach strand habitats on Guam is typically sparse and generally ranges from 6 to 10 feet in height (GDAWR 2006a). Salt tolerant species, such as *Pemphis, Tournefortia,* and *Casuarina*, are characteristically found in this area. Other beach strand vegetation in Guam includes *Cocos, Ipomoea, Canavalia, Scaevola,* and *Triumfetta* (USFWS 1993). Beach strand also supports nesting by green and hawksbill sea turtles, as well as providing habitat for seabirds, geckos, skinks, and invertebrate species (GDAWR 2006a).

Coastal Back Strand

Back strand is a mixture of strand and native limestone forest vegetation. The coastal and back strand habitat is a lush jungle of vegetation often covered with vines. Coastal strand vegetation is typically comprised of relatively widespread plant species and is highly resistant to disturbance (Lobban and Schefter 1997). Three endemic species (*Aglaia mariannensis, Guamia mariannae,* and *Tournefortia argentia*) are abundant and dominate this habitat at Ritidian. Indigenous trees in the coastal and back strand areas include breadfruit (*Artocarpus* sp.), banyan (*Ficus* sp.), *Guettarda speciosa,* and *Pisonia grandis*. Ground ferns as well as epiphytic ferns on senescent coconut trees are also found within the back strand. Several medicinal herbs and the cycad Cycas revolute are found here (P. Ha, NOAA, personal communication).

Limestone Forest

Northern Guam is primarily flat limestone with abrupt cliffs and drop-offs toward the ocean. The underlying limestone may be strongly weathered into a karst formation (Mylroie et al. 2001). Primary limestone forest is relatively tall with a canopy to 60 feet and a relatively thick understory, dominated by *Artocarpus mariannensis, Ficus prolixa, Aglaia mariannensis, Guamia mariannae, Cycas circinalis, Premna obtusifolia, Ochrosia mariannensis, Macaranga thompsonii, Elaeocarpus joga, Neisosperma oppositifolia, Pisonia grandis,* and *Mammea odorata* (Fosberg 1960). *Intsia bijuga* and *Tristiropsis obtusangula* are less common. In addition, grasses, ferns and orchids litter the forest floor (Stone 1970). Many of the same species are present in secondary forest, albeit in lower densities, with the addition of *Carica papaya, Cestrum diurnum, Hibiscus tiliaceus, Morinda citrifolia, Pandanas tectorius,* and *P. dubius.* Some land adjacent to the cliff lines is virtually pristine, possibly because the karst topography and steep cliffs made the area difficult to clear and the sharp karst limits ungulate use. These areas contain some of the best species composition and structure found in the primary growth limestone forest that once covered now-cleared areas of Guam.

Typhoons have shaped the vegetation on Guam. In limestone forest, winds have blown down clusters of trees, opening gaps in the forest canopy where understory vegetation proliferate (Quinata 1994). Typhoons can enhance forest regeneration by inhibiting shade tolerant invasive plants and increasing vegetative reproduction (Craig 1992). Regenerating typhoon-modified limestone forest is composed of dense understory vegetation, including ferns, herbaceous vegetation, and small shrubby species (Quinata 1994) which support native bird and animal species. Some portions of the Ritidian Unit contain forests that can be considered primary growth forest and typhoon-modified forest (Fosberg 1960, Quinata 1994).

Not all modification can be considered beneficial to the vegetative ecosystems of the Ritidian Unit. Activities associated with World War II (WWII) and subsequent military operations in the 1960s lead to the clearing of native limestone forest and surface grading. Imported fill of crushed coral and argillaceous clay was placed and compacted over pulverized limestone to stabilize runways, taxiways, and aprons on parts of the Air Force Refuge overlay (USAF 2006). Further, invasive ungulate species greatly reduced recruitment of native limestone woody species into the upper canopy, thereby altering forest composition and structure. As discussed previously, the BTS indirectly affected forest composition and structure by eliminating many forest bird species. The loss of most insectivorous birds may leave secondary limestone forests vulnerable to a variety of insect pests.

Arguably, the limestone forest provides high quality, essential habitat for a number of endangered forest birds and bats (Wiles et al. 1995, Cox and Elmqvist 2000). Mariana crows reside primarily in these forest types, frequently nesting in *Aglaia mariannensis, Artocarpus mariannensis, Elaeocarpus joga, Ficus prolixa, Guamia mariannae, Intsia bijuga, Premna obtusifolia,* and *Tristiropsis obtusangula* (Wiles et al. 1995). Mariana fruit bats forage and roost primarily in limestone forest and have been found primarily roosting in tree species including *Mammea odorata, Ficus prolixa, Neisosperma oppositifolia, Aglaia mariannensis, Barringtonia asiatica, Casuarina equisetifolia, Elaeocarpus joga, Cocos nucifera, Pandanus tectorius, Terminalia catappa, Artocarpus mariannensis, Erythrina variegate, Ceiba pentandra, Pisonia grandis,* and *Guettarda speciosa* (USFWS 1990, Janeke 2006. N. Johnson, SWCA, unpublished data).

Caves

The porosity of the northern Guam Pleistocene karst lends itself to the formation of caves (Mylorie et al. 2001). Most karst caves are formed by the dissolution of limestone by water percolating through the rock, erosion, and collapse (Taboroši 2004). Sea caves are created by erosion rather than dissolution.

The clifflines of Ritidian and surrounding areas are littered with many caves. Located at the base of the cliffs and in the cliff-faces, these caves contain impressive stalactites, partially dissolved when the caves were flooded with seawater. The largest known flank margin cave (a coastal cave created by dissolution by forceful mixing of fresh and salt groundwater) on Guam is Ritidian Cave (Taboroši 2004). The cave is some 130 feet wide and 30 feet high, with a floor covered with flowstones, large stalagmites and a freshwater pool. Perhaps the most visited cave area at the Ritidian Unit is the pictographs in the Ritidian cave and the dot-drawings in the adjoining Star Cave. The pictographs represent human figures. In 1999, a cave drawing of rows of 16 dots, placed horizontally and vertically, perhaps representing a 16-month calendar based on the stars, was discovered in Star Cave (http://guam.org.gu/starcave). These pictographs are not well understood, partly due to the uncertainty of their age (April 2006).

Apart from their cultural value, these caves also provide an essential habitat for the Guam swiftlet. Because the swiftlet is non-migratory, occupation of caves is year-round (Pratt et al. 1987). Historically, these caves provided a predator-free environment with stable temperature and humidity deep within the caves where the swiftlet normally roosts and nests (USFWS 1991b). Although it is unclear why the swiftlet is currently absent from caves at the Ritidian Unit, the removal of BTS and limitation of access of humans to the caves may improve the chances that the swiftlet will once again utilize the Refuge's caves as habitat.

Native Plants

Other native forest plant species have also fared poorly on Guam and, like *Serianthes nelsonii*, are declining rapidly. Declines in plant communities on the Ritidian Unit and surrounding areas can be attributed to many causes, including loss of forest due to agricultural and wartime activities (Baker 1946, Fosberg 1960), introduction of invasive animals and plants (Conry 1988; Wiles et al. 1990; 1996, Moore et al. 2005), plant pathogens, and declines or extirpations of some bird, bat, and insect pollinators and seed dispersers (Savidge 1987, Wiles et al. 1989; Cox et al. 1991). The introduced BTS indirectly affected forest composition and structure by eliminating many forest bird species (Savidge 1987). Birds and fruit bats are important in secondary limestone forests because they naturally pollinate and disperse seeds of shrubs and trees and thereby help maintain forest diversity (Wiles et al. 1995; Cox and Elmqvist 2000), contributing to recovery after typhoons and perturbations. Rodents and feral pigs disperse some seeds.

Listed as vulnerable on the 2007 IUCN Red list, *Heritiera longipetiolata* is endemic to Guam, Rota, and Saipan (Stone 1970). Known locally as "ufa halomtano," the species is primarily found in northern Guam, restricted to limestone cliffs and plateaus, almost always within 330-660 feet of coastal limestone cliffs. A few isolated trees have been identified along the north and east coasts from Ritidian Point to Pagat point (Wiles et al. 1995). Heavy predation by introduced deer and coconut crab (*Birgus latro*) on the seed, as well as browsing on seedlings by deer and pigs are considered reasons for decline of this species (Wiles et al. 1995). As with *Serianthes nelsonii*, typhoons have destroyed some trees. As a consequence there is limited recruitment of trees into the population.

The joga tree (*Elaeocarpus joga*) occurs only on Guam and Rota in the Mariana Islands and Palau in the western Caroline Islands. On Guam, it grows on limestone and limestone-based soils and clay loam soils (Marler and Lawrence 2004) and is present on the Guam Refuge. It is a relatively large tree (up to 50 feet tall) with distinct horizontal branching and large edible fruits (Stone

1970). Seeds fall near the parent tree, resulting in a dense seedling bank beneath the parent tree (Ritter and Naugle 1999). However, Schreiner (1997) observed these seedling banks were absent and speculated that the feral pig was responsible. The factors adversely affecting *E. joga* are likely similar to those identified in the decline of hayun lagu (*S. nelsonii*).

Many of the same pressures that affected hayun lagu, ufa halomtano, and joga declines on Guam have caused population reductions in other native species. Wiles (2005) identified ungulate predation pressure as the major factor for inhibiting recruitment of the native *Artocarpus mariannensis*. The author documented a 65.4 percent decrease in trees within Andersen AFB Munitions Storage Area between 1989 and 1999. Ungulate predation, typhoons, and low recruitment hinder the recovery of dwindling populations of *Merrilliodendron megacarpum* (GDAWR 2006a). Populations of *Tabernaemontana rotensis*, recently considered for Federal listing, were discovered on the Airforce Overlay Unit in the late 1990s (USEPA 2000). Lack of reproductive vigor and seed distribution due to low numbers of pollinators; large, incongruent distances between individual trees; and competition with nonnative plants have been associated with the species decline.

Pisonia grandis and *P. umbrellifera* are severely pruned by typhoons, and as a component of the ever-dwindling native limestone forest habitat on Guam, these species need protection (Raulerson and Rinehart 1991). *Casuarina equisetifolia*, although considered an invasive species in many parts of the world, is classified as indigenous to Guam (Raulerson and Rinehart 1991). The species is hardy but reports by the University of Guam, Guam Department of Agriculture and the Natural Resource Conservation Service of thousands of trees dying in recent years is disturbing. A seemingly healthy stand of *C. equisetifolia* on the Refuge may be of interest for further study into the species' decline. The major threat to the once common *Cycas micronesica* is the introduced Asian cycad scale (*Aulacaspis yasumatusi*), which has caused significant mortality of the cycad since 2003 (A. Moore, University of Guam, personal communication).

Marine Vertebrates and Invertebrates

There are no federally listed endangered or threatened marine fish, invertebrates, or algae in the marine waters of the Ritidian Unit (Stojkovich 1977, USFWS 1993); however, NOAA Fisheries designated the bumphead parrotfish (*Bolbometopon muricatum*) and the humphead wrasse (*Cheilinus undulates*) 'species of concern' due to overfishing and habitat loss (USFWS 2007d).

The number of individual fish and species present (richness) was greater in the closed reef flats compared to those of the open reef flats. Species diversity values, which consider the abundance of each species present at a site, were also higher in the closed sites (Donaldson and Rongo 2006). The nearshore sandy reef flat supports foraging and resting areas for marine turtles.

Donaldson and Rongo (2006) counted fish along four transect lines within the reef flats of the Ritidian Unit. The most dominant fish species found during this survey were damselfishes (*Pomacentridae*), wrasses (Abridge), parrotfishes (*Scarinae*), and surgeonfishes (*Acanthuridae*). The most abundant species recorded were *Stegastes albifasciatus, Halichoeres trimaculatus, Chlorurus sordidus*, and *Chrysiptera brownriggi*. A list of fish species observed during surveys of the reef flats by Donaldson and Rongo (2006) is provided in Appendix L. Fish that have been observed during surveys to the west of the Ritidian Channel include damselfishes (Pomacentridae) such as *Pomachromis guamensis* and *Dascyllus reticulatus*; hawkfishes

(Cirrhitidae) such as *Paracirrhites arcatus*, *Paracirrhites forsteri* and *Cirrhitichthys falco*; the surgeonfish *Acanthurus nigrofuscus* (Acanthuridae), and the small grouper *Cephalopholis urodeta* (Serranidae). Abundance and diversity increased to the east of the reef channel.

In addition to damselfishes and hawkfishes, the following species were commonly observed in the open fore reef: surgeonfishes (Acanthuridae) such as *Acanthurus nigrofuscus, Acanthurus nigoris, Ctenochaetus striatus, Naso literatus, Naso vlagmingi*; parrotfishes (Scarinae) such as *Chlorurus sordidus, Scarus psittacus,* and *Scarus schlegeli*; wrasses (Labridae) such as *Cheilinus trilobatus, Halichoeres margaritaceus, Labroides dimidiatus, Oxycheilinus unifasciatus,* and *Thalassoma amblycephalum*; butterflyfishes (Chaetodontidae) such as *Chaetodon auriga, Chaetodon citrinellus, Chaetodon lunula,* and *Chaetodon reticulatus*; triggerfishes (Balistidae) such as *Balistapus undulatus, Odonus niger, Melichthys vidua, Sufflamen bursa,* and *Sufflamen chrysiptera*; blennies (Blenniidae) such as *Ecsenius bicolor* and *Plagiotremus tapeinosoma*; the pygmy angelfish *Centropyge flavissimus* (Pomacanthidae), and the emperor fish *Monotaxis grandoculis* (Lethrinidae) (Donaldson and Rongo 2006).

Other marine invertebrates on Guam include 59 flatworms, 1722 molluscs, 104 polychaetes, 840 arthropods, and 196 echinoderm species (Kelty and Kuartei 2004). Although the tide pools exposed at low tide at the Ritidian Unit have been reported to support crabs and shrimps, no surveys of these invertebrates for the site could be found.

Threats to Habitats, Plants, and Wildlife

Habitat destruction, resource exploitation, and siltation are threatening the marine ecosystems of Guam and the Ritidian Unit. Corals and sea shells are often collected for souvenirs, private collections, and commercial use in the tourist industry. Coral assemblages are also harmed by dynamite, chlorine, and fish poisons that are used to capture fish species (USFWS 1994c). Other threats to the marine and coral reef environment include invasive species and marine debris that may smother or break coral. *Acanthaster planci* (crown-of-thorns starfish) outbreaks may occur, causing shifts in the reef community (Kelty and Kuartei 2004). In addition to anthropogenic threats such as nearby coastal development, the coral and marine communities at Ritidian are susceptible to damage by typhoons (Donaldson and Rongo 2006).

Despite the good condition of the marine resources compared to other locations on Guam, the general public and marine scientists have suggested increased monitoring and assessment of the marine resources at the Refuge are necessary. These activities could provide more detailed information on existing conditions in order to develop sound management programs (Donaldson and Rongo 2006, USFWS 2007d).

Threatened and Endangered Species

Endangered and threatened species are federally protected by the Endangered Species Act (ESA) of 1973. The ESA grants protection to any species deemed "in danger of extinction throughout all or a significant portion of its range" (ESA 1973 Section 3-6). This Act was designed to "conserve the ecosystems upon which endangered and threatened species depend and to conserve and recover listed species" (USFWS 2005a). Any activities with the potential to affect listed species require review by the Service, National Marine Fisheries Service (NMFS), or both, in accordance with Section 7 of the ESA.

There are three species of bats, seven birds, two marine reptiles, and one plant that are threatened or endangered speces that have been documented as either occurring or potentially occurring on all units of the Guam Refuge (Table 3). In addition, at least three of seven species of tree snail and two of three insects which are listed as candidate species or species of concern have been found on the Refuge.

Bats

Pacific sheath-tailed bat

The Pacific sheath-tailed bat (*Emballonura semicaudata rotensis*) is a nocturnal bat that roosts in caves during daylight hours. Pelage is dull grayish-brown and it is the smallest of the Guam bat species. The following measurements were recorded from two female Pacific sheath-tailed bats captured on Aguiguan in 1984: body length - 2.7 in, 2.8 in; tail - 0.7 in, 0.7 in; hind foot - 0.3 in, 0.3 in; ear - 0.4 in, 0.4 in; forearm - 1.7 in, 1.8 in; weight - 0.18 ounces (oz), 0.25 oz. (Lemke 1986). This species is the only insectivorous bat found in the Mariana Islands. The Pacific sheath-tailed bat was once present on the islands of Saipan, Tinian, Aguiguan, Rota, and Guam, but currently the only remaining population consists of approximately 400-500 individuals on Aguiguan (Esselstyn et al. 2004).

The Pacific sheath-tailed bat was listed as endangered by the Government of Guam in 1982 (Lemke 1986) and is presently listed as a Federal candidate in the Mariana Islands by the Service (USFWS 2005d). Observations of small bats (presumably Pacific sheath-tailed bats) have been recorded on Rota and Aguiguan between the 1940s and late 1960s, and on Saipan, Anatahan, and the East Island of Maug as recently as 1976 (Lemke 1986). One of the earliest records of the Pacific sheath-tailed bat on Guam was noted by A. Marche near the mouth of the Talofofo River in 1887. Marche stated, "Ipan Cave is inhabited by a species of small bats [sic] of which I was able to catch a few specimens" (Lemke 1986). Six small bats (presumably Pacific sheath-tailed bats) were apparently reported by a hunter in one of the Ritidian Point caves on Guam in March 1968 (Drahos 2006);, this species utilized the forest and caves comprising the Guam Refuge. The last known observation of the Pacific sheath-tailed bat on Guam was in the Tarague Basin in May 1972 (Lemke 1986; Wiles et al. 1995). A comprehensive survey of limestone caves on Guam by G. Wiles in 1984 did not detect any Pacific sheath-tailed bats (Lemke 1986). Consequently, the Pacific sheath-tailed bat appears to be extirpated from Guam (Chiroptera Specialist Group 2000; Wiles 2005).

It is uncertain what caused the demise of the Pacific sheath-tailed bat in the Mariana Islands. However, population losses on Saipan, Rota, and Guam nearly all coincided with declines or extirpations of Guam swiftlets, implying that analogous feeding and roosting habits potentially made both species equally vulnerable to existing threats (Wiles and Worthington 2002). The Chiroptera Specialist Group (2000) and Wiles and Worthington (2002) outlined a few potential reasons for the decline and disappearance of Pacific sheath-tailed bat in the Mariana Islands. These included the human occupation and warfare near and within caves during WWII, pesticides, deforestation, predators (including monitor lizards (*Varanus indicus*) and other introduced species), typhoons, and guano mining. All of these factors likely contributed to the extirpation of Pacific sheath-tailed bats on Guam (including the Ritidian Unit); however, pesticides and deforestation may have played a major role. Between the 1940s and 1970s, moderate application

Table 3. Guam's Listed, Proposed or Candidate species, as designated under the U.S. Endangered Species Act (updated August 29, 2005).

Species Name	Common Name and (Chamorro name)	Status
BATS		
Emballonura semicaudata	Pacific sheath-tailed bat (Payesyes)	C*
Pteropus tokudae	Little Mariana fruit bat (Fanihi)	E*
Pteropus mariannus mariannus[2,3]	Mariana fruit bat (Fanihi)	T
BIRDS		
*Acrocephalus luscinia***	Nightingale reed warbler (Ga'ga' karisu)	E*
Aerodramus bartschi[3]	Guam swiftlet (Yayaguak)	E
Corvus kubaryi[2]	Mariana crow (Aga)	E
Gallinula chloropus guami[3]	Mariana moorhen (Pulattat)	E
Halcyon cinnamomina cinnamomina[1]	Guam Micronesian kingfisher (Sihek)	E
Megapodius laperouse	Micronesian megapode (Sasangat)	E*
Rallus owstoni[1]	Guam rail (Koko)	E
Zosterops conspicillatus	Bridled white-eye (Nosa)	E*
REPTILES		
Chelonia mydas	Green turtle (Haggan Bed'di)	T
Eretmochelys imbricate	Hawksbill turtle (Haggan Karai)	E
PLANTS		
Serianthes nelsonii	No common name (Trongkon guafi)	E
INVERTEBRATES		
Partula gibba[2]	Mariana Islands tree snail (Akaleha)	C
Partula radiolata[2]	Pacific tree snail (Akaleha)	C
Partula salifana	Guam tree snail (Akaleha)	SOC*
Samoana fragilis[2]	Mariana Islands fragile tree snail	C
Succinea guamensis	No common name	SOC*

Species Name	Common Name and (Chamorro name)	Status
Succinea piratarum	No common name	SOC*
Succinea quadrasi	No common name	SOC*
INSECTS		
Catacanthus sp. nov.	Guam bronze boony bug	SOC
Hypolimnus octocula	Mariana eight spot butterfly	C
Vagrans egestina	Mariana wandering butterfly	C*
Species status: E=endangered; T=threatened; C=candidate for listing; SOC=species of concern; *=possibly extirpated from Guam; **=not known from the Guam NWR. [1] Occurs only in captivity: [2] Occurs on Andersen AFB overlay refuge: [3] Occurs on Navy overlay refuge. Extracted from http://www.fws.gov/pacificislands/wesa/pacificislandslisting.pdf		

of pesticides (DDT and malathion) were likely more intense on Guam, because of the presence of a larger human population and American military installations (Wiles and Worthington 2002). Additionally, deforestation for construction of American military installations on Guam during and after WWII probably resulted in extensive loss of foraging habitat and reduced prey availability for the Pacific sheath-tailed bat (Wiles and Worthington 2002).

Little Mariana fruit bat

The Little Mariana fruit bat "Fanihi" (*Pteropus tokudae*) is a small fruit bat that was first discovered in 1931 (USFWS 1990a) and endemic to Guam (Chiroptera Specialist Group 1996). The Little Mariana fruit bat is considerably smaller than the Mariana fruit bat (*Pteropus mariannus mariannus*) with a body length between 5.5-9.9 in, forearm length 3.7 in, wingspan between 25.6-27.9 in, and body weight around 5.4 oz (USFWS 1990a). Other than a few white hairs, the wings and abdomen are brown to dark brown in color. The sides of the neck and the mantle exhibit a brown to pale golden coloration. The chin and throat are dark brown, while the cap is gray to yellow (USFWS 1990a).

Ecological and natural history information are essentially lacking for this species. Only three Little Mariana fruit bat specimens have been collected, the last being a female that was shot by hunters below Tarague Point on June 5, 1968 (Wiles 1987). Despite intensive search efforts since then by Wheeler in 1978 and 1979 and Wiles from 1981 to 1990, no additional confirmed observations of Little Mariana fruit bat have occurred on Guam, except a single potential sighting in June 1979 at Ritidian Point by M. Wheeler (USFWS 1990a). Consequently the Little Mariana fruit bat now appears extirpated from the island (Chiroptera Specialist Group 1996, Wiles 2005). Hunting this species as a food source is believed to be the primary cause of extinction (Chiroptera Specialist Group 1996).

Considering the location where the Little Mariana fruit bat was shot in 1968 (Tarague Point) and the proximity and similar forest composition to the Ritidian Unit, the Little Mariana fruit bat probably utilized forest comprising the Refuge for either roosting or foraging purposes.

Mariana fruit bat

The Mariana fruit bat "Fanihi" (*Pteropus mariannus mariannus*) is a medium-sized colonial flying fox, with body length of 7.7 to 9.8 in, forearm length between 5.3-6.1 in, a wingspan of 33.9 to 41.9 in, and body weight ranging between 11.6 and 20.4 oz (USFWS 1990a). In 1984, the Mariana fruit bat was listed as endangered on Guam by the Service (USFWS 1984). However, in 2005 the Service determined that movement of fruit bats between all islands in the Mariana archipelago occurs, resulting in exchange of genetic material. Consequently, Mariana fruit bats on Guam and throughout the CNMI comprise one subspecies and are presently listed as federally threatened throughout their entire range (USFWS 2005c). In the Mariana Islands, Mariana fruit bat is known to occur on all islands extending northward from Guam to Maug (Wiles et al. 1989; Johnson 2001).

In 1931, W. Coultas (in USFWS 1990a) reported that fruit bats were most abundant in northern Guam. However, in 1945, R. Baker (in USFWS 1990a) determined fruit bats to be uncommon in northern Guam. Baker reported they were primarily restricted to the forested clifflines, but described the species as scarce in southern Guam. In 1958, D. Woodside (in USFWS 1990a) estimated Guam's entire Mariana fruit bat population to be less than 3,000. Throughout the 1960s and 1970s, Guam's Mariana fruit bat population decreased dramatically, plummeting to less than 50 animals in 1978 (Wiles et al. 1989). However, between 1980 and 1982, the population rapidly increased to approximately 850-1,000 individuals, potentially resulting from immigration of Mariana fruit bats due to illegal hunting activities on neighboring Rota (Wiles 1987, Wiles et al. 1989). Following a 1984 Guam bat census, 425-500 individuals were tallied, indicating a population decline since the early 1980s (Wiles 1987).

From 1987 to 1995, the Mariana fruit bat population fluctuated between 200 and 750 individuals on Guam and was mainly confined to the limestone forest near the clifflines on Andersen AFB (Wiles et al. 1995). Throughout 1981-1994, Mariana fruit bat colonies were documented at 21 sites on Andersen AFB, 11 at Pati Point, and 10 between Ritidian Point and the northern region of Tarague basin (Wiles et al. 1995). Presently, less than 100 Mariana fruit bats remain on Guam, primarily restricted to a single colony and satellite individuals inhabiting the limestone forest on Andersen AFB (Janeke 2006). Illegal hunting appears to be the key cause of their dramatic decline, while habitat destruction and predation by introduced BTS may also be contributing factors (Wiles et al. 1989).

Mariana fruit bats have been historically and recently detected in the forest comprising the Guam Refuge, and the Ritidian Unit specifically (Wiles 1987, Wiles et al. 1995, Wiles 1998a, Wiles 1999). This region has been, and still appears to be, essential for Mariana fruit bat roosting and foraging activities. With suitable habitat available at the Ritidian Unit, the Refuge may be an important factor for the conservation and recovery of the Mariana fruit bat on Guam.

Birds

Nightingale reed-warbler

The Service listed the nightingale reed-warbler (*Acrocephalus luscinia*) as endangered in 1970 (USFWS 1998b). It is a yellowish, medium-sized (7 in), long-billed passerine historically found on six islands in the Mariana archipelago: Guam, Tinian, Aguiguan, Saipan, Alamagan, and Pagan

(Pratt et al. 1987; USFWS 1998b). The reed-warbler was considered extirpated from Guam in the late 1960s (Wiles 2005) and from Pagan prior to 1981 (Jenkins 1983; USFWS 1998b). Populations of nightingale reed-warblers presently persist on the islands of Saipan and Alamagan (USFWS 1998b; Cruz et al. 2000; Vogt and Williams 2004). Sightings of one or two reed-warblers were recorded in 1992, 1993, and 1995 on Aguiguan; however, during subsequent visits to the island, biologists have not located individuals or a small population (USFWS 1998b; Cruz et al. 2000).

The Guam population of the nightingale reed-warbler resided primarily in wetland habitat, with the Agana Swamp, Atanotano River marsh, near the mouth of the Masso River, and Agat comprising a significant portion of the reed-warbler's total range (Baker 1951; USFWS 1998b). However, by 1968 the reed-warbler was restricted to the Agana Swamp and Atanotano River, and the last documented observation on Guam was recorded in the Agana Swamp in 1969 (Reichel et al. 1992). Fire and wetland modification, such as conversion to rice paddies during WWII and drainage of wetlands for development following the war, likely contributed to the demise of the nightingale reed-warbler on Guam (Baker 1951; Jenkins 1983; USFWS 1998b).

With no wetland habitat present on the Ritidian Unit, the nightingale reed-warbler is unlikely to have occupied this region of the island.

Guam Swiftlet [2]

The Guam swiftlet (*Aerodramus bartschi*) was federally listed as an endangered species throughout the Mariana archipelago in 1984 (USFWS 1984). It is 1 of 9 species and 62 subspecies of Aerodramus swiftlets recognized world-wide. The group is widely-distributed throughout the Indo-Pacific region from the Seychelles Islands, Reunion Island, and Mauritius, throughout Southeast Asia and Queensland, Australia, to islands in Melanesia, Micronesia, and Polynesia, reaching as far east as the Marquesas archipelago (Dickinson 2003).

The Guam swiftlet is a small (4 inches), mostly sooty-black slender-winged bird historically found on Saipan, Tinian, Aguiguan, Rota, and Guam (Chantler and Driessens 2000). Presently, the species is found only on Saipan, Aguiguan, and Guam (Vogt and Williams 2004), although an introduced population persists on the island of O'ahu in the Hawaiian Islands (Wiles and Woodside 1999, Chantler and Driessens 2000). The species is thought to have colonized the Mariana Islands from the Malayan region probably by way of the Philippines and Palau (Baker 1951).

Guam swiftlets are non-migratory and occupy natural and man-made caves year round (Pratt et al. 1987). They have the unique ability to echolocate, which allows them to penetrate, orientate, and navigate within the dark regions of caves where roosting and nesting normally occur (USFWS 1991b).

Caves containing guano have been located at the Ritidian Unit. However, there is some uncertainty whether the guano is that of the Guam swiftlet or the Pacific sheath-tailed bat (Drahos 2006). D.W. Steadman and G. Pregill found numerous swiftlet bones during excavations in caves on the Ritidian Unit (D. Steadman, Florida University of Natural History, personal communication). Currently, no Guam swiftlet colonies occupy the caves on the Refuge. There are

---

[2] Recent taxonomic revision has raised the formerly named Mariana gray swiftlet subspecies of the Vanikoro swiftlet (*Aerodramus vanikorensis bartschi*) to a full species called the Guam Swiftlet (*Aerodramus vanikorensis*), and separated it from the gray swiftlet of the south Pacific (AOU 1995).

presently three known Guam swiftlet colonies on Guam. All are located on the Navy overlay refuge in the southern region of the island (A. Brooke, U.S. Navy, personal communication). Because the Ritidian Unit was once swiftlet habitat, the area could be considered for relocation of the species.

Mariana Crow

The Mariana crow "Å'ga" (*Corvus kubaryi*) is a small, forest-dwelling crow (15 in) endemic to Guam and Rota and is the only corvid in Micronesia (Baker 1951; Jenkins 1983; Pratt et al. 1987). It was listed as endangered in 1984 by the Service (USFWS 1984). The Mariana crow is black in coloration with some gloss on the back, wing, and tail (Jenkins 1983). The crow is omnivorous, essentially foraging in the understory and forest canopy, and occasionally on the ground (Marshall 1949; Baker 1951; Jenkins 1983; Michael 1987). Mariana crows are gregarious, most often observed in groups of 2-5 birds (Jenkins 1983). However, on Guam, flocks of 7 and 14 were noted by Jenkins (1983), and two aggregations of at least 66 and 25 crows were recorded by Wiles (1998b).

On Guam, the Mariana crow historically inhabited most habitat types, principally mature forest (Stophlet 1946, Marshall 1949). However, in 1978 and 1979, crows were detected in relatively similar numbers throughout mature forests, second growth, and mixed woodland in the north-westernmost region of Guam (Jenkins 1983). In the 1960s, Mariana crows were considered common in the ravine and coastal forests, and the riparian regions in southern Guam (Stophlet 1946; Jenkins 1983). Unfortunately, the last sightings of the Mariana crow in southern Guam occurred in the mid-1960s, and the species has not been detected in central Guam since the 1970s (Jenkins 1983).

An island-wide forest bird survey in 1981 found the Guam crow population consisted of 357 crows, all restricted to the northern cliffline forests and occupying just 25 percent of their 1950s range (Engbring and Ramsey 1984) and just 4 estimated to inhabit the Ritidian basin. By 1985, the crow population was confined to Northwest Field and the Conventional Weapons Storage Area on Andersen AFB, with a population estimated at 100 birds (Michael 1987; USFWS 1990b). Subsequent to 1990, the Mariana crow population on Guam was never estimated to be higher than 57 individuals; the lowest estimate of just 7 birds was recorded in 1999 (USFWS 2005a). In 1997, translocation of crow eggs and nestlings from Rota to Guam commenced (USFWS 2005b). Consequently, the Mariana crow population on Guam no longer consists of solely Guam-born birds. Between 2000 and 2004, Guam's population fluctuated between 10 and 13 crows (USFWS 2005b). The most recent population estimate for Guam's crows is 10 birds (3 females and 7 males), all confined to Northwest Field and the Conventional Weapons Storage Area on Andersen AFB (GDAWR 2006b).

Guam's Mariana crow population started to decline around 1950, shortly after the introduction of BTS (USFWS 2005b). Morton et al. (1999) outlined potential reasons preventing recovery of the crow population on Guam. Predation by BTS; infertility; predation by rats (*Rattus sp.*) and monitor lizards (*Varanus indicus*); mobbing by black drongos; typhoons; and anthropogenic disturbances have all been suggested as explanations for the species' decline. They are now part of the GDAWR captive breeding program (S. Medina, GDAWR, personal communication)

Mariana crows have been historically and recently detected at the Ritidian Unit, at Ritidian Basin and Ritidian Point (Stophlet 1946; Engbring and Ramsey 1984; DAWR 2006, others). This region has been and still appears to be instrumental in the possible release of captive crows and ultimate recovery of the Mariana crow on Guam.

Mariana Common Moorhen

The Mariana subspecies of the common moorhen (*Gallinula chloropus guami*) was listed as an endangered species in 1984 by the Service (USFWS 1984). It is a mostly dark to sooty gray waterbird (13 in) possessing a red bill with a yellow tip, red frontal shield and yellow legs (Baker 1951; Pratt et al 1987). The moorhen was historically restricted to wetlands on Pagan, Saipan, Tinian, and Guam (USFWS 1991a). Populations of the Mariana common moorhen currently persist on Saipan, Tinian, Rota, and Guam (Takano and Haig 2004a; Vogt and Williams 2004). On Guam, the moorhen inhabits emergent vegetation within freshwater habitats including marshes, swamps, ponds, and calm rivers (Marshall 1949; Baker 1951; Jenkins 1983; USFWS 1991a; Takano and Haig 2004a; Takano and Haig 2004b). In 1945, the largest concentrations of moorhen were in the Agana Swamp and along the Ylig River (Baker 1951). In 2001, Takano and Haig (2004a) estimated a total population of 90 adult birds on Guam, with 37% recorded at the Fena Valley Reservoir on the Navy overlay refuge, the largest permanent body of water on the island.

Current threats to Guam's moorhen population include wetland degradation, reduction of open water due to encroachment by the reed *Phragmites karka*, disturbance of emergent wetland vegetation by feral pigs and carabao, and egg and nestling loss, possibly due to predation by BTS (Takano and Haig 2004a).

With no wetland habitat present at the Ritidian Unit, the Mariana common moorhen is not likely to have occupied this region of Guam.

Guam Micronesian Kingfisher

The Guam Micronesian kingfisher or "Sihek" (*Halcyon cinnamomina cinnamomina*) is endemic to Guam and is one of three extant subspecies of *Halcyon cinnamomina* found in Micronesia (Pratt et al. 1987; USFWS 2004). The species was listed as endangered in 1984 by the Service (USFWS 1984). It is a small (8 in), sexually dimorphic species. Males are distinguished by their blue upperparts and rusty cinnamon belly while females are similar except their ventral feathers are white (Pratt et al. 1987; USFWS 2004).

Historically, the Guam Micronesian kingfisher nested and fed in all habitat types except wetlands and pure savanna (Marshall 1949; Baker 1951; Jenkins 1983). It occurred primarily in mature limestone forest, mixed woodland, and second growth stands, with a preference for edges separating woodlands and openings (Baker 1951; Jenkins 1983). The Guam Micronesian kingfisher is a cavity nester known to excavate nests in decaying standing wood, arboreal termitaria, or arboreal fern root masses (Marshall 1949; Baker 1951; Jenkins 1983; Marshall 1989). Known tree species in which kingfishers have been documented excavating nests include *Pisonia grandis, Cocos nucifera, Ficus* sp., *Artocarpus* sp., and *Tristiropsis acutangula* (Marshall 1989).

Guam Micronesian kingfishers were a common sight throughout the island in 1945 (Watson 1946; Baker 1951). They were frequently observed throughout southern Guam's ravine and coastal forests, in addition to riparian regions adjacent to rivers and streams (Stophlet 1946; Jenkins 1983). By the 1970s, the Micronesian kingfisher was absent from southern Guam (USFWS 2004). In 1978, 1979, and 1981, the kingfisher was, nonetheless, considered the most widely distributed native forest bird on Guam; in 1981 it still occupied nearly 40 percent of its 1950s range, albeit restricted to the northern one-third of the island (Jenkins 1983; Engbring and Ramsey 1984). Engbring and Ramsey (1984) estimated 3,022 kingfishers present on Guam (58 within the Ritidian basin) in 1981.

By 1984 to 1985, the Guam population of the kingfisher consisted of less than 50 individuals, all restricted to Northwest Field and the Conventional Weapons Storage Area on Andersen AFB (USFWS 1990b). The Guam Micronesian kingfisher was last observed in the wild in 1988 (USFWS 2004). Presently, the kingfisher is extinct in the wild and with less than 50 maintained in captivity on Guam and in zoos across the U.S. mainland (USFWS 2004; Wiles 2005).

Guam Micronesian kingfishers were detected in the primary limestone forest along the northwestern and northernmost cliffs of Guam at Ritidian Basin and Ritidian Point, and were considered to be common in those areas (Stophlet 1946; Jenkins 1983; Engbring and Ramsey 1984). Furthermore, it is believed that this region was one of the last strongholds for the kingfisher prior to extinction in the wild (Marshall 1989). Thus, this species historically utilized the forest comprising the Ritidian Unit. If the kingfisher were to be re-released on Guam, the Ritidian Unit might well be considered suitable location for restoration.

Micronesian megapode

The Micronesian megapode "Sasangat" (*Megapodius laperouse*) was listed as endangered in 1970 by the Service (USFWS 1984). It is a dark, brownish-black bird approximately 15 inches in length (Pratt et al. 1987). The Micornesian megapode was historically widespread and has been documented on all 15 islands in the Mariana archipelago (USFWS 1998a). Populations currently persist on 12 islands in the archipelago: Aguiguan, Tinian, Saipan, Farallon de Medinilla, Anatahan, Sarigan, Guguan, Alamagan, Pagan, Agrihan, Asuncion, and Maug (USFWS 1998a; Vogt and Williams 2004).

The Micronesian megapode has always been considered rare on Guam from the time the first European naturalists visited the island until its demise in the 1930s (USFWS 1998a). The species was not found on Guam by J. Marshall or the Naval Medical Research Unit No. 2 (NAMRU2) party in 1945 (Marshall 1949; Baker 1951), nor was it detected during intensive bird surveys in the 1980s (Jenkins 1983; Engbring and Ramsey 1984). The Micronesian megapode is considered to be extirpated from Guam (Wiles 2005).

It is unclear whether the Micronesian megapode ever occurred on the Ritidian Unit. However, megapodes are known to occur in native limestone forest (USFWS 1998a), a relatively common habitat type found at the Ritidian Unit. It is possible the Micronesian megapode could be translocated from other islands to Guam in an effort to re-establish the species on the island.

Guam Rail

The endemic Guam rail "Koko" (*Rallus owstoni*) was listed as endangered in 1984 by the Service (USFWS 1984). It is a large (11 in), flightless rail with mainly grayish-brown upperparts and black with white barring on the lower breast, abdomen, under tail coverts, and tail (Baker 1951; Pratt et al. 1987). It is the only rail found in the Mariana Islands and is known to inhabit mixed woodland, secondary growth, scrub, grassland, and fern thickets (Marshall 1949; Jenkins 1979; Pratt et al. 1987).

The Guam rail was formerly distributed throughout most of Guam (USFWS 1990b). In 1945, it was frequently observed crossing roads or along the roadside (Watson 1946; Baker 1951). Tubb (1966) also noted its common presence along roadsides in 1965. By the mid-1970s, the rail was absent from southern Guam (Jenkins 1979). A 1981 island-wide survey by the Service found that Guam rails were only distributed throughout northern Guam including the Ritidian Basin region, and presumably what is presently the Guam Refuge. The largest numbers were recorded from Andersen AFB (Engbring and Ramsey 1984). Using playback data, Guam's rail population was estimated to be 2,329 birds in 1981 (Engbring and Ramsey 1984). After repeating the 1981 survey in 1984, the rail was found to be very rare in Northwest Field, and the only viable population was confined to a 70-acre region within the flightline on Andersen AFB. In July 1985, just one rail was detected in this area (USFWS 1990b). Currently, the Guam rail is considered extinct in the wild but a re-introduced population is being established and supplemented on Rota and additional individuals are maintained in captivity.

In addition to the Guam rail detections in the Ritidian Basin by Engbring and Ramsey (1984) in 1981, Jenkins (1983) also documented rails in the Ritidian region in 1978 and 1979. This species historically utilized habitat comprising the Guam Refuge including the Ritidian Unit, potentially a consideration for rail reintroduction. In fact, two previous attempts to reintroduce the Guam rail to northern Guam have occurred. The first release was at "Area 50," a fenced, ungulate proof, 60-acre plot of mixed forest on Andersen AFB. Sixteen Guam rails (8 males, 8 females) were released in 1998 and survived an average of 198 days (http://www.guamdawr.org/wildlife/railrelease/document_view), although some birds survived between 541 to 607 days (S. Medina, GDAWR, unpublished data). Four females and five males nested during the monitoring period producing 17 nests of which 84 percent of the 50 eggs successfully hatched. However, predation by feral cats following typhoons that compromised the integrity of the fence eradicated the remaining population. Nevertheless, the release was considered successful as the birds were able to adapt to foraging and surviving in the wild. A second release in the Munitions Storage Area on Andersen AFB in 2003 was less successful, primarily due to feral cat predation at the release site. Nevertheless, with feral cat and BTS control, introduction to the Ritidian Unit could be successful.

Bridled White-eye

The Guam subspecies of the bridled white-eye (*Zosterops conspicillatus conspicillatus*) was listed as endangered in 1984 by the Service. It is a small (4 in) white-eye with green upperparts, yellow-green underparts, and a wide, white ring surrounding the eye (Jenkins 1983, Pratt et al. 1987). In recent history, the Guam bridled white-eye was apparently common and widespread throughout the island (Jenkins 1983). After a 1981 island-wide survey, Engbring and Ramsey (1984) estimated 2,220 birds (179 within the Ritidian basin). During the survey, white-eyes were recorded in, and confined to, primary limestone forest, broken forest, and scrub forest habitats in the following regions of northern Guam: Pajon Basin and Plateau, Ritidian Basin, Uruno Basin, and Tarague Basin (Engbring and Ramsey 1984). In addition to the species' detections in the

Ritidian Basin by Engbring and Ramsey (1984), other authors have documented white-eyes in the forest near Ritidian Point (Stophlet 1946, Jenkins 1983). Thus, this species historically utilized forest on the Guam Refuge including the Ritidian Unit.

Following the introduction of BTS to Guam, the bridled white-eye population experienced one of the most rapid declines of any native forest bird on the island (Wiles et al. 2003). The last confirmed Guam record of the species in the wild appears to be 1984 (Wiles et al. 2003). Since no birds have been recorded since then, the Guam subspecies of the bridled white-eye is presumed to be extinct (Wiles 2005, USFWS 2006).

Sea Turtles

There are seven known species of sea turtles, of which three have been recorded inhabiting the waters off Guam (Eldredge 2003). Nests of the green turtle (*Chelonia mydas*) and the hawksbill turtle (*Eretmochelys imbricata*) have been found on Guam, but only green turtles have been recorded nesting at the Ritidian Unit (Cummings 2002). Leatherback turtles (*Dermochelys coriacea*) are extremely rare around Guam and have yet to be recorded at the Ritidian Unit. The last sighting of a leatherback around Guam was in 1985 (Cummings 2002). As the species is considered an unlikely vagrant to the Guam Refuge, it will not be specifically addressed here.

Green Turtle

Green turtles (*Chelonia mydas*) are characterized by a smooth carapace with four pairs of lateral scutes and a coarsely serrated lower jaw-edge. The carapace is keel-less and variable brown in color, with darker blotches or patchy markings. The name green turtle is derived not from their external color but from the green coloration of their subdermal fat (NMFS-USFWS 2007b). Adults often reach a maximum carapace size of about 3.3 feet and weigh approximately 220 pounds (NMFS-USFWS 1998a). Juveniles have streaked dorsal patterns of various colors ranging from yellow-gold to black. Hatchlings have a black carapace and pure white underbody. The carapace length of hatchlings ranges from 1.8 to 2.2 in, with body mass between 0.8 and 1.1 oz (Limpus and Chaloupka 1997).

Estimates based on mark-recapture and skeletochonology research indicate that green turtles reach maturity around 20-40 years from birth (Limpus and Chaloupka 1997; Chaloupka et al. 2004) and are reproductive for approximately 17-23 years (Carr et al. 1978; Chaloupka et al. 2004). Hirth (1997) estimated a reproductive female can lay about three nests of 100 eggs per season. Survivorship is lower in juveniles and subadults (0.88 and 0.85, respectively) than adults (0.95; Chaloupka and Limpus 2005), although average survival ratios differ substantially from region to region (NMFS-USFWS 2007b).

While adult green turtles prefer fairly shallow waters, except when migrating to their nesting grounds, juveniles reside primarily in pelagic or open-ocean habitats. When they reach around an 8-in carapace length, they move back into shallow feeding habitat (USFWS 2007b). This highly mobile species travels vast distances through incongruent habitats during their periodic migration between foraging and nesting sites (Plotkin 2003). Carr et al. (1978) found that females are philopatric to specific nesting beaches. Later studies demonstrated that females return, up to 40 years later, to their natal hatching beach to nest (Meylan et al. 1990; Limpus and Chaloupka 1997).

Green turtles are not obligate herbivores as once believed, but instead feed on seagrass, algae, jelly fish, sponges and other pelagic prey (Hatase et al. 2006). Hatchlings have been observed eating only invertebrates and fish eggs (NMFS-USFWS 1998a). Akin to nesting migrations, green turtles often return to the same foraging areas following nesting (Godley et al. 2002). Once at these areas, individuals demonstrate strong site fidelity to these foraging sites for extended time periods (Godley et al. 2002; Makowski et al. 2006). Not all green turtles utilize coastal foraging sites; some remain in the open ocean (Pelletier et al 2003).

Within the Pacific area, green turtles are found along the coasts of Hawai'i, American Samoa, Guam, and the Commonwealth of the Northern Mariana Islands (CNMI). The species has been reported as the principal sea turtle in the CNMI (Pritchard 1982; Wiles et al. 1989, 1990; Pultz et al. 1999; Kolinski et al. 2005). Although Guam breeding populations may not contribute substantially to the overall global density of green turtles, the island still contributes to the genetic diversity of the species (NMFS-USFWS 2007b). The number of nesting females on Guam is highly variable but ranged from 2 to 60 individuals annually between 1990 and 2002 (Cummings 2002). The author presented data from aerial surveys conducted between 1990 and 2002 which showed relatively constant near-shore abundances ranging from 80 to 250 turtles. Ritidian Point has been noted as an important habitat for the green turtle, based on numerous sightings, nests and crawls (Wiles et al. 1995).

Hawksbill Turtle

The hawksbill turtle's (*Eretmochelys imbricata*) name derives from its prominent hooked beak. As one of the smaller sea turtles, the distinguishing characteristics of hawksbill turtles are their small size, narrow head, and thick overlapping shell scutes (NMFS-USFWS 1998b). Adults range in carapace size from 2.6 to 3.3 ft, and weigh between 100 and 200 pounds (USFWS 2007c). The scutes of the carapace are thick and usually dark brown in color with light yellow lines and markings and a yellow plastron (NMFS-USFWS 1998b). Hatchlings have a tan carapace ranging in size from 1.5 to 1.6 in (NMFS-USFWS 1998b).

Based on various studies of different populations, age to maturity in the Indo-Pacific hawksbill is estimated at least 30-35 years (Limpus and Miller 2000). Hawksbills are a slow growing species averaging 0.4-1.2 in growth per year, although growth is non-monotonic, being greater before sexual maturity than after (Chaloupka and Limpus 1997). The species is generally reproductively active for about 17-20 years (Mortimer and Bresson 1999; Limpus 1992). Typically females lay clutches at 14-day intervals (Witzell 1983), with 3-5 clutches per nesting season (Richardson et al. 1999; Mortimer and Bresson 1999). Clutch size averages 160 eggs (Ehrhart 1982). Nesting hawksbills are rare on Guam; in 2003 less than 5-10 nesting events were recorded (NMFS-USFWS 2007c), none at the Ritidian Unit.

Like green turtles, hawksbills are highly migratory and travel vast distances through disparate habitats during their periodic foraging to nesting site migration (Plotkin 2003). To cover these vast areas, this highly maneuverable species can reach speeds up to 15 mph. Once believed to exhibit disperse nesting patterns, this phenomenon is currently thought to be a direct result of reduction of previously large colonies through overexploitation (Limpus 1995; Meylan and

Donnelly 1999). Female hawksbill turtles show strong site fidelity in their choice of nesting sites (Witzell 1983) which are usually their natal hatching beach site (Broderick et al. 1995).

Post hatching, juvenile hawksbills move from the beach to the open ocean. These young sea turtles are often found in association with Sargassum in the Pacific Ocean (Musick and Limpus 1997). During their oceanic phase, turtles feed on a combination of plant and animal material (Bjornal 1997). Post-oceanic phase feeding occurs in a variety of habitats including coral reefs, seagrass fields, algal beds, and mangroves (Musick and Limpus 1997). During this phase, hawksbills feed on jellyfish, sea urchins, sea sponges, and algae growing on reefs (Bjornal 1997).

Hawksbill turtles are found predominately in warm tropical waters including the Pacific islands of Hawai'i, American Samoa, Guam, and the CNMI. Micronesia is thought to support some 300 females annually (NMFS-USFWS 1998b). There are 83 known nesting concentrations of hawksbills in the Indo-Pacific Ocean, of which Guam is one (NMFS-USFWS 1998b). Since hawksbill turtles are typically found near river mouths, they tend to congregate in southern Guam and around Apra Harbor. Such habitat is unavailable in northern Guam, which may explain the lack of nesting and relatively few sightings of the species around Ritidian Point (Wiles et al. 1995).

Threats to Sea Turtles

Green, hawksbill, and leatherback turtles were once abundant globally, but have declined dramatically over the past 100 years (NMFS-USFWS 2007b, 2007c, 2007d). On Guam, the historical and recent population trends show that local populations of nesting green turtles are relatively stable (NMFS-USFWS 2007b), but hawksbill nesting continues to decline (NMFS-USFWS 2007c). These population declines are due primarily to direct take of turtles and eggs. Cummings (2002) anecdotally reported the most significant threats to the Guam population of sea turtles was by-catch and illegal take by fishermen, primarily for consumption at celebrations for the patron saints of local villages. Predation on sea turtle nests by monitor lizards (*Varanus indicus*), wild pigs (*Sus scrofa*), rats (*Rattus* sp.) and ghost crabs (*Ocypode* sp.) are also considered a threat (Cummings 2002). As leatherback turtles have been so infrequently found in Guam waters, it is unclear what impact humans or feral animals have had on the local population.

A newly emerging and potentially significant threat to the demography of all three sea turtles is the increasing sex bias toward females (Hays et al. 2003; Baker et al. 2006; NMFS-USFWS 2007c, 2007d). Because sex determination is temperature dependent in these turtles (Mrosovsky 1994), an increase in water and nesting site temperatures brought about by global warming could further skew ratios to a point where viable populations cease to exist (Hays et al. 2003). Additionally, the loss of rookeries can lead to a decline in genetic diversity and resilience to extirpation of this species (Bowen 1995). Fibropapillomatosis (FP) has been reported in some sub-populations of green turtles, including those in neighboring Federated States of Micronesia (Seminoff 2004).

The listing of green, hawksbill, and leatherback turtles as threatened or endangered under the ESA throughout all areas under U.S. jurisdiction and their inclusion in CITES has increased the level of protection afforded to these species. NMFS and the Service have recently completed comprehensive 5-year reviews for each species (NMFS-USFWS 2007b, 2007c, 2007d) which will guide managers and policy makers in protecting sea turtles. The Guam Refuge has taken steps to protect the individuals that use its beaches and shoreline. A large area of beach front is closed to visitors to protect nesting turtles. The visitor center provides material to educate the public about sea turtles and perhaps dissuade individuals from consuming them. Feral animal control is currently being addressed and measures to reduce their numbers will certainly help to sustain and perhaps increase the current sea turtle population.

Endangered Plants

Deterioration of Guam's native vegetation is multifactorial: human exploitation (Lawrence and Dougherty 1993); invasive plant species (Lee 1974); loss of pollinators and seed dispersal (Cox et al. 1991; Dougherty and Falanruw 1993); nonnative ungulates (Lawrence and Dougherty 1993; Schreiner 1997; Morton et al. 2000); and damaging storms (Fosberg 1960; Lawrence and Dougherty 1993) have all been implicated to some degree. Large areas of forest and woody vegetation on and adjacent to the Refuge have been replaced by vines, herbs, and grasses (Lee 1974; Morton et al. 2000), particularly following typhoons that create openings in the forest canopy and allow invasion of fast-growing exotics (Horvitz et al. 1998). Donnegan et al. (2004) estimated that about 20 percent of Guam's trees have been damaged, primarily from weather, other vegetation, and insects. Still, some native vegetation exists, and intact forest remnants can be found on the Refuge. The only federally listed plant species is found on the Ritidian Unit.

Serianthes Nelsonii

The genus *Serianthes Bentham* (*Mimosoideae, Fabaceae*) is composed of 10 species spread from Sumatra and the Malay Peninsula in the west to French Polynesia and Micronesia in the east (Fosberg 1960). Endemic to Guam and Rota, *Serianthes nelsonii*, locally known as "trongkon guafi," was listed as endangered in February 1987 (GDAWR 2006a). The species was first collected in the late 1800s but not described until 1919 from a holotype that was destroyed during a World War II bombing raid in Manila (Merrill 1919; Fosberg 1960).

Serianthes nelsonii is one of the largest native trees in the Marianas, reported to grow to 66 feet on Guam and 118 feet on Rota. It has a sprawling canopy as large as 75 feet in diameter (Merrill 1919; Raulerson and Rinehart 1991). The leaves are long and pointed, the seed pod hard, and the light pink flowers brush-like (Stone 1970). Surviving trees are found in limestone forests on soils derived from limestone substrate (Fosberg 1960; USFWS 1994b). Most grow on or near cliffs or steep hillsides but not in the extreme karst forests on either island (Fosberg 1960). Two trees were found growing in the volcanic soils of central Guam (USFWS 1994b).

The original distribution of *Serianthes nelsonii* is unknown, but it is clear that the species has always been considered rare (Merrill 1919; Stone 1960). Of the six mature trees ever found on Guam, the majority were located in the north, on or near the Ritidian Unit (Wiles et al 1996). Currently, the species is represented by 121 mature trees on Rota but only one mature, naturally occurring tree on Guam, located on the Air Force Overlay Unit (USFWS 1994b; Wiles et al. 1995). A second tree, in Northwest Field adjacent to the Ritidian Unit, was destroyed by Typhoon Omar in 1992; however, a small number of its seedlings survived (Wiles et al. 1996). Seeds from Rota *Serianthes nelsonii* are being propagated by Guam Forestry and will be out-planted on the Ritidian Unit and possibly the Air Force Overlay Unit (C. Bandy, USFWS, personal communication).

Populations of *Serianthes nelsonii* remain senescent, with little or no successful regeneration occurring. When a population is endangered, the loss of a few individuals can cause a serious problem to the overall viability of that population. Although inadequately studied, the lack of regeneration is likely caused by a number of factors including browsing, trampling, and rooting of seedlings by the introduced Philippine deer (*Cervus mariannus*) and feral pigs (*Sus scrofa*). Evidence of animal herbivory, most likely deer, was found in Guam where seedlings beneath a mature tree were bitten off at ground level (Schreiner and Nafus 1991). Herbivory on trees and seedlings by mealybugs (*Dysmicoccus brevipes, D. neobrevipes, Ferrisia virgata and Planococcus sp.*) and a butterfly (*Eurema blanda*) have also been implicated as threats to *Serianthes nelsonii* (Wiles et al. 1996) as has *Tetraleurodes acaciae* (A. Moore, University of Guam, unpublished data). These pest species have been observed feeding on the leaves, leaf buds, branch tips, and roots of trees and seedlings (Schreiner and Nafus 1991). The ant *Pheidole megacephala* has been observed carrying *D. brevipes* to a group of propagated seedlings. The ensuing infestation of the mealy bug subsequently killed 19 of the 20 seedlings (Wiles et al. 1996). The caterpillar of *E. blanda* easily defoliates *Serianthes nelsonii*, removing as much as 25% of the foliage from a single tree (Schreiner and Nafus 1991). Control using herbicides proved problematic for small seedlings, which were negatively affected by the poison application (Schreiner and Nafus 1991). Predation on seed pods is significant in the Rota population of *Serianthes nelsonii* but has not been noted on Guam (USFWS 1994b). Unknown species of termites have attacked at least three *Serianthes nelsonii* on Guam in recent years and contributed to their deaths. Termite and other insect damage can severely weaken branches and trunks leaving them vulnerable to storm and typhoon damage.

Native habitat destruction in northern Guam, including military construction during WWII and the subsequent urbanization of the area since, undoubtedly influenced the decline of *Serianthes nelsonii*, although no direct links between the two have been described. The construction of Andersen AFB following WWII probably destroyed some trees, particularly associated with airport runway clearings (USFWS 1994b). The Air Force inadvertently destroyed a mature tree adjacent to the road on Ritidian Point in the early 1970s. However, the Northwest Field tree avoided destruction when the proposed radar system project was withdrawn (USFWS 1994b). Andersen AFB initiated a *Serianthes nelsonii* recovery effort in collaboration with the University of Guam and out-planted seedlings in the Tarague Embayment and Area 50 in 1997. The seedlings were protected from ungulate predation with mesh wire fences, although eventually, they were infested with mealy bugs and vines (H. Hirsh, SWCA, personal communication). Although all seedlings in Area 50 subsequently perished, four survived at Tarague (A. Brooke, NAVFACMAR, pers. comm. 2006). The Guam Refuge later erected an ungulate proof fence around the trees.

Other factors such as lack of pollinators, inbreeding, storms, and wildfires may have contributed to the species' demise. Methods of pollination are unreported for this species, but Mariana fruit bats have been observed feeding on *Serianthes nelsonii* flowers and may play a role in pollination (Wiles et al. 1996). Lack of genetic diversity has undoubtedly restricted opportunities for out-breeding. With so few individuals, the opportunity for self-pollination increased and cross pollination decreased, possibly leading to reduced reproductive quality and output. Further, typhoons and tropical storms damage and destroy healthy trees. At least two Guam trees have been killed by typhoons, but both had previously been weakened by either termite infestation (Northwest Field, Typhoon Omar 1992) or mealybug herbivory (Yona, Typhoon Russ 1990). Although not so prevalent in northern Guam, southern Guam is particularly susceptible to wildfires. In fact, fire is responsible for the death of a *Serianthes nelsonii* in the Tarzan River Valley and for severely damaging a second tree in the area, undoubtedly contributing to its death in 1982 (USFWS 1994b).

The formation of the Guam Refuge has afforded some level of protection of *Serianthes nelsonii*. The last remaining mature tree is located within the Air Force Overlay Unit. In 1981, *Serianthes nelsonii* was placed on the Guam Endangered Species List and consequently is protected by the Endangered Species Act of Guam (P.L. 15-36) as well as the ESA. In collaboration with Guam Forestry, searches for new trees have occurred and fences have been placed around existing trees. Seeds have been collected (most from the Rota population) and propagated by various organizations and individuals including the Division of Forestry and Soil Resources. Further efforts to preserve maximum genetic diversity by selecting robust parental stock are intended (Wiles et al. 1996). Recovery efforts should focus on preventing or reducing browsing by both vertebrate and invertebrate herbivores. The erection of additional ungulate-proof fencing and plantings within the fenced areas are planned for the immediate future. Other management activities, such as the removal of strangler figs (*Ficus prolixa*) from trees and saplings, mechanical cross fertilization to enhance out-breeding, and further caging of seedlings should also be considered (USFWS 1994b).

Other Species of Concern

Tree snails are found in cool, shaded forest habitats with high humidity and low air movement (Cowie 1992). Although none of Guam's native partulid tree snails are currently federally listed as threatened or endangered, all are drastically declining or extirpated. As a consequence, three species are candidates for Federal listing (*Partula gibba, P. radiolata,* and *Samoana fragilis*) and one (*P. salifana*), now considered extinct (B. Smith, University of Guam, personal communications), as a species of concern. Hopper and Smith (1992) found no known living partulids on the Ritidian Unit. However, in 1996 a small colony of *P. radiolata* was found inhabiting a small grove of trees along the beach road at the Refuge (B. Smith, University of Guam, personal communication). Colonies of partulids are currently known from the Navy Overlay Unit (NTCS). This area supports the only known colony of *S. fragilis,* as well as *P. gibba,* and *P. radiolata* (Hopper and Smith 1992). Hopper and Smith (1992) attribute the introduction in 1978 of a predatory flat worm (*Platydemus manokwari*), and several carnivorous land snails (*Euglandina rosea, Gonaxis kibweziensis,* and *G. quadrilateralis*) in the 1950s and 1960s as major reasons for tree snail decline. In addition, habitat for all tree snail species has been seriously degraded by ungulates, causing further threat to the viability of surviving populations.

The Mariana eight-spot butterfly (*Hypolimnus octocula mariannensis*) is endemic to the islands of Guam and Saipan in the Mariana archipelago, and the Mariana wandering butterfly (*Vagrans egestina*) to Guam and Rota (Schreiner and Nafus 1997). The abundance of both species decreased rapidly and they were thought to be endangered by the 1970s. Both were federally listed as candidate species in 1997, by which time the butterflies may have been extirpated from Guam and populations reduced elsewhere (http://www.biologicaldiversity.org/swcbd/Programs/international/butterflies.html). Although it is not known whether either species occurred on the Ritidian Unit, *H. octocula* was recorded at nearby Hilaan point (Schreiner and Nafus 1997). *Vagrans egestina* is strongly associated with the tree *Maytenus thompsonii* (Schreiner and Nafus 1997) which is common in limestone forests (Stone 1970). Therefore, it is likely that both butterflies were present on the Guam Refuge.

Although the Guam bronze boony bug (*Catacanthus* sp.) is listed as a species of concern under the Endangered Species Act (ESA) (see Table 4), there is no available information on the species (A. Moore, University of Guam, personal communication).

Two marine fishes, the humphead wrasse (*Cheilinus undulatus*) and bumphead parrotfish (*Bolbometopon muricatum*) are classified as species of concern. *C. undulatus* is currently listed as vulnerable by the IUCN (NOAA 2007) and under consideration for CITES listing. These species are slow growing and long-lived but have delayed reproduction and low recruitment. Generation periods of 10 years or more render them particularly susceptible to overexploitation (Donaldson and Sadovy 2001). *C. undulatus* has a particularly patchy distribution; adults are rarely seen in Guam waters (Myers 1999). *B. muricatum* is more likely to be seen off Ritidian Point than *C. undulatus* because of its preference for clear outer lagoons and seaward reefs (Myers 1999). However, the species has almost completely disappeared from Guam's reefs and is increasingly difficult to find (NOAA 2007).

Even in preferred habitats, *B. muricatum* densities are never high (Donaldson and Sadovy 2001). Night-time spear fishing is also a problem for *B. muricatum* because of its habit of sleeping in schools (GDAWR 2006a). Both species are particularly vulnerable to intensive fishing pressure for the reef-fish food trade because of their sedentary nature (NOAA 2007). Being large fish, these species are important to divers and have a high tourism value (Rudd and Tupper 2002). Without public outreach to reduce take of these species and further protection of their preferred habitats, populations of both *C. undulatus* and *B. muricatum* will be further jeopardized.

Seabirds

Waters near the Ritidian Unit likely serve as important flyways for breeding and non-breeding seabirds. The brown noddy (*Anous stolidus*) and white tern (*Gygis alba*) are Guam's only resident breeding seabirds. Non-breeding seabirds that may roost on Guam and are also frequently attracted to Guam's nearshore waters (possibly including the waters near the Guam Refuge), include wedge-tailed shearwater (*Puffinus pacificus*), white-tailed tropicbird (*Phaethon lepturus*), red-tailed tropicbird (*Phaethon rubricauda*), brown booby (*Sula leucogaster*), red-footed booby (*Sula sula*), great frigatebird (*Fregata minor*), black noddy (*Anous minutus*), black-naped tern (*Sterna sumatrana*), and sooty tern (*Sterna fuscata*) (Wiles 2005).

Non-breeding seabirds that are pelagic and primarily occur farther offshore Guam include Tahiti petrel (*Pseudobulweria rostrata*), Juan Fernandez petrel (*Pterodroma externa*), streaked shearwater (*Calonectris leucomelas*), short-tailed shearwater (*Puffinus tenuirostris*), Townsend's shearwater (*Puffinus auricularis*), Audubon's shearwater (*Puffinus lherminieri*), Leach's storm-petrel (*Oceanites leucorhoa*), Matsudaira's storm-petrel (*Oceanodroma matsudairae*), masked booby (*Sula dactylatra*), and greater crested tern (*Sterna bergii*) (Wiles 2005). Other non-breeding seabirds that have been detected in the waters near Guam include common black-headed gull (*Larus ridibundus*), common tern (*Sterna hirundo*), little tern (*Sterna albifrons*), white-winged tern (*Chlidonias leucopterus*), and whiskered tern (*Chlidonias hybrida*) (National Audubon Society Christmas Bird Counts 1989-2006; Wiles 2005).

Migratory Waterfowl and Waterbirds

With no standing water sources present, migratory waterfowl and waterbirds are rare observations on the Ritidian Unit. However, migratory waterbirds using open field regions of the Refuge include cattle egret (*Bulbulcus ibis*), little egret (*Egretta garzetta*), and intermediate egret (*Egretta intermedia*) (Pratt et al. 1987). Two resident breeding waterbirds that are documented in forest edge and exposed coral reef regions on the Ritidian Unit are yellow bittern (*Ixobrychus sinensis*) and Pacific reef-heron (*Egretta sacra*) (Pratt et al. 1987).

Migratory Shorebirds

Guam serves as an important stop-over location for migratory shorebirds during the non-breeding season. Shorelines, exposed coral reef, and open field habitats are common observation locations for shorebirds on the Ritidian Unit. Sightings during the fall migration have been recorded on the Refuge for Pacific golden-plover (*Pluvialis fulva*) and wandering tattler (*Heteroscelus incanus*).

5.4 Pest and Nonnative Species

Pest Species

Invasive species are infiltrators that invade ecosystems beyond their historic range and threaten biological diversity. Introductions are usually human-mediated and cause harm to the economy, environment, or human health (Executive Order 13112). Direct competition with native species for resources such as food, water, and space has a major impact on the environments to which the species is introduced. Invasive species may also destroy or modify crucial habitat leading to greater exposure of native species to predators, competition for food resources, and removal of important Refuge attributes (Priddel and Carlile 1998). In addition, invasives are often vectors for the spread of pathogens and disease (Geering et al. 1995; Dickman 1996).

Island ecosystems are exceptionally fragile and adversely impacted by invasives due to their intricate trophic structure (Fritts and Rodda 1998b). Endemic island species that have evolved in the absence of a particular invasive predator are at risk because they lack the necessary defenses to impede their predation (Dickman 1996, Fritts and Rodda 1998a) or survive resultant ecosystem imbalance. Guam is a notable example of island invasion success, with the introduction and establishment of at least 9 mammal and 32 amphibian and reptile species since European settlement (Savidge 1987; McCoid 1993; 1999, Stinson 1994; Christy et al. 2007). However, not all species establish and are considered invasive. There are currently over 80 invasive species listed for Guam (Appendix A), and the number is growing rapidly (e.g., the recent discovery in September 2007 of the coconut rhinoceros beetle *Oryctes rhinoceros*; A. Moore, University of Guam, personal communication). However, only a subset is present on Guam Refuge (Table 4).

Table 4. Terrestrial nonnative species present at the Ritidian Unit known to have negative impacts. Data compiled from: R. Miller and A. Moore, UOG field collections and http://www.invasivespecies.net/database/species/search.asp?sts=sss&st=sss&fr=1&sn= &rn=guam&hci=-1&ei=-1&x=33&y=10

Species Name	Common Name	Chamorro Name
MAMMALS		
Cervus mariannus	Philippine deer	Binadu
Sus scrofa	feral pig	Babuen hålomtåno'
Felis catus	feral house cat	Katón machalek
Canis familiaris	feral dog	Gálagon machalek
Suncus murinus	shrew	Chå'ka
Rattus rattus	black rat	Chå'ka
Rattus norvegicus	Norway rat	Chå'ka
Mus musculus	house mouse	Chå'ka
HERPETOFAUNA		
Varanus indicus	monitor lizard	Hilitai
Boiga irregularis	brown treesnake	Kulepbla
Hemidactylus frenatus	house gecko	Guali'ek
Carlia ailanpalai	curious skink	Achi'ak
Ramphotyphlops braminus	brahminy blind snake	Ulo' åttelong
Chaunus (=Bufo) marinus	marine toad	Tot
BIRDS		
Dicrurus macrocercus	black drongo	Salin Taiwan
Francolinus francolinus	black francolin	
Passer montanus	Eurasian tree sparrow	Ga'ga' pale'
Streptopelia bitorquata	Island collared dove	Paluman Senesa
Gallus gallus	feral chicken	Mannok
INVERTEBRATES		
Adoretus sinicus	Chinese rose beetle	
Popilla lewisi	scarab beetle	

Species Name	Common Name	Chamorro Name
Protaetia orientalis	oriental flower beetle	
Protaetia pryeri	Midway emerald beetle	
Bactrocera cucurbitae	melon fly	
Tetraleurodes acacia	acacia whitefly	
Leptoglossus australis	leaf-footed bug	
Physomerus grossipes	spine-footed bug	
Aulacaspis yasumatsui	Asian cycad scale	
Aphis mellifera	honey bee	
Quadrastichus erythrinae	erythrina gall wasp	
Campsomeris sp.		
Delta campaniforme	yellow potter wasp	
Polistes olivaceous	paper wasp	
Pareuchaetes pseudoinsulata		
Chilades pandava	cycad blue butterfly	
Eudocima fullonia	fruit-piercing moth	
Diaphania sp.		
Stenocatantops splendens	short-horned grasshopper	
Pison, Sceliphron, and Chalybion sp.	mud dauber wasps	
Formidae	ant, up to 26 species	

Pest Mammals

The flora and fauna of oceanic islands that have evolved without mammals have fared particularly poorly compared to those that have evolved with mammals. The feral pig (*Sus scrofa*) and Philippine deer (*Cervus mariannus*) were intentionally introduced to Guam for hunting between the late 1600s and 1700s (Conry 1988; Wiles et al. 1999). Arriving on Guam with no natural predators, both species proceeded to destroy native vegetation and increase vulnerability of the now open habitats to other species invasions (Morton et al. 2000). In the nearby area of Andersen AFB Munitions Storage Area 1, ungulate densities were reported to be 183 Philippine deer per square kilometer, and 38 feral pigs per square kilometer (Knutson and Vogt 2002). Both are responsible for considerable damage to the Refuge's vegetative structure through foraging, rooting, and wallowing. Feral pigs are omnivorous and can feed on native sea turtles, sea birds, and reptiles, putting these vulnerable species at risk. Complete eradication of pigs and deer on Guam is not culturally acceptable to a large number of people because the community values these species for hunting and food.

Rodents, particularly rats, have been implicated in 40-60 percent of recorded bird and reptile extinctions (e.g., Wanless et al. 2007). Introduced rodents also contribute to the decline of native vegetation by consuming native seed or seedlings (e.g., DeMattia et al. 2004). Rodents are predators of nesting birds, land invertebrates, and plants, as well as a reservoir of disease and disperser of invasive plant seeds (Amori and Clout 2003). Due to the benign climate and ample abundance of food on Guam, rodents and shrews are capable of breeding year round (A. Wiewel, USGS, personal communication). The black rat (*Rattus rattus*), Norway rat (*Rattus norvegicus*), house mouse (*Mus musculus*) and shrew (*Suncus murinus*) have been recorded on Guam Refuge (Table 3, Peterson 1956; A. Wiewel, USGS, personal communication). Small mammals have not posed as great a threat to the Refuge and its environs because densities have remained relatively low. We speculate this to be caused, in part, by high predation pressure by BTS and foraging by introduced ungulates causing low recruitment of fruit and seed-bearing plants used as food. Feral cats (*Felis catus*) and dogs (*Canis familiaris*) have been observed on the Ritidian Unit from time to time but have not to-date posed any major problems. However, cats have the ability to prey on reptiles and ground birds (Dickman 1996) and thus may require containment or control if the Guam rail is to be reintroduced to the area.

Pest Reptiles and Pest Amphibians

By far the most notorious invader to Guam is BTS. BTS is native to Australia, Papua New Guinea, Indonesia, and the Solomon Islands, and was accidentally introduced to Guam shortly after WWar II (Savidge 1987; Rodda et al. 1999). It spread rapidly, with populations peaking at about 100 snakes per hectare in the early 1980s (Rodda et al. 1999; Fritts 2002). As a consequence, populations have successfully established island-wide and extirpated or severely reduced most of Guam's native terrestrial vertebrates, including bats, lizards, and virtually all of the island's forest birds (Fritts 1988, Fritts and Rodda 1998, Rodda et al. 1999, Wiles et al. 1995). Since its peak in the 1980s, the number of snakes has declined slightly (Fritts and Rodda 1998), although it is extremely unlikely to be extirpated from the island any time soon. BTS is common to the Ritidian Unit.

Other invasive reptiles and amphibians found on the Ritidian Unit include the monitor lizard (*Varanus indicus*), curious skink (*Carlia ailanpalai*), house gecko (*Hemidactylus frenatus*) and marine toad (*Chaunus marinus*). Most likely the greatest impact of monitor lizards on the Refuge is the propensity for the species to predate and scavenge sea turtle nests (Read and Mosby 2006). In addition, the lizard may feed on ground-dwelling birds and their eggs (Bennett 1995), which may pose a problem if the Guam rail is reintroduced to the Refuge. Marine toads have substantially impacted ecosystems via direct and indirect mechanisms (Crossland 2000) and are likely a threat to native fauna. The toad is a voracious, opportunistic feeder (Hinkley 1962), possessing large parotoid glands that excrete poison and kill the potential prey (Crossland 2000). Small invasive geckos and skinks impact the ecosystem by preying on native invertebrates and providing food for other invasives such as the marine toad or the BTS (Fritts and Rodda 1998a, b).

Pest Birds

Five introduced bird species are found at the Ritidian Unit (Table 2). Of these, the Eurasian tree sparrow (*Passer montanus*) and Philippine turtle dove (*Streptopelia bitorquata*) are the most conspicuous. Introduced between 1945 and 1960 (King 1962), the Eurasian tree sparrow is now very common in urban areas. It is frequently observed on Refuge buildings and congregating in the highly disturbed areas on the Ritidian Unit. The Philippine turtle dove was introduced by the Spanish, probably in the 1700s (Baker 1951). The species is now common island-wide, and like the black francolin, is hunted as game (Jenkins 1983). Engbring and Ramsey (1984) estimated a population size of at least 104 individuals in the Ritidian basin. The black francolin (*Francolinus francolinus*) was introduced to Guam from Southeast Asia, also as a game animal (Jenkins 1983). Francolin abundance increased to almost 5,000 birds in 1980 prior to the onset of hunting (Engbring and Ramsey 1984). The feral chicken (*Gallus gallus*), is a combination of many races of domestic chicken likely introduced by the Chamorro people (Engbring and Ramsey 1984). Baker (1951) found no feral chicken in 1945 and Engbring and Ramsey (1984) reported chickens only in the region of Northwest Field (Andersen AFB) in 1981. However, chickens were commonly observed during the early morning and late afternoon at the Ritidian Unit between 2002 and 2007 (M. Christy, personal observation).

A strongly territorial and aggressive bird, the black drongo (*Dicrurus macrocercus*) is perhaps the most concerning of all introduced birds on the Guam NWR. The species was originally introduced to Rota but quickly spread to Guam (Baker 1951). By 1981 the species was considered one of the most common bird species island-wide (Engbring and Ramsey 1984) but numbers rapidly fell shortly thereafter. Engbring and Ramsey (1984) estimated a population size of at least 28 individuals in the Ritidian basin in 1981. The species is known to displace smaller birds that might otherwise nest in the area (Fritts and Rodda 1998). If reintroduction of small, native bird species at the Refuge is considered, further studies on the likely impact of the black drongo on these native species and eventually their control or eradication may be necessary.

Pest Insects

A cycad scale insect (*Aulacaspis yasumatsui*) native to Southeast Asia (Howard et al. 1999; Muniappan 2005) was first detected on Guam in 2003 (Moore et al. 2005). It quickly spread to native populations of the cycad (*Cyca micronesica*) and by 2005 had infested most of the island's wild and cultivated cycads (Moore et al. 2005). It is not harmful to humans, but covers the cycad with a white film and eventually kills the plant. During cycad scale surveys at the Ritidian Unit, Moore et al. (2005) found a lycaenid butterfly (cycad blue butterfly, *Chilades pandava*) also attacking the cycad. In 2005, the first release of the black lady beetle (*Rhyzobius lophanthae*) as bio-control for the scale occurred on the Refuge. The release was moderately successful and thus far, the only control of the cycad scale insect on Guam.

At least three species of mud dauber (*Sphecidae and Vespidae*) inhabit the caves on the Ritidian Unit (A. Moore, University of Guam, personal communication). As elsewhere, the mud dauber poses a problem at the Ritidian Unit because it has built nests at rock art sites, specifically on the Refuge's ancient pictograph paintings. The nests consist of locally derived sediment, and although there is no evidence that these insects erode the rock surface, present nests attract more nest-building activity which will ultimately damage the paintings (Naumann and Watson 1987). Since the pictographs have great historical value, Refuge staff is actively working on ways to clean nests from the paintings and inhibit the insect from building new nests.

All Guam's ant species are a direct result of accidental introduction (Moore et al. 2005). There are some 26 species of ant currently found on the Ritidian Unit (R. Miller, University of Guam, unpublished data). The rise in Guam's invasive ant diversity and abundance is a prime suspect in the decline in recruitment of some of the island's endangered and threatened plant species. While most ants are opportunistic foragers, some feed on plant exudates, seeds, fruit, leaf, and stem material, and inhabiting arthropods. Invasive ants frequently have drastic disruptive effects on the native invertebrates and small animals and upon the general ecology of the habitat they invade. Invasive ants may exclude competing native invertebrates from food resources, raid their nests, or directly compete for resources. The loss of key invertebrate species may have cascading effects that lead to subsequent loss of species. The African big-headed ant (*Pheidole megacephala*) and yellow crazy ant (*Anoplolepis gracilipes*) are examples of species with known negative ecological impacts, arguably greater than any other invasive ant species in the Pacific (Wetterer 2007). In areas where they occur in high densities, few native invertebrates persist. Although a few species of invasive ants occur on the Guam NWR, their impact is generally unknown. There are currently no control mechanisms in place for any ant species.

Only 7 of Guam's 24 species of mosquitos are endemic (Ward 1984). These non-indigenous species are represented within six genera including *Anopheles, Aedes, Culex, Armigeres, Mansonia,* and *Aedeomyia* (Lounibos 2002). Certain species are primary vectors for spreading West Nile Virus and other diseases to humans, and avian diseases to seabirds. The Asian tiger mosquito (*Aedes albopictus*) may be found at the Ritidian Unit from time to time. It is associated with the transmission of diseases such as Dengue, West Nile and Japanese Encephalitis. Because of the Refuge's lack of sizeable pools of standing water, mosquitoes are not likely to become a major threat to visitors or the ecosystem.

Pest Plants

Some clearing and habitat modification occurred at the Ritidian Unit associated with WWII and military build-up in the late 1940s. After clearing, forested areas were exposed to invasion by nonnative plant species, including *Bidens alba, Chromolaena odorata, Stachytarpheta cayennensis, Ipomaea indica, Passifolia foetida, Passifolia suberosa, Operculina ventricosa, Cestrum diurnum, Muntingia calabura, Triphasia trifolia, Leucanea leucocephala,* and *Caesalpinia major*. Woody species such as *L. leucocephala* (tangan tangan) quickly formed a major component of open xeric areas, and *Vitex parviflora* dominated upper and mid-canopies of denser forests (Fosberg 1960). Invasive ungulates reduced recruitment of native limestone woody species into the upper canopy, thus altering forest composition and structure (Wiles et al. 1999). Management of invasive plant species is necessary to maintain the integrity of the Ritidian Unit's remaining native vegetation.

Chapter 6. Refuge Facilities, Archaeology, and Socioeconomic Environment

6.1 Infrastructure and Administrative Facilities

Guam NWR Headquarters

The headquarters of the Guam Refuge is located on the Ritidian Unit (Figures 1 and 2). Naval buildings constructed between the 1960s and the 1980s have been renovated beginning in 2000. The Administrative Building with offices, a conference room, and a classroom is shared with the USGS Biological Research Division Brown Treesnake Research Project. A maintenance shop and flammables storage building support Refuge operations. A Nature Center was opened to the public in 2007.

Utilities have had recent renovations. Electric lines coming from the high voltage lines on Route 3A are now underground to provide protection from typhoon damage. A backup generator with an automatic transfer switch is able to power the entire headquarters site when island power is lost. A solar system provides electricity to most of the administration building offices. Water is collected from the roofs of the buildings, stored in tanks, and made potable through filters and ultraviolet light treatment. Septic tanks and leachfields were replaced in 2008. The septic tank and leachfield at the Nature Center were built to size for the construction of a public restroom facility. Currently portable restroom facilities are maintained through a rental company.

The entrance road and Nature Center parking are planned to be upgraded as funds become available. The entrance road is to be straightened where it enters the Nature Center parking lot and a sharp curve just inside the Refuge boundary is to be widened by shaving off a rock face.

6.2 Operation and Maintenance

Guam Refuge has high maintenance requirements due to Guam's high ambient temperatures, high humidity, the location of the buildings near the shoreline, and the direction of the prevailing winds. Corrosion of metal, even stainless steel, requires constant repair and replacement. Vehicles and equipment are stored inside when not in use.

A rooftop solar system provides power for most offices in the administration building. A switch allows transfer of that load when cloudy days limit power collection. The solar system cannot meet the electric load requirements of the air conditioning system.

Although there is a wet season and a dry season, the tropical vegetation grows throughout the year and requires constant cutting and trimming. Routine requirements of staff, community service persons, and volunteers are in Table 5.

Table 5. Refuge maintenance activities

Description of routine maintenance	Daily	Weekly	Monthly	# of Hours
Tree Trimming		X		2
Bush cutting (sidewalks, fences, etc.)			X	3
Mowing (roads, trails, etc.)			X	3
Trash pick-up	X			1
Trash disposal		X		3
Vehicle maintenance (service, vacuuming, washing, etc.)		X		3
Fueling vehicles off-site		X		1
Equipment maintenance (fire extinguishers, solar batteries, etc.)			X	2
Building maintenance (sweeping, mopping, painting, etc.)		X		3
Generator maintenance (oil/filter change, fueling, etc.)			X	2
Air-conditioning units maintenance			X	3
Water system maintenance		X		1
Trail structure maintenance		X		1

6.3 Recreation Overview

Public Use Conditions

This section describes public use opportunities currently occurring on the Ritidian Unit of the Refuge, as well as recreational activities in the surrounding area. Island-wide recreational demands and potential opportunities at the Refuge are also discussed.

Existing Refuge Recreation

The Administration Act identifies six wildlife dependent visitor uses: hunting, fishing, wildlife observation and photography, environmental education, and interpretation. According to the Refuge Recreation Act of 1962 and the Administration Act, all recreational activities must be compatible with the primary purpose of the Refuge.

In April 2007, a Nature Center was opened at the Ritidian Unit to promote the importance of conserving Guam's indigenous natural resources. This center is open seven days a week from 8:30 a.m. to 4:00 p.m. (closed Federal holidays) and admission is free. Since the opening of the Nature Center, approximately 20 people visit the Nature Center daily (C. Bandy, USFWS, personal communication). Additionally, over a thousand students visit annually as part of the environmental education program provided by Refuge staff.

Public recreational activities are permitted on approximately 120 acres, or 10 percent, of the Ritidian Unit during open hours. Visitor programs include certain types of fishing, wildlife observation/photography, natural and cultural resources interpretation, and environmental education. Public programs occurring on the Ritidian Unit are discussed in the following section. Refuge staff members carefully monitor these activities to ensure visitor safety and preservation of the natural and cultural resources of the Refuge. Public programs are designed to "foster an understanding of and support for stewardship of Guam's natural environment" (USFWS 2007a). Additionally, the public may picnic, swim, snorkel, scuba dive, and hike in open portions of the Ritidian Unit. Refuge staff members estimate that between 75,000 and 80,000 individuals visit the Refuge annually (E. Sablan, USFWS, personal communication).

The remaining 90 percent of the Refuge (including the coral reef, beach, and forest east of Ritidian Cut) is closed for public safety, protecting native habitat and cultural resources, and sea turtle nesting areas. Closed areas further provide a marine sanctuary for coral and other marine species. These areas are patrolled by a full time law enforcement officer and staff.

6.4 Fishing

At a minimum, all regulations developed by the Government of Guam apply to all fishing activities on the Ritidian Unit. Refuge regulations further restrict some aspects. Fishing using rod and reel, talaya (traditional throw net), spears, hand collecting, and Hawaiian slings is permitted in the open area of the Ritidian Unit (http://www.fws.gov/policy/605fw4.html).

The Service considers fishing a priority wildlife-dependent activity when found compatible with the purpose of the Refuge. However, coral trampling can cause significant damage to the reef and should be controlled. Though no creel surveys have been conducted, an estimated 100 visitors per week are engaged in fishing, the majority of which is rod and reel with some throw netting, spear fishing, and simple collecting (such as octopus). Almost all fishing is by local residents rather than tourists. Heavy seasonal use may occur when certain species of fish are present.

6.5 Wildlife Observation and Photography

Wildlife viewing and observation is a primary visitor activity at Guam Refuge. These programs, if compatible, then become priority general public uses of the System and receive consideration in Refuge planning and management. Park rangers stationed at the center provide guided wildlife walks through the native limestone forest and archaeological sites on request.

Quality wildlife observation is defined by the following elements: (1) opportunities exist to view wildlife in their habitats and in a natural setting; (2) observation opportunities promote public understanding of Guam Refuge resources and the Refuge's role in managing and protecting those resources; (3) observations occur in places with the least amount of disturbance to wildlife; (4) facilities are safe, fully accessible, and available to a broad spectrum of the public; (5) viewing opportunities are tied to interpretive and educational opportunities; and (6) observers have minimal conflict with other visitors or Refuge operations (http://www.fws.gov/policy/605fw4.html).

Opportunities for enhanced wildlife observation and photography are plentiful at the Ritidian Unit and will increase through the development and maintenance of trails, boardwalks, and observation sites. Wildlife viewing opportunities could be provided for a portion of the one million tourists who visit Guam annually (GVB 2007). Visitors would continue to be guided in order to minimize disturbance to sensitive wildlife and their habitats.

6.6 Environmental Education

Since its establishment, educators and youth professionals have been using the Refuge as an outdoor classroom to study endangered species and natural resource management, cultural history and conservation. High school and middle school students have participated in daylong events at the Refuge to learn about Guam plants (http://www.reeis.usda.gov/web/areera/ Combined.GU.re-port.2002.pdf). Regular Refuge guided walks also included a session in an indoor classroom. Reservations are required for classroom orientations and group size can range to over 100 people. Group sizes on staff-led tours to the pictograph cave are limited to 20 people. Larger groups are broken up to accommodate this requirement. University of Guam science students also utilize the Refuge and adjacent USGS Brown Treesnake Project for field trips to receive credit as part of their study program. In 2007, 1,109 people participated in educational programs on the Refuge, and 2,105 people in outreach programs off-site (E. Sablan-Torres, USFWS, personal communication).

6.7 Interpretation

Natural areas and the Nature Center on the Ritidian Unit offer the opportunity to connect visitors to the natural heritage and natural resources of the island. Archaeological remnants of the native Chamorro people on the Refuge provide an attraction for both visitors and locals. Cultural artifacts and sites include pottery shards, cave pictographs, lusong and lommok (mortar and pestle), and latte stones. Guided walks are led by staff from the Nature Center to the main cave featuring ancient Chamorro pictographs and sometimes stopping at another cave along the way with cave formations and a few pictographs.

In addition, the Ritidian area is particularly important to the Chamorro culture for the collection of plant foods, medicinal plants, firewood, and native plants specific to northern Guam. Traditionally, important plant parts are allowed to be collected for non-economic uses in a designated area with a Special Use Permit (SUP) (72 FR 37037). Maintaining these cultural practices allows local people to continue traditional use of native natural resources, allows the Refuge staff to interact with, involve, and learn from suruhana (traditional healing practitioners), and provides opportunities for individuals not of Chamorro descent to experience the cultural link that these indigenous people had with the land.

6.8 Non Wildlife-dependent Recreation

Ritidian Beach is a popular destination for both tourists and locals offering over a mile of sandy beach (http://www.visitguam.org/guide/?pg=northern&site=ritidian). Public access to the beach is provided from designated parking areas. Visitors are also able to participate in unstructured, non-wildlife-oriented family and friend gatherings in the clean, uncrowded, undeveloped beach environment. Activities include swimming and picnicking. Facilities at Ritidian beach include 18 beach-side picnic areas with parking and portable restrooms (http://www.fws.gov/refuges/profiles/ observephotog.cfm?ID=12518). Approximately 75,000-80,000 people visit the Refuge annually. Refuge staff members estimate that during the week, foreign tourists such as Japanese and Koreans account for 60 percent of visitors. During the weekends 300 visitors or more, mostly local people, visit the Refuge (C. Bandy, USFWS, personal communication).

6.9 Illegal Uses

During closed hours, trespassing for poaching is a problem. Illegal aliens have come to Guam, by boat, to the remote Ritidian Unit three times in the last four years. Guam Refuge is a "Pack your trash" site and most visitors comply, though the trash left by a few is a constant problem. All staff members participate in constant cleanup.

6.10 Adjacent Area Outdoor Recreational Opportunities and Trends

The coastal and inland areas surrounding the Ritidian Unit of the Guam Refuge have high potential for public recreation. Located adjacent to one of Guam's main population centers, the area provides nearby public access to both aquatic and terrestrial natural resources. Area recreation activities include beach-going, fishing, scuba diving, snorkeling, boating, environmental education, and wildlife observation and photography.

In general, existing public recreation areas in northern Guam are limited to day use activities. Increased demand for recreation areas is anticipated due to the impending population increase forecast over the next 5 years (USAF 2006). In particular, there is high public demand for access to northern Guam since this area has historically been restricted because of Department of Defense security (USFWS 1994). At the same time, strict security has allowed for the preservation of natural and cultural resources in this area. The following section provides detail on existing and potential recreational opportunities in the area surrounding the Ritidian Unit.

Wildlife Observation/Photography

There are natural areas adjacent to the Ritidian Unit where wildlife observation may occur. However, conservation areas have limited accessibility to the public (GDAWR 2006a). The Anao Conservation Area, administered by the Government of Guam, lies to the southeast of Andersen AFB. Encompassing approximately 764 acres, this area must be accessed through private lands and is mostly used by the hunting community (GDAWR 2006a).

Several natural areas managed by the Federal government also have limited public access. The 750-acre Pati Point Natural Area is located along the northern edge of Andersen AFB. Public use and access to this area is highly restricted in order to protect endangered wildlife (USFWS and USAF 2001). Some hiking is allowed on approved hiking trails at Andersen AFB with recreational passes issued by the Air Force to persons with access to military bases. These activities are carefully monitored by the Air Force Conservation Officers (ATSDR 2002). Camping at Tarague Beach is permitted and the campground rules are provided in Air Force Regulation 126-1 (USFWS and USAF 2001).

In addition, The Haputo Ecological Reserve Area, located along the northwest coast of Guam, includes beach and submerged lands, supporting a healthy and diverse reef community (http://www3.mpa.gov/exploreinv/SiteProfile4.aspx?SiteID=GU16). This area is also part of the Navy Overlay Unit. Use of this area is only for persons with access to military bases.

Natural and Cultural Resources Interpretation

The Guam Visitors Bureau describes opportunities to explore both ecological areas and cultural sites throughout Guam's northern landscape (http://visitguam.org/guide/?pg=northern&site =eco). Historical and cultural sites of interest in the area include the Tarague/Jinapsan Communities, Hila'an (an archaeological site), and the South Pacific Memorial Park (Unipingo 2005). The Department of Parks and Recreation and Guam Boonie Stompers also offer public hikes throughout the island every Saturday to various beaches including Ritidian, snorkeling spots, waterfalls, mountains, caves, and cultural and historical sites (http://visitguam.org/ activities/?pg=stomp).

Diving and snorkeling

Due to the highly diverse assemblage of coral and marine fish species, diving is an important recreational activity on Guam for tourists and local residents. Of the estimated 300,000 dives on Guam per year, one third consists of local divers and the remaining two third are international visitors to the island (Van Beukering et al 2007); Asian travelers are the most frequent (Puglise and Kelty 2007). In 2004, over 5,000 entry level certifications were issued in Guam (Porter et al 2005). The most popular dive spots on the northern portion of Guam include Pati Point on the eastern side, and The Pinnacle, Northern Caves, and Double Reef on the northwestern side of Guam (http://www.visitguam.org/dive/). Strong currents limit diving spots along the northern coastline range to more advanced level divers.

Fishing

Fishing is also a common activity throughout Guam's reefs (Puglise and Kelty 2007). Methods include traditional hook-and-line, cast nets (talaya), spearfishing, and surround nets (chenchulu), as well as more controversial methods such as "throw-away" gill-nets and nighttime scuba spearfishing (Porter et al 2005). It is estimated that roughly 35 to 45 percent of the local population fish on a weekly basis (Van Beukering et al 2007).

Coastal inaccessibility and fishing restrictions limit the amount of fishing in the area surrounding the Refuge. Hook and line fishing is permitted from the shore in some areas of the Andersen AFB Marine Resources Preserve (Pati Point) with annual fishing permits. Spearfishing and nets are prohibited in this area (USFWS and U.S. Air Force 2002). Boat-based offshore fishing activities on Guam include trolling and bottomfishing. There are approximately 10 locally-based charter fishing boats that operate regularly from the island (Porter et al. 2005). Local recreation and charter boats usually operate from the Agana Boat Basin, Apra Harbor, and Agat Marina (Guam EPA 2000).

Hunting

The GDAWR and Andersen AFB environmental staff coordinate a public hunting program on the installation with designated areas for gun and archery hunting (Figure 9). Game-hunting on the base includes feral pigs and deer. Hunters must purchase a hunting license and permit, and attend a briefing on safety and regulations (USFWS and USAF 2001). Approximately 500 hunters attend the safety briefings given by the Andersen AFB Conservation Officers each year and more than 80 percent of the attendees are Guam residents. The Anao Conservation Area

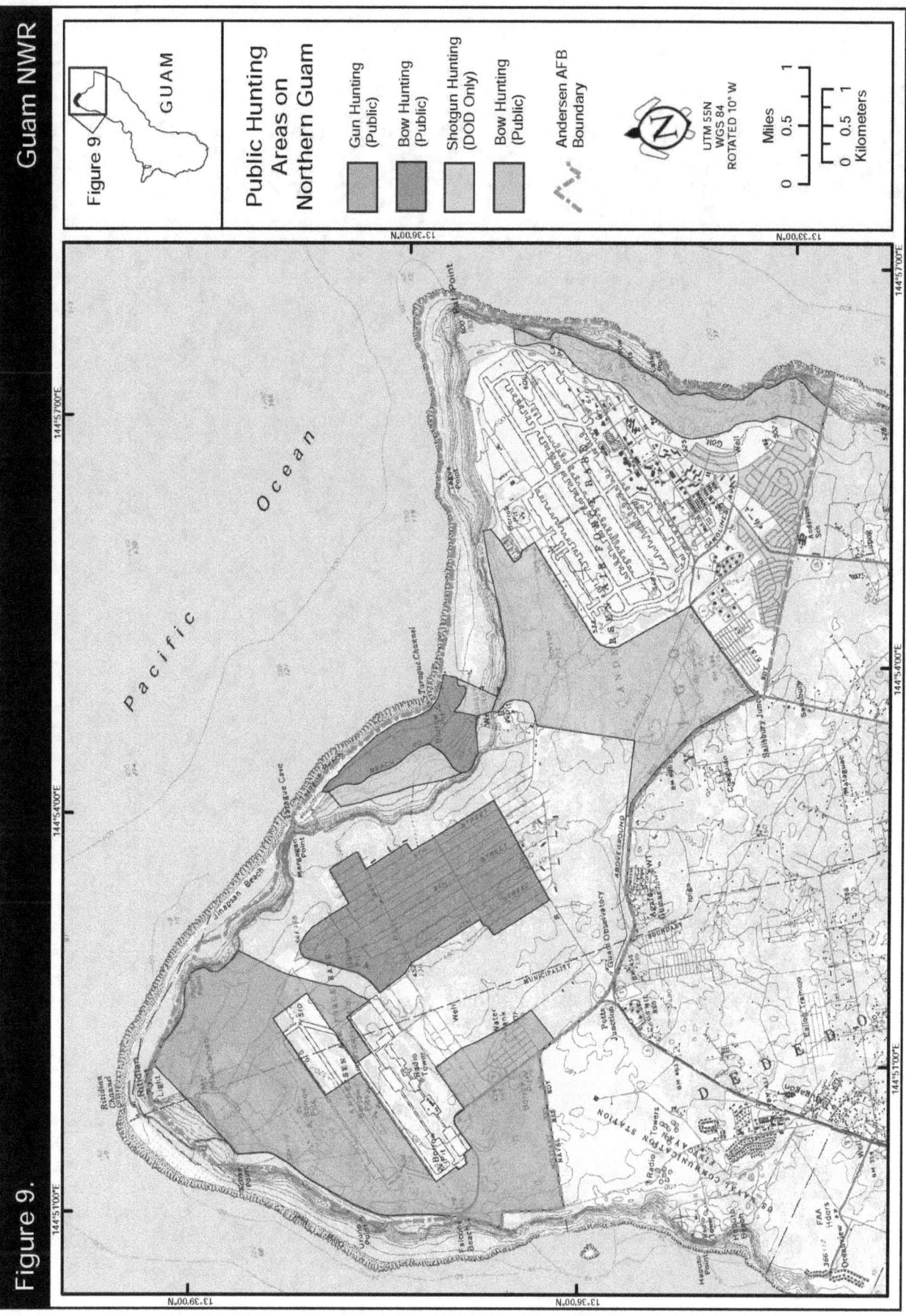

Figure 9.

Guam NWR

Figure 9

GUAM

Public Hunting Areas on Northern Guam

Gun Hunting (Public)

Bow Hunting (Public)

Shotgun Hunting (DOD Only)

Bow Hunting (Public)

Andersen AFB Boundary

UTM 55N
WGS 84
ROTATED 10° W

Miles
0   0.5   1

Kilometers
0   0.5   1

5-20-09, DH, 09-122-7.MXD

The back sides of pages with maps are blank to facilitate map readability.

is another area utilized by hunters in the northern region (GDAWR 2006a). The Guam Refuge does not have any involvement in the hunt programs at Andersen AFB. This activity occurs near the Refuge and on the Air Force Overlay Unit. The animals taken in the hunt programs are considered feral and invasive by Refuge management.

Beach Usage

The Guam Department of Parks and Recreation administers a total of 29 public beaches and parks along the coastline of Guam (Prasad and Manner 1994). Guam locals enjoy swimming and barbeques at the beach. It is estimated that as many as 92 percent of households regularly (more than twice per year) have barbeques on the beach. The public considers clean, clear, safe ocean water, and good public facilities the most important recreational amenities in Guam (Van Beukering et al 2007).

Some public access restrictions occur in areas of private and military land ownership. Beaches east of the Ritidian Unit include Jinapsan, Tarague, Sirena, and Pati. Urunao and Falcona Beaches are found to the west of the Ritidian Unit. Access to Tarague Beach is permitted for DOD employees, dependents, authorized guests, and active duty personnel (USFWS and USAF 2002). Recreational activities at Tarague Beach include swimming, picnicking, volleyball, barbecues, and camping. There is a concession stand, indoor seating, a sand volleyball court, a stage area, and a restroom/shower structure. Three lifeguards are present on the beach between 8:00 a.m. and 5:00 p.m. daily during summer and on weekends during the remainder of the year (USFWS and USAF 2002). The beach has 50 camp sites that are open by reservation only (ATSDR 2002). Although the campsites satisfy the current demand, parking and overcrowding is a problem during heavy use on summer weekends.

Sirena Beach, located to the east, is a secluded area available only for private parties. Sirena Beach is accessed from a footpath from the parking area roughly 100 feet from the shore. Facilities include a 900 square-foot pavilion, a restroom/shower structure, and a grassy picnic area (USFWS and USAF 2002). Hook and line fishing is permissible in the waters off Pati Beach; however, landing of beach-craft like kayaks, sailboats, and jetskis is prohibited.

6.11 Archaeological and Cultural Resources

The Ritidian area is known to have been used by the ancient Chamorro people, the indigenous people of Guam. A Cultural Resources Overview and Management Plan (CROM Plan) was developed in 2006 and is incorporated into this CCP as Appendix I. Current activities on the Ritidian Unit include staff-led interpretive walks to a cave or two with pictographs, ancient Chamorro cave drawings, and implementation of the CROM Plan through systematic field investigations by the UoG Micronesian Area Research Center (MARC). The recent excavation of a latte site (see Appendix I) by MARC and University of Hawaii staff and students presents another opportunity for interpretation by way of a longer trail, which some visitors ask for, but none has been built before this.

The Nature Center displays are written in English and Chamorro and cultural panels interpret former uses. The bilingual Park Ranger on staff weaves cultural education throughout presentations and educational activities. A short, accessible, self-guided trail is being developed across the road from the Nature Center. The trail will have interpretive signs for native plants still used by suruhana (traditional medicine practitioners) and lead to a cave with pictographs. It goes through representative coastal strand habitat and next to limestone cliff habitat.

In order to maintain natural habitat, minimize disturbance to wildlife, and protect cultural resources, most of the Ritidian Unit is not open to visitor use. Protective measures, such as fences, are being used since some negative impacts to archaeological and cultural resources have occurred. Before the Refuge was established there was vandalism of a cave by persons making their own drawings in a cave with ancient pictographs. Invasive mud-dauber wasps built nests on pictographs in a cave. The cave entrance has now been covered with netting to minimize wasp activity. As visitor use increases, remote monitoring of some sites will be developed. Due to the richness of cultural resource deposits, all earth disturbing activities will be required to comply with Section 106 of the National Historic Preservation Act.

6.12 Social/Economic Environment

This section discusses the social and economic environment surrounding the Ritidian Unit within the context of the local area and the island as a whole. In addition, the economic contribution of the Refuge itself to the surrounding area is discussed.

Population

Guam is the most populated island in Micronesia. Between 1980 and 1990, the island's population rose 25.6 percent from 105,979 to 133,152 individuals. By 2000, the total population grew an additional 16.3 percent to 154,805 persons, with a rise in population density from 634.5 to 737.7 individuals per square mile (Guam Bureau of Statistics and Plans 2006). The most recent population estimate of Guam in 2005 was 168,564 people, an 8.16 percent increase from the 2000 estimate. Although the population has been increasing, the total number of military personnel and their dependents has decreased on the island since the late 1980s, but will increase over the next few years due to U.S. Marines relocating from Japan (see section 3.2.6). Military personnel and their families comprised roughly 7.5 percent (or 12,642 individuals) of the resident population on Guam in 2005. This percentage was almost double in 1990 when approximately 14.7% of the population (19,573 individuals) was military and their dependents (Guam Bureau of Statistics and Plans 2006). In 2000, the median age of residents island-wide was 25 years (Guam Bureau of Statistics and Plans 2006).

Guam Refuge's headquarters is located in the village of Yigo (Figure 1). Yigo has had substantial population growth over the past three decades. Between 1980 and 1990, Yigo's population increased by 37.2 percent from 10,359 to 14,213. By 2000, the population expanded by an additional 37 percent (Guam Bureau of Statistics and Plans 2006). Approximately 19,474 people resided in the 35.41 square-miles of Yigo in 2000, a density of 550 individuals per square-mile.

The Dededo village, on which almost half of the Refuge is located, is adjacent to Yigo (Figure 1). Dededo houses the greatest population on Guam. The village accommodates almost 28 percent of the total island population (Guam Bureau of Statistics and Plans 2006). Although not reflected in data by the Guam Bureau of Statistics and Plans, it is anticipated that the population of Dededo may increase by as much as 40 percent, attributed to the upcoming relocation of military forces and their dependents from Okinawa (First Hawaiian Bank 2006). Past and projected population figures for both the Yigo and Dededo villages are provided in Table 6.

Table 6. Population figures, both actual and projected for villages of Yigo, Dededo, and Guam island-wide. Source: Guam Bureau of Statistics and Plans (2006).

Area	1980	% change	1990	% change	2000	% change	2006 (Projected)
Guam	105,979	25.6	133,152	16.3	154,805	10.47	171,020
Yigo	10,359	37.2	14,213	37.0	19,474	10.47	21,514
Dededo	23,644	34.2	31,728	35.5	42,980	10.47	47,482

Island-wide, the population is expected to increase by 17,000 military service and family members by 2010 due to the DOD relocating Command, Air, Ground, and Logistics units from Okinawa, Japan, to Guam (72 FR 10186). However, military spokesmen have since reported numbers around 40,000, including estimates for contractor and service persons (C. Bandy, USFWS, personal communication).

The ethnic composition of Guam is highly mixed and intermarriage among these groups has resulted in a blend of many cultures. The population is composed of roughly 37 percent indigenous Chamorro, 26 percent Filipino, and 7 percent Caucasian (Figure 10). The remaining 30 percent is made up of Koreans, Japanese, Chinese, and other Pacific Islanders (First Hawaiian Bank 2004).

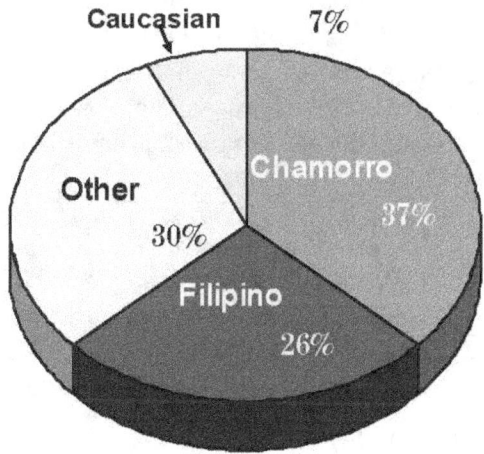

Figure 10. Breakdown of different cultures that make up the population of Guam. "Other" includes Koreans, Japanese, Chinese, and other Pacific Islanders

Housing

The number of households on Guam increased by 23.6 percent between 1990 (31,373) and 2000 (38,769). During this same time period, the average island household size decreased from 3.97 to 3.89 persons (Guam Bureau of Statistics and Plans 2006). In Yigo, there was a 37.5 percent increase from 1990 to 2000 of 4,634 households. Unlike the island average, household size increased in Yigo by 5.4 percent to 4.09 persons per household (Guam Bureau of Statistics and Plans 2006).

The mean sales value of single family residences on Guam in 2000 was $135,682, while condominiums averaged $106,413. During 2000, 20,022 units were renter-occupied. The median monthly rent of these units was $774 (Guam Bureau of Statistics and Plans 2006). The volume and value of real estate market sales decreased throughout the early 21st century. The median sales prices of single family homes and condominiums reached the lowest levels in 2003. The following year, total real estate market sales rose to $244,956,530, an increase of 67.9 percent (Guam Bureau of Statistics and Plans 2006).

Housing prices have recently attained pre-recession levels in Guam. The median sales prices for single family dwellings and condominiums in 2005 were $144,254 290 and $115,000, respectively. At the same time, home ownership became more affordable due to low interest rates. Rising housing demands are expected to continue due to anticipated growth from military expansion. According to an assessment of Guam's economy by the First Hawaiian Bank (2006), real estate prices continued to rise substantially through the first half of 2006. Anticipated military expansion, in combination with increasing construction costs and new regulations, suggests housing prices will continue to rise (First Hawaiian Bank 2006).

Education

There are 37 public schools, 18 private schools, one university, and one community college on Guam (First Hawaiian Bank 2006). Enrollment in primary and secondary schools has remained stable from 2000 to the present, with the majority of students attending classes in the Guam public school system. From 2000 to 2005, the average pupil to student ratio in the public system ranged from 14.1 to 25.6 (Guam Bureau of Statistics and Plans 2006). Catholic schools, Department of Defense Education Activity, and other private schools show substantially smaller total enrollment number than public schools. New elementary, middle, and high schools are being planned in response to the rising population (Guam Bureau of Statistics and Plans 2006).

In 2000, roughly 79 percent of the community of Yigo over 25 years of age had received a high school diploma, compared to 73 for Dededo (Guam Bureau of Statistics and Plans 2006). The island average was 76.3 percent. The percentage of Yigo and Dededo's population with a Bachelor's degree or higher during the same year was 19.3 and 18.9 percent respectively. The island average was slightly higher, with approximately 20.0 percent of residents holding a Bachelor's degree or higher (Guam Bureau of Statistics and Plans 2006).

Income

The median household income on Guam in 2003 was $33,457, compared to the 2000 estimate of $37,605. Island-per-capita income increased from $10,872 in 2001 to $11,254 in 2003 (Guam Bureau of Statistics and Plans 2006). Average earnings increased in both the public and private sector of Guam between 2000 and 2005. Hourly Government of Guam earnings rose from $15.35 to $16.98 between 2000 and 2005, while the mean hourly rate in the private sector increased from $10.07 to $11.08 (Guam Bureau of Statistics and Plans 2006). Individuals in the Yigo district experienced an 11.8 percent decrease in the average personal income between 1990 and 2000, from $12,490 to $11,018. This decrease was less significant in the main population center of Dededo, which suffered a 4.8 percent decrease (Guam Bureau of Statistics and Plans 2006). At the same time, the median household income in Yigo rose 2.5 percent between 1990 and 2000 to $37,415. The median household income dropped 9.4 percent in Dededo during the same time period. In

1999, approximately 18.1 and 20.3 percent of total families were living below the poverty level in Yigo and Dededo, respectively (Guam Bureau of Statistics and Plans 2006).

Employment

Guam's total estimated payroll employment in 2007 was 59,780 jobs. Public sector employment, including the Federal Government and the Government of Guam, generated 15,390 jobs. The remaining 44,390 jobs were private sector positions (Hiles 2007). Of these, the service and retail industries were the largest employers providing 15,920 and 11,780 jobs, respectively (Hiles 2007). The next leading employer was the construction industry, with approximately 5,150 jobs. Transportation and public utilities provided 4,970 jobs in 2005 (Hiles 2007). Other industries in the private sector include finance/insurance and real estate (2,550 jobs), wholesale trade (2,040 jobs), manufacturing (1,700 jobs), and agriculture (280 jobs) (Hiles 2007).

Employment decreased throughout Guam to the early 2000s. Unemployment rates increased between 1990 and 2000 to 12.0 percent (Guam Bureau of Statistics and Plans 2006). Similar increases occurred in Yigo and Dededo during these years, rising from 4.0 to 11.6 percent (Yigo) and 3.3 to 12 percent (Dededo). Island unemployment peaked in 2003 at 15.3 percent (Guam Bureau of Statistics and Plans 2006). In 2004, an estimated 4,710 Guam residents (7.7 percent of the population) were unemployed although job growth has been flat since 2004; the island unemployment rate is anticipated to decline markedly due to the new surge in military growth (First Hawaiian Bank 2006).

Economy

Beginning in 2002, Guam's economy fell into a recession due to a myriad of factors including the terrorist events of September 11, 2001; Severe Acute Respiratory Syndrome (SARS); and the typhoons of Chata'an and Pongsona. The estimated Gross Territorial Product (GTP) of Guam in 2002 was $3.4 billion (First Hawaiian Bank 2006). Job growth and gross revenue remained negative until 2004. The economy has since recovered and expanded over the recent fiscal years achieving pre-recession levels. Stable growth has brought the estimated 2007 GTP to $3.9 billion (First Hawaiian Bank 2006, Guam Bureau of Statistics and Plans 2006). This recovery is largely due to substantial Federal assistance and investments from private businesses, Government of Guam, and Federal Government projects. Increased tourist arrivals, civilian employment, and consumer and investor confidence are additional factors facilitating recovery (Guam Bureau of Statistics and Plans 2006). Assuming current economic activity, the Bank of Hawaii (2006) projected that GTP may grow by 18 percent during 2008.

Tourism and the U.S. military are currently the principle components driving Guam's economy. Since the 1960s, tourism has generated a significant income for the island. The industry first expanded in the late 1980s and early 1990s due to Japan-financed investment in hotels. Visitor arrivals, particularly from Japan and Korea, continued to increase and reached the highest level of 1,381,510 visitors in 1997 (First Hawaiian Bank 2006; GVB 2006). The tourism industry suffered a severe setback in the 1990s because of a number of super-typhoons, an 8.1 earthquake, and the crash of Korean Air flight 801 from Seoul, Korea, to Guam, which killed 228 of the 254 passengers and crew on board. The visitor rate fell to a considerable low in 2003 during the economic recession, but has been steadily increasing. In 2005, total air and sea visitors were estimated at

1,227,587 (GVB 2007). In 2005, over 80 percent of the island's visitors were from Japan, followed by South Korea (9 percent) and Taiwan (2 percent) (Guam Bureau of Statistics and Plans 2006).

Guam's total visitor expenditure in fiscal year 2006 was $772,297,000, some 60 percent of the island's revenue (GVB 2007). Coral reef related tourism has been valued near $94.63 million per year. The total annual revenue generated from marine-related water sport activities, including snorkeling, surfing, dolphin watching, and scuba diving is estimated at $8.7 million. Van Beukering et al. (2007) found that approximately 28.5 percent of tourist sector revenues on Guam depend on healthy marine ecosystems. The tourism industry not only generates revenue from off-island money markets, but is the largest contributor of private sector jobs (USFWS 1992). In 2006, the industry provided more than 20,000 direct and indirect jobs, about 35 percent of Guam's total employment (First Hawaiian Bank 2006).

Positive and negative indicators provide a mixed forecast for the tourism industry on Guam. According to the Guam Hotel and Restaurant Association, room rates increased by 3 percent and occupancy rates by 6 percent in 2005 (Guam Bureau of Statistics and Plans 2006). Furthermore, new hotels have opened and significant renovations of existing hotels are underway, demonstrating business confidence for the future. Concurrently, high fuel costs, suspended airline services, and the potential of an avian influenza outbreak threaten the future of Guam's tourist industry (First Hawaiian Bank 2006, Guam Bureau of Statistics and Plans 2006).

The U.S. military activity on Guam is the second largest economic contribution to the island. Military expenditures were the most substantial component of the private business sector in 1990, providing over $327 million (USWS 1992). Contributions include indirect spending by personnel, civilian employment, construction contracts, materials and services purchases, and Federal income tax paid by military employees. Military expenditures have climbed from $431.2 million in 2000 to $624.3 million in 2004 (Guam Bureau of Statistics and Plans 2006).

In 2006, Washington confirmed its decision to relocate about 8,000 Marines and their dependents from Okinawa to Guam. The government estimates that the military sector will be generating significant economic growth since $15 billion in military spending has already been announced for Guam over a 10-year period. Areas of spending will include housing, schools, infrastructure, and training sites (First Hawaiian Bank 2006).

The construction sector is cyclically important, fluctuating significantly with changes in other areas of the economy. Increases in this industry are anticipated with the new military developments. The total value of building permits in 2005 was $167,599,164, a 36 percent increase from 2004 and a 75 percent increase from 2002 (Guam Bureau of Statistics and Plans 2006). The Government of Guam has scheduled over $86 million in Department of Public Works projects for 2006 and 2007. Additionally, the Air Force is planning on approximately $100 million in construction projects (Guam Bureau of Statistics and Plans 2006). The industry estimates that 20,000 to 25,000 construction workers may eventually be needed on Guam, compared to the 5,000 currently employed on the island (First Hawaiian Bank 2006).

Other sectors of Guam's economy, such as fisheries and agriculture, contribute insignificantly to the economy. Guam's total fishery value was estimated at $3.96 million, with the reef-related market value comprising only $ 0.54 million (Van Beukering et al 2007). The total value of commercial landings of fish in 2004 was estimated at $753,678, reef fish representing the largest contributor at $164,919 (Guam Bureau of Statistics and Plans 2006). The total dollar value of agriculture produced on Guam in 2000 was $1,556,098, vegetables being the most valuable home-grown resource. This number has declined substantially from the peak value of $12,015,125 in 1993. Similarly, livestock value also declined between 1993 and 2000, falling substantially from $26,929 to $9,128 (Guam Bureau of Statistics and Plans 2006). Guam is hoping to diversify its economy by expanding into new areas such as bonded warehousing and legal arbitration (First Hawaiian Bank 2006).

Refuge Contribution

Recreational spending near Guam Refuge generates economic activity for local economies. These expenditures can include food, lodging, transportation, and other purchases from local businesses while engaging in Refuge activities (Caudill and Henderson 2005, Carver and Caudill 2007). In 2006, approximately 34.8 million people visited refuges around the U.S., generating an estimated $1.7 billion in regional economies. Nationwide, Refuge employment contributed $542.8 million in income and recreational spending generated about $185.3 million in tax revenue at the local, state, territorial, and Federal level (Carver and Caudill 2007).

Recreational expenditures of visitors to the Guam Refuge have undoubtedly contributed to the local economy. However, the exact contribution of resident and non-resident Refuge visitors to the economy is not known. Some revenue can be assumed from the 75,000 to 80,000 annual visitors (E. Sablan, USFWS, personal communication). Carver and Caudill (2007) found that refuges with similar visitation rates had total non-consumptive visitor expenditures ranging from $275,000 to $1,292,500. Although this range estimates the potential contribution of a refuge similar in size to the Guam Refuge, the specific recreational activities occurring at the Ritidian Unit and the distinct elements of Guam's economy would most likely influence the total amount of expenditures. Additional revenue is also derived from local taxes and employment income from the Refuge (Caudill and Henderson 2005). Collecting information on expenditures and revenue can give an estimate of the potential impact the Refuge has on Guam's economy.

Similar to other refuges, the Guam Refuge is managed primarily for the protection of endangered and threatened species. This purpose is not obviously compatible with most commercial uses (USFWS 1994). At this stage, it is unlikely that the Guam Refuge will permit commercial uses, except photography and videography, therefore, the capacity of economic contribution to the local economy beyond that already discussed is unlikely.

6.13 Special Designation Lands

Guam Refuge offers a unique opportunity to influence the future of a variety of threatened and endangered species. Currently, the Refuge contains 385 acres (terrestrial) of critical habitat for the Sihek, Aga, and fruit bat (fanihi).

The staff conducted a wilderness review (Appendix D), the results of which indicated that Guam Refuge does not contain resources and lands that are appropriate for inclusion in the National Wilderness Preservation System. In addition, the level of disturbance, invasive species, and impacts to native species would not provide the necessary characteristics for designation as a Research Natural Area.

Appendix A: Response to Comments

The Refuge received 3 comments submitted in writing at the public open houses, 6 e-mails, 3 faxes, and 2 topics that were of much interest at the open houses in response to the Draft CCP/EA. Comments are summarized below by topic. The comment is either quoted directly or paraphrased based upon comments received. We have included only substantive comments in this appendix. General expressions of support or disapproval have not been included. A comment is considered substantive if it raises specific issues or concerns regarding the preferred alternative or the evaluation process, but not if it merely expresses support for or opposition to the project or a particular alternative.

Wildlife impacts

Comment: "The reason we support Alternative A is the impact on surrounding lands (particularly on private properties) the barriers that are going to be constructed for Alternative B and C. These barriers will keep unwanted animals (species) from entering the Refuge, thus limiting their habitat, and will result in increased of their population in the surrounding properties. The Refuge staff's current effort in the status quo (Alternative A) of eliminating the unwanted species in the Refuge is contributing in keeping their population in check. Also, Alternative A still has positive impacts as current and future plan improvements take place."

Response: We appreciate the concern about pest species, however, we disagree that there would be an appreciative difference in the number of animals outside of the Refuge boundary. Certainly, there is some movement of individuals between Refuge lands and private lands, but it is unlikely that there is a constant influx of individual animals that would then be cut off from Refuge lands and impact surrounding lands any more greatly than is already the case. The relative acreage of habitat for pest species on the Refuge versus the surrounding landscape is small.

Hours of Operation

Comments: "Our additional comment is on the hours when the Refuge is open to the public. The current hours of 8:30 a.m. to 4:00 p.m., and closed on Federal holidays, are very limited. As you know, the Refuge is very popular with the local community and tourists. Recommend to have the Refuge open from 7:00 a.m. to 6:00 p.m., and open on Federal holidays. I'm sure this operating hours is in keeping with other national refuge and parks hours in the states; as citizens and tourists go to the park daily, and especially during a 3 day weekend and other holidays."

"Open the gates early for fishermen 6:00 a.m. till the sun goes down or 6:00 p.m."

Response: Given existing staff levels, it is difficult to offer additional hours at this time. We will constantly evaluate this ability and are open to the idea of extending the hours to accommodate individuals hoping for high quality fishing experiences.

Maintenance

Comment: "Additionally, though the maintenance in the Refuge itself is somewhat adequate, some maintenance is needed on Route 3A; from pothole repairs on the road to cutting of overgrown trees and grass along Route 3A. The numerous potholes and overgrown trees and grass are a safety hazard for people going to and returning from the refuge. Because of the overgrown, some areas on Route 3A is reduced from a 2 lane road, to about a 1 lane; made more dangerous with potholes. Since the Refuge is a Federal entity, hopefully it can work with the Air Force (as the landowner of Route 3A) in repairing the potholes and cutting the overgrown trees and grass."

Response: Route 3A is under the jurisdiction of the territory of Guam. We agree that there is a need for maintenance and will offer whatever assistance that we are able to.

Overlay Refuge

Comment: "Although not addressed in the CCP, I also with to strongly encourage the USFWS to work aggressively on all Refuge overlay lands occurring on military property. Part of the original intention of the Guam NWR was to improve the management of all natural resources on these lands, but this goal seems to have been lost for a number of years now, especially on Andersen Air Force Base."

Response: We agree. The bases on Guam are in the process of developing Integrated Natural Resources Management Plans. The Service is a part of the planning for resource management and hopes that the INRMPS will provide the opportunity for increased resource management on these lands.

Additional information

Comment: "I want to draw your attention to the following published paper, which was not cited in the CCP: Wiles, G. J. 2005, Decline of a population of wild seeded breadfruit (Artocarpus mariannensis) on Guam, Mariana Islands. Pacific Science 59:509-522. It will hopefully provide information that may be useful in managing the refuge for native tree species, especially seeded breadfruit, which is a valuable wildlife food plant."

Response: We appreciate the information.

Land ownership/Refuge disposition

Comment: "There have been two considerations for land swaps with other private land owners near the Jinapsan and Uranao areas, which is proof that Ritidian is not conducive for the regenerating of birds, bees and fauna."

"Just compensation was never given or completed. The land does not belong to the government and is in fact still private property."

Adjacent and former landowners from Ritidian Point attended both public meetings in Guam to express their desire to re-acquire the lands that were taken by eminent domain during the 1950s. They do not believe that the land was acquired legally and request that the U.S. Government vacate the land and return and/or sell the land back to the original owners. Some individuals claim continued ownership of the property.

Response: The issue of federal land ownership at Ritidian Point has been contentious for a number of years and includes litigation. The Service considers the issue of land ownership resolved through the courts. Guam National Wildlife Refuge is an important natural resource for the United States and the territory of Guam. The conservation priorities and strategies outlined in the Comprehensive Conservation Plan offer the possibility of re-introducing the extirpated bird and bat species of Guam. We are committed to managing the land for the benefit of native wildlife and their habitats. Given the benefit to native birds that the Refuge can provide, we cannot consider disposition of the Refuge.

Uranao Right-of-Way

Comment: A number of individuals expressed concern during the public meetings about the proposal to move the Uranao Right-of-Way that provides access to private property across the Refuge. Concerns raised included impacts to additional Refuge habitat, grade of the area of the proposed re-alignment, materials that would be used for the road, width of the access road, and the logistics of negotiating the change to a consent decreed Right-of-Way.

Response: After careful consideration, we have removed the proposal to move the right-of-way. The cost, effort, and habitat disturbance would likely not have commensurate benefits to wildlife in the long run.

Activities

Comment: "Guam EPA recommends the development of a self-guided snorkeling trail."

Response: We will consider this opportunity in the future as staff and resources allow.

Fishing

Comment: "The Guam DOA suggests requiring permits or licenses to fish on the Refuge. This could be a way to monitor sale or trade of fish caught on the Refuge."

Response: In addition to the specific requirements and restrictions listed in the Code of Federal Regulations, territorial regulations apply in Refuge waters. Requiring a fishing license or Refuge permit will require changing the Code of Federal Regulations. There are a number of items in the CCP that will require such a change, such as eliminating take of humphead wrasse and humphead parrotfish. The Refuge will evaluate the necessity of requiring a permit in conjunction with these changes. In the meantime, as the Refuge staff collect data during the planned creel surveys outlined in the CCP, we hope to track the amount of fish taken off the Refuge and refine additional Refuge-specific regulations in the future as necessary.

Plan Revision

Comment: "Guam DOA suggests that the CCP be revised in a shorter time frame (5 or 10 years or as needed)."

Response: The intent of CCPs to be 15 year management plans comes from the National Wildlife Refuge Improvement Act, which has been stepped down to the Service planning policy. While the maximum length of time for plan revision is 15 years, the planning policy requires the staff to review the plan every five years and revise as necessary.

Interpretive Materials

Comment: "Guam DOA suggests translation of interpreive materials into Chuukese."

Response: We appreciate the suggestion about how to best reach relevant local audiences. We would hope to translate interpretive materials into those languages that are most relevant to the public visiting the refuge.

Appendix B. Appropriate Use and Compatibility Determinations

Federal law and Service policy provide the direction and planning framework to protect the Refuge System from incompatible or harmful human activities, and to ensure that Americans can enjoy Refuge System lands and waters. The Administration Act, as amended by the Refuge Improvement Act (Act), is the key legislation regarding management of public uses and compatibility. The compatibility requirements of the Refuge Improvement Act were adopted in the Service's Final Compatibility Regulations and Final Compatibility Policy published October 18, 2000 (Federal Register, Vol. 65, No. 202, pp 62458-62496). This Compatibility Rule changed or modified Service Regulations contained in Chapter 50, Parts 25, 26 and 29 of the Code of Federal Regulations (USFWS 2000c). To view the policy and regulations online, go to http://policy.fws.gov/library/00fr62483.pdf.

The Act and Regulations require that an affirmative finding be made of an activity's "compatibility" before such activity or use is allowed on a national wildlife refuge. A compatible use is one, "...that will not materially interfere with or detract from the fulfillment of the mission of the Refuge System or the purposes of the refuge" (Act). Not all uses that are determined compatible must be allowed. The Refuge has the discretion to allow or disallow any use based on other considerations such as public safety, policy and available funding. However, all uses that are allowed must be determined compatible. Except for consideration of consistency with State laws and regulations as provided for in subsection (m) of the Act, no other determinations or findings are required to be made by the refuge official under this Act or the Refuge Recreation Act for wildlife-dependent recreation to occur Act.

We have completed appropriateness findings and compatibility determinations (CDs) for five priority public uses (wildlife observation, wildlife photography, environmental education, environmental interpretation, and fishing), traditional gathering, and research for Guam NWR under existing Service regulations and policy, the Act, and the recent revisions of our Compatibility Regulations. Each (with some restrictions) was found to be compatible with both the mission of the Refuge System and the purposes for which the Refuge was established.

Additional CDs will be developed when appropriate new uses are proposed. CDs will be re-evaluated by the Refuge Manager when conditions under which the use is permitted change significantly; when there is significant new information on effects of the use; or at least every 10 years for non-priority public uses. Priority public use CDs will be re-evaluated under the conditions noted above, or at least every 15 years with revision of the CCP.

Additional detail on the CD process is in Parts 25, 26, and 29 of Title 50 of the Code of Federal Regulations, effective November 17, 2000.

Compatibility Determination

Use: Wildlife Observation and Photography

Refuge Name: Guam National Wildlife Refuge (NWR)

City/County and State: Unincorporated U.S. Territory of Guam

Establishing and Acquisition Authority(ies):

The refuge authorizing authorities most relevant to the four principle reasons Guam NWR was established are the Endangered Species Act (ESA), Fish and Wildlife Act, Migratory Bird Conservation Act, and Refuge Recreation Act.

Refuge Purpose(s):

Ritidian Unit

The Administration Act directs the Service to manage each refuge to fulfill the mission, to maintain and where appropriate, restore the refuge's ecological integrity; and achieve the specific purposes for which the refuge was established. The Refuge purposes for the Ritidian Unit are as follows:

... to conserve (A) fish or wildlife which are listed as endangered species or threatened species ... or (B) plants ...16 U.S.C. §1534 (Endangered Species Act of 1973)

... for the development, advancement, management, conservation, and protection of fish and wildlife resources ...16 U.S.C. § 742f (a) (4), (Fish and Wildlife Act of 1956)

... for use as an inviolate sanctuary, or for any other management purpose, for migratory birds. 16 U.S.C. § 715d (Migratory Bird Conservation Act)

... suitable for (1) incidental fish and wildlife-oriented recreational development, (2) the protection of natural resources, (3) the conservation of endangered species or threatened species... 16 U.S.C. 460k-1 (Refuge Recreation Act (16 U.S.C. 460k-460k-4), as amended).

National Wildlife Refuge System Mission:

To administer a national network of lands and waters for the conservation, management, and where appropriate, restoration of the fish, wildlife, and plant resources and their habitats within the United States for the benefit of present and future generations of Americans (Administration Act of 1966, as amended (16 U.S.C. 668dd-668ee)).

Description of Use(s):

The 1997 amendments to the Administration Act (Act) defined wildlife observation and photography as wildlife-dependent public uses. In that Act, the U.S. Congress charged that such uses be given special consideration in planning for and management of the National Wildlife Refuge System. When determined compatible on a refuge-specific basis, these uses are priority general public uses of that national wildlife refuge. National wildlife refuges are to seek opportunities to allow these uses in an appropriate and compatible manner.

Public recreational activities are permitted on approximately 120 acres or 10 percent of the Ritidian Unit between the hours of 8:30 a.m. to 4:00 p.m daily (closed Federal holidays). Refuge staff carefully monitors these activities to ensure visitor safety and preservation of the natural and cultural resources of the Refuge. Public programs are designed to "foster an understanding of and support for stewardship of Guam's natural environment" (USFWS 2007). Staff members at the Ritidian Unit estimate that between 75,000 and 80,000 individuals visit the Refuge annually (E. Sablan, USFWS, personal communication).

Guam Refuge offers opportunities for visitors to observe wildlife in a natural environment. Park rangers stationed at the center provide guided wildlife tours through the native limestone forest and archaeological sites on request. Self-guided nature trails allow visitors to observe wildlife and their natural surroundings in a forested habitat. Ritidian Beach, as it is known to the local public, provides an opportunity for the public to enjoy the beach and marine portion of the Refuge. Individuals and family groups park in dedicated areas adjacent to the beach. Visitors use select portions of the beach for walking, picnicking, beachcombing, and swimming in the course of observing the natural environment, seabirds, shorebirds, butterflies, invertebrates (e.g. coconut crab) and occasional marine mammals. Visitors participate in snorkeling activities, which offer opportunities to observe coral, fish, turtles, and invertebrate marine life. By allowing visitors to access only certain areas of the beach and water and monitoring visitor behavior, any adverse effects associated with Refuge visitation can be minimized.

Wildlife viewing and observation is a primary visitor activity at Guam Refuge and these uses, if compatible, then become priority general public uses of the System and therefore receive consideration in Refuge planning and management.

Quality wildlife observation is defined by the following elements: (1) opportunities exist to view wildlife in their habitat and in a natural setting; (2) observation opportunities promote public understanding of Guam Refuge resources and its role in managing and protecting those resources; (3) observations occur in places with the least amount of disturbance to wildlife; (4) facilities are safe, fully accessible, and available to a broad spectrum of the public; (5) viewing opportunities are tied to interpretive and educational opportunities; and (6) observers have minimal conflict with other visitors or Refuge operations (http://www.fws.gov/policy/605fw4.html).

All interpretive materials in English and Chamorro would be translated into Japanese and Korean. A self-guided trail which is accessible would continue to be constructed. Information about conservation of natural resources and habitat restoration would be shared with the visitors to educate and reduce the impact visitors have on the Refuge. The fishing program would be re-evaluated based on information obtained during creel and reef surveys. A wildlife observation and photography clinic would be implemented. A display area will be created for local wildlife photographs.

Opportunities for enhanced wildlife observation and photography are plentiful at the Ritidian Unit and will increase through the development and maintenance of trails, boardwalks, and observation sites. Wildlife viewing opportunities could be provided for a portion of the one million tourists who visit Guam annually (GVB 2007). Visitors would continue to be guided in order to minimize disturbance to sensitive wildlife and their habitats.

Availability of Resources:

The Refuge has sufficient staff time and other resources to allow this use at the current levels. Currently the Refuge has a Visitor Services Professional and Law Enforcement Officer to administer and monitor the activities, and a Maintenance Worker to maintain public facilities and access points.

Category and Itemization	One-time ($)	Annual ($ per year)
Administration and Management		$41,896
Maintenance		$36,130
Monitoring		$9,474
Special equipment, facilities or improvements		$0
Offsetting revenues		$0

The numbers above reflect the current estimated costs. Estimated costs were calculated using 25% of the base cost of a GS-11 Visitor Services Professional and 10% of a GS-13 Refuge Manager for Administration and Management; 35% of the base cost of a WG-10 Maintenance Worker for maintenance; and 10% of the base cost of a GS-11 Refuge Biologist for monitoring, assuming that this priority activity would use that "portion of a year" to administer.

Anticipated Impacts of the Use(s):

Minor impacts to terrestrial and marine life would occur on the Refuge in the form of disturbance. Movement and behavior patterns could be altered by the presence of visitors. Some trampling of vegetation could occur as visitors stray to the edges of trails and access roads.

Use of the waters of Guam Refuge increases the potential for introductions of nonnative species and interactions (some negative) by snorkelers and divers with sea turtles, fish, invertebrates, and live corals. One accidental introduction of a nonnative species on a boat or dive equipment could devastate the marine environment.

There are a number of alien species on Guam in general and many of those (e.g., BTS, feral pigs, monitor lizards) have become established on the Refuge. As the Refuge staff work to eliminate or reduce pest species, it is possible that invasive plants and animals could be transported onto the Refuge in vehicles or from seeds that are trapped in clothing or vehicle wheels. Protocols could reduce this risk.

Public Review and Comment:

This determination was issued for public review and comment as part of the Guam NWR Draft Comprehensive Conservation Plan. The plan and associated compatibility determinations were made available through printed copies upon request and through the Refuge website. The 30-day review occurred from July 21 through August 24. We did not receive specific comments regarding the compatibility determinations. However, a number of individuals suggested that the hours of operation for the Refuge be extended to include Federal holidays. No change has been made at this time, but the Refuge staff will consider opportunities to expand operating hours as staff positions are re-filled and potentially expanded.

Determination:

___ Use is Not Compatible

X Use is Compatible with Following Stipulations

Stipulations Necessary to Ensure Compatibility:

Refuge hours are 8:00 a.m. to 4:30 p.m. Use outside of these hours is not allowed

Wildlife observation and photography may occur only in those areas that have been opened to the public. Approximately a ½ mile of beach area along the west end of the Refuge, self-guided trails, access roads, access paths, parking areas, and the area around the nature center are currently open to the public. The ocean and coral reef areas adjacent to the beach are open for swimming and snorkeling.

A Visitor Services Professional and Law Enforcement Officer administer and monitor the activities of visiting public.

A maintenance worker maintains public facilities and access points to direct visitors to areas open to public use.

Refuge staff will close portions of the beach [and water] as necessary to protect nesting turtles.

Visitors are not allowed to touch, take, or stand upon any reef material.

Amplified sound is not allowed.

Justification:

Individuals and groups are able to spend time outdoors and provide the Service an opportunity to expose the general population to the Refuge System, habitat management, and the impacts of invasive species on the native ecosystem. Guam Refuge provides a unique opportunity in this regard, particularly in light of the increasingly limited opportunities for the public to engage in such activities on Guam with military buildup. Relationships with the government of Guam, while positive at the staff level, could be improved through grassroots outreach to the public. Offering opportunities for wildlife observation and photography presents a wildlife conservation message to members of the public who are not likely to be reached by other means. In addition, allowing these activities supports the "connecting people with nature" initiative within the Service. When determined compatible on a refuge-specific basis, wildlife observation and photography are priority public uses of that national wildlife refuge. As endangered species recovery activities increase, it may be necessary to limit this activity and/or re-evaluate for compatibility.

The combination of limiting visiting hours, properly maintaining visitor access points, allowing visitors to access only certain areas of the beach and water, and monitoring visitor use and behavior allows the Refuge to minimize any adverse effects associated with Refuge visitation. By applying the stipulations described above, it is anticipated that wildlife populations will find sufficient food resources and resting places such that their abundance and use of the Refuge will not be measurably lessened from wildlife observation and photography activities. The relatively limited number of individuals expected to be adversely affected due to wildlife observation and photography will not cause wildlife populations to materially decline, the physiological condition and production of native bird and bat species and marine species will not be impaired, their behavior and normal activity patterns will not be altered dramatically, and their overall welfare will not be negatively impacted. Thus, allowing wildlife observation and photography to occur with stipulations will not materially detract or interfere with the purposes for which the Refuge was established or the Refuge System mission. The stipulations included herein would allow such uses to occur in a compatible manner.

Mandatory 10- or 15-year Reevaluation Date:

X   Mandatory 15-year re-evaluation date (for wildlife-dependent public uses)

_   Mandatory 10-year re-evaluation date (for non-wildlife-dependent public uses)

NEPA Compliance for Refuge Use Decision (check one below)

_   Categorical Exclusion without Environmental Action Statement

_   Categorical Exclusion and Environmental Action Statement

X   Environmental Assessment and Finding of No Significant Impact

_   Environmental Impact Statement and Record of Decision

Refuge Determination:

Project Leader,
Guam National Wildlife Refuge

Joseph Schwagerl
(Signature)   Date: 9/25/09

Project Leader,
Hawaiian and Pacific
Islands NWRC   _Barry W. Stieglitz_
(Signature)   Date 9/25/09

Concurrence:

Regional Chief,
National Wildlife
Refuge System   _Carolyn J. Bohan_
Pacific Region   (Signature)   Date 9/28/09

Compatibility Determination

Use: Environmental Education and Interpretation

Refuge Name: Guam National Wildlife Refuge (NWR)

City/County and State: Unincorporated U.S. Territory of Guam

Establishing and Acquisition Authority(ies):

Guam NWR was established administratively in 1993. At the time of establishment, Service policy did not require a notice to be posted in the Federal Register. The best record regarding Refuge establishment is the "Final Environmental Assessment for the Proposed Guam National Wildlife Refuge" and the associated "Finding of No Significant Impact" (U.S. Fish and Wildlife Service 1993). The Refuge authorizing authorities most relevant to the four principle reasons Guam NWR was established are the Endangered Species Act (ESA), Fish and Wildlife Act, Migratory Bird Conservation Act, and Refuge Recreation Act.

Refuge Purpose(s):

Ritidian Unit Purposes

The Administration Act directs the Service to manage each refuge to fulfill the mission, to maintain and where appropriate, restore the refuge's ecological integrity; and achieve the specific purposes for which the refuge was established. The Refuge purposes for the Ritidian Unit of Guam NWR are as follows:

... to conserve (A) fish or wildlife which are listed as endangered species or threatened species ... or (B) plants ...16 U.S.C. §1534 (Endangered Species Act of 1973)

... for the development, advancement, management, conservation, and protection of fish and wildlife resources ...16 U.S.C. 742f (a) (4), (Fish and Wildlife Act of 1956)

... for use as an inviolate sanctuary, or for any other management purpose, for migratory birds. 16 U.S.C. 715d (Migratory Bird Conservation Act)

... suitable for (1) incidental fish and wildlife-oriented recreational development, (2) the protection of natural resources, (3) the conservation of endangered species or threatened species ... 16 U.S.C. 460k-1 (Refuge Recreation Act (16 U.S.C. 460k-460k-4), as amended).

National Wildlife Refuge System Mission:

To administer a national network of lands and waters for the conservation, management, and where appropriate, restoration of the fish, wildlife, and plant resources and their habitats within the United States for the benefit of present and future generations of Americans (Administration Act).

Description of Use(s):

The 1997 amendments to the Administration Act defined environmental education and interpretation as wildlife-dependent public uses. In that Act, the U.S. Congress charged that such uses be given special consideration in planning for and management of the National Wildlife Refuge System. When determined compatible on a refuge-specific basis, these uses are priority general public uses of that national wildlife refuge. National wildlife refuges are to seek opportunities to allow these uses in an appropriate and compatible manner.

Both environmental education and interpretation strive to convey an understanding and appreciation of national wildlife refuge resources, the issues that affect them, and the techniques and programs pursued in their management. For this reason these two uses have been combined in one compatibility determination (CD).

On-site environmental education opportunities would include an outdoor classroom setting for local school classes that would range from 15-30 students. Components of the education opportunities would include a combination of staff-led hikes, classroom activities, and hands-on experiences.

Interpretive opportunities include the self-guided interpretive trails that are under development, interpretive panels at various locations around the Refuge, and the visitor center.

To share the ecology and management practices necessary to recover and preserve the Refuge's natural and cultural resources with the public the Refuge would extend its outreach efforts. Refuge outreach is limited to schools with budgets large enough to transport students to the Refuge. For schools who cannot afford to bring the students to the Refuge, Refuge staff would go to them. Refuge staff along with other agencies would develop schoolyard habitat programs. This would bring Refuge staff to the schools so that the environmental education and wildlife conservation can take place locally at the school.

Availability of Resources:

The Refuge has sufficient staff time and other resources to allow this use at the current levels. Currently the Refuge has a Visitor Services Professional to administer and monitor the activities and a Maintenance Worker to maintain public facilities and access points.

Category and Itemization	One-time ($)	Annual (per year)
Administration and Management		$41,896
Maintenance		$36,130
Monitoring		$9,474
Special equipment, facilities or improvements		$0
Offsetting revenues		$0

The numbers above reflect the current estimated costs. Estimated costs were calculated using 40% of the base cost of a GS-11 Visitor Services Professional and 10% of a GS-13 Refuge Manager for Administration and Management; 25% of the base cost of a WG-10 Maintenance Worker for maintenance assuming that this priority activity would use that "portion of a year" for administration, participation, and maintenance associated with environmental education and interpretation.

Anticipated Impacts of the Use(s):

Minor impacts to terrestrial species would occur on the Refuge in the form of disturbance. Movement and behavior patterns could be altered by the presence of visitors. Some trampling of vegetation could occur as visitors stray to the edges of trails and access roads.

There are a number of alien species on Guam in general and many of those (e.g., brown treesnake, feral pigs, monitor lizards) have become established on the refuge. As the Refuge staff work to eliminate or reduce pest species, it is possible that invasive plants and animals could be transported onto the Refuge in vehicles or from seeds that are trapped in clothing or vehicle wheels. Protocols could reduce this risk.

Public Review and Comment:

This determination was issued for public review and comment as part of the Guam NWR Draft Comprehensive Conservation Plan. The plan and associated compatibility determinations were also made available through printed copies upon request and through the Refuge website. The 30-day review occurred from July 21 through August 24. We did not receive specific comments regarding the compatibility determinations. However, a number of individuals suggested that the hours of operation for the Refuge be extended to include Federal holidays. No change has been made at this time, but the Refuge staff will consider opportunities to expand operating hours as staff positions are re-filled and potentially expanded.

Determination:

_____   Use is Not Compatible

_X_   Use is Compatible with Following Stipulations

Stipulations Necessary to Ensure Compatibility:

Environmental education and interpretation generally occur only in those areas that have been opened to the public. There may be a limited number of environmental education opportunities offered in closed areas. These programs will be conducted only by Refuge staff and will be limited to a maximum of 30 participants. Approximately ½ mile of beach area along the west end of the Refuge, self-guided trails, access roads, access paths, parking areas, and the area around the nature center are currently open to the public. The ocean and coral reef areas adjacent to the beach are open for swimming and snorkeling.

A Visitor Services Professional and Law Enforcement Officer administer and monitor the activities of visiting public.

A maintenance worker maintains public facilities and access points to direct visitors to areas open to public use.

Refuge staff will close portions of the beach [and water] as necessary to protect nesting turtles.

Visitors are not allowed to touch, take, or stand upon any reef material.

Justification:

When determined compatible on a refuge-specific basis, environmental education and interpretation are priority public uses of that national wildlife refuge. The promotion of environmental education and interpretation when compatible supports the "connecting people with nature" initiative within the Service. As endangered species recovery activities increase, it may be necessary to limit this activity and/or re-evaluate for compatibility.

The combination of limiting visiting hours, properly maintaining visitor access points, allowing visitors to access only certain areas of the beach and water, Refuge staff administration and supervision of group activities, and monitoring visitor use and behavior allows the Refuge to minimize any adverse effects associated with Refuge visitation. By applying the stipulations described above, it is anticipated that wildlife populations will find sufficient food resources and resting places such that their abundance and use of the Refuge will not be measurably lessened from wildlife observation and photography activities. The relatively limited number of individuals expected to be adversely affected due to wildlife observation and photography will not cause wildlife populations to materially decline, the physiological condition and production of native bird and bat species and marine species will not be impaired, their behavior and normal activity patterns will not be altered dramatically, and their overall welfare will not be negatively impacted. Allowing wildlife observation and photography to occur with stipulations will not materially detract or interfere with the purposes for which the Refuge was established or the Refuge mission. The stipulations included herein would allow such uses to occur in a compatible manner.

Mandatory 10- or 15-year Reevaluation Date:

X   Mandatory 15-year re-evaluation date (for wildlife-dependent public uses)

_   Mandatory 10-year re-evaluation date (for non-wildlife-dependent public uses)

NEPA Compliance for Refuge Use Decision (check one below)

_   Categorical Exclusion without Environmental Action Statement

_   Categorical Exclusion and Environmental Action Statement

X   Environmental Assessment and Finding of No Significant Impact

Refuge Determination:

Project Leader,
Guam National Wildlife Refuge

(Signature)   Date: 9/25/09

Project Leader,
Hawaiian and Pacific
Islands NWRC   _(Signature)_   Date 9/25/09

Concurrence:

Regional Chief,
National Wildlife
Refuge System
Pacific Region   _(Signature)_   Date 9/29/09

Compatibility Determination

Use: Fishing

Refuge Name: Guam National Wildlife Refuge (NWR)

City/County and State: Unincorporated U.S. Territory of Guam

Establishing and Acquisition Authority(ies):

The refuge authorizing authorities most relevant to the four principle reasons Guam NWR was established are the Endangered Species Act (ESA), Fish and Wildlife Act, Migratory Bird Conservation Act, and Refuge Recreation Act.

Refuge Purpose(s):

Ritidian Unit

The Administration Act directs the Service to manage each refuge to fulfill the mission, to maintain and where appropriate, restore the refuge's ecological integrity; and achieve the specific purposes for which the refuge was established. The Refuge purposes for the Ritidian Unit of Guam NWR are as follows:

... to conserve (A) fish or wildlife which are listed as endangered species or threatened species ... or (B) plants ...16 U.S.C. §1534 (Endangered Species Act of 1973)

... for the development, advancement, management, conservation, and protection of fish and wildlife resources ...16 U.S.C. 742f (a) (4), (Fish and Wildlife Act of 1956)

... for use as an inviolate sanctuary, or for any other management purpose, for migratory birds. 16 U.S.C. 715d (Migratory Bird Conservation Act)

... suitable for (1) incidental fish and wildlife-oriented recreational development, (2) the protection of natural resources, (3) the conservation of endangered species or threatened species...16 U.S.C. 460k-1 (Refuge Recreation Act (16 U.S.C. 460k-460k-4), as amended).

National Wildlife Refuge System Mission:

To administer a national network of lands and waters for the conservation, management, and where appropriate, restoration of the fish, wildlife, and plant resources and their habitats within the United States for the benefit of present and future generations of Americans (Administration Act).

Description of Use(s):

The 1997 amendments to the Administration Act defined fishing as a wildlife-dependent public use. In that Act, the U.S. Congress charged that such uses be given special consideration in planning for and management of the National Wildlife Refuge System. When determined compatible on a refuge-specific basis, these uses are priority general public uses of that national wildlife refuge. National wildlife refuges are to seek opportunities to allow these uses in an appropriate and compatible manner.

Public recreational activities are permitted on the Ritidian Unit between the hours of 8:30 a.m. to 4:00 p.m daily (closed Federal holidays). Refuge staff members carefully monitor these activities to ensure visitor safety and preservation of the natural and cultural resources of the Refuge. Public programs are designed to "foster an understanding of and support for stewardship of Guam's natural environment" (USFWS 2007). Refuge staff members at the Ritidian Unit estimate between 75,000 and 80,000 individuals visit the Refuge annually (E. Sablan, USFWS, personal communication).

Anglers may fish and collect marine life on designated areas of the Refuge only in accordance with Refuge and Government of Guam laws and regulations. A leaflet is available at the Refuge headquarters.

Availability of Resources:

The Refuge has sufficient staff time and other resources to allow this use at the current levels. Currently the Refuge has a Visitor Services Professional and Law Enforcement Officer to administer and monitor the activities, and a Maintenance Worker to maintain public facilities and access points. These costs would be the same as those for wildlife observation and photography. They are listed here, but should not be considered additive to those costs.

Category and Itemization	One-time ($)	Annual (per year)
Administration and Management		$41,896
Maintenance		$36,130
Monitoring		$9,474
Special equipment, facilities or improvements		$0
Offsetting revenues		$0

The numbers above reflect the current estimated costs. Estimated costs were calculated using 25% of the base cost of a GS-11 Visitor Services Professional and 10% of a GS-13 Refuge Manager for Administration and Management; 35% of the base cost of a WG-10 Maintenance Worker for maintenance; and 10% of the base cost of a GS-11 Refuge Biologist for monitoring, assuming that this priority activity would use that "portion of a year" to administer.

Anticipated Impacts of the Use(s):

Minor impacts to terrestrial and marine life would occur on the Refuge in the form of disturbance. Movement and behavior patterns could be altered by the presence of visitors. Some trampling of vegetation could occur as visitors stray to the edges of trails and access roads.

Use of the waters of Guam Refuge increases the potential for introduction of nonnative species and interactions (some negative) by snorkelers and divers with sea turtles, fish, invertebrates, and live corals. One accidental introduction of a nonnative species on a boat or dive equipment could devastate the marine environment.

There are a number of alien species on Guam in general and many of those (e.g., BTS, feral pigs, monitor lizards) have become established on the Refuge. As Refuge staff members work to eliminate or reduce pest species, it is possible that invasive plants and animals could be transported onto the Refuge in vehicles or from seeds that are trapped in clothing or vehicle wheels. Protocols could reduce this risk.

Fishing inherently impacts fish species that are targeted. Individuals experience mortality and are consumed. Due to the limited number of fish and invertebrates which would be allowed to be taken and consumed, impacts to fish and invertebrate species populations as a whole are not expected.

Public Review and Comment:

This determination was issued for public review and comment as part of the Guam NWR Draft Comprehensive Conservation Plan. The plan and associated compatibility determinations were made available through printed copies upon request and through the Refuge website. The 30-day review occurred from July 21 through August 24. We did not receive specific comments regarding the compatibility determinations. However, a number of individuals suggested that the hours of operation for the Refuge be extended to include Federal holidays. No change has been made at this time, but the Refuge staff will consider opportunities to expand operating hours as staff positions are re-filled and potentially expanded.

Determination:

___   Use is Not Compatible

X   Use is Compatible with Following Stipulations

Stipulations Necessary to Ensure Compatibility:

Anglers are subject to the following conditions:

Refuge and territory fishing regulations apply.

Anglers may fish while the Refuge is open from 8:30 a.m. until 4:00 p.m. daily, except Federal holidays.

We prohibit overnight camping on the Refuge.

Anglers may not possess surround or gill nets on the Refuge.

We prohibit the collection of corals, giant clams (*Tridacna and Hippopus spp.*), and coconut crabs (*Birgus latro*) on the Refuge.

We prohibit use of Self Contained Underwater Breathing Apparatus (SCUBA) to take fish or invertebrates.

We prohibit anchoring boats on the Refuge.

We prohibit sailboards or motorized personal watercraft on the Refuge.

Take of humpback wrasse bumphead parrotfish is prohibited.

Refuge staff will periodically review regulations and make adjustments as necessary.

Justification:

When determined compatible on a refuge-specific basis, fishing is a priority public use of that national wildlife refuge. The promotion of fishing when compatible supports the "connecting people with nature" initiative within the Service. As endangered species recovery activities increase, it may be necessary to limit this activity and/or re-evaluate for compatibility. Because numbers and types of species which can be taken by refuge visitors is very limited, it is anticipated that wildlife populations will find sufficient food resources and resting places such that their abundance and use of the Refuge will not be measurably lessened from fishing activities. The relatively limited number of individuals expected to be adversely affected due to fishing will not cause wildlife populations to materially decline, the physiological condition and production of marine turtle and fish species will not be impaired, their behavior and normal activity patterns will not be altered dramatically, and their overall welfare will not be negatively impacted. Fishing with stipulations will not materially detract or interfere with the purposes for which the Refuge was established or the Refuge mission. The stipulations included herein would allow such uses to occur in a compatible manner.

Mandatory 10- or 15-year Reevaluation Date:

X   Mandatory 15-year re-evaluation date (for wildlife-dependent public uses)

_   Mandatory 10-year re-evaluation date (for non-wildlife-dependent public uses)

NEPA Compliance for Refuge Use Decision (check one below)

_   Categorical Exclusion without Environmental Action Statement

_   Categorical Exclusion and Environmental Action Statement

X   Environmental Assessment and Finding of No Significant Impact

_   Environmental Impact Statement and Record of Decision

Refuge Determination:

Project Leader,
Guam National Wildlife Refuge

Joseph Schnagel
(Signature)   Date: 9/25/09

Project Leader,
Hawaiian and Pacific
Islands NWRC   *Barry W. Stieglitz*
                      (Signature)   Date 9/25/09

Concurrence:

Regional Chief,
National Wildlife
Refuge System   *Carolyn J. Bohan*
Pacific Region   (Signature)   Date 9/29/09

FINDING OF APPROPRIATENESS OF A REFUGE USE

Refuge Name: Guam National Wildlife Refuge

Use: Scientific Research

This form is not required for wildlife-dependent recreational uses, take regulated by the State, or uses already described in a refuge CCP or step-down management plan approved after October 9, 1997.

Decision Criteria:	YES	NO
(a) Do we have jurisdiction over the use?	✓	
(b) Does the use comply with applicable laws and regulations (Federal, State, tribal, and local)?	✓	
(c) Is the use consistent with applicable Executive orders and Department and Service policies?	✓	
(d) Is the use consistent with public safety?	✓	
(e) Is the use consistent with goals and objectives in an approved management plan or other document?	✓	
(f) Has an earlier documented analysis not denied the use or is this the first time the use has been proposed?	✓	
(g) Is the use manageable within available budget and staff?	✓	
(h) Will this be manageable in the future within existing resources?	✓	
(i) Does the use contribute to the public's understanding and appreciation of the refuge's natural or cultural resources, or is the use beneficial to the refuge's natural or cultural resources?	✓	
(j) Can the use be accommodated without impairing existing wildlife-dependent recreational uses or reducing the potential to provide quality (see section 1.6D, 603 FW 1, for description), compatible, wildlife-dependent recreation into the future?	✓	

Where we do not have jurisdiction over the use ("no" to (a)), there is no need to evaluate it further as we cannot control the use. Uses that are illegal, inconsistent with existing policy, or unsafe ("no" to (b), (c), or (d)) may not be found appropriate. If the answer is "no" to any of the other questions above, we will **generally** not allow the use

If indicated, the refuge manager has consulted with State fish and wildlife agencies. Yes ___ No ___

When the refuge manager finds the use appropriate based on sound professional judgment, the refuge manager must justify the use in writing on an attached sheet and obtain the refuge supervisor's concurrence.

Based on an overall assessment of these factors, my summary conclusion is that the proposed use is:

Not Appropriate ___   Appropriate ✓

Refuge Manager: *Joseph Schnagerl*   Date: 9/25/09

If found to be Not Appropriate, the refuge supervisor does not need to sign concurrence if the use is a new use.

If an existing use is found Not Appropriate outside the CCP process, the refuge supervisor must sign concurrence.

If found to be Appropriate, the refuge supervisor must sign concurrence.

Refuge Supervisor: _____   Date: _____

A compatibility determination is required before the use may be allowed.   FWS Form 3-2319
02/06

Compatibility Determination

Refuge Name: Guam National Wildlife Refuge

City/County and State: Unincorporated Organized Territory of Guam

Establishing and Acquisition Authority(ies):

The refuge authorizing authorities most relevant to the four principle reasons Guam NWR was established are the Endangered Species Act (ESA), Fish and Wildlife Act, Migratory Bird Conservation Act, and Refuge Recreation Act.

Refuge Purpose(s):

Ritidian Unit

The Administration Act directs the Service to manage each refuge to fulfill the mission, to maintain and where appropriate, restore the refuge's ecological integrity; and achieve the specific purposes for which the refuge was established. The refuge purposes for the Ritidian Unit of Guam NWR are as follows:

... to conserve (A) fish or wildlife which are listed as endangered species or threatened species ... or (B) plants ...16 U.S.C. §1534 (Endangered Species Act of 1973)

... for the development, advancement, management, conservation, and protection of fish and wildlife resources ...16 U.S.C. § 742f (a) (4), (Fish and Wildlife Act of 1956)

... for use as an inviolate sanctuary, or for any other management purpose, for migratory birds. 16 U.S.C. § 715d (Migratory Bird Conservation Act)

... suitable for (1) incidental fish and wildlife-oriented recreational development, (2) the protection of natural resources, (3) the conservation of endangered species or threatened species ... 16 U.S.C. § 460k-1 (Refuge Recreation Act (16 U.S.C. § 460k-460k-4), as amended).

National Wildlife Refuge System Mission:

To administer a national network of lands and waters for the conservation, management, and where appropriate, restoration of the fish, wildlife, and plant resources and their habitats within the United States for the benefit of present and future generations of Americans (Administration Act).

Description of Use(s):

When determined compatible on a refuge-specific basis, research, scientific collecting, and surveys (research) are allowable uses and are conducted on Refuge lands and waters by independent researchers, partnering agencies, and educational groups. The Service defines these uses as:
- Research: Planned, organized, and systematic investigation of a scientific nature.
- Scientific collecting: Gathering of refuge natural resources or cultural artifacts for scientific purposes.
- Surveys: Scientific inventory or monitoring.

The types of research vary greatly, but could revolve around birds, marine animals, sea turtles, coral reefs, the marine environment, marine debris, invasive species, habitat classification and restoration, and cultural and historic resources.

Research proposals may be for any time of the year and on any of the habitat types and/or surrounding waters within the Refuge. However, the Refuge may limit the time and location of research projects to ensure that negative impacts to Refuge resources are avoided or limited.

Each research, scientific collection, or survey project would undoubtedly have different protocols and methodologies; therefore, each study necessitates its own scientific review. Each research project would be carefully reviewed to prevent any significant short-term, long-term, or cumulative impacts. New research requests would be evaluated by Refuge staff by comparing them to ongoing or recently completed research on the Refuge to determine if the species studied, methodologies used, or habitat type and locations used may lead to undesirable cumulative impacts. All projects would be subjected to the Refuge permitting process. This level of review would help ensure all levels and types of impacts are carefully considered before any permit for research is issued. Within the permit, conditions would be clearly defined to protect and conserve the existing natural, cultural, and historic resources found on the Refuge. Standard and specific conditions are included in this CD under Stipulations Necessary to Ensure Compatibility.

The Service will encourage and support research and management studies on Refuge lands that improve and strengthen natural resource management decisions. The Refuge manager will encourage and seek research relative to approved Refuge objectives that clearly improves land management and promotes adaptive management. Information that enables better management of the nation's biological resources and is generally considered important to agencies of the Department of the Interior, including the Service, the Refuge System, and State Fish and Game Agencies, and/or that addresses important management issues or demonstrates techniques for management of species and/or habitats, will be the priority.

The Refuge may also consider research for other purposes which may not be directly related to Refuge-specific objectives, but would contribute to the broader enhancement, protection, use, preservation, and management of populations of fish, wildlife, plants, and their natural diversity within the region or flyway. These proposals must comply with the Service's compatibility policy.

The Refuge may develop a list of research needs that will be provided to prospective researchers or organizations upon request. Refuge support of research directly related to Refuge objectives may take the form of funding, in-kind services such as housing or use of other facilities, direct staff assistance with the project in the form of data collection, provision of historical records, conducting of management treatments, or other assistance as appropriate.

Availability of Resources:

The bulk of the cost for research is incurred in staff time to review research proposals, coordinate with researchers, write Special Use Permits (SUPs), and review the research results. In some cases, a research project may only require one day of staff time to write an SUP. In other cases, a research project may require weeks of staff time. Under a modest scenario, a Refuge biologist would spend an average of 80 hours a year working on research projects conducted by outside researchers. This adds up to about $3,800 annually for resources spent on outside research.

Anticipated Impacts of the Use(s):

Disturbance to wildlife and vegetation by researchers could occur through observation, a variety of wildlife capture techniques, banding, and accessing the area by foot or vehicle. It is possible that direct or indirect mortality could result as a by-product of research activities. Mist-netting or other wildlife capture techniques, for example, can cause mortality directly through the capture method or in trap predation, and indirectly through capture injury or stress caused to the organism.

Although a single research project for a single year may cause few, if any, negative resource impacts, it may in fact cause cumulative impacts over multiple years or when considered additively with all activity on the Refuge. Therefore, it is critical for the Refuge manager to examine all projects with a multi-year timeframe in mind and consider all activities that are planned concurrently on the Refuge before approval is granted. It may be appropriate to set a limit to the number of research projects occurring in a particular habitat or relative to a single species or species group, even if staff are available to coordinate the projects.

Overall, however, allowing well designed and properly reviewed research to be conducted by non-Service personnel is likely to have very little impact on Refuge wildlife populations. If the research project is conducted with professionalism and integrity, potential adverse impacts are likely to be outweighed by the knowledge gained about an entire species, habitat, or public use.

Public Review and Comment:

This determination was issued for public review and comment as part of the Guam NWR Draft Comprehensive Conservation Plan. The plan and associated compatibility determinations were made available through printed copies upon request and through the Refuge website. The 30-day review occurred from July 21 through August 24. We did not receive specific comments regarding the compatibility determinations. However, a number of individuals suggested that the hours of operation for the Refuge be extended to include Federal holidays. No change has been made at this time, but the Refuge staff will consider opportunities to expand operating hours as staff positions are re-filled and potentially expanded.

Determination:

___ Use is Not Compatible

X Use is Compatible with Following Stipulations

Stipulations Necessary to Ensure Compatibility:

SUPs will be issued for all research conducted by non-Service personnel. The SUP will list the conditions that the Refuge manager determines to be necessary to ensure compatibility. The SUPs will also identify a schedule for progress reports and the submittal of a final report or scientific paper.

Regional Refuge biologists, other Service Divisions, State agencies, or non-governmental organizations and biologists may be asked to provide additional review and comment on any research proposal.

All researchers will be required to obtain appropriate State and Federal permits.

All research related SUPs will contain a statement regarding the Service's policy regarding disposition of biotic specimen. The current Service policy language in this regard (USFWS, 1999) is, *"You may use specimens collected under this permit, any components of any specimens (including natural organisms, enzymes, genetic material or seeds), and research results derived from collected specimens for scientific or educational purposes only, and not for commercial purposes unless you have entered into a Cooperative Research and Development Agreement (CRADA) with us. We prohibit the sale of collected research specimens or other transfers to third parties. Breach of any of the terms of this permit will be grounds for revocation of this permit and denial of future permits. Furthermore, if you sell or otherwise transfer collected specimens, any components thereof, or any products or any research results developed from such specimens or their components without a CRADA, you will pay us a royalty rate of 20 percent of gross revenue from such sales. In addition to such royalty, we may seek other damages and injunctive relief against you."*

Any research project may be terminated at any time for non-compliance with the SUP conditions, or modified, redesigned, relocated or terminated, upon a determination by the Refuge manager that the project is causing unanticipated adverse impacts to wildlife, wildlife habitat, approved priority public uses, or other Refuge management activities.

Justification:

Research on the Refuge is inherently valuable to the Service, since it is intended to expand the knowledge base of those who are given the responsibility of managing the resources found within. This is particularly true in this case where many of the resources remain in pristine condition and detailed information is lacking for a portion of these species. In many cases, if it were not for the Refuge providing access to the lands and waters along with some support, the research would never take place and less scientific information would be available to the Service to aid in managing and conserving the Refuge resources.

Because each SUP will contain specific permit conditions for minimizing adverse effects to Refuge resources while the research project is being conducted, it is anticipated that wildlife populations will find sufficient food resources and resting places such that their abundance and use of the Refuge will not be measurably lessened from research activities. The relatively limited number of individuals expected to be adversely affected due to research will not cause wildlife populations to materially decline, the physiological condition and production of native bird and bat species and marine species will not be impaired, their behavior and normal activity patterns will not be altered dramatically, and their overall welfare will not be negatively impacted. Thus, allowing research to occur with stipulations will not materially detract or interfere with the purposes for which the Refuge was established or the Refuge System mission.

Mandatory 10- or 15-year Reevaluation Date:

X   Mandatory 15-year re-evaluation date (for wildlife-dependent public uses)

_   Mandatory 10-year re-evaluation date (for non-wildlife-dependent public uses)

NEPA Compliance for Refuge Use Decision (check one below)

_   Categorical Exclusion without Environmental Action Statement

_   Categorical Exclusion and Environmental Action Statement

X   Environmental Assessment and Finding of No Significant Impact

_   Environmental Impact Statement and Record of Decision

References Cited:

U.S. Fish and Wildlife Service. 1985. Refuge Manual. Washington, D.C.: U.S. Government Printing Office.

U.S. Fish and Wildlife Service. 1999. Director's Order No. 109: Use of Specimens Collected on Fish and Wildlife Lands. March 30, 1999.

Refuge Determination:

Project Leader,
Guam National Wildlife Refuge

Joseph Schwagerl
(Signature)   Date: 9/25/09

Project Leader,
Hawaiian and Pacific
Islands NWRC   _Barry W. Stieglitz_
(Signature)   Date 9/25/09

Concurrence:

Regional Chief,
National Wildlife
Refuge System   _Carolyn J. Bohan_
Pacific Region   (Signature)   Date 9/29/09

FINDING OF APPROPRIATENESS OF A REFUGE USE

Refuge Name: Guam National Wildlife Refuge

Use: Traditional Gathering

This form is not required for wildlife-dependent recreational uses, take regulated by the State, or uses already described in a refuge CCP or step-down management plan approved after October 9, 1997.

Decision Criteria:	YES	NO
(a) Do we have jurisdiction over the use?	✓	
(b) Does the use comply with applicable laws and regulations (Federal, State, tribal, and local)?	✓	
(c) Is the use consistent with applicable Executive orders and Department and Service policies?	✓	
(d) Is the use consistent with public safety?	✓	
(e) Is the use consistent with goals and objectives in an approved management plan or other document?	✓	
(f) Has an earlier documented analysis not denied the use or is this the first time the use has been proposed?	✓	
(g) Is the use manageable within available budget and staff?	✓	
(h) Will this be manageable in the future within existing resources?	✓	
(i) Does the use contribute to the public's understanding and appreciation of the refuge's natural or cultural resources, or is the use beneficial to the refuge's natural or cultural resources?	✓	
(j) Can the use be accommodated without impairing existing wildlife-dependent recreational uses or reducing the potential to provide quality (see section 1.6D, 603 FW 1, for description), compatible, wildlife-dependent recreation into the future?	✓	

Where we do not have jurisdiction over the use ("no" to (a)), there is no need to evaluate it further as we cannot control the use. Uses that are illegal, inconsistent with existing policy, or unsafe ("no" to (b), (c), or (d)) may not be found appropriate. If the answer is "no" to any of the other questions above, we will **generally** not allow the use.

If indicated, the refuge manager has consulted with State fish and wildlife agencies. Yes ___   No ___

When the refuge manager finds the use appropriate based on sound professional judgment, the refuge manager must justify the use in writing on an attached sheet and obtain the refuge supervisor's concurrence.

Based on an overall assessment of these factors, my summary conclusion is that the proposed use is:

Not Appropriate _____   Appropriate ✓

Refuge Manager: _Joseph Schnagel_   Date: _9/25/09_

If found to be **Not Appropriate**, the refuge supervisor does not need to sign concurrence if the use is a new use.

If an existing use is found **Not Appropriate** outside the CCP process, the refuge supervisor must sign concurrence.

If found to be **Appropriate**, the refuge supervisor must sign concurrence.

Refuge Supervisor: _____   Date: _____

A compatibility determination is required before the use may be allowed.   FWS Form 3-2319
                                                                                    02/06

Attachment to
Finding of Appropriateness of a Refuge Use

Use: Traditional Gathering

On Guam NWR, island people developed medicinal remedies and practices that existed for hundreds of years before the islands were discovered by western civilizations. These traditional practices have typically involved collection of plant material for consumption or use off Refuge lands. Medicinal plant collection involves taking cuttings from live plants through clipping leaves or stems. Plant material is collected in small amounts and no plant mortality occurs. Other gathering includes coconut and breadfruit which are in such abundance that the amount of gathering does not impact the plant community or animal species that use the fruits. The occurrence of these activities is currently infrequent and is not expected to grow significantly in the near future. Impacts to the Refuge are expected to be minimal.

Additional information regarding the Service evaluation of proposed Traditional Gathering for Guam National Wildlife Refuge:

    i.   The project may not appear to contribute to the public's understanding and appreciation of the Refuge's natural or cultural resources or be beneficial to the Refuge's natural or cultural resources. Consistent with relevant policy (603 FW 1.11 B.), the Refuge has completed an "Exceptional or Unique Circumstances Analysis" (see below).

Exceptional or Unique Circumstances Analysis for Traditional Gathering at Guam National Wildlife Refuge (603 FW 1.11 B.).

The "Finding of Appropriateness of a Refuge Use" determination caused the Refuge to further clarify that Traditional Gathering could contribute to the public's understanding and appreciation of the Refuge's natural or cultural resources. Following the Refuge conditions for compatibility will establish that Traditional Gathering will not materially detract from these resources or the public's understanding and appreciation of them. Consistent with relevant policy (603 FW 1.11 B.), the Refuge has made a determination that the use is appropriate for the following reasons:

- The use would not materially interfere with or detract from the fulfillment of the Refuge System mission or the purposes of the Refuge in providing for the conservation and management of fish and wildlife and their habitats, as well as historic and cultural resources.
- The use could positively impact the public's understanding and appreciation of the Refuge's natural or cultural resources. The Refuge has interpretive materials and signs to which those members of the public participating in the use would be exposed. Law enforcement and management staff would be able to expose these individuals to information specific to wildlife conservation and habitat management at Guam NWR.
- The use would only be allowed if it were also determined compatible.
- All individuals are required to obtain permits. Information about Guam NWR will be provided to the permittees.

Compatibility Determination

Use: Traditional Gathering

Refuge Name: Guam National Wildlife Refuge (NWR)

City/County and State: Unincorporated Organized U.S. Territory of Guam

Establishing and Acquisition Authority(ies):

Guam NWR was established administratively in 1993. At the time of establishment, Service policy did not require a notice to be posted in the Federal Register. The best record regarding the Refuge establishment is the "Final Environmental Assessment for the Proposed Guam National Wildlife Refuge" and the associated "Finding of No Significant Impact" (U.S. Fish and Wildlife Service 1993). The refuge authorizing authorities most relevant to the four principle reasons Guam NWR was established are the Endangered Species Act (ESA), Fish and Wildlife Act, Migratory Bird Conservation Act, and Refuge Recreation Act.

Refuge Purpose(s):

Ritidian Unit Purposes

The Administration Act directs the Service to manage each refuge to fulfill the mission, to maintain and where appropriate, restore the refuge's ecological integrity; and achieve the specific purposes for which the refuge was established. The refuge purposes for the Ritidian Unit of Guam NWR are as follows:

... to conserve (A) fish or wildlife which are listed as endangered species or threatened species ... or (B) plants ...16 U.S.C. §1534 (Endangered Species Act of 1973)

... for the development, advancement, management, conservation, and protection of fish and wildlife resources ...16 U.S.C. § 742f (a) (4), (Fish and Wildlife Act of 1956)

... for use as an inviolate sanctuary, or for any other management purpose, for migratory birds. 16 U.S.C. § 715d (Migratory Bird Conservation Act)

... suitable for (1) incidental fish and wildlife-oriented recreational development, (2) the protection of natural resources, (3) the conservation of endangered species or threatened species ... 16 U.S.C. § 460k-1 (Refuge Recreation Act (16 U.S.C. § 460k-460k-4), as amended).

National Wildlife Refuge System Mission:

To administer a national network of lands and waters for the conservation, management, and where appropriate, restoration of the fish, wildlife, and plant resources and their habitats within the United States for the benefit of present and future generations of Americans (Administration Act).

Description of Use(s):

On Guam NWR, the native population developed medicinal remedies and practices that existed for hundreds of years before the islands were discovered by western civilizations. These traditional practices have typically involved collection of plant material for consumption or use off Refuge lands. Medicinal plant collection involves taking cuttings from live plants through clipping leaves or stems. Plant material is collected in small amounts and no plant mortality occurs. Other gathering includes coconut and breadfruit which are in such abundance that the amount of gathering does not impact the plant community or animal species that use the fruits. The occurrence of these activities is currently infrequent and is not expected to grow significantly in the near future. Impacts to the Refuge are expected to be minimal.

Additional information regarding the Service evaluation of proposed Traditional Gathering for Guam National Wildlife Refuge:

ii.   The project may not appear to contribute to the public's understanding and appreciation of the Refuge's natural or cultural resources or be beneficial to the Refuge's natural or cultural resources. The following explanation, consistent with relevant policy (603 FW 1.11 B.) the Refuge has completed an "Exceptional or Unique Circumstances Analysis" (see below).

Exceptional or Unique Circumstances Analysis for Traditional Gathering at Guam National Wildlife Refuge (603 FW 1.11 B.).

The "Finding of Appropriateness of a Refuge Use" determination caused the Refuge to further clarify that Traditional Gathering could contribute to the public's understanding and appreciation of the Refuge's natural or cultural resources. Following the Refuge conditions for compatibility will establish that Traditional Gathering will not materially detract from these resources or the public's understanding and appreciation of them. Consistent with relevant policy (603 FW 1.11 B.), the Refuge has made a determination that the use is appropriate for the following reasons:

- The use would not materially interfere with or detract from the fulfillment of the Refuge System mission or the purposes of the Refuge in providing for the conservation and management of fish and wildlife and their habitats, as well as historic and cultural resources.
- The use could positively impact the public's understanding and appreciation of the Refuge's natural or cultural resources. The Refuge has interpretive materials and signs to which those members of the public participating in the use would be exposed. Law enforcement and management staff would be able to expose these individuals to information specific to wildlife conservation and habitat management at Guam NWR.
- The use would only be allowed if it were also determined compatible.
- All individuals are required to obtain permits. Information about Guam NWR will be provided to the permittees.

Relationships with the government of Guam, while positive at the staff level, could be improved through grassroots outreach to the public.

No facilities are dedicated solely to these uses that need to be covered by this compatibility determination.

Availability of Resources:

No funding presently exists specifically for this use. However, the occurrence of this activity is currently infrequent and is not expected to grow significantly in the near future, thus the costs to the Refuge are minimal and can be accommodated within the existing budget.

Anticipated Impacts of the Use(s):

Impacts to the Refuge are expected to be minimal. Plant material is collected in small amounts through clipping leaves or stems. No plant mortality occurs. Coconuts and breadfruit are in such abundance that the amount of gathering that occurs does not impact the plant community or animal species that use the fruits.

Public Review and Comment:

This determination was issued for public review and comment as part of the Guam NWR Draft Comprehensive Conservation Plan. The plan and associated compatibility determinations were made available through printed copies upon request and through the Refuge website. The 30-day review occurred from July 21 through August 24. We did not receive specific comments regarding the compatibility determinations. However, a number of individuals suggested that the hours of operation for the Refuge be extended to include Federal holidays. No change has been made at this time, but the Refuge staff will consider opportunities to expand operating hours as staff positions are re-filled and potentially expanded.

Determination:

___	Use is Not Compatible
_X_	Use is Compatible with Following Stipulations

Stipulations Necessary to Ensure Compatibility:

A permit is required.

No more than 20 coconuts and 20 breadfruits may be collected per individual per day.

Justification:

Because collecting will be limited to no more than 20 coconuts and 20 breadfruits per individual per day, and plant material is collected in small amounts through clipping leaves or stems, no plant mortality occurs. Coconuts and breadfruit are in such abundance that the amount of gathering that occurs does not impact the plant community or animal species that use the fruits.

Mandatory 10- or 15-year Reevaluation Date:

_____ Mandatory 15-year re-evaluation date (for wildlife-dependent public uses)

__X__ Mandatory 10-year re-evaluation date (for non-wildlife-dependent public uses)

NEPA Compliance for Refuge Use Decision (check one below)

_____ Categorical Exclusion without Environmental Action Statement

_____ Categorical Exclusion and Environmental Action Statement

__X__ Environmental Assessment and Finding of No Significant Impact

_____ Environmental Impact Statement and Record of Decision

Refuge Determination:

Project Leader,
Guam National Wildlife Refuge

(Signature)   Date: __9/25/09__

Project Leader,
Hawaiian and Pacific
Islands NWRC   Date __9/25/09__
(Signature)

Concurrence:

Regional Chief,
National Wildlife
Refuge System   Date __9/29/09__
Pacific Region   _(Signature)_

Appendix C. Plan Implementation and Costs

Staffing

Necessary staffing as projected by the Service's National Staffing Model, generated 13 positions for the Guam NWR. The existing, core-funded staff is six, so seven additional positions are justified. However, as a part of the modeling exercise, one Full-Time Equivalent (FTE) was moved to the Hawaiian and Pacific Islands NWRC to support a Writer/Editor to benefit all 20 Refuge System units, leaving six additional positions. The increased staffing would provide increased coordination with other Federal agencies, Territorial agencies, and the local public; additional capacity to conduct biological inventory, monitoring, and research; improved maintenance capability for visitor facilities and Refuge buildings; visitor safety and law enforcement to reduce wildlife disturbance; environmental education and interpretation of Refuge resources; and invasive species control.

Current and Necessary Permanent Full-Time Staffing for Guam NWR[*]

Staff position	Salary Rating
Project Leader	GS-13
Deputy Project Leader	GS-11/12
Supervisory Park Ranger	GS-7/9/11
Park Ranger (bilingual)	GS-5
Wildlife Biologist	GS-9/11
Wildlife Biologist	GS-5/7/9
Wildlife Biologist	GS-5/7/9
Maintenance Worker	WG-6
Maintenance Worker	WG-5/6
Maintenance Worker	WG-5/6
Administrative Support	GS-7
Park Ranger (LE)	GS-5/7/9

[*]Shaded cells indicate positions that are either currently filled or in the process of being filled.

Additional Permanent Full-Time Staff under Alternative B

Staff position	Salary Rating
Maintenance Worker	WG-5/6
Volunteer Coordinator	GS-5/7
Visitor Services Specialist	GS-5/7
Wildlife Biologist	GS-5/7/9

Additional Permanent Full-Time Staff under Alternative C

Staff position	Salary Rating
Maintenance Worker	WG-5/6
Wildlife Biologist	GS-5/7/9
Wildlife Biologist	GS-5/7/9
Volunteer Coordinator	GS-5/7

Administration

Guam NWR is administered and supervised as a part of the Hawaiian and Pacific Islands NWR Complex, headquartered in Honolulu, Hawai'i. This arrangement will continue, with the staff from the Honolulu office providing support as needed.

Refuge Funding

Successful implementation of the CCP relies on our ability to secure funding, personnel, infrastructure, and other resources to accomplish the actions identified. Full implementation of the actions and strategies in this CCP will incur costs including staffing, construction projects, and individual resource program expansions. Most of these projects have been identified as Tier 1 or Tier 2 Projects in the Refuge System's Refuge Operations Needs System database (RONS).

Budget Requests

The following table represents budget requests for RONS (Refuge Operating Needs System) projects. These guide the funding of CCP goals and strategies and will financially enable the Guam NWR to carry out its plans under the CCP. The RONS system will be updated with new items that are presented in the CCP.

Project Number	Title	Cost
FY08-5125	Control invasive predators	$106,000
FY08-5151	Establish a friends group	$38,639
FY08-5150	Promote restoration of *Serianthes nelsonii*	$55,639
FY08-5131	Monitor coral reef and marine area	$48,639

Appendix D. Wilderness Review for Guam National Wildlife Refuge

I. General Information on Wilderness Reviews

A wilderness review is the process used to determine whether or not to recommend lands or waters in the National Wildlife Refuge System (System) to the United States Congress (Congress) for designation as wilderness. Planning policy for the System (602 FW 3) mandates conducting wilderness reviews every 15 years through the Comprehensive Conservation Planning (CCP) process.

The wilderness review process has three phases: inventory, study, and recommendation. After first identifying lands and waters that meet the minimum criteria for wilderness, the resulting wilderness study areas (WSA) are further evaluated to determine if they merit recommendation from the Service to the Secretary of the Interior for inclusion in the National Wilderness Preservation System (NWPS). Areas recommended for designation are managed to maintain wilderness character in accordance with management goals, objectives, and strategies outlined in the final CCP until Congress makes a decision or the CCP is amended to modify or remove the wilderness proposal. A brief discussion of wilderness inventory, study, and recommendation follows.

Wilderness Inventory

The wilderness inventory consists of identifying areas that minimally meet the requirements for wilderness as defined in the Wilderness Act of 1964 (Wilderness Act). Wilderness is defined as an area which:

- Has at least 5,000 acres of land or is of sufficient size as to make practicable its preservation and use in an unimpaired condition, or be capable of restoration to wilderness character through appropriate management at the time of review, or be a roadless island;
- Generally appears to have been affected primarily by the forces of nature, with the imprint of man's work substantially unnoticeable;
- Has outstanding opportunities for solitude or a primitive and unconfined type of recreation; and
- May also contain ecological, geological, or other features of scientific, educational, scenic, or historical value. These features and values, though desirable, are not necessary for an area to qualify as a wilderness.

Wilderness Study

During the study phase, lands and waters qualifying for wilderness as a result of the inventory are studied to analyze values (ecological, recreational, cultural, spiritual), resources (e.g., wildlife, water, vegetation, minerals, soils), and uses (habitat management, public use) within the area. The findings of the study help determine whether to recommend the area for designation as wilderness.

Wilderness Recommendation

Once a wilderness study determines that a WSA meets the requirements for inclusion in the NWPS, a wilderness study report that presents the results of the wilderness review, accompanied by a Legislative Environmental Impact Statement (LEIS), is prepared. The wilderness study report and LEIS that support wilderness designation are then transmitted through the Secretary of the Interior to the President of United States, and ultimately to the United States Congress for approval.

The following section summarizes the inventory phase of the wilderness review for Guam NWR.

II. Wilderness Inventory

The wilderness inventory is a broad look at the planning area to identify WSAs. These WSAs are roadless areas within refuge boundaries, including submerged lands and their associated water column, that meet the minimum criteria for wilderness identified in Section 2(c) of the Wilderness Act. A WSA must meet the minimum size criteria (or be a roadless island), appear natural, and provide outstanding opportunities for solitude or primitive recreation. Other supplemental values are evaluated, but not required.

Two inventory units were identified in order to evaluate whether the lands and waters of Guam NWR meet the minimum criteria for a WSA. These inventory units are identified as Inventory Unit A: Guam NWR, Ritidian Unit, terrestrial area; and Inventory Unit B: Guam NWR, Ritidian Unit, marine area.

<u>Evaluation of Size Criteria for Roadless Areas, Roadless Islands, and Submerged Lands and Associated Water Column</u>
Identification of roadless areas, roadless islands, and submerged lands and associated water column required gathering land status maps, land use and road inventory data, satellite imagery, aerial photographs, and personal observations of areas within Refuge boundaries. "Roadless" refers to the absence of improved roads suitable and maintained for public travel by means of motorized vehicles primarily intended for highway use.

Inventory units meet the size criteria for a WSA if any one of the following standards applies:

- An area with over 5,000 contiguous acres. State and private lands are not included in making this acreage determination.
- A roadless island of any size. A roadless island is defined as an area surrounded by permanent waters or that is markedly distinguished from the surrounding lands by topographical or ecological features.
- An area of less than 5,000 contiguous Federal acres that is of sufficient size as to make practicable its preservation and use in an unimpaired condition, and of a size suitable for wilderness management.
- An area of less than 5,000 contiguous Federal acres that is contiguous with a designated wilderness, recommended wilderness, or area under wilderness review by another Federal wilderness managing agency such as the Forest Service, National Park Service, or Bureau of Land Management.

Inventory Unit A is composed of a highly modified land management unit totaling 385 acres on the island of Guam. It is bounded and bisected by state-owned and refuge-owned roadways maintained for travel by passenger vehicles. Inventory Unit B is composed of an 832 acre marine and coral reef area on the shoreline of Guam. These inventory units do not meet the size criteria.
<u>Evaluation of the Naturalness Criteria</u>

A WSA must meet the naturalness criteria. Section 2 (c) of the Wilderness Act defines wilderness as an area that "...generally appears to have been affected primarily by the forces of nature with the imprint of man's work substantially unnoticeable." The area must appear natural to the average visitor rather than "pristine." The presence of ecologically accurate, historic landscape conditions is not required. An area may include some man-made features and human impacts provided they are substantially unnoticeable in the unit as a whole. Human-caused hazards, such as unexploded ordnance from military activity, and the physical impacts of refuge management facilities and activities are also considered in the evaluation of the naturalness criteria. An area may not be considered unnatural in appearance solely on the basis of "sights and sounds" of human impacts and activities outside the boundary of the unit. The cumulative effects of these factors were considered in the evaluation of naturalness for each wilderness inventory unit.

In the wilderness inventory, specific man-made features and other human impacts need to be identified that affect the overall apparent naturalness of the tract. The following factors were primary considerations in evaluating the naturalness of the inventory units:

Inventory Unit A
- Administrative, maintenance and visitor services buildings,
- Gates, parking lots, and roadways

Inventory Unit B
- Scattered anchor blocks/pilings

Inventory Unit A contains numerous buildings, an entrance roadway, and parking lots. Inventory Unit B is a relatively pristine coral reef and marine ecosystem. Scattered old and rusting pilings are visible. Otherwise, the effects of human activity are relatively unnoticed.

Evaluation of Outstanding Opportunities for Solitude or Primitive and Unconfined Recreation
In addition to meeting the size and naturalness criteria, a WSA must provide outstanding opportunities for solitude or primitive recreation. The area does not have to possess outstanding opportunities for both solitude and primitive and unconfined recreation, and does not need to have outstanding opportunities on every acre. Further, an area does not have to be open to public use and access to qualify under these criteria. Congress has designated a number of wilderness areas in the NWPS that are closed to public access to protect ecological resource values.

Opportunities for solitude refer to the ability of a visitor to be alone and secluded from other visitors in the area. Primitive and unconfined recreation means non-motorized, dispersed outdoor recreation activities that do not require developed facilities or mechanical transport. These primitive recreation activities may provide opportunities to experience challenge and risk, self reliance, and adventure.

These two opportunity "elements" are not well defined by the Wilderness Act but in most cases can be expected to occur together. However, an outstanding opportunity for solitude may be present in an area offering only limited primitive recreation potential. Conversely, an area may be so attractive for recreation use that experiencing solitude is not an option. Due to their size and location, neither inventory units offer opportunities for solitude or primitive and unconfined recreation. Daily management activities occur on these inventory units. These activities include road maintenance, law enforcement patrol, predator control, conducting interpretative and educational programs, and mowing of fields.

Evaluation of Supplemental Values
Supplemental values are defined by the Wilderness Act as "ecological, geological, or other features of scientific, educational, scenic, or historic value." Based upon the findings of the required components for WSA designation, supplemental values were not evaluated.

Inventory Findings
Inventory units A and B do not meet the minimum criteria for WSA consideration (see Table 1).

Table 1. Wilderness Inventory Summary

Components	Inventory Unit A: Ritidian Unit, Guam NWR, terrestrial portion (385 acres)	Inventory Unit B: Ritidian Unit, Guam NWR, marine portion (832 acres)
Required Components		
(1) Has at least 5,000 acres of land or is of sufficient size to make practicable its preservation and use in an unconfined condition, or is a roadless island.	No. Does not contain 5,000 acres, is not a roadless island, and is not practicable to manage as a wilderness.	No. Does not contain 5,000 acres, is not a roadless island, and is not practicable to manage as a wilderness.
(2) Generally appears to have been affected primarily by the forces of nature, with the imprint of man's work substantially unnoticeable.	No. Landscape is highly modified and actively managed.	Yes. Marine landscape appears relatively pristine and affected primarily by the forces of nature.
(3a) Has outstanding opportunities for solitude.	No. Unit is actively and regularly managed.	No. Unit is actively and regularly visited by the public and refuge staff.
(3b) Has outstanding opportunities for a primitive and unconfined type of recreation.	No. Recreation is highly regulated and requires staff presence.	No. Recreation is highly regulated with limited area in which to participate in recreational activities.
Other Components		
(4) Contains ecological, geological or other features of scientific, educational, scenic, or historical value.	Not evaluated.	Not evaluated.
Summary		
Parcel qualifies as a wilderness study area (meets criteria 1, 2 and 3a or 3b).	No	No

Appendix E. Glossary of Acronyms

List of Acronyms

ABW	Air Base Wing
Andersen AFB	Andersen Air Force Base
ACOE	Army Corps of Engineers
ARPA	Archaeological Resource Protection Act
BCE	Base Civil Engineer (Andersen Air Force Base)
BMP	Best Management Practices
BRD	Biological Resources Discipline (see also USGS)
BTS	Brown Treesnake
BSP	Bureau of Statistics and Plans, Government of Guam
CCP	Comprehensive Conservation Plan
CD	Compatibility Determination
CITES	Convention on International Trade in Endangered Species of Wild Fauna and Flora
CNMI	Commonwealth of the Northern Mariana Island
COMNAVMAR	Commander, U.S. Naval Forces, Marianas
CZMA	Coastal Zone Management Act
DOA	Department of Agriculture, Government of Guam
DOD	Department of Defense
DODD	Department of Defense Directive
DPR	Department of Parks and Recreation, Government of Guam
EA	Environmental Assessment
EEC	Estimated Environmental Concentration
EIS	Environmental Impact Statement
EOD	Explosives Ordnance Division
EPA	Environmental Protection Agency
ERA	Ecological Reserve Area
ESA	Endangered Species Act
ESQD	Explosive Safety Quantity-distance
FIFRA	Federal Insecticide, Fungicide and Rodenticide Act of 1996
FISC	Fleet Industrial Supply Center (Navy)
FSRD	Forestry and Soil Resources Division, Government of Guam
FUDS	Formerly Used Defense Site
GCWCS	Guam Comprehensive Wildlife Conservation Strategy
GEPA	Guam Environmental Protection Agency

GDAWR	Guam Division of Aquatic and Wildlife Resources, Government of Guam
GDPR	Guam Department of Parks and Recreation, Government of Guam
Guam NWR	Guam National Wildlife Refuge
GVB	Guam Visitors Bureau
HQ USAF	Headquarters, U.S. Air Force
HMP	Habitat Management Plan
INRMP	Integrated Natural Resources Management Plan
IPM	Integrated Pest Management
IRP	Installation Restoration Program
MAJCOM	Major Commander (Andersen Air Force Base)
MBTA	Migratory Bird Treaty Act
MMPA	Marine Mammal Protection Act
MRW	Morale, Recreation, and Welfare
NAVACTS	Naval Activities
NCTS	Navy Computer and Telecommunications Service
NEPA	National Environmental Policy Act
NHPA	National Historic Preservation Act
NMFS	National Marine Fisheries Service, U.S. Department of Commerce
NRCS	Natural Resources Conservation Service, USDA
NWR	National Wildlife Refuge (see also Refuge)
NWRS	National Wildlife Refuge System
NOAA	National Oceanographic and Atmospheric Administration
OIA	Office of Insular Affairs, U.S. Department of the Interior
PACAF	Pacific Air Force Command
PACDIVNAVFACENGCOM	Pacific Division Naval Facilities Engineering Command (Navy)
PPE	Personal Protective Equipment
PRP	Preplanning Report
PUP	Pesticide Use Proposal
Refuge	National Wildlife Refuge (see also NWR)
Refuge System	National Wildlife Refuge System
SUP	Special Use Permit
SHPO	State Historic Preservation Office
Service	U.S. Fish and Wildlife Service

UOG	University of Guam
USA	United States of America
USAF	U.S. Air Force
USDA	U.S. Department of Agriculture
USDA-WS	U.S. Department of Agriculture, Wildlife Services
USN	U.S. Navy
USFWS	U.S. Fish and Wildlife Service
USGS	U.S. Geological Service
USAF	United States Air Force
USA	United States Army
USN	United States Navy
UXO	Unexploded Ordnance
WSA	Wilderness Study Area

Appendix F. Refuge Purposes Research

Refuge Purpose(s) ensure that the Guam Refuge will be managed to fulfill the mission of the National Wildlife Refuge System and the specific purposes for which the Refuge was established. The Refuge purpose is used to derive management goals and objectives, prioritize Refuge activities, and to ensure secondary uses do not detract from the purpose of the Refuge. The Refuge Purpose also allows the Service to give priority to achieving a unit's purpose(s) when conflicts with the System mission or a specific goal exist." (601 FW1).

A. Guam NWR: Ritidian Unit Refuge Purpose

Guam Refuge was established administratively in 1993. At the time of establishment, Service policy did not require a notice to be posted in the Federal Register. In order to determine the Refuge purposes, the CCP Planning team searched the administrative record on the establishment of the Guam Refuge. Files in the Guam Refuge, the Pacific Islands Refuge Planning Office, and the Regional Office (Region 1) were also searched.

The best record regarding Refuge establishment is the "Final Environmental Assessment for the Proposed Guam National Wildlife Refuge" and the associated "Finding of No Significant Impact" (Finding of No Significant Impact) (USFWS 1993). These two key administrative memoranda document the acquisition authorities, and while they address the "purpose for the proposed action" (in accordance with NEPA); neither document stated the official 'Refuge Purpose(s).' Section III, below, provides the NEPA statements from the EA and FONSI.

At the time the Refuge was established (1993) there was no planning requirement for a Land Protection Plan or a Conceptual Management Plan. There is no Land and Water Conservation Fund budget request on file (and no Land Acquisition Priority System evaluations) because fee title to the Ritidian Unit was acquired through a no-cost transfer of surplus Navy land. A number of internal correspondence documents refer to 'Refuge Purposes,' but the statements vary widely and these memoranda do not meet the definition in the CCP Preplanning Guidance of "administrative memoranda that authorize or expand a Refuge." Furthermore, because the statements vary and are not rooted in an official legal document, these internal memoranda were not included in the Refuge Purpose review.

In the absence of specific Refuge purposes being documented in administrative memoranda and in accordance with Service policy, Refuge Purposes are derived from the acquisition authorities through which the Refuge was established. Guam Refuge arose as a consequence of the listing in 1984 of six endangered species pursuant to the ESA, 16 U.S.C. §1531 et seq. The Service has a statutory obligation of conserving the ecosystems upon which threatened and endangered species depend for their survival 16 U.S.C. §661, et seq.; ESA, 16 U.S.C. § 1531, et seq.

According to the Service's Refuge Mission, Goals, and Purposes policy, the Service uses refuge establishing authorities to derive refuge purposes, which can be further refined through examination of administrative memoranda. In the case of Guam, we do not have an administrative memoranda decision document (such as Migratory Bird Commission meeting notes or other planning documents) that clearly articulates refuge purposes.

From the research, the paramount reason for establishing Guam is to protect endangered species and the habitat upon which they depend and contribute to recovery. Based on the administrative memoranda, protection of native wildlife, including migratory species (part of conserving native biodiversity) is another main reason for establishing the Refuge. Various administrative memoranda also make it clear that another primary reason for Refuge establishment is to provide wildlife-dependent recreation.

The refuge authorizing authorities most relevant to the four principle reasons Guam NWR was established are the ESA, Fish and Wildlife Act, Migratory Bird Conservation Act (MBCA) and Refuge Recreation Act; these four statute purposes represent the Refuge purposes.

The research also documents that native wildlife, migratory species, and biological diversity are important reasons for establishing the Refuge, but clearly secondary to threatened and endangered species. Since the administrative record appears to give equal weight to native wildlife, migratory species, and biological diversity considerations, we believe it is appropriate to include both Fish and Wildlife Act and Migratory Bird Conservation Act (MBCA) as Refuge purposes. Although migratory birds are not common on the Refuge, the MBCA is important, because the opportunity to protect and conserve the migratory birds of Guam was cited in the initial justification for the transfer of land from the Navy to the Service.

The following Refuge purpose(s) statement is consistent with the Service's statutory obligations, establishing authorities for the Refuge, the mission and the approach contained in Refuge Policy 601 FW 1, System, Mission, Goals, and Purposes Policy:

The Purposes of the Ritidian Unit, Guam National Wildlife Refuge

The Administration Act directs the Service to manage each refuge to fulfill the mission, to maintain and where appropriate, restore the refuge's ecological integrity; and achieve the specific purposes for which the refuge was established. The Refuge purposes for the Ritidian Unit of Guam NWR are as follows:

... to conserve (A) fish or wildlife which are listed as endangered species or threatened species .... or (B) plants ...16 U.S.C. §1534 (Endangered Species Act of 1973)

... for the development, advancement, management, conservation, and protection of fish and wildlife resources ...16 U.S.C. § 742f (a) (4), (Fish and Wildlife Act of 1956)

... for use as an inviolate sanctuary, or for any other management purpose, for migratory birds. 16 U.S.C. § 715d (Migratory Bird Conservation Act)

... suitable for (1) incidental fish and wildlife-oriented recreational development, (2) the protection of natural resources, (3) the conservation of endangered species or threatened species ... 16 U.S.C. § 460k-1 (Refuge Recreation Act (16 U.S.C. § 460k-460k-4), as amended).

B. Navy and Air Force Overlay Refuge Units Purposes.

The purposes of the Guam Refuge military overlay Refuge units are separate from the purpose of the Ritidian unit (U.S. Fish and Wildlife Service memo dated March 25, 1994). The overlay Refuge purposes here are specified in the Cooperative Agreements for the Navy and Air Force Overlay Units of the Guam Refuge (dated March 4, 1994, and March 10, 1994, respectively), and are:

A. "... to conserve (A) fish or wildlife which are listed as endangered species or threatened species ... or (B) plants ... (C) the ecosystems upon which endangered species and threatened species depend ..." (Endangered Species Act of 1973, 16 U.S.C., 1534);

B. "... shall be administered by him [Secretary of the Interior] directly or in accordance with cooperative agreements ... and in accordance with such rules and regulations for the conservation, maintenance, and management of wildlife, resources thereof, and its habitat thereon..." (Fish and Wildlife Coordination Act, 16 U.S.C. 664);

C. "... for the development, advancement, management, conservation, and protection of fish and wildlife resources" (Fish and Wildlife Act of 1956, 16 U.S.C. 742f(a)(4));

D. "... for the benefit of the United States Fish and Wildlife Service, in performing its activities and services. Such acceptance may be subject to the terms of any restrictive or affirmative covenant, or condition of servitude, if such terms are deemed by the Secretary to be in accordance with law and compatible with the purposes for which acceptance is sought." (Fish and Wildlife Act of 1956, 16 U.S.C. 742f(b)(1));

E. "... (1) incidental fish and wildlife-oriented recreational development, (2) the protection of natural resources, (3) the conservation of endangered species and threatened species" (Refuge Recreation Act, 16 U.S.C. 460k-l);

F. "... the Secretary ... may accept and use ... donations of ... real ... property. Such acceptance may be accomplished under the terms and conditions of restrictive covenants imposed by the donors...." (Refuge Recreation Act, 16 U.S.C. 460k-2); and

G. "To ensure that [Air Force and Navy] lands within the Guam National Wildlife Refuge remain available for the use of the [Air Force and Navy] to carry out its responsibilities to organize, supply, equip, train, service, mobilize, demobilize, administer, and maintain forces" (10 U.S.C. 8013).

I.   Supplemental Information

The following excerpts from administrative memoranda provide background on the purpose for establishing the Refuge and were rejected from being considered the official Refuge purpose statements for reasons provided:

    A.   Source 1. U.S. Fish and Wildlife Service, 1993. Final Environmental Assessment for the Proposed Guam National Wildlife Refuge, Territory of Guam. Dept. of the Interior, Region 1, Portland, OR. 153 pp. page 3.

"B. Purpose of the Proposed Action [Land acquisition and Refuge establishment]"

The primary purposes of the proposed Refuge are to halt and reverse the decline of Guam's endangered and threatened species and to protect migratory birds and other native wildlife. Protection and recovery of endangered and threatened species and the conservation of Guam's native biological diversity are dependent upon securing the best remaining wildlife habitats and implementing restoration and enhancement projects. Brown treesnake control and anti-poaching initiatives would be high priorities of initial protection and recovery programs. A secondary purpose of the proposed Refuge is to develop and implement educational and other public informational programs concerning Guam's wildlife and habitat resources. Including submerged lands in the proposed Refuge would contribute to the protection and recovery of endangered and threatened sea turtles and complement programs to manage near shore marine resources of biological, recreational, and commercial value." (Final EA, page 3)

Justification for rejecting this as the official Refuge purpose statement: The CCP Planning Team found that this is a purpose of establishing the refuge as defined under NEPA, rather than the Refuge purpose. The statement provides information that the priority is for the Service to conserve and recover listed species, and conserve migratory birds and other native wildlife through the Refuge. It documents the intention of the Refuge to provide education and information opportunities to members of the public as a subordinate use to wildlife conservation.

B.   Source 2. U.S. Fish and Wildlife Service, 1993. Finding of No Significant Impact. In: U.S. Fish and Wildlife Service, 1993. Final Environmental Assessment for the Proposed Guam National Wildlife Refuge, Territory of Guam. Dept. of the Interior, Region 1, Portland, OR. 153 pp. (FONSI page 2).

"The purposes for establishing the proposed Guam National Wildlife Refuge are to: (1) protect and restore essential habitats and provide for recovery actions for several endangered and threatened species; (2) conserve migratory species and their habitats; (3) protect and manage migratory species and other native wildlife and their habitats in order to conserve the biological diversity of Guam; (4) control predation upon native species, particularly by the brown treesnake; (5) complement ongoing Government of Guam and Department of Defense programs in natural resource management, conservation, law enforcement, research, and education; (6) provide opportunities for public education, enjoyment of wildlife, cultural use of resources and scientific research; and (7) maintain the scenic values of the protected areas." (FONSI, page 2.)

Justification for rejecting this as the official Refuge purpose statement: The CCP Planning Team found that this is a purpose of establishing the Refuge as defined under the National Environmental Policy Act (NEPA), rather than the Refuge purpose. The statement documents a clear priority for the Refuge to conserve and recover listed species, and conserve migratory birds and other native wildlife. It documents the intention of the Refuge to provide education and information opportunities to members of the public as a subordinate use to wildlife conservation.

It documents the commitment to working with Guam and DOD partners. The statement points to the intention of the Service to implement programs for public education, enjoyment of wildlife, cultural use of resources and scientific research, and demonstrates a commitment to maintaining scenic values of the protected areas. This list includes concepts that are intended to be part of the Refuge management program, but are not establishing Refuge purposes.

C. Source 3. U.S. Fish and Wildlife Service. March 25, 1994. Memorandum from Ray Rauch, Project Leader, Hawaiian and Pacific Islands National Wildlife Refuge Complex, Hawaii, to Chief, Division of Refuges Fish and Wildlife Service, Washington D.C.

The memo from Mr. Rauch clarifies that Overlay Refuge purposes are different than the purpose of the Ritidian Point Unit of Guam NWR. The memo notes "significant endangered species resources at the Ritidian Point Unit that will be the focus of our management strategy on Guam."

The memo informed the Chief that the Cooperative Agreements to establish overlay Refuge Units have been signed. It informs the Chief that the list of purposes of the Guam NWR needs to reflect the purposes as stated in the respective final Cooperative Agreements with the Air Force and Navy and transmits an updated list of purposes of the Guam NWR.

The memo notes that, "The purposes of the Department of Defense overlay units of the Guam NWR are different than the purpose of the Ritidian Point Unit of the Guam NWR. However, there are significant endangered species resources at the Ritidian Point Unit that will be the focus of our management strategy on Guam."

D. Source 4. U.S. Fish and Wildlife Service national database of Refuge purposes.

The following information was retrieved on March 01, 2007 from: http://refugedata.fws.gov/databases/purposes.taf?_function=detail&Layout_0_uid1=33610&_Use rReference=62470F2DF80C3BE4C991CBDE [Note: the odd symbols are actually part of the posted Web site source.]

"Unit Purposes"

Guam NWR

The purposes shown here are based upon land acquisition documents and authorities. The unit purposes may also include purposes included as deed restrictions, management agreements with primary land managers, and congressional established wilderness designations which were not part of the acquisition documents and authorities.

"...particular value in carrying out the national migratory bird management program." 16 U.S.C. 667b (An Act Authorizing the Transfer of Certain Real Property for Wildlife)

"... to conserve (A) fish or wildlife which are listed as endangered species or threatened species.... or (B) plants ..." 16 U.S.C. 1534 (Endangered Species Act of 1973)

"... for the development, advancement, management, conservation, and protection of fish and wildlife resources ..." 16 U.S.C. 742f(a)(4) "... for the benefit of the United States Fish and Wildlife Service, in performing its activities and services. Such acceptance may be subject to the terms of any restrictive or affirmative covenant, or condition of servitude ..." 16 U.S.C. 742f(b)(1) (Fish and Wildlife Act of 1956)

"... shall be administered by him [Secretary of the Interior] directly or in accordance with cooperative agreements ... and in accordance with such rules and regulations for the conservation, maintenance, and management of wildlife, resources thereof, and its habitat thereon, ..." 16 U.S.C. 664 (Fish and Wildlife Coordination Act).

"... suitable for (1) incidental fish and wildlife-oriented recreational development, (2) the protection of natural resources, (3) the conservation of endangered species or threatened species ..." 16 U.S.C. 460k-1 "... the Secretary ... may accept and use ... real ... property. Such acceptance may be accomplished under the terms and conditions of restrictive covenants imposed by donors ..." 16 U.S.C. 460k-2 (Refuge Recreation Act (16 U.S.C. 460k-460k-4), as amended).

To ensure that Navy lands within the Guam NWR remain available for the use of the Navy to carry out its responsibilities to supply, equip, train, service, mobilize, demobilize, and maintain forces. (10 U. S. C. 5013)

To ensure that Air Force lands within the Guam NWR remain available for the use of the Air Force to carry out its responsibilities to supply, equip, train, service, mobilize, demobilize, and maintain forces. (10 U. S. C. 8013)

[end of "Unit Purposes" from National database]

Justification for rejecting this as the official Refuge purpose statement: While this statement has strong credibility for being the official Refuge purpose, there is no documentation to point to the source of these Refuge purpose statements. The Guam CCP Planning Team concludes that a staff person tried to do research to include generic Refuge purpose statements in the database based on the various authorities cited in both the EA for the Proposed Guam NWR and the Cooperative Agreements for the Overlay Refuge Units. It is our belief that this was the draft Refuge Purpose statement that Ray Rauch was referring to in a memorandum dated March 25, 1994, in which he provided clarification that the Refuge purposes listed were different for the Ritidian Unit and the overlay Refuge Units. This Refuge purposes list combines the purpose for the Overlay Refuge units with the purposes of the Ritidian Unit.

III.   Other statements of benefits from various records in the administrative record for the establishment of the Guam NWR.

A.   Source #1. U.S. Fish and Wildlife Service, 1993. Final Environmental Assessment for the Proposed Guam National Wildlife Refuge, Territory of Guam. Dept. of the Interior, Region 1, Portland, OR. 153 pp. (page 3)

"Establishment of a Refuge would provide a coordinated program for the protection of endangered and threatened species and other native flora and fauna, unique ecosystems, and the conservation of native biological diversity in coordination and cooperation among the Guam

DAWR, the Service, and the DOD. In addition to providing increased opportunities for wildlife management, a Refuge would provide the public with increased opportunities for access to northern Guam for natural history education and other uses that are compatible with the proposed Refuge." (page 3).

Note: This statement describes the benefits of the Refuge.

> B. Source #2. U.S. Fish and Wildlife Service, 1993. Final Environmental Assessment for the Proposed Guam National Wildlife Refuge, Territory of Guam. Dept. of the Interior, Region 1, Portland, OR. 153 pp. (page 88)

"For example, the Endangered Species Act directs the Service to take action on behalf of endangered and threatened species, and to manage these species and their habitats to provide for recovery and eventual de-listing. The proposed Refuge would provide for the long-term survival and protection of Guam's unique and endangered wildlife and habitats." (page 88).

> C. Source #3. U.S. Fish and Wildlife Service memorandum, Circa March 23, 1994. Memo from Marvin Plenert, Regional Director, Region 1, to Deputy Director, Service, Washington DC.

The memo transmitted a copy of the executed Cooperative Agreements for the Guam NWR overlay units. It states that, "The establishment of the Guam NWR is a significant contribution by the U.S. Fish and Wildlife Service (Service), the U.S. Air Force, and the U.S. Navy toward protecting endangered species and conserving the native biodiversity on Federal Lands on Guam."

> D. Source #4. U.S. Fish and Wildlife Service 1993. Executive Summary of the Decision Document for the Proposed Guam National Wildlife Refuge.

"Objectives

The U.S. Fish and Wildlife Service (Service) is proposing to establish a National Wildlife Refuge (Refuge) on certain lands owned by the Department of Defense (DOD) and the Government of Guam, and certain submerged lands on Guam. The proposed Refuge would be established to: (1) protect and recover endangered and threatened species; (2) protect and restore essential habitats for federally listed species and implement recovery actions; (3) protect and manage migratory species and other native wildlife and their habitats in order to conserve Guam's biological diversity; (4) control predation upon native wildlife by harmful alien species, particularly by the brown treesnake, and protect wildlife from poaching; (5) complement ongoing Government of Guam and Federal programs in natural resources management, conservation, law enforcement, research, and education; (6) provide opportunities for public education, enjoyment of wildlife, cultural use of resources and scientific research; and (7) maintain the scenic values of the protected areas."

> E. Source #5. U.S. Fish and Wildlife Service. 1993. Final Environmental Assessment for the Proposed Guam National Wildlife Refuge, Territory of Guam. Dept. of the Interior, Region 1, Portland, OR. 153 pp. (page 3)

"Establishment of a Refuge would provide a coordinated program for the protection of endangered and threatened species and other native flora and fauna, unique ecosystems, and the conservation of native biological diversity in coordination and cooperation among the Guam DAWR, the Service, and the DOD. In addition to providing increased opportunities for wildlife management, a Refuge would provide the public with increased opportunities for access to northern Guam for natural history education and other uses that are compatible with the proposed Refuge."

Appendix G. Statement of Compliance

The following executive orders and legislative acts have been reviewed as they apply to implementation of the Comprehensive Conservation Plan (CCP) for Guam National Wildlife Refuge (Refuge).

National Environmental Policy Act (1969) (NEPA) (42 U.S.C. 4321 et seq.). The CCP planning process has been conducted in accordance with NEPA implementing procedures,DOI and Service procedures, and is performed in coordination with the affected public. Procedures used to reach this decision meet the requirements of NEPA and its implementing regulations in 40 CFR Parts 1500-1508. These procedures include the development of a range of alternatives for the CCP, analysis of the likely effects of each alternative, and public involvement throughout the planning process.

The CCP management strategies and activities have been integrated into an Environmental Assessment (EA) document and process, including the release of a Draft CCP/EA for a 30-day public comment period. Public notices of availability of the Draft CCP/EA include a Federal Register notice, news releases to local media outlets, the Service's refuge planning website, and planning updates. Copies of the Draft CCP/EA and planning updates were distributed to an extensive mailing list. Public comment was received and information provided at two public open houses on Guam. Revisions to the final CCP are based on public comments received on the Draft CCP/EA. We received 12 written comment letters and emails on the Draft CCP, including two from Territorial agencies. A summary of comments and responses can be found in Appendix A.

National Historic Preservation Act (1966) (NHPA)(16 U.S. C.470 et seq.). This Act requires Federal agencies to consult with the President's Advisory Council on Historic Preservation, State or Territorial Historic Preservation Officers, and the National Park Service for any proposed actions that may affect cultural resources eligible for the National Register of Historic Places.

The management of archaeological and cultural resources of Guam Refuge complies with the regulations of Section 106 of the National Historic Preservation Act (NHPA). No historic properties are known to be affected by the proposed action based on the criteria of an effect or adverse effect as an undertaking defined in 36 CFR 800.9 and Service Manual 614 FW 2. Determining whether a particular action has a potential to affect cultural resources is an ongoing process that occurs as step-down and site-specific project plans are developed. Activities in the CCP address further coordination in Section 106 compliance with the Territory. Should historic properties be identified in the future, the Service will comply with the NHPA if any management actions have the potential to affect any these properties.

Executive Order 12372. Intergovernmental Review. Coordination and consultation with other affected Federal agencies, Territorial agencies, and local mayors has been completed through personal contact by Service planners, the acting Refuge manager, and supervisors. The Refuge manager determined there are no local or tribal governments associated with Guam Refuge.

Executive Order 12898. Federal Actions to Address Environmental Justice in Minority and Low-Income Populations. All Federal actions must address and identify, as appropriate, disproportionately high and adverse human health or environmental effects of its programs, policies, and activities on minority populations, low-income populations, and Indian Tribes in the

United States. The CCP was evaluated and no adverse human health or environmental effects were identified for minority or low-income populations, Indian Tribes, or other populations.

Migratory Bird Treaty Act (MBTA)(16 U.S.C. 703-712) Guam Refguge is an important site for migratory shorebirds and nesting seabirds. Protecting nesting seabird habitat is the major purpose of the Refuge and is consistent with the provisions of MBTA. All of the proposed alternatives would be consistent with the Refuge purposes and the MBTA in protecting these birds. The proposed action, however, would afford more benefits. This planning effort is being coordinated with other offices of the Service and DOI that have responsibilities pertaining to the MBTA.

Executive Order 13186. Responsibilities of Federal Agencies to Protect Migratory Birds. This Order directs departments and agencies to take certain actions to further implement the MBTA. A provision of the Order directs Federal agencies to consider the impacts of their activities, especially in reference to birds on the Service's list of Birds of Conservation (Management) Concern (BCC). It also directs agencies to incorporate conservation recommendations and objectives found within the North American Waterbird Conservation Plan and bird conservation plans developed by Partners in Flight into agency planning. Species selected as conservation targets in the CCP were identified from multiple sources including pertinent BCC lists, applicable Flyway Management Plans, and regional seabird and shorebird conservation plans. The effects of all alternatives on focal conservation targets were assessed during this planning process.

Endangered Species Act (ESA) (16 U.S.C. 1531-1544). The ESA provides for the conservation of threatened and endangered species of fish, wildlife, and plants by Federal action and by encouraging the establishment of state programs. It provides for the determination and listing of endangered and threatened species and the designation of critical habitats. Section 7 requires refuge managers to perform consultation before initiating projects which affect or may affect endangered species. The Service will conduct consultation under Section 7 of the ESA for any refuge management program actions which have the potential to affect listed species.

National Wildlife Administration Act of 1966, as amended by The National Wildlife Refuge System Improvement Act of 1997 (16 U.S.C. 668dd-668ee). The National Wildlife Refuge System Improvement Act requires the Service to develop and implement a CCP for each refuge. These conservation plans identify and describe a refuge purpose; refuge vision and goals; fish, wildlife, and plant populations and related habitats; archaeological and cultural values of the refuge; issues that may affect populations and habitats of fish, wildlife, and plants; actions necessary to restore and improve biological diversity of the refuge; and opportunities for wildlife-dependent recreation. This CCP meets the Service's requirements for Guam Refuge. The CCP includes appropriateness findings and compatibility determinations for all relevant activities.

Wilderness Preservation Act of 1964 (Wilderness Act). The Wilderness Act requires the Service to evaluate the suitability of Guam NWR for wilderness designation. A Wilderness Review is included as an appendix to the CCP.

Executive Order 13089, Coral Reef Protection (June 11, 1998). The purpose of this Executive Order is "...to preserve and protect the biodiversity, health, heritage, and social and economic value of U.S. coral reef ecosystems and the marine environment..." It directs all Federal agencies to identify actions that may affect U.S. coral reefs; utilize their programs and authorities to protect and enhance coral reef ecosystems; and assure their actions would not degrade those ecosystems. Federal agencies whose actions affect U.S. coral reef ecosystems are further directed to implement measures needed to research, monitor, manage, and restore affected ecosystems, including, but not limited to, measures reducing impacts from pollution, sedimentation, and fishing. Executive Order 13089 also initially established the U.S. Coral Reef Task Force, co-chaired by the Secretaries of the Interior and Commerce, through the Administrator of NOAA. The Task Force has oversight responsibility for implementation of policy and Federal agency responsibilities found in this Order, and support activities under the U.S. Coral Reef Initiative. In addition, the Order directs the Task Force to work cooperatively with State, territory, commonwealth, and local government partners to map, monitor, conserve, mitigate, and restore coral reef ecosystems.

The Proposed Action is fully consistent with the spirit and intent of the Executive Order. Implementation of the Proposed Action would materially improve surveillance and enforcement and discourage unauthorized take of fish and wildlife within the Refuge and improve the capacity of the Service to monitor fish and wildlife and manage their protection within the Refuge.

Coral Reef Conservation Act and Executive Order 13158, Marine Protected Areas (16 U.S.C. 6401-6409) (May 26, 2000). These statutes collectively direct Federal agencies to coordinate among themselves and State and territorial governments via the Coral Reef Task Force to protect and enhance coral reefs and avoid actions that degrade reefs, promote marine protected area development and reef restoration, and provide conservation grants and cooperative agreements (including States and institutions) to conduct research and development of existing and candidate marine protected areas located on coral reefs.

The Proposed Action and other alternatives are consistent with the spirit and intent of these policies. Implementation of the Proposed Action would materially improve surveillance and enforcement and discourage unauthorized take of fish and wildlife within the Refuge and improve the capacity of the Service to monitor fish and wildlife and manage their protection within the Refuge.

Coastal Zone Management Act, Section 307. The proposed project was coordinated with the Territory of Guam's Coastal Zone Management Program (CZMP). The Draft CCP/EA was sent to the office for review in early August. The CZMP is reviewing the plan, which includes a 60-day review process. CZMP may add conditions for the consistency determination. The Service will adopt the finding of Federal Consistency for the plan and will consult with the CZMP as needed when implementing specific provisions of the CCP. The consistency determination for the Guam CCP is anticipated during the first week of October 2009.

_____   9-28-09
Chief, Division of Planning,   Date
Visitor Services, and Transportation

Appendix H. CCP Core Team Members

Name	Role
Chris Bandy	Former Project Leader, contributing writer for all chapters
Chris Eggleston	Wildlife Biologist, environmental effects
Bill Perry	Refuge Planner, contributing writer for all chapters and planning process coordination
Charlie Pelizza	Former Refuge Planner, Refuge goals and objectives, Refuge purposes research
David Hoy	Cartographer, maps
Carrie Eggleston	Wildlife Biologist, maps
Emily Sablan-Torres	Visitor Services Specialist, Chapter 5

Appendix I. Cultural Resource Overview

Guam National Wildlife Refuge Ritidian Unit

Cultural Resources Overview and Management Plan - 2006

Guam National Wildlife Refuge Ritidian Unit

Cultural Resources Overview and Management Plan - 2006

Prepared by:

Lou Ann Speulda

Virginia Parks

Nick Valentine

Anan Raymond, Regional Archaeologist

August 2006

Cultural Resources Team, Region 1
U.S. Fish and Wildlife Service
20555 SW Gerda Lane
Sherwood, OR 97140
503/625-4377 or fax 503/625-4887

Table of Contents

Figures and Tables

Figures

Tables

Introduction

Ranging from evidence of prehistoric latte architecture to Cold War-era structures, Guam National Wildlife Refuge (NWR) manages several important cultural resources within its boundaries. This overview provides a summary of the known cultural history of the refuge. Included is information regarding the prehistoric and modern environment of the region, a summary of the ethnographic and ethnohistoric setting, an overview of cultural resource inventory projects, a list of all known historic properties, information regarding federal laws and regulations applicable to cultural resources on federal lands, and a contact/consultation list.

This document also outlines a management plan with specific information regarding the location and integrity of cultural resources in order to appropriately preserve and protect the important resources and to enhance visitor appreciation of the island's cultural history through interpretation.

This overview focuses on the Ritidian Unit, which covers approximately 375 acres of land and 400 acres of submerged lands (Figure 1). The approved boundary of the Refuge encompasses noncontiguous parcels on both northern and southern portions of the island, totaling approximately 22,500 acres (Figure 2). Most of these lands are owned by the military (U.S. Air Force and U.S. Navy), and while the Service assists in protecting wildlife and habitat in an overlay refuge arrangement in some locations, the military mission remains the priority.

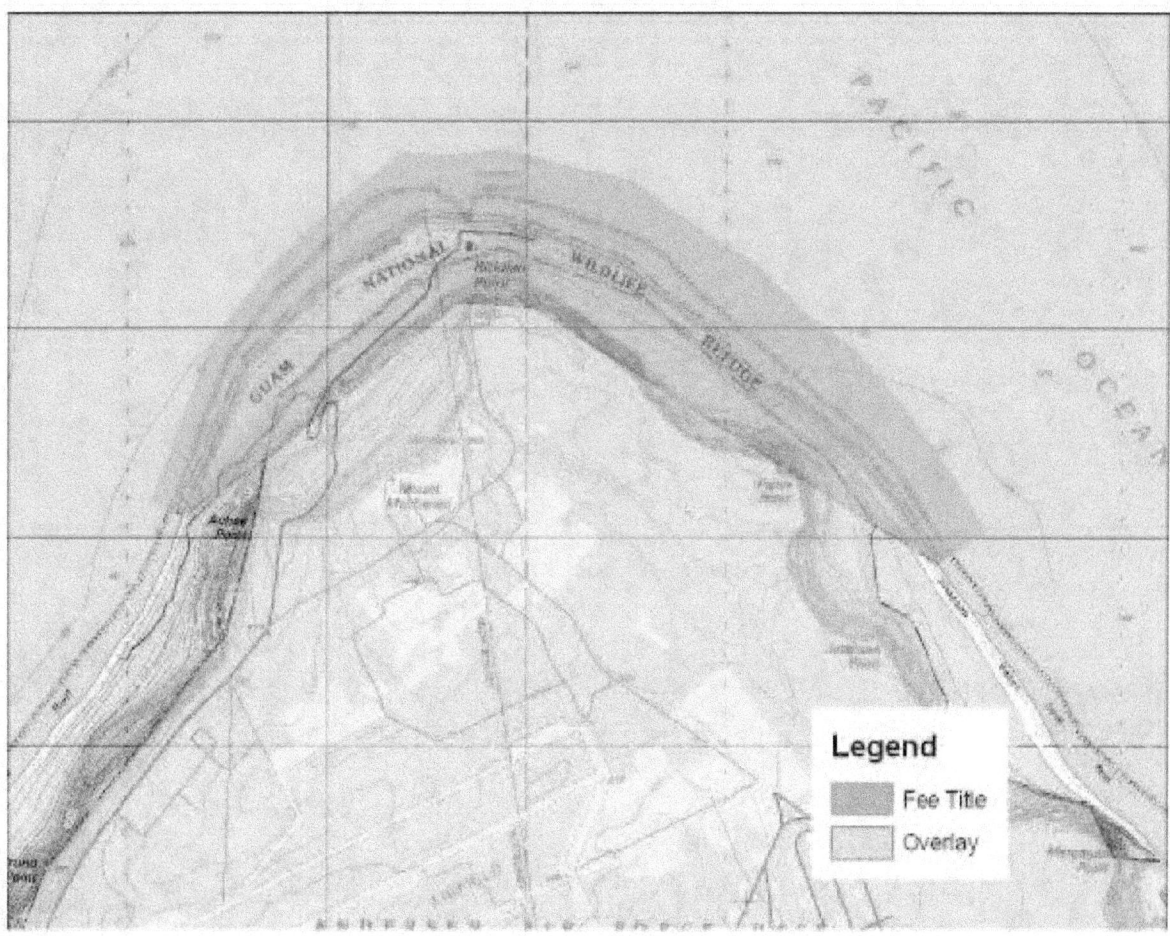

Figure 1. Acquired refuge lands, Ritidian Unit, Guam NWR.

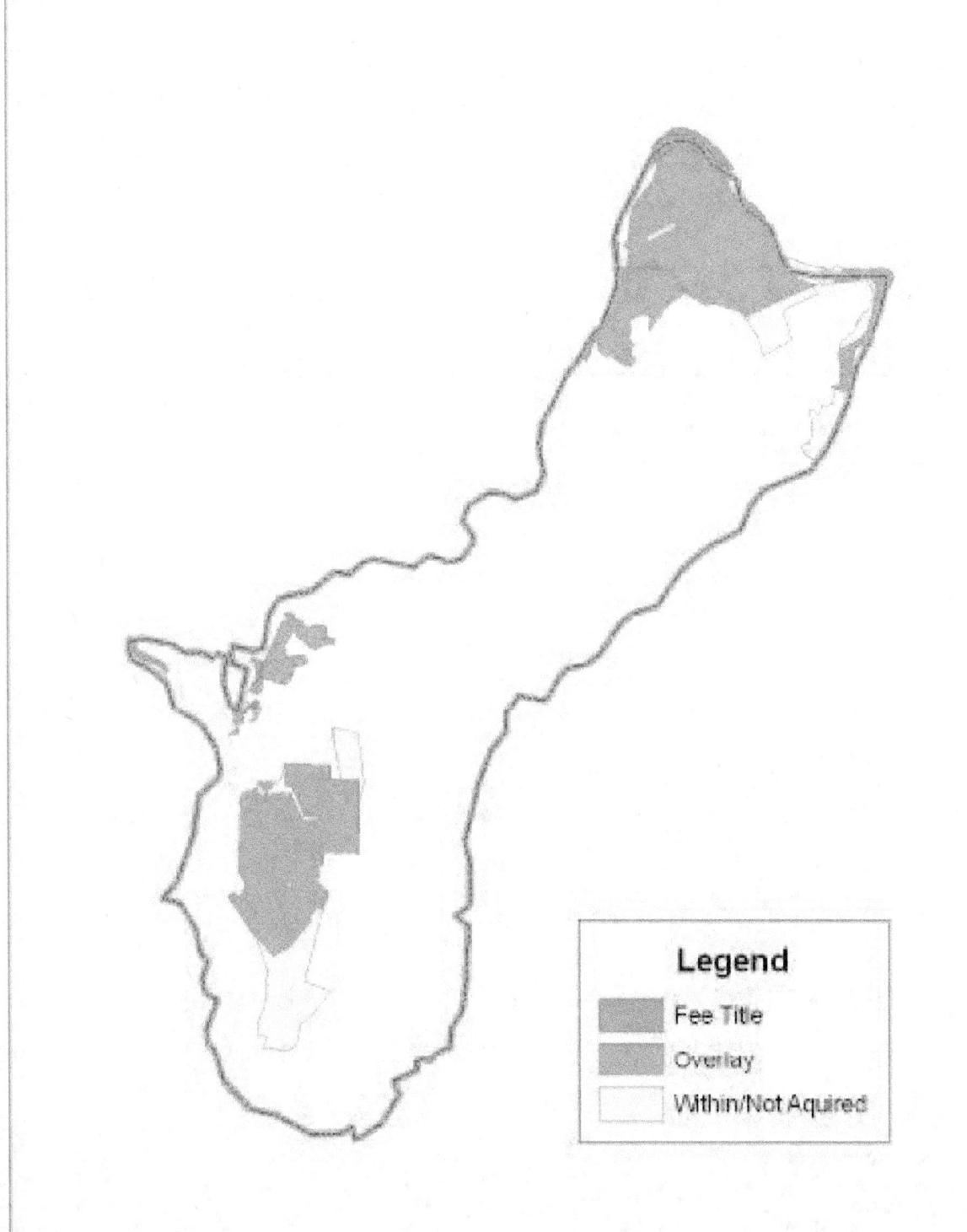

Legend

Fee Title

Overlay

Within/Not Aquired

Figure 2: Approved boundaries of Guam NWR.

Background

Environmental Setting

Guam is the largest and southernmost of the Mariana Islands, roughly 30 miles long and 4-8 miles wide. The Mariana Islands, along with Palau and Yap, are the exposed tips of an extensive submerged mountain chain situated to the east of the Philippine Sea. This immense range stretches for more than 1,400 miles. The chain forms the western edge of the Pacific northwest tectonic plate subduction zone along the rim of the Philippine Sea. The subduction zone forms the deepest canyon on earth, the Marianas Trench, which begins approximately 200 miles east of Saipan and curves south to its deepest point at 36,198 ft below sea level southwest of Guam (Liston 1996:17).

The archipelago is composed of 15 widely dispersed volcanic and coralline reef islands. The southern islands are older and larger than the northern islands. A noteworthy characteristic of Guam is the presence of limestone cliffs, rising dramatically from the ocean in a series of stepped coastal terraces (Liston 1996:17). Seismic activity contributed to the cliff height, especially pronounced along the northern end of the island at Ritidian Point.

The island has two distinct physiographic provinces: the dry, generally flat karst plateau in the north, and the higher, gently rolling uplands and descending slopes associated with alluvial valley floors in the volcanic south. The two regions are separated by the Adelup Point-Pago Bay fault that extends from Adelup Point on the western side of the island, down the Pago River drainage to Pago Bay on the eastern side (Liston 1996:17).

The tectonic uplift of the northern end of Guam has consequences to archaeological resources. "Beach areas within reef embayments are subject to infilling and extension seaward as the reef gradually grows. The violent typhoons on Guam have been shown to contribute to both beach accretion and destruction. Because of this alteration in land mass, cultural deposits representative of earlier human occupation on beach environments are often found further inland than later settlements" (Liston 1996:20).

Guam has a humid tropical climate with the majority of rainfall occurring during the four month long wet season extending from about mid-July to mid-November. Vegetation ranges from forests to swamps to grasslands. Ritidian Unit vegetation is associated with forest communities and heavily modified landforms with introduced species. "Forest species include pago (*Hibiscus tiliaceus*), fadang (*Cycas circinalis*), betel nut palm (*Areca sp.*), coconut palm (*Cocos nucifera*), screwpine (*Pandanus spp.*), and banyan (*Ficus sp.*).

The Ritidian Unit of Guam NWR wraps narrowly around the northern tip of Guam, extending from 30 meters depth below sea level to the top of Pajon Point at a height of 500 feet. The cliff face is pock-marked with small caves and crevices and a series of step-like terraces. The limestone also served as a water source for prehistoric inhabitants, with rain water percolating through the porous rock to recharge freshwater springs and seeps at the base of the cliff. A fringing reef protects the beach from low level storms although a channel cut through the coral is turbulent and dangerous. Within the refuge, the vegetation has adapted to the limestone bedrock and fairly narrow beach strand that is often pummeled by typhoons. Tangantangan (*Leucaena glauca*), introduced after World War II, currently dominates portions of the beach area.

Historical and Cultural Setting

There are six historic periods or themes defined by the Guam State Historic Preservation Office (SHPO) that provide a context for evaluating the significance of resources. The themes are: Initial Settlement Period 1,500 to 500 B.C.; Late Prehistoric Period 800 to 1600 A.D.; Spanish Period 1521-1898; First American Period 1898-1941; Japanese Period 1941-1944; Second American Period 1944 - [present]. Buildings, sites, and objects that represent these themes are important to identify and interpret for the benefit of the public. At least two of these themes are represented at the Ritidian Unit by tangible, although deteriorated, remains: the Late Prehistoric Period and Spanish Period. Additionally, evidence associated with the Initial Settlement Period and Second American Period may be found at the Ritidian Unit, Guam NWR.

Initial Settlement Period 1,500 to 500 B.C.

The question of when the Mariana Islands were first settled and from where has been of great interest for many decades. "Oceania, including the islands of Micronesia, comprise the last major portion of the globe to be colonized by man. This colonization, which was launched into the vast unknown Pacific Ocean, ranks as one of mankind's most daring exploits" (Russell and Fleming 1989:1). Inhabitants of Southeast Asia, Philippines, and Indonesia contributed to a series of migrations beginning about 4,000 B.C. Migrations of various island groups, through time, complicate the settlement patterns on Guam.

> *"Based on the linguistic evidence and the presence of the thin-walled, red slipped ceramics found at early sites, it is very likely that initial settlement of the Marianas can be traced directly to the Philippines....Chamorro is only distantly related to the eastern Micronesian languages. Based on these points, it is very likely that rather than serving as stepping stones for easterly or southerly expansion, settlement in the Marianas in fact was a cultural cul de sac" (Russel and Fleming 1989:8).*

It is likely that the first inhabitants of the Mariana Islands arrived about 3,500 years ago as documented by archaeological excavations in Saipan (Butler 1994; Butler and DeFant 1989:42-22; Moore et al. 1992; Liston 1996:29). The location of Pre-Latte Period sites on Guam suggests that the population lived in coastal areas during the initial phase of immigration and settlement of the island. "Pre-Latte sites have been found inland from Latte Period sites in some coastal lowland settings. The difference in site location is a result of changes in sea level and beach progradation over the long period of prehistoric occupation. The archaeological sites of the two different periods are in the same geomorphological location; that is, the nearshore strand that existed at the time of their occupation" (Liston 1996:29).

Evidence of early settlements have been recovered from Guam, Rota, and Saipan. The sites contain a limited amount of material probably because the population density was small. From a subsistence standpoint, these early populations probably relied heavily on marine resources that were abundant in the shallow reefs and offshore waters adjacent to their settlements (Russel and Fleming 1989:29). Only a handful of sites have been found and excavated by archaeologists. One of the sites studied is a deeply stratified deposit at Tarague. The earliest sites found on Guam, such as Tarague, are located in coastal beach environments (Liston 1996).

> *"Moore has identified five primary environmental zones at Tarague which include 1) the open ocean; 2) the reef; 3) the sand flat; 4) the limestone terraces; and 5) the plateau. Each of these zones offers specific resources that would have been useful to humans (Moore 1983:22).*
> *"Tarague's key advantages are the availability of freshwater, the rich floral and faunal populations, the presence of the channel and fringing reef, the close proximity to the nearest neighbor-*

ing island of Rota and the natural fortification created by the 500-foot cliffline. All of these natural features combine to make Tarague one of the most optimal areas for human habitation on Guam" (Kurashina and Clayshulte 1983:3).

Sites associated with this early period possess virtually the only surviving information with which to piece together man's initial settlement in the Marianas as well as in other parts of Micronesia and Polynesia. They also possess important information that will allow for the establishment of a cultural baseline against which to measure subsequent cultural change in the Marianas over a 3,000-year period. These questions can only be addressed through the systematic documentation and study of these sites. Enhancing their significance is the fact that there appear to be only a very small number of surviving sites associated with this context, making those that are extant especially valuable (Russel and Fleming 1989:34-35).

The resources and features that made Tarague a valuable location for initial settlement are to a lesser degree present at Ritidian, suggesting that it may contain evidence of early habitation. The disadvantages of Ritidian include the strong northeast trade winds which blow for most of the year, heavy surf, and severe currents at this meeting point of the Pacific Ocean and Philippine Sea.

Early Occupation Period 500 B.C. to A.D. 800

The people of the Marianas used pottery throughout the entire prehistoric period. Pottery and the technology of how to make it was brought to the Mariana Islands with the first settlers, and perhaps with subsequent emigrations. The pottery found on Guam is unique to the Mariana Islands and is an important direct connection to earlier generations.

Fragments of pottery vessels are found in nearly every archaeological site on Guam and are therefore, key to defining the cultural sequence. Pottery can be used to date sites and understand the changes that have occurred over the past several thousand years. Different vessel shapes, decoration, thickness, and tempering additives provide clues to the variety of food resources used and the social dynamics.

Ceramic vessels could have been used for cooking, transporting, storing, serving, and ceremonial purposes. For instance, preparing the swamp taro (*Cyrtosperma chamissonis*) for consumption involves peeling the tubers, cutting them in pieces and cooking them in coconut milk over a slow fire for at least three hours (Moore 1983:169). A ceramic vessel with an inverted or constricted rim would keep moisture from evaporating too rapidly during this long cooking session. Whereas, the thick walled (robust) type of vessel with open rim may have been used to boil saltwater to obtain salt. Ceramic vessels may have been required to soak the nuts of the fadang (*Cycas circinalis*) which were leached to remove the toxins prior to consumption. And, very large containers may have been used to make coconut syrup and oil or served as water catchment and storage devices.

Around 500 B.C., perhaps as a result of contact with other regions, the arrival of new groups of people, or changes in food resources the ceramic vessels changed. Large, thick-walled (robust) vessels and decoration with Lime Impressed patterns are found at several sites on Guam and other islands of the Marianas, suggesting that inter-island voyages were occurring during this time. Shell peelers are often found with the robust and Lime Impressed wares, indicating that tubers were part of the diet. Processing tubers is the first sign of agriculture. Additionally, shellfish, reef fish, and perhaps fruit bat were exploited (Moore 1983:219).

Another interesting point is that the pottery vessels, especially large ones, would be difficult to transport empty and very difficult if they were full. This suggests that activities took place within villages by 500 B.C. with work parties bringing collected foods or resources back to the settlement. The large size of the containers also may indicate that large quantities of foods were being processed and stored (Moore 1983:170).

Sometime after 150 B.C., pottery with lime inlaid designs disappeared. Moore speculates that because of an increasing population density the Chomorro did not travel as much and distinctive pottery designs became associated with individual villages or areas. Although vessels with decorated rims continued to be manufactured, the complexity of the designs decreased. Rims were decorated with simple indentations. Typical forms were open bowls with vertical or slightly flaring walls. The most common temper was mixed sands (Moore 1983:220).

Moore also notes variations in the vessel morphology over time. Pottery vessels with rounded bottoms and thinner walls are present in some of the early period assemblages. Some experimentation with tempering agents also occurred. These variations in pottery form may have been due to changes in diet caused by fewer resources or new food processing activities (Moore 1983:220)

Identifying the ceramic vessel forms at Ritidian would greatly enhance our understanding of the periods of use at the site. The Early Occupation Period is not well documented and archaeological evidence retrieved in a controlled study would be invaluable for addressing research questions regarding settlement of Ritidian. Studies of pottery from the Tarague site provides a wealth of information that can be associated with the pottery fragments found at Ritidian.

Late Prehistoric Period (aka. Latte Period) A.D. 800 to A.D. 1600

Liston observed that:

"Beginning roughly eleven hundred years ago, a number of changes began which would result in the distinctive Chamorro culture flourishing in the islands at the time of initial European contact in the early sixteenth century. The most important change (or at least the most distinctive) was the emergence of latte architecture. The columns are made from coral, limestone, and volcanic rock, usually cut from nearby reef or rock outcrops. Latte stones are composed of two parts, an upright shaft called a helege, *and a hemispherical cap called a* taza. *They are usually found in parallel rows of from six to 14 shafts. At present, latte are rarely found with* taza *in place above the* helege, *and only sometimes are the* helege *found in an upright position, time and events often combining to have toppled them" (Liston 1996:31).*

A 1565 diary entry by a member of the Miguel de Legazpi expedition, commissioned by the Spanish crown to sail from Mexico to the Philippines, provides a description of Chamorro housing:

"Their houses are high, well kept and well made. [They] stand the height of a man off the ground, atop large stone pillars, upon which they lay the flooring. . .These are the houses in which they sleep. They have other low houses, on the ground, where they cook and roast food. . .They have other large houses which are used for boathouses. These are not dwellings, but communal [houses] in which they store the large proas [double-ended sailing canoes with a single outrigger] and [which] shelter [their] canoes. In each barrio [a group of buildings forming a distinctive unit] there is one of these boathouses" (Plaza 1973:7 in Morgan 1988:119-120).

It is also suggested by some researchers that only the chief or higher status members of the community lived in the houses supported by latte. And, indeed the extra time and skill involved in building such a structure would have made it fairly costly. The latte expression became more elaborate over time and by the time they were recorded by the Spanish the taller helege may have been used for ceremonial or high-status individuals. However, placing living quarters on a raised platform supported with sturdy piers that would withstand storm surges and constructed with readily available limestone and coral seems like an obvious adaptation for beach front villages.

Russell and Fleming identified the Latte Period as being marked by "significant changes in ceramic manufacture, by a growing reliance on starchy plant foods, and by the expansion of settlement areas outside of the optimal coastal environments" (Russel and Fleming 1989b:3). This increasing reliance on starchy foods is evidenced by a number of stone and shell implements which appear more frequently during the Latte Period. Particularly prevalent are stone scrapers which may have been used for processing breadfruit, yam and taro, as well as several types of stone pounders. The emergence of more globular ceramic vessel forms, suitable for boiling and water storage, lends support to the increased utilization of starchy food plants. Although definitive data are lacking, there is some evidence to support the proposition that rice was being cultivated during the Latte period. Early ethnohistorical accounts document that rice was being grown on Guam at least by the middle decades of the sixteenth century. The presence of large stone mortars (*lusong*), found associated exclusively with latte sites, is circumstantial evidence for the cultivation of rice and perhaps for some form of contact with the islands of the Philippines late in prehistory. It has been proposed that these mortars were used for husking rice, a function they serve in the Philippines. They may also have been associated with processing the nut of the toxic cycad palm (*fadang*) (Russel and Fleming 1989b:4).

The development of the latte culture is closely tied with increasing population causing the marine resources such as fish and shellfish to be depleted. Therefore, reliance on plant foods expanded to maintain a stable food source. This also helps to explain why latte sites are found in various environmental settings, rather than just along the beaches. And, as marine resources declined they were used more intensively. Population growth and competition for resources, social stratification, and organized culturally proscribed behaviors are suggested by the latte stone architecture, burial practices, and village locations (Liston 1996:32-33).

Latte settlement sites in optimal coast locations are often built over early pre-latte habitation sites. The latte-structure habitations are also reflective of villages and often of extended family units with stratified classes. As competition for resources became more intense, so did aggressive behavior between villages. There is evidence that villages at Tarague and Ritidian were often at war with each other and that the Spanish missions caused even more friction between the two factions (Rogers 1995). The Chamorro did not maintain ownership property and land rights according to the mother's lineage (matrilineage). Rogers noted, "property rights extended beyond the shore and included portions of the fringe reefs, offshore submerged reefs, and fishing rights far out to sea. . . . Spaniards and later the Americans were unaware or indifferent to this custom" (Rogers 1995: 34, 36).

The Chamorro were a communal matrilineal culture where the married couple moved to the village of the groom's maternal uncle, not with the parents from either side. This social structure did not develop lineages or village headmen for more than one generation. The social network was complex and interwoven, but not set up to meet the hierarchical structure of the Spanish government. Religious beliefs were based on ancestor traditions and were village specific. The "political autonomy of Chamorro clans from each other did not lend itself to unified political or military efforts to maximize power. If a Chamorro was killed by Spaniards, only the members of that Chamorro's clan were obligated to redress the wrong; other clans would go on dealing with the Spaniards as if nothing had occurred" (Rogers 1995:39). This lack of national unity was confusing for the Spanish who were living in a very structured, power-maximizing system.

Latte-period sites date between 300 and 1200 years ago. The terminal date for latte occupation is based on the assumption that most prehistoric village sites were abandoned during the intensive colonization period that forced the native Chamorro into Spanish missions by about 1700 AD. "The *latte* period ended abruptly after the arrival of Father San Vitores in 1668" (Rogers 1995:33). The Spanish Period overlaps the Late Prehistoric Period by nearly a century (see Spanish Period, below).

Russel and Fleming observed that "by far, the most common and abundant artifact found on the surface at latte settlements is pottery, particularly in coastal areas. Less frequently found but still fairly common are stone and shell tools, and food remains" (Russel and Fleming 1989b:21).

One site type often found in association with latte settlements consists of caves and rockshelters. These are naturally created overhangs and cavities found along limestone clifflines. These features may contain midden deposits of subsistence remains and artifacts, and human burials. The exact function or functions of these sites are unclear although it can be assumed that they were possibly used as temporary habitation areas, as well as for mortuary activities. Also found at such sites (although very rarely) are petroglyphs and pictographs, attesting to the possible ritual function of these areas. It is likely that some of these sites were used by the latte settlement inhabitants as places of refuge during typhoons and tropical storms. It is also very likely that caves and rockshelters contain materials associated with use during the Pre-Latte Phase (Russel and Fleming 1989b:23).

Latte sites can be viewed as significant because of their potential to yield information concerning late prehistoric life. Chief among the research questions are changing subsistence strategies and social organization in response to a growing population. Of special interest are questions relating to the significance, origin, and technical specifications of latte architecture. Were latte the result of a more formal social differentiation? What food resources were important or available? Sites associated with the Late Prehistoric Period are numerous, but are especially susceptible to vandalism and destruction from modern development.

Latte stones have been identified within the Ritidian Unit, Guam NWR and reflect the presence of a large village and differential status occupants at some point in the past. Ritidian is known as a village site during contact with the Spanish, but it is not known if the latte structures were still being occupied at contact. A different type of architectural feature associated exclusively with northwestern coastal settlements is a prehistoric well, described as a stone lined depression:

These wells, faced with rock, were excavated to tap the shallow freshwater lens which floats atop the seawater. These features may be hard to identify due to post-abandonment filling...Former well features have been reported to measure 15 ft in diameter and appear to be lined with regular courses of stone to a depth of about 5 to 6 ft (Russel and Fleming 1989b:21).

Ceramic forms after A.D. 800 include jars with restricted openings and thickened rims. A variety of new surface treatments appeared including combed, trailed, incised, wiped, and lime plastered. Calcareous sands as tempering materials became nearly obsolete. The Latte occupation involved expansion into inland areas on Guam. Mortars are commonly associated with Latte sets and it seems likely that much of the food items were processed in the mortars. Evidence for other changes in the types of foods used is suggested by the greater numbers of fishhooks and shell adzes found in archaeological assemblages (Moore 1983:223).

Spanish Period 1521-1898

Guam's history was documented by a variety of visitors, each with their own biases, including representatives of the Spanish colonial government and military, religious emissaries, adventurers, participants of scientific expeditions, and the American military (Arago 1823; de la Corte y Ruano Caleron 1870; Corzet 1891; Garcia 1985; Stafford 1899-1901; Shurz 1959).

In March 1521 Magellan sighted the islands of Guam and Rota. The expedition traveled to the southwest coast and spent four days re-supplying their ships with fresh food and water. After receiving the supplies the natives considered a small skiff to be payment. Magellan's crew determined it was a theft and they burned the village and killed several natives. The ships set sail the next morning while the furious Islanders hurled slingstones and spears. In 1526 another ship was provisioned in the channel between Rota and Guam, this time iron was traded for food and water. By the time Spain claimed Guam in 1565, the indigenous people of the Marianas would be called *Chamurres*, the Spanish version of the local term, *chamorri*, which is what the islanders called members of their high caste (Rogers 1995:6). In January 1565, the Legazpi Expedition landed near Umatac Bay and stayed for about a month. This expedition gathered a great deal of information about the island including the name of *Goam*. The Legazpi expedition formally claimed the entire Mariana archipelago as a possession of the Spanish Crown and established the route between Acapulco to Manila through the Mariana chain between Rota and Guam. Legazpi continued on to claim the Philippines for the Spanish Crown (Liston 1996:33). Guam was well situated to re-provision the ships, but lacked the spices, silks, gold, and sandalwood that were valued items in the Orient. Visits to Guam were routine and brief until the late 1600s when Spanish Jesuit missionaries arrived.

In 1668, Father Luis Diego San Vitores arrived with a detachment of five Jesuits, a garrison of Spanish troops, and a group of lay catechists. A mission was established in Agana, the largest village on the island. After a few years of essential servitude the Chamorro began resisting Spanish control. During the command of Don Damian de Esplana, harsh punishments were commonly meted out to the villagers and additional churches were constructed to convert and control the native Chamorro. The missionaries tried to settle the inter-village conflict between Tarague and Ritidian by constructing churches at both villages and controlling the populations. Catechism records show 500 adults attending the Tarague church and 400 attending the Ritidian church. While these numbers may be inflated, it suggests that this area was densely populated (Liston 1996:35).

"A wooden church was built on this site [Ritidian] sometime between August and November, 1674. In the first part of 1675, the original church was torn down and a new, larger church was built on the site, together with a priests' house and a school for boys. And, in the latter part of 1675, a school for girls was added" (Haynes and Wuerch 1993:13). However, the Chamorro along the northern coast were not used to religious service to the priest and began to rebel. Tension between the villagers at Tarague and Ritidian also probably led to the uprising that ended with burning of the church and schools later that year (Haynes and Wuerch 1993:13). Another report described the incident:

> On 8 December 1675, Chamorros in the supposedly converted village of Ritidian killed Brother Pedro Diaz and his assistant when they tried to suppress uritao activities. The Chamorros then burned the church and the priests' residence, and all the villagers took off in proas for Rota to escape the reprisal that they knew would come. The reprisal came from converted Chamorros in the nearby village of Tarague, who took advantage of the situation to settle an old clan revenge against their neighbors, burning the Ritidian houses and cutting down all fruit trees (Rogers 1995:60).

In other accounts, the Spanish revenged this by setting fire to the nearby Chamorro village of Ritidian (Driver 1992:44). Whoever set fire to the village may never be known and it is also unclear if a village continued to exist at Ritidian after this event. The records are clear, however, that the rival village at Tarague was still occupied and its church continued to serve the natives.

The Spanish missionaries found it difficult to convert the Chamorro and from about 1671 to 1695 there was nearly continuous guerilla warfare between the Catholic missionaries and native Chamorro people. Unfortunately, during this period many villages were destroyed and in particular the latte stone houses were torn down, because they represented the chief or high status personage of the village. In this way the Spanish missionaries tried to control the Chamorro and force them into the Christian lifestyle.

In 1680, a shift in the Spanish control of Guam occurred when additional military arrived and established a formal government with the title of governor which was separate from the clergy. There were 60 Spanish governors, or acting governors of the Mariana Islands who served for varying lengths of time at Agana on Guam, most served for about two years (Nelson and Nelson 1992:113). Soon after this change in organization, the missionaries began a program of moving all the Chamorro people into more centralized villages where stricter control by the government and military authority was achieved. A report of hostilities in 1681 indicates that the Ritidian Church had been rebuilt and was in operation, because the priest attempted to flee to Rota and was caught and hanged by the villagers (Rogers 1995:67-68).

The twenty-five year period of "pacification" reduced the native population to a small fraction of the approximately 12,000 estimated for Guam in 1668 to fewer than 2,000 by 1690 (Rogers 1995:70). Chamorro men were killed in higher numbers as they fought against the Spanish military. Then in 1700 a smallpox epidemic further reduced the population. In 1710, the first census was taken and only 3,678 Chamorro were recorded, mostly women and children. Finally, in 1769, the Jesuits were expelled from the Marianas by Carlos III of Spain and replaced by Augustinian Recollects, who with far fewer priests lessened the extent of their religious instruction (Liston 1996:39).

The Spanish governor between 1771 and 1774, Don Mariano Tobias was one of the few leaders who attempted to educate and re-introduce agricultural practices to the Chamorro. "To him is ascribed the distinction of re-introducing the cultivation of rice, maize, and surgarcane, of importing cacao, indigo, and cotton plants on the island as well as every variety of European vegetables, . . . watermelons. . . and mangoes, . . . which were brought from Manilla" (Nelson and Nelson 1992:114). Don Mariano also introduced deer into Guam and Rota from the Philippines (Thompson 1932:63).

The 1800s were transition years as the Spanish government became more settled and Guam's port cities were visited by whaling ships and European explorers. The latter part of the century was marked by natural disasters, increasing visits from European countries, the establishing of an American consul, and the continued oppressive control of the Spanish rule. The demographics of Guam changed throughout the Spanish Period, as Chamorro populations decreased and the Spanish government imported workers from the Carolina Islands, Philippines, China, and Japan, and other Pacific Islands to fill jobs because there were not enough Chamorro laborers. The common culture on Guam became a mixture of ancient Chamorro ways tempered by Spanish Catholicism and further enlivened by the diverse traditions of the southwest Pacific (Liston 1996:41). It is interesting to note, however, that the Chamorro language continued to be used as the primary family language.

Sites that are associated with the Spanish Period include forts, outposts, and missions. Many of these were destroyed during World War II or by storms, and those that survived are now threatened by new development. Early mission sites such as the one at Ritidian are extremely rare and have not been well documented. As noted previously, the Ritidian church was burned in about 1675 but was active again by 1681. The continued aggression between Chamorro and Spanish missionaries ended in about 1700 as the population decreased and Spanish rule expanded. No mention of the mission at Ritidian or a Chamorro village is made after this period and it is assumed that the area was essentially abandoned. Neither ownership nor land use during this period has been documented.

First American Period 1898-1941
The Spanish residing on Guam were unaware of the declaration of war between Spain and the United States, and were taken by surprise when the cruiser USS *Charleston* steamed into Apra Harbor and opened fire on the fort. In fact, the Spanish Governor thought the ship was merely saluting the fort and was planning to fire a return salute but was not prepared with loaded weapons. Luckily a battle was avoided because of their unpreparedness and the island was captured for the United States without incident (Nelson and Nelson 1992:139-140).

The initial transition to a United States possession was not entirely smooth. After capture, the Spanish military governor and troops were removed, but no official government was established for fourteen months, creating a chaotic situation. The official ownership of the island was determined by treaty and Executive Order, although not with any input from the local population. Rather than establishing a civil authority on Guam, President McKinley placed the island under the control of the Department of the Navy (Nelson and Nelson 1992:143-144). Captain Richard P. Leary arrived in August 1899 to serve as the first American governor of Guam. The transition also was the first time the islands in the Marianas chain were ruled separately. For the following 42 years the U.S. Navy was in charge of governing Guam. The years were turbulent as the Navy tried to establish order, alter many of the Catholic traditions, and set up a democracy where most of the population didn't speak English and lacked education or adequate health services.

The Navy automatically acquired all Spanish crown lands, although the precise locations of the property boundaries had not been accurately recorded so there was general confusion regarding land status. There was no complete cadastral survey of Guam until the 1990s, which contributed to the confusion regarding property boundaries and caused protracted litigation and fraud (Rogers 1995:130). The Navy also constructed roads, built schools, improved sanitation and water quality, and revised the land and taxation laws. During this period camphor, Jamaica mangoes, naval oranges, vanilla, black pepper, coral vines, fire trees, blue water lilies and various other plants and shrubs were introduced by Lieutenant Stafford (Nelson and Nelson 1992:150). Coconut palms grew well on the island and nearly every part of the tree and fruit was used. Production of copra, the dried meat, of the coconut, was promoted as an industry base to help lift the island's economic condition.

In the early 1900s Japanese entrepreneurs acquired or leased large tracts of land to develop as coconut plantations. The Japanese would then transport the copra back to Japan for final processing into the variety of products including soap, cosmetic items, and fuel oil. Processing coconut for copra required a fairly rudimentary system of air drying the cracked nuts. Drying racks on elevated platforms covered with an A-frame roof of corrugated metal or canvas was a common feature at the plantations. The U.S. Government tried to limit the Japanese by restricting their ability to own land to just five years, but by the 1910s Japanese business interests dominated the economy of Guam. A plantation was established at Tarague and possibly at Ritidian during this period. In 1917 the Atkins, Kroll and Company of San Francisco acquired the Tarague plantation (Liston 1996:47).

World War I had little effect on Guam, except to increase the demand in Japan for copra, and production doubled. The U.S. military increased personnel only slightly.

From 1898 until 1941 the whole island was one enormous naval station, operated principally in the interests of the United States by a series of governors who ran the island as they would a warship (Kraft 1961:3). The economy stabilized after the turn of the century for most of Guam's population. The urban center of Agana grew as many residents found employment with the U.S. Navy. The Commercial Pacific Cable Company established a station on Guam in 1903 to link with Manila and Midway. Guam's Cable Station was nearly identical to the one on Midway, but was abandoned after World War II and is no longer standing. In 1935, Pan American airlines constructed a hotel and began commercial air service to the Far East with refueling/ rest stops at Honolulu, Midway, Wake, Guam, and Manila.

Following World War I, Japan secured a mandate over all the former German islands north of the equator, which left Guam nearly surrounded by Japanese holdings (Kraft 1961:6). By 1936, world conditions in the Far East were unstable, but no clear policy for Guam's future was formulated. With the Depression devastating the U.S. mainland, little attention was given to this remote Pacific Island. The Depression caused a drop in copra prices and the plantation at Tarague was closed.

At Ritidian there is no recorded evidence of copra production from the pre-World War II era. However, the land ownership records have not been reviewed. Judging by the successful plantation at Tarague it is likely that a coconut plantation was also planted at Ritidian. The 1940 census records noted that "the northeast plateau (now Anderson AFB) had 80 farms averaging 17.6 acres each" suggesting that other areas besides Tarague were farmed (Bureau of the Census 1951:1, in Carrico et al. 1993:26). Also by 1940, over one-third of the island was owned by the naval government, a 30 percent increase since the U.S. took over in 1899 (Liston 1996:51).

Japanese Period 1941-1944

Just hours after the attack on Pearl Harbor on 7 December 1941, Japanese forces numbering 5,000 invaded Guam. The American naval government surrendered after a brief fire fight, as it was ill-prepared to repulse a Japanese invasion…Guam was essentially one link in the chain of Japanese bases that were positioned to cripple the American fleet should it enter the western Pacific.

During the 2½ year Japanese occupation, the northern section of Guam was not heavily fortified due to the natural protection of the high cliffs. The Japanese built a few pillbox-type defensive positions, lookouts, and may have improved caves for defensive positions. The War Department reported that "the 2d Battalion, 18th Infantry Regiment of the Japanese Imperial Army was known to be located in northern Guam for the period of June and July 1944, but saw no action" (War Dept. 1946:21). The Battalion was garrisoned at Tarague. No fortifications have been identified at Ritidian.

U.S. forces landed at two approaches on 21 July 1944 and began the conquest to recapture Guam. After the initial beach invasion at Apra Harbor, the military began a drive to the outer edges of the island to complete the re-occupation. The 22nd Marines and the 1st Provisional Brigade advanced towards Ritidian Point, and by mid-afternoon on 8 August, Ritidian Point was reached in the wake of a series of aerial bombing attacks (Liston 1996:54). A sketch map of the final drive shows a road to the Ritidian Light, on the cliff top, along with a road down to the beach, near today's western refuge boundary. The last official battle for the recapture of Guam was joined on August 10th at Tarague where Japanese and U.S. tanks met and the U.S. forces were victorious. Although the battle was officially over, small skirmishes continued between Japanese stragglers and the U.S. military. "Between August 1944 and the end of WWII a year later, 8,500 Japanese were either killed or captured on Guam" (O'Brian 1966:43).

The remote northern fringe of Guam, characterized by its limestone cliffs with caves and fresh water and thick jungle, created an advantageous area for surviving Japanese military to hide and await the return of their countrymen. The U.S. military tried to convince the Japanese to surrender voluntarily, but this was seen as dishonorable and many men committed suicide.

At Ritidian, the gun barrel and firing mechanism of a Japanese type 99 short rifle was recovered from an archaeological test unit located along the base of the limestone terrace directly south of the main NAVFAC security compound during a 1987 excavation. The rifle was similar to the classic type 38 Arisaka 6.5mm that the Japanese adopted for use in 1942:

> *Since no battles were fought in the Ritidian Point area during 1944-1945, there is a strong possibility that this particular type 99 short rifle was discarded, buried or remained from a suicide of a Japanese soldier. X-ray of this weapon revealed that two live bullets remain in the magazine. This lends credence to the hypothesis that the rifle was hidden or buried for possible future use…A surviving Japanese soldier in the Ritidian area would have been part of the Japanese 31st Army Infantry units (Kurashina, et al. 1990:99).*

Sixty-seven men surrendered with Lt. Col. Hideyuki Takeda in September 1945 near Tarague and 46 more soldiers surrendered the following year (Kurashina, et al. 1990:99). Of course it is also possible that the gun was lost during the period of Japanese occupation, perhaps forgotten during a reconnaissance mission. Additional survey of the cliff face and caves is needed to determine if Japanese soldiers took shelter in this rugged environment.

Second American Period 1944-to present

At the close of WWII in 1945, Guam was heavily damaged by the bombings and invasions. Rebuilding infrastructure was a high priority. In 1949, control of Guam passed to the U.S. Department of the Interior, and a civilian government was established. On 1 August 1950, by an Act of Congress, Guam became an unincorporated organized Territory of the United States through the passage of the Organic Act. Congressional --although not constitutional-- citizenship was conferred upon the residents of Guam (Liston 1996:60). Distribution of lands followed, with the U.S. government retaining about 36% of the land base.

At the northern end of the island an air field had been developed and was reactivated after the re-occupation of Guam. In 1947, North Field was redesignated by the newly formed U.S. Air Force as North Guam Air Force Base (AFB) and in 1949 the base became Andersen AFB (AAFB), in honor of Brigadier General James Roy Andersen, who was lost on a flight to Hawaii in February of 1945 (Liston 1996:60-61). AAFB continued to develop and was strategically located for the Korean Conflict and Vietnam War.

Guam was essentially a military installation with controlled access until 1962 when restrictions were relaxed and tourists, including Japanese tourists, were allowed to enter Guam. Tourism has grown dramatically over the years with huge hotels and shopping mall constructed along the coastal fringe, especially near Agana and Tumon Bay. The U.S. military continues to be a dominant presence on the island.

"The Navy facilities were commissioned as NAVFAC Guam in December 1968 as part of Task Group 30.4 of the Commander, Oceanographic System, Pacific (COMOCEANSYSPAC). The site was originally used by the Army as a Topo Scatter Communications Facility. There were 10 buildings associated with NAVFAC Guam, including Building 800 the main Operations building. Public Works functions were in Buildings 801 and 802, and Administrative activities in Building 803" (Kurashina et al. 1990:51). The buildings were of simple blok concrete construction. Other facilities included a gate house, water tanks, storage, and outdoor recreational facilities including a softball field, and a beach pavilion with picnic tables. No family housing or barracks were constructed as these facilities were available elsewhere on the island.

In 1993, the Navy transferred property at Ritidian Point to the U.S. Fish and Wildlife Service for inclusion in the newly created Guam NWR. The Ritidian Unit of the Refuge retains several buildings constructed by the Navy, including the Administration office (803), Operations building (800), Public Works buildings (801 and 802) and two gate houses. Building 803 has been converted for use as the Refuge offices. The antennas, beach structures, and lesser buildings have been removed.

Cultural Resource Investigations

Summary of Previous Surveys and Research

A summary of previous surveys and research directly associated with what is now Guam NWR is provided in Table 1. The first professional archaeological studies of Guam and the Mariana Islands were sponsored in the 1920s by the Bishop Museum in Honolulu. Subsequent fieldwork, both on a landscape level and specific to Ritidian, has been conducted by the military, the National Park Service, and most recently, the Service. For those projects dating 1990 and later, the survey location information is adequate for mapping purposes. The total area of the Ritidian Unit for which documentation of systematic survey exists is approximately 14 acres, as presented in Figure 3.

1925 - Hans Hornbostel

Hans Hornbostel surveyed Ritidian and excavated a fairly extensive area, in addition to investigating other islands in the Marianas. Hornbostel's work provided the first documented evidence of a Chamorro village and Spanish mission on the beach at Ritidian. Nearly 10,000 artifacts collected by Hornbostel constitute the Marianas collection curated by the Department of Anthropology at the Bishop Museum.

1932 - Laura Mead Thompson

In 1932, Dr. Laura Thompson published a synthesis of Hornbostel's collection, photographs, and field notes entitled *Archaeology of the Mariana Islands* as Bishop Museum Bulletin 100.

1947 - Douglas Osborne

In 1947, Douglas Osborne, an officer assigned to the Military Police Battalion on Guam, conducted a series of surveys and limited excavations around the island. He found little evidence of lattes intact on the beaches, but observed more intact evidence on the inland rivers in the southern half of Guam. The beach sites appear to have been heavily impacted by the war years and perhaps even earlier by the Spanish. Osborne briefly visited the northern coast and notes that "from Oruno around the whole northern to northeastern coast on the island there is a continual archaeological area" (Osborne 1947:47 in Liston 1996:65). Osborne also described several small latte groups at Ritidian in a state of poor preservation (Osborne 1947:47 in Liston 1996:67).

1952 - Erik Reed

Reed surveyed areas of Guam for the U.S. National Park Service with an aim to protect, preserve, and possibly develop prehistoric and historic sites for interpretation. He focused on relocating the sites identified by Hornbostel and Osborne rather than making new discoveries. Reed did not relocate the latte set at Ritidian. However, he did describe the surviving Spanish structure as being located on the beach strand below Ritidian Point.

1977 - Fred Reinman

In 1977, F. R. Reinman, sponsored by a National Science Foundation Grant and the Field Museum of Natural History in Chicago, conducted a comprehensive survey of large portions of Guam and test excavated five sites. He also prepared standardized site forms for the archaeological sites he visited.

1990 - Kurashina et al

Archaeological investigations conducted by the Navy in 1987-1989 in compliance with the National Historic Preservation Act revealed pockets of intact cultural deposits, several burials, and areas that had been truncated by previous building projects (Kurashina et al. 1990). Based on their field efforts, Kurashina noted that while cultural deposits exist close to the forebeach, the western portion of the midbeach appears to have been the location of the main prehistoric occupation.

Date	Investigator/ Organization	Title/ Location	Methods	Results
1924	Hornbostel, H	Unpublished field notes and artifact catalogs on file at Bernice Pauahi Bishop Museum Library	Survey and excavation at several locations throughout the Marianas Islands	17th century Spanish church ("blockhouse" or Casa Real) No evidence observed since 1952 Lattes, burials
1932	Thompson, L.M.	Archaeology of the Mariana Islands	Published review and synthesis of Hornbostel's notes and collections	n/a
1947	Osborne, D	Chamorro Archaeology	Survey and limited excavations around Guam	"Casa Real," chapel or religious school
1952	Reed, E.K.	War in the Pacific: Archaeology and History of Guam	Survey, revisited previously documented sites	Identified sites no longer visible since previous surveys
1977	Reinman, F	An Archaeological Survey and Preliminary Text Excavations on the Island of Guam, Mariana Islands, 1965-1966.	Systematic site survey and recording on standardized site forms	Ritidian Point – 66-08-0612 (5 latte groups)) Pajon Site – 66-08-0613 (6 latte groups)
1990	Kurashina, H. et al	Archaeological Investigations at the Naval Facility (NAVFAC) Ritidian Point, Guam, Mariana Islands	Monitoring and excavation	Lithics, human remains, pottery, fish and shellfish, shell artifacts
1997a	Olmo, R. International Archaeological Institute, Inc.	Archaeological Assessment of Reptile Recovery Project Area – Letter Report Location: Ritidian Point	Survey	Location 1: no artifacts, organically enriched sands Location 2: surface scatter and midden including: adze fragments, ground stone fragments, food shell, pottery (Latte Period). Appears to be village site.
1997b	Olmo R. International Archaeological Institute, Inc.	Snake Trap Installation – Letter Report	Monitoring	Midden deposit and human remains
2000	Dixon, B International Archaeological Institute, Inc.	Archaeological Survey and Testing at a Proposed Brown Tree Snake Pen, Guam NWR, Ritidian Point, Territory of Guam, Mariana Islands Location: Ritidian Point	Survey Limited subsurface testing	Buried post WWII concrete pad Sparse subsurface prehistoric ceramic and shell layer
2005	Carson, M International Archaeological Institute, Inc.	Letter Report: Salvage of Disturbed Human Skeletal Remains at Guam NWR, Ritidian, Guam Location: Ritidian Point	Salvage excavation	Human remains in two pits disturbed by pig or human activity Coarse potsherds characteristic of Latte Period; thin, fine potsherds that could predate AD 1000; shell adze fragment; flaked volcanic stone and limestone; midden and ecofacts

Table 1. Summary of previous research and surveys associated with the Ritidian Unit.

1997a and 1997b - Richard Olmo, IARII

Under contract with the U.S. Fish and Wildlife Service, Richard Olmo conducted a Section 106 survey (1997a) and a monitoring project (1997b) for the development of brown tree snake control facilities and research areas. The results of these projects were presented in a letter report format.

2000 - Boyd Dixon, IARII

A small testing project was undertaken in 2000 at Ritidian prior to construction of several snake pens (Dixon 2000). The project area was east of the compound of buildings, within a closed portion of the refuge where antennas had been stationed. No features or artifact concentrations were identified and it appears that this area of the beach strand was not heavily occupied or that storms and construction disturbances have obliterated the evidence.

Figure 3. Previously surveyed areas of the Ritidian Unit, Guam NWR.

2005 - Michael Carson, IARII

Archaeological salvage of disturbed human skeletal remains which involved: mapping the project area; recovery of loose skeletal elements, traditional artifacts, and midden on the surface; sifting through 1/8" wire mesh of loose dirt; and controlled excavation in two pits that appeared most likely to contain in situ burial remains.The location for this project plotted on Figure 3 is approximate. It will be updated with UTM coordinates when available

Other Relevant Studies

A study of the nearby Tarague Embayment provides an excellent data set for comparing with Ritidian (Liston et al. 1996). The intensive level of historical research, survey, and testing has revealed a long and complex cultural history exhibiting many parallels with the Ritidian Unit of Guam NWR. Especially useful is the documentation prepared for each site and detailed descriptions of features and site constituents.

Documented Cultural Resources

Sites Located on the Refuge

There are two recorded archaeological sites on Guam NWR -- Ritidian Site and Pajon Point Site. Both could more accurately be described as "districts," characterized as they are by multiple locales and feature types representing a broad spectrum of prehistoric and historic periods. A third location – though it has a long history of informal documentation and has been described in relation to both the recorded sites -- does not appear to be officially a part of either one. For the purposes of this overview, therefore, the discussion of the "Mission Site" will be presented independently of the recorded sites. The locations of these sites are presented in Figure 4.

Ritidian Site (66-08-0012)

Status: Listed to the Guam Register of Historic Places on August 14, 1974, as Ritidian Dededo. Nominated but not listed on National Register of Historic Places.

Description: The National Register nomination form for the Ritidian Site describes its boundaries thus: "the site covers the entire beach between the 20 to 40 foot contours from Achae Point north to the edge of the ... area below Ritidian Point where the U.S. Naval Communications Station has been erected...The sea forms the western boundary and the cliffline the Eastern. The area slopes gently to the cliffline which rises abruptly to a height of 600 ft (Moore 1979).

The Ritidian area, situated on a rocky coastal shelf, is the site of a large prehistoric Chamorro settlement with numerous *latte* remains, a stone-lined well, mortars, midden mounds, tools, and heavy pottery concentrations. Hornbostel's investigations and testing revealed intact cultural deposits and burials associated with latte stones.

Thompson, working from Hornbostel's notes, describes one of the caves at Ritidian Point:

> *Excavations below the surface of the floor of a cave at Ritidian, Guam revealed the following stratification: a layer of bat manure 1.5 feet thick superimposed upon a 1-foot layer of fragments from the walls of the cave; under these fragments, a 1.5-foot stratum of sand containing scattered human bones, potsherds, stone and shell implements, and fragments of charcoal. No drawings were found in this cave (Thompson 1932:20 in Liston 1996:65).*

In 1952, when Reed attempted to relocate sites first identified by Hornbostel he was unsuccessful in locating the latte set at Ritidian,

Several large storms and construction of the Naval facility in the late-1960s obliterated any remaining surface features at the center of the point. In 1977, Reinman noted five sets of latte in varying stages of disturbance in the southern half of the site area between Achae Point and Ritidian Point. Reinman also observed features and artifact concentrations that he included in a site record which was recognized by the Guam Register of Historic Places as an important cultural area. The site was listed on Guam's Register of Historic Places on August 14, 1974. A subsequent nomination for the National Register of Historic Places was prepared and submitted in 1980. The office of the Chief, Branch of Registration returned the nomination along with a list of items to be addressed prior to resubmittal. It does not appear that the changes were made nor was the nomination resubmitted.

Kurashina also uncovered burials during testing for improvements at the Naval facility on Ritidian (Kurashina 1991). Kurashina identified one large shaped limestone rock that might be associated with a latte, but it was not in a context that could support the theory conclusively. A gun barrel and firing mechanism of a Japanese type 99 short rifle was recovered from an archaeological test unit located along the base of the limestone terrace directly south of the main NAVFAC security compound. It is possible that the gun was lost during the period of Japanese occupation, or by one of the survivors after the end of the war. Kurashina's investigations suggest that while the Naval facility may have damaged the integrity of the archaeological deposit, it has not completely obliterated it. The potential to recover information about the early Chamorro and initial missionary period on Guam appears to be high.

During the small testing project undertaken in 2000 at Ritidian prior to construction of several snake pens, excavation revealed:

> "the partially buried remains of three post-WWII concrete structures; one probably 'deadman' with three metal cable supports, and two small concrete pads. Fragments of metal roofing and possible cable supports were located near the easternmost concrete pad just outside the northeast corner of the pen, and a pile of discarded wooden posts was located in the approximate center of the snake pen area. Limited subsurface testing was then conducted at regular 10 m intervals along the boundaries of the proposed 20 x 20 m pen where the trench for the wall footings would be placed. The purpose of the excavation was to determine the horizontal and vertical extent of any subsurface deposits, as well as the time period and nature of buried prehistoric remains. One test unit encountered the buried remains of a post-WWII concrete pad beneath several layers of probable storm disturbed sands. The remaining seven test units revealed the presence of one thin but undisturbed prehistoric horizon situated between two layers of natural dune sands. This cultural layer contained very sparse remains of traditional ceramics and marine shell, indicating that the snake pen area was located at the fringes of a prehistoric habitation zone during the Latte Phase, between approximately AD 1000 and European Contact in 1521" (Dixon 2000:iii).

No features or artifact concentrations were identified in this area. It appears that this area of the beach strand was not heavily occupied or that storms and construction disturbances have obliterated the evidence.

Pajon Point Site (66-08-0013)

Status: Listed on the Guam Register of Historic Places on July 3, 1974. Nominated but not listed on the National Register of Historic Places

Description: Located on the eastern side of Ritidian Point and extending toward Pajon Point are the concentrated remains of a village-type assemblage. The entry for the Pajon Point site in the National Register Form indicates that disturbed latte structures and extensive midden deposits are found at the site and it appears to be a prehistoric Chamorro settlement. Reinman identified the site and completed the documentation for Guam Register of Historic Places status. The site is, by consensus, deemed a historic property because of its research potential, but while it was submitted for listing on the NRHP in 1980, the Chief of the Branch of Registration returned it with a list of items to be addressed prior to resubmittal. It does not appear that the changes were ever made or the form resubmitted. It is therefore not formally listed on the National Register of Historic Places.

Documentation of the Pajon Point site is extremely limited. The types of artifacts, presence of features, and location of latte stones are not detailed on a sketch map. While the Ritidian Point site has been tested several times with subsurface information indicating a long period of use and complexity of the deposits, no similar studies have been conducted at Pajon Point. The site is within a restricted zone and may contain intact deposits, so its research potential, while not adequately evaluated, may be high.

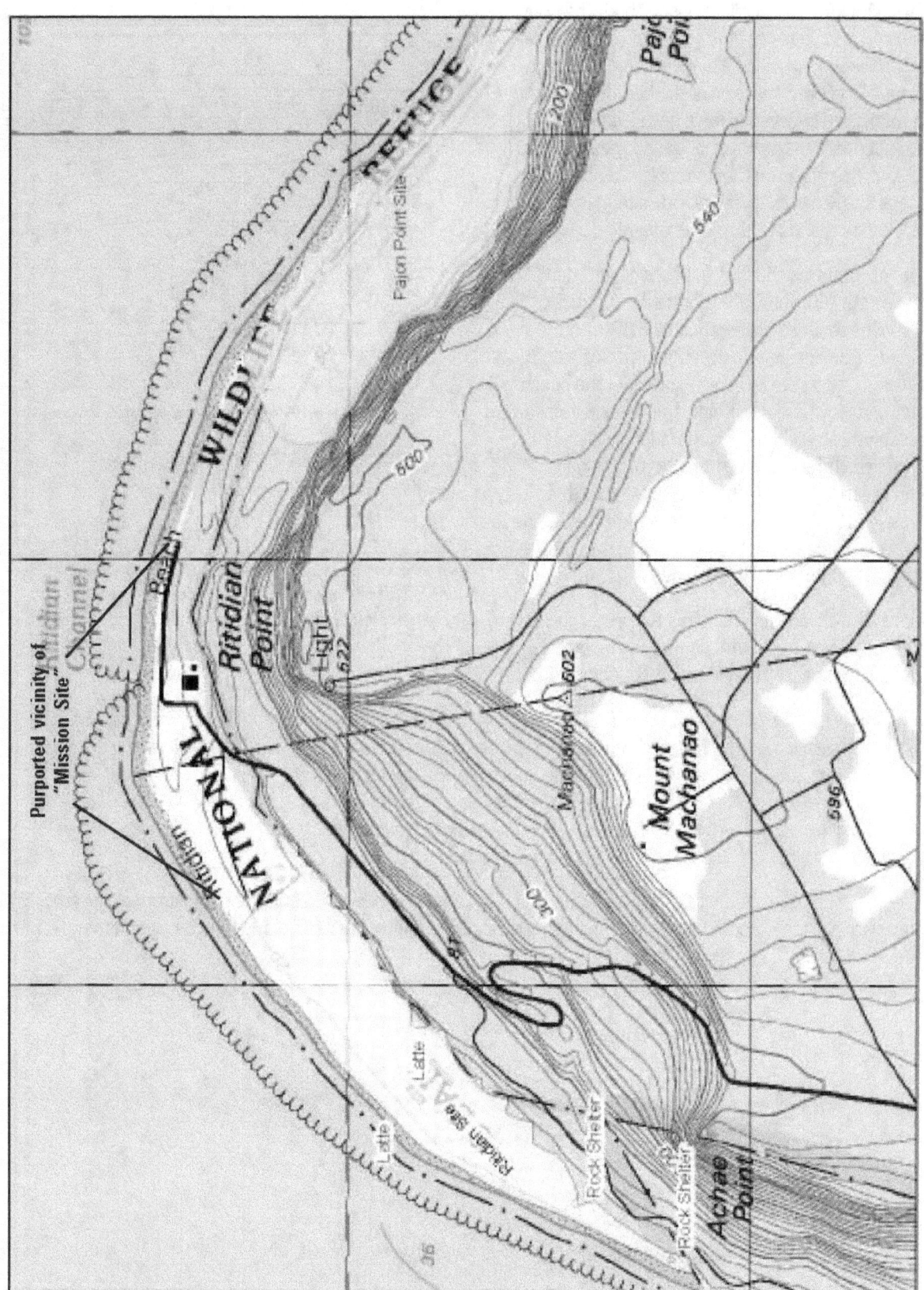

Figure 4. Recorded sites on Ritidian Unit of Guam NWR.

"Mission Site"

Status: remains have not been relocated, additional research and testing is necessary

Description: The nominations for both the above sites make reference to the remains of a Spanish structure, a "mission," "blockhouse," or "Casa Real." However, the area of the beach where the remains are believed to have been located is not included within the physical boundaries of either site, as described on the nominations (nor do the maps in the nominations provide adequate information to make any determination).

Hornbostel was the first to describe and mark the relative location of the structure (Figure 5). Osborne revisted the location in 1947, as did Reed in 1952, when he described the surviving Spanish structure as being located on the beach strand below Ritidian Point. Reed found ruins of an oblong stone building 39 ft in length and 15 ft wide which he described as a "typical small church structure," with a doorway located at the west end and three windows along each side; the east end had no opening and the 6 ½ ft tall walls were 29-30 in. thick (Reed 1952).

In his list of recommendations for protection and interpretation of Guam's significant resources, Reed says of the "Casa Real" at Ritidian Point:

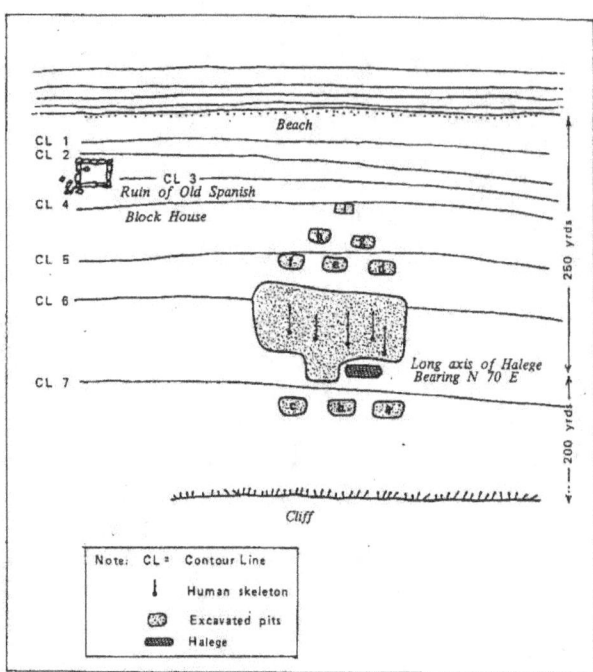

Figure 5. Sketch map showing the location of Latte 7-20-23 Ritidian (Halege), Hornbostel's excavations and the Spanish block house at Ritidian, after Hornbostel's field map. Reproduced from Kurashina, 1990.

> *This very interesting ruin, close to a house belonging to Juan Castro of Toto and presumably on his property, certainly should be acquired, protected, and preserved, if at all possible, even if it is not surprisingly old as suggested above. No special interpretive or other development, beyond clearing it and keeping it brushed off, is recommended at the present time; but it could well be designated nevertheless as a territorial historical park for primarily protective purposes." (Reed 1952)*

The following managememt plan outlines future steps for research and testing in the vicinity of the structure with the aim to positively identifying its location and defining the site boundaries in relation to the other recorded sites.

Management Plan/Recommendations

Guam NWR encompasses a fairly undeveloped region of Guam and retains many features related to early human use of the island and the initial contact between Chamorro and Spanish cultures. Protecting this legacy and developing a plan to investigate and interpret the cultural heritage represented at the Ritidian Unit is one of the goals of this study.

Data Gaps

There are several areas in our research where what we know is overshadowed by what we do not know. Therefore, we are recommending that management goals are directed toward filling the gaps in the information.

For instance, archaeological studies beginning in the 1920s found substantial remains of the latte-period and a Spanish Mission at Ritidian. In the 1930s and 1940s much of northern Guam was used for Copra production. Of the 80 farms reported in the 1940 census it is unknown if any were located at Ritidian. Potential evidence of copra production at Ritidian could include remnant stands of coconut palms and artifacts relating to Japanese workers. Further research is warranted to fill this void in our knowledge of land use on the Ritidian Unit.

Activities at Ritidian during World War II have not been documented, although a Japanese rifle was found (Kurashina et al. 1990:99) Survey of the cliff face and caves may reveal evidence of use during this period. After World War II, the beach area was cleared and several U.S. Navy buildings were constructed, many of which are still in use. Unfortunately, the area cleared by the Navy may be the area where the Spanish Mission was located. We will need to excavate through the disturbed surface to determine the exact location of the mission. The records and collections of the Hornbostel study are stored at the Bishop Museum in Honolulu and reviewing the original maps and field notes might also shed more light on the location of the mission.

The location of the Spanish Mission is also important to establish because it is not included in the boundaries drawn for the Ritidian archaeological site (66-08-0012). The National Register nomination form includes it in the discussion of the importance of the site, but lacks the crucial bit of information about its location. At this juncture we do not know where the mission was located and therefore cannot determine it's integrity, nor can we protect this important resource or manage if effectively. The Spanish Mission is emblematic of all of the features at the Ritidian and Pajon Point sites where records and descriptions of features suggest the importance of the site and capture the public's imagination, but are so poorly documented that we do not have the tools to protect or share the information effectively. Management of the site is nearly impossible under these circumstances.

Revising the National Register nomination forms for both Ritidian and Pajon Point sites is obviously needed. The boundaries for both sites appear to be randomly drawn with no justification or discussion of the features that they encompass. Both nominations were rejected by the National Park Service because of the unsubstantiated boundary. One of the primary goals of the research and fieldwork recommended below is to determine the size, boundary, and constituents of the Ritidian and Pajon Point sites. The information potential is good, but our actual knowledge is very poor.

And, while our knowledge of the cultural resources at the Ritidian site is meager, our knowledge of the Pajon Point site is even more scant. The Pajon Point side of the refuge has been closed to the public and was closed to most military since the 1950s. Therefore, no survey since the 1920s has been completed and the information about the integrity of features has not been updated. While we know even less about Pajon Point, we are not recommending survey and testing procedures until the Ritidian site has been completed.

This recommendation is based on the assumption that Pajon Point will remain closed to the public and therefore protected from most intrusions. If the management of Pajon Point anticipates changes to include a public use or is opened to the public then the concern for investigating, recording, and revising the National Register nomination would be raised to a high level of priority. The same procedures would be needed including, survey of the Lower and Middle Pajon Point Units and test excavation of features identified to define integrity. The boundary would need to be clearly demarked and justified. And, the information collected could be added to the interpretation of the refuge.

Another recommendation is for the protection and appropriate treatment of the cultural features and exposed surface artifacts on Ritidian and Pajon Point. The caves located at Ritidian contain cultural features and artifacts that are fragile and finite. They need to be protected and interpreted to the public. The survey and testing of the caves should lead to a management strategy for installing fencing and protective ground cover, and defining a tour route that will provide the public with access to the caves without damaging the cultural remains. Artifacts such as ceramic vessel fragments litter the surface along the trail to the cave and on the beach strand. The fragmented vessels provide the cultural chronology of prehistoric use at Ritidian and are therefore a valuable resource that requires protection and further study. Restoring cultural features like one of the wells and perhaps a latte structure could be a strong link to a dynamic interpretive program.

Recommendations for the long-term management of Guam NWR's cultural resources are three-fold. First, conduct research and fieldwork to identify and explain the features of the site; second, protect the features from damage and deterioration; and three, interpret and possibly restore elements of the site to provide the public access to the rich history that is present at this site.

Summary of Tasks

Guam NWR has a critical need for specific information regarding the location and integrity of cultural resources within the refuge boundaries in order to appropriately preserve and protect the important resources and to enhance visitor appreciation of the island's cultural history through interpretation. Therefore, the tasks summarized below and itemized in Table 2 provide suggestions for various steps that would substantially augment the current knowledge of the Ritidian Unit and facilitate a more successful management strategy.

There are seven types of tasks outlined below, with notes about the type of work, cost estimates and priority. They include: research, collections management, survey, testing, excavation, restoration, and interpretation/outreach. These tasks can be grouped together or performed in phases. The accompanying table's description column includes information about the task, expectations, and methodology. The cost estimates are truly ball-park estimates as costs can vary widely. The estimate also includes an approximate amount of time to complete the task which may provide the refuge with a means of estimating costs. The last column provides the level of priority with a justification in some cases.

Research:
Most of the information known about the area is from surveys completed more than 50 years ago. Updating the current site information and integrating it into the refuge planning and interpretive program are essential to preserve and protect what remains of the cultural history. This task will be ongoing. However, it would be useful to systematically locate and copy all reports and documents that are pertinent to Ritidian and Pajon Point. For instance, the unpublished field notes of Hornbostel are on file at the Bishop Museum in Honolulu and on microfilm at the Micronesian Area Research Center. Locating photographic records and copying the documents could aid in the interpretive panels. One facet of the research should provide a clear document of the land use and ownership chain so that twentieth century features can be placed into their appropriate context. Long-term or special research might include the repositories on other islands in the Pacific and even the archives of Spain. Research should be linked with projects to provide detailed information to augment fieldwork.

Task	Description/Notes	Cost/Time Estimates	Priority
Research – local repositories	Create list of plant and animal species introduced during the Spanish and American periods. Review oral histories and land use records. For instance, when were copra plantations established?	Volunteers, contractors, refuge staff – 2 weeks of time per year, for 5 years.	Low – On-going
Research – Hawaii & Other repositories	Develop a research library at the Refuge for material pertinent to Ritidian Point. Material to assist with interpretation.	Volunteers, contractors, refuge staff – 2 weeks of time per year, for 5 years.	Low – On-going
Collections Management – Hawaii	Review previous collections from 1920s to 1960s (Hornbostel, etc.)	10 days in Hawaii at Bishop Museum to inventory and photograph collection. (~ $ 3,000)	Medium
Collections Management – Refuge	Develop research lab for objects found at Ritidian Point. Build storage facility for artifacts that is secure, temperature/humidity controlled.	Cabinets and secure area – (~ $ 6,000)	Medium
Survey – Beach front	Pedestrian intensive, map to scale, photographs, id. all features, artifacts, plants (native, Spanish, and American). Record stone-lined well located on beach.	Contractor & volunteers – 1 week fieldwork; 3 weeks report/feature map preparation; 1 week final report (~ $ 15,000)	**High** Because of public use and need for protecting/interpreting features.
Survey – Middle strand	Pedestrian intensive, map to scale, photograph all features; map and sample collect surface artifact scatters. Record artifact clusters that may relate to latte.	Contractor & Volunteers – 2 week fieldwork; 4 weeks report/feature map preparation; 2 weeks artifact descriptions/ceramic typology; 1 week final report (~$ 25,000)	**High** Because artifact scatters are on the surface and are being vandalized.
Survey – Base of cliff	Pedestrian intensive, map to scale, photograph all features; map and sample collect surface artifact scatters. Record cave locations.	Contractor – 1 week fieldwork; 3 weeks report/ feature map preparation; 2 weeks artifact descriptions; 1 week final report (~ $20,500)	**High** Because of caves are subject to vandalism, artifacts to trampling and collection.
Survey – Cliff face	Pedestrian intensive, map to scale, photograph all features; map and sample collect surface artifact scatters. Look for higher caves, roads, and features. This would complete the survey of the refuge and provide information not previously collected.	Contractor – 2 weeks fieldwork; 2 weeks report/feature map preparation; 1 week artifact analysis; 1 week final report (~ $17,500)	Low Rugged conditions, so probability of features is low and not very much disturbance from public.
Testing – Spanish Mission area	Set up grid and excavate small units to try to locate evidence of mission, such as foundation stones, Spanish ceramic, glass	Contractor and volunteers 2 weeks fieldwork, 4 weeks artifact analysis; 2 weeks report/map preparation; 1 week final report (~ $35,000)	**High** Public use and visibility of this area would be greatly improved if the mission site was located, protected, and interpreted.

Table 2. Priority list of cultural resource management tasks with associated time/cost estimates.

Task	Description/Notes	Cost/Time Estimates	Priority
Testing -- Latte area	Test where latte were reported, based on description in 1930s and 1950s reports and results of Middle Strand survey. Artifacts should include pottery, shell, and fish hooks.	Contractor and volunteers. 2 weeks fieldwork; 4 weeks artifact analysis; 2 weeks report/map preparation; 1 week final report (~ $35,000)	Medium. Information would assist with protection and interpretation.
Testing -- Cave area	Excavate small area of cave to determine depth and type of deposits.	Contractor. 1 week fieldwork; 3 weeks artifact analysis; 1 week report/map preparation, 1 week final report (~ $25,500)	Medium. Information would assist with protection and interpretation.
Excavation -- Depending on results of testing in Mission area, Latte, or Cave.	More intensive excavation to recover data	Project specific	Project specific
Excavation -- As mitigation for refuge projects	Data recovery	Project specific	Project specific
Restoration -- Beach front	Well feature could be cleaned out, restored, and interpreted as a link with early settlement. Document before, during and after, develop restoration plan.	Contractor and volunteers. 1 week preparation of plan; 3 weeks fieldwork; 1 week report preparation/maps; 1 week final report (~ $25,500)	Medium. Project would provide information for interpretation.
Restoration -- Middle Strand	Spanish mission building if remains are found. Or restore a latte building.		Low
Interpretation/Outreach	Include information in visitor center panels and brochures.	Interpret features such as the well, mission location, caves.	High -- but only possible after completing survey and testing to provide the information needed for interpretation.

Table 2 continued. Priority list of cultural resource management tasks with associated time/cost estimates.

Collections Management:

There are really three components to this task. The most critical task is to build or find a facility for storing artifacts found at the refuge in a secure, temperature controlled environment. The Refuge can either build an appropriate archive storage area in its current facility or contract to a collections repository, such as the University of Guam, for this service. Collections management is ongoing, as there are several surface scatters of artifacts that should be sampled before the information (artifacts) is lost. A third element of collections management is closely tied with research – reviewing the materials that were collected in the 1920s to 1950s by previous archaeologists and using this data to assist in interpreting the site. The artifacts collected in the 1920s that constitute the Hornbostel Collection are curated by the Department of Anthropology at the Bishop Museum. An inventory, photographic record, and assessment of their condition would greatly assist interpretation of the latte- and mission-periods at Ritidian. Analysis of the ceramic vessel fragments that have been collected and turned into the refuge headquarters would be a useful first step toward building a comparative collection and developing the chronological sequence for the site.

Survey:

An intensive, pedestrian survey of the entire Refuge is lacking and is desperately needed. A survey to identify all of the surface cultural features would substantially increase the Refuge's ability to protect sensitive areas, plan projects, and integrate important cultural resources into interpretive materials. The survey should map and photograph all features, identify plants from the different periods, and document artifact scatters. Because survey of the entire Refuge is a large task, it might be easier to divide it into zones and survey small pieces at a time. The survey areas could be arranged geographically, such as along the beach front, middle strand, base of cliff, and cliff face.

Testing:

Testing is useful for excavating a small sample in a controlled method to determine if a location has subsurface integrity. Testing is also valuable for determining stratigraphy, absolute depth, and for obtaining samples for various analyses as a means of characterizing a site's excavation potential and developing a research design. The areas chosen for testing procedures are usually associated with surface evidence, such as concentrations of pottery. However, there are several locations that were reported in the 1920s and 1950s, such as the Spanish Mission and latte remains, that currently lack any surface expression. Testing for the Spanish Mission is well worth the effort, any evidence of the mission would greatly add to our knowledge, interpretation, and appropriate treatment of the site. And, if building stones are found, then a partial reconstruction of the mission might be possible. The same is true for the latte remains noted in the 1950s.

Excavation:

Excavation differs from testing in that it is more comprehensive and exhaustive. Testing is used to pinpoint a location and assess integrity, while excavation is used to systematically collect information. For instance, if testing reveals evidence of the Spanish mission, then the excavation phase would recover as much information about the mission site as possible. Because of the complexity involved with excavations they may take several years to complete and require an extended period of analysis prior to publishing the results.

Restoration:

Restoration – bringing intact but deteriorated cultural features back to their original state – has limited applicability. However, the well feature, for example, might be an interesting project to clean out and restore. Restoration can be a useful tool for interpretation.

Interpretation/Outreach:

There are various avenues for presenting information about the cultural history of Ritidian. Brochures and panels within the visitor center are useful for reaching a percentage of the audience. Yet, providing a more authentic experience for visitors allows them to take what they've learned in the visitor center and create a personal memory that is associated with a place. This "sense of place" is usually established through obvious structures, ruins, or landscape features that transmit various levels of information. At Ritidian several features are available to integrate into the interpretive plan. For instance, the stone-lined well located on the beach is in a high traffic area, and after restoration, the feature could be interpreted for the public to explore an interesting component of the cultural development at Ritidian. Additionally, the caves along the base of the cliff and the remains of the Spanish mission and latte structures (if located) would add significantly to the long and colorful history of Ritidian.

A Note Regarding Contracting Work vs. FWS Cultural Resource Team:

Due to the costs associated with travel for Oregon-based FWS Cultural Resource Team (CRT) members, contracting instead with qualified local archaeological consulting firms would be appropriate for much of the fieldwork required for Section 106 compliance projects. There are several contracting firms on Guam that would meet the professional requirements. The CRT can assist in developing management plans, scopes of work, and providing oversight of contracts. The CRT can also contribute to the ongoing interpretation and educational program by synthesizing and summarizing information garnered from archaeological investigations for use in a variety of media and formats.

Future Management - Comprehensive Conservation Planning:

In compliance with the National Wildlife Refuge System Improvement Act of 1997, every Refuge within the National Wildlife Refuge System will develop a Comprehensive Conservation Plan to provide long-term guidance and management direction to achieve Refuge purposes and to meet other applicable mandates. Appendix B presents a set of draft goals and objectives that may be considered for incorporation into Guam NWR's CCP, the development of which which is scheduled to begin in 2006.

References

Allen, S. Jane

1988   *Geoarchaeological Analysis, NAVFAC Archaeological Site Area, Ritidian Point, Guam.* Bishop Museum, Honolulu.

Carson, Michael T.

2005   *PTransmittal of letter report and recovered materials for salvage of disturbed human skeletal remains at Guam National Wildlife Refuge, Ritidian, Guam.* IARI, Inc., Guam.

Carucci, James

1993   *The Archaeology of Orote Peninsula: Phase I and II Archaeological Inventory Survey of Areas Proposed for Projects to Accomodate Relocation of Navy Activities from the Philippines to Guam, Mariana Islands.* IARI, Inc., Guam.

Craib, John L.

1995   *Pre-Final Report: Archaeological Survey at U.S. Naval Magazine Guam in Conjunction with U.S.F.S. and Gov Guam Reforestation Project.* Ogden Environmental, Guam.

Craib, John L., and Richard Nees

1995   *Preliminary Report: Archaeological Survey and Subsurface Testing of Prehistoric Inland Chamorro Settlement Systems at Naval Magazine Guam.* Ogden Evironmental, Guam.

Craib, John L., and Ann Yoklavich

1992   *Preliminary Report: Cultural Resources Management Overview Survey, Naval Supply Depot.* Ogden Environmental, Guam.

Driver, Marjorie G.

1985   *Guam: A Nomenclatural Chronology.* Micronesian Area Research Center, University of Guam, Mangilao.

1992   *The History of the Marianas, with Navigational Data, and of the Caroline, and Palau Islands: From the Time of their Discovery by Magellan in 1521 to the Present,* translation from Colonel of the Infantry Luis de Ibanez y Garcia, translated and annotated by Marjorie G. Driver. Micronesian Area Research Center, University of Guam, Mangilao.

Haynes, Douglas E. And William L. Wuerch

1993   *Historical Survey of the Spanish Mission Sites on Guam 1669-1800,* Second Edition. Micronesian Area Research Center, University of Guam, Mangilao

Kraft, Charles Edwin

1961   *Guam, 1939-1945: American Indifference and Japanese Occupation.* MA thesis, Department of History, University of Oregon, Eugene.

Kurashina, Hiro, Jeannette A. Simons, James A. Toenjes, Jane Allen, Steven S. Amesbury, Gary M. Heathcote, Richard H. Randall, Barry D. Smith, Rebecca A. Stephenson, and Eleanor F. Wells

1990   *Archaeological Investigations at the Naval Facility (NAVFAC) Ritidian Point, Guam, Mariana Islands.* Micronesian Area Research Center, University of Guam.

Lauter-Reinman, Gloria

1994   *Pre-Final Report: Management Plan for World War II Resources at Navy Installations in Guam.* Ogden Environmental, Guam.

Liston, Jolie

1996   *The Legacy of Tarague Embayment and Its Inhabitants, Anderson AFB, Guam, Volume I: Archaeology.* Prepared by International Archaeology, Inc., Honolulu. Prepared for Andersen Air Force Base, Guam.

Moore, Darlene

1983   *Measuring Change in Marianas Pottery: The Sequence of Pottery Production at Tarague, Guam.* Master's Thesis in Behavior Science, University of Guam.

Morgan, William N.

1988   *Prehistoric Architecture in Micronesia.* University of Texas Press, Austin, Texas.

Nelson, Evelyn Gibson and Frederick Jens Nelson

1991   *The Island of Guam: Description and History from a 1934 Perspective.* Ana Publications, Washington, D.C.

Rogers, Robert F.

1995   *Destiny's Landfall: A History of Guam.* University of Hawaii Press, Honolulu.

Russel, Scott and Michael A. Fleming

1989   *The Initial Settlement of Guam 1,050 to 500 B.C.* Unpublished report, on-file Guam Historic Preservation Office, Barrigada.

Russel, Scott and Michael A. Fleming

1989b   *Late Prehistoric Cultural Changes on Guam, 800 to 1600 A.D.* Unpublished report, on-file Guam Historic Preservation Office, Barrigada.

Thompson, Laura Maud

1932   *Archaeology of the Mariana Islands* Bernice P. Bishop Museum Bulletin 100, Honolulu, Hawaii.

1991   *MARC Monograph Series, No. 2.* Beyond the Dream: A Search for Meaning. Micronesian Area Research Center, University of Guam, Mangilao.

Wheeler, Joseph, Brig. General, U.S. Army

1900   No. XXVIII: *Report on the Island of Guam.* Adjutant-General's Office, Government Printing Office, Washington, D.C.

Appendix A
Regulatory Considerations

National Historic Preservation Act of 1966, as amended, 16 U.S.C. 470-470w-6.

Section 106: The NHPA is set forth in a series of regulations in 36 CFR 800. Section 106 of the NHPA requires a Federal agency head with jurisdiction over a Federal, federally assisted, or federally licensed undertaking to take into account the effects of the agency's undertakings on properties included in or eligible for the National Register of Historic Places and, prior to approval of an undertaking, to afford the Advisory Council on Historic Preservation a reasonable opportunity to comment on the undertaking.

The Section 106 process attempts to accommodate historic preservation concerns with the needs of Federal undertakings. It is designed to identify potential conflicts between the two and to help resolve such conflicts in the public interest.

Integration of the Section 106 process into the normal administrative process used by agencies for project planning ensures early, systematic consideration of historic preservation issues. Steps for administrating the Section 106 process are clearly defined in 36 CFR 800. Essentially, any undertaking that has the potential to effect historic properties must proceed through the identification, evaluation, and assessment of project effects steps prior to completion of the activity. Consultation and reviewing existing information is part of this process.

Section 110: This section requires Federal agencies to create a program to identify and protect historic properties. This program includes the nomination of eligible properties to the National Register of Historic Places; the designation of a qualified agency historic preservation officer; conducting agency programs and activities so that preservation values are considered; and the authority of Federal agencies to include the costs of preservation activities within overall project costs during undertakings.

NHPA and the Ritidian Unit: Based on previous archaeological surveys and excavations an extensive site underlies the Ritidian Unit of the Guam NWR. Features associated with the archaeological site include artifacts (ceramic pottery, shell, stone tools), latte stones, a Spanish period building, caves, pictographs, and a well. Essentially, the site has been "identified" as meeting eligibility guidelines and is considered a "historic property," although the features are not well documented. Therefore, when the "Area of Potential Effects" for an undertaking is defined, then the archaeological extent, potential research values, and level of integrity need to be assessed prior to the undertaking.

One of the "Needs" for the Refuge is a complete and thorough documentation of all surface features that will assist with planning. And, because much of the archaeological evidence is buried, assessing the effects of each project will require subsurface testing within the proposed APE. While not all areas of the Ritidian Unit retain archaeological materials, the expectation of archaeological materials should be routinely addressed by Refuge Managers and planning staff.

Archaeological Resources Protection Act of 1979, as amended 1988, 16 U.S. Code 460 and 43 CFR part 7.

The purpose of this Act is to secure, for the present and future benefit of the American people, the protection of archaeological resources and sites which are on public lands and Indian lands and to foster increased cooperation and exchange of information between governmental authorities, the professional archaeological community, and private individuals having collections of archaeological resources and data which were obtained before the date of the enactment of this Act. ARPA also attaches criminal penalties for the excavation, removal, or damage of an archaeological resource located on public lands, or the selling, purchasing, exchanging, transporting, or receiving of an archaeological resource removed from public lands is in violation of this Act.

Appendix B
Contacts and Consultation List

In fulfilling its historic preservation responsibilities, the Service strives to consult with and keep informed a wide variety of agencies and organizations who have an interest in the cultural resources the Service manages. The following is an evolving list. Omissions are unintentional and should be brought to the attention of the Refuge Manager.

Government of Guam Agencies

State Historic Preservation Office
Guam Historic Preservation Office
Lynda Bordallo Aguon
Dept of Parks and Recreation
Government of Guam
490 Chalan Palasyo
Agana Heights, Guam 96910
(671) 475-6294/95/72
FAX: (671) 4747-2822

Dept of Chamorro Affairs
Dr. Katherine B. Aguon
Research, Publication & Trng
P.O. Box 2950
Hagatna, GU 96932

KGTF - Guam Edu & Telecom Corp
Jackie Ronan - Director
jronan@kgtf.org
PH: (671) 734-2207
Fax: (671) 734-5483
Johnny Sablan (Asst Gen Mgr)
jsablan@kgtf.org

Mayor's Council of Guam
Paul McDonald, President
P.O. Box 786
Hagatna, Guam 96932
(671) 472-6940/477-8461
FAX: (671) 477-8777

Municipality of Dededo
Mayor Melissa B. Savares
P.O. Box 786
Hagatna, GU 96932
Ph: (671) 632-5203

Municipality of Yigo
Mayor Robert Lizama
P.O. Box 11670
Yigo, GU 96929
PH: (671) 653-5248/653-9446

Municipality of Dededo
Mayor Melissa B. Savares
PO Box 786
Hagatno, GU 96932
Phone: (671-632-5203

University of Guam
R.F. Taitano Micro Area Research Center
P.O. Box 5205 UOG Station
Mangilao, GU 96923
PH: 671-735-2150/51 or 734-2153 thru55

U.S. Government Agencies

Department of the Navy
Department of the Navy
U.S. Naval Base Guam
PSC 455 BOX 152
FPO AP 96540-1000

Anderson AFB
Natural Resource Division
36 CES/CEV
Unit 14007
APO AP 96543

Dept of the Interior
National Park Service
War in the Pacific NHP
Superintendent Sara Creachbaum
Casa de Espana
Hagatna, GU 96932
PH: (671) 477-7278 ext 1003

Native Organizations and Historic Preservation Organizations

Chamorro Land Trust Commission
Thomas Elliott, Director
Phone: 475-4251/4292/4281

Nasion Chamoru
c/o Ms. Debbie Quinata
debbiq@rocketmail.com

J. Lawrence Cruz
President, Dept. of Chamorro Affairs
(671) 475-4378/4279
dcapres1@ite.net

Eddie Benavente
Administrator
Guam Ancestral Lands Commission
P.O. Box 2950
Hagatna, Guam 96932
(671) 472-5263/5265

Commission on Decolonization
Ed Benavente, Director
Phone: 473-5265

Mrs. Hope Cristobal
(671) 649-0097
ecris@teleguam.net

Mr. Leonard Iriarte
Director, Guma' Palo Li'c
(671) 735-5578/652-5964
Fax: (671) 734-4356

Mr. Frank Rabon
1 Taotao Tano
(671) 565-9877
frankguahan@hotmail.com

Mr. Rufo Lujan
Ma'gas, Organization of People
for Indigenous Rights
(671) 734-3942/3943
Fax: 734-6569
rufoj@yahoo.com

Chamorro Artists Association
Filamore P. Alcon, Director
Phone: 472-9659
Fax: 472-1659

Stebisio Para I Manamko'
Ann San Nicolas, Chairman
Sigundo Aguon, Director
Phone: 473-1013
Fax: 477-9015

Appendix C
Comprehensive Conservation Planning Draft Goals and Objectives

The comprehensive conservation planning (CCP) process for Guam NWR is scheduled to begin in 2006. The CCP represents an opportunity to improve management for the refuge, and cultural resource management should be an integral part of habitat and people management, not just because the law mandates it but for the unique information it can bring to understanding the environment and land use history for which the refuge is responsible. The following issues are very important:

1. How do we maintain the integrity of the refuge's cultural resources while managing and restoring wildlife habitat?

2. How do we work and consult with Guam SHPO and concerned parties on the management of cultural resources in a manner that facilitates the mission of the refuge and addresses issues of importance?

3. How do we work and consult with Guam SHPO and concerned parties on the disposition of human remains and burial objects?

4. How do we incorporate cultural resources into an interpretive and recreation program that explore humankind's interaction with the natural world?

These issues illustrate some of the Service's legally-mandated responsibilities for cultural resource management. They are an integral element of the process of meeting the refuge's obligations, and consequently, of fulfilling its stated purpose. To this end, we recommend that the CCP include the following goal:

Goal: Protect, preserve, evaluate, and interpret the cultural heritage and resources of the Refuge while consulting with appropriate groups and preservation organizations, and complying with historic preservation legislation.

With this goal in mind, we recommend the following objectives and strategies:

Objective CR1: Implement a proactive cultural resource management program that focuses on meeting the requirements of the National Historic Preservation Act, including consultation, identification, inventory, evaluation, and protection of cultural resources.

Achievement Strategies

A. Identify archaeological sites that coincide with existing and planned roads, facilities, public use areas, and habitat projects. Evaluate threatened and impacted sites for eligibility to the National Register of Historic Places. Prepare and implement activities to mitigate impacts to sites as necessary.

B. Implement a program to evaluate eligibility to the National Register of Historic Places those archaeological sites that may be impacted by Service undertakings, management activities, erosion, or neglect.

C. Coordinate with the habitat restoration and research programs to ensure that cultural resources are not impacted by such activities.

D.   Develop a GIS layer for cultural resources that can be used with other GIS layers for the Refuge, yet contains appropriate security features to protect sensitive information.

Discussion: Various federal historic preservation laws and regulations require the Service to implement the kind of program described under this objective. Inattention to these responsibilities may obstruct the Refuge in its other land, habitat, and wildlife management efforts.

RONS: We recommend that development of a cultural resource management plan as defined above be submitted to the Refuge Operations Needs System.

Applicable Alternatives: This objective and accompanying strategies apply equally to all action alternatives.

Objective CR2:   Develop, in partnership with preservation partners, a program for the education and interpretation of cultural resources of the Refuge.

Achievement Strategies

A.   Prepare interpretive media (e.g., pamphlets, signs, exhibits) that relate the cultural resources and use history of the Refuge.

B.   Prepare environmental/cultural education materials for use in local schools concerning cultural resources, the discipline of archaeology, the perspective of indigenous peoples, the history of the area, and conservation of natural and cultural resources. These materials could include an artifact replica kit with hands-on activities and curriculum prepared in consultation with preservation partners and the local school district.

C.   Consult with preservation partners to identify the type of cultural resources information appropriate for public interpretation.

D.   Develop an outreach program and materials so that the cultural resource messages become part of cultural events in the area, including: the State's Archaeology Month, National Wildlife Refuge Week, and appropriate local festivals.

E.   Develop Museum Property Inventory. Create storage and use plans for museum property as part of the outreach program.

Discussion: Cultural resources are not renewable. Thus, interpretation of cultural resources can instill a conservation ethic among the public and those who encounter or manage them. The goals of the cultural resource education and interpretive program are fourfold: (1) translate the results of cultural research into language and media that can be understood and appreciated by a variety of audiences, (2) relate the connection between cultural resources and natural resources and the role of humans in the environment (3) foster an awareness and appreciation of native cultures, and (4) instill an ethic for the conservation of our cultural heritage.

Applicable Alternatives: This objective and accompanying strategies apply equally to all action alternatives.

Objective CR3:   Create and utilize a Memorandum of Agreement (MOA) with Guam SHPO to address inadvertent discoveries of human remains.

Achievement Strategies

A.   Identify groups and direct lineal descendants that may be affiliated with the Refuge lands.

B.   Open consultation process with affiliated groups and direct lineal descendants.

C.   Define burial objects.

D.   Develop procedures to follow or intentional and inadvertant discoveries.

Discussion: Development of an MOA prior to inadvertant discovery is strongly suggested. Such an agreement can greatly facilitate and speed up consultations after an inadvertant discovery.

RONS: It is expected that one quarter of a full-time equivalent (FTE) position will be required for two years to negotiate and complete an MOA. It is recommended that a 1/8 FTE and a budget for travel expenses be submitted to the Refuge Operation Needs System.

Applicable Alternatives: This objective and accompanying strategies must be followed regardless of action alternatives.

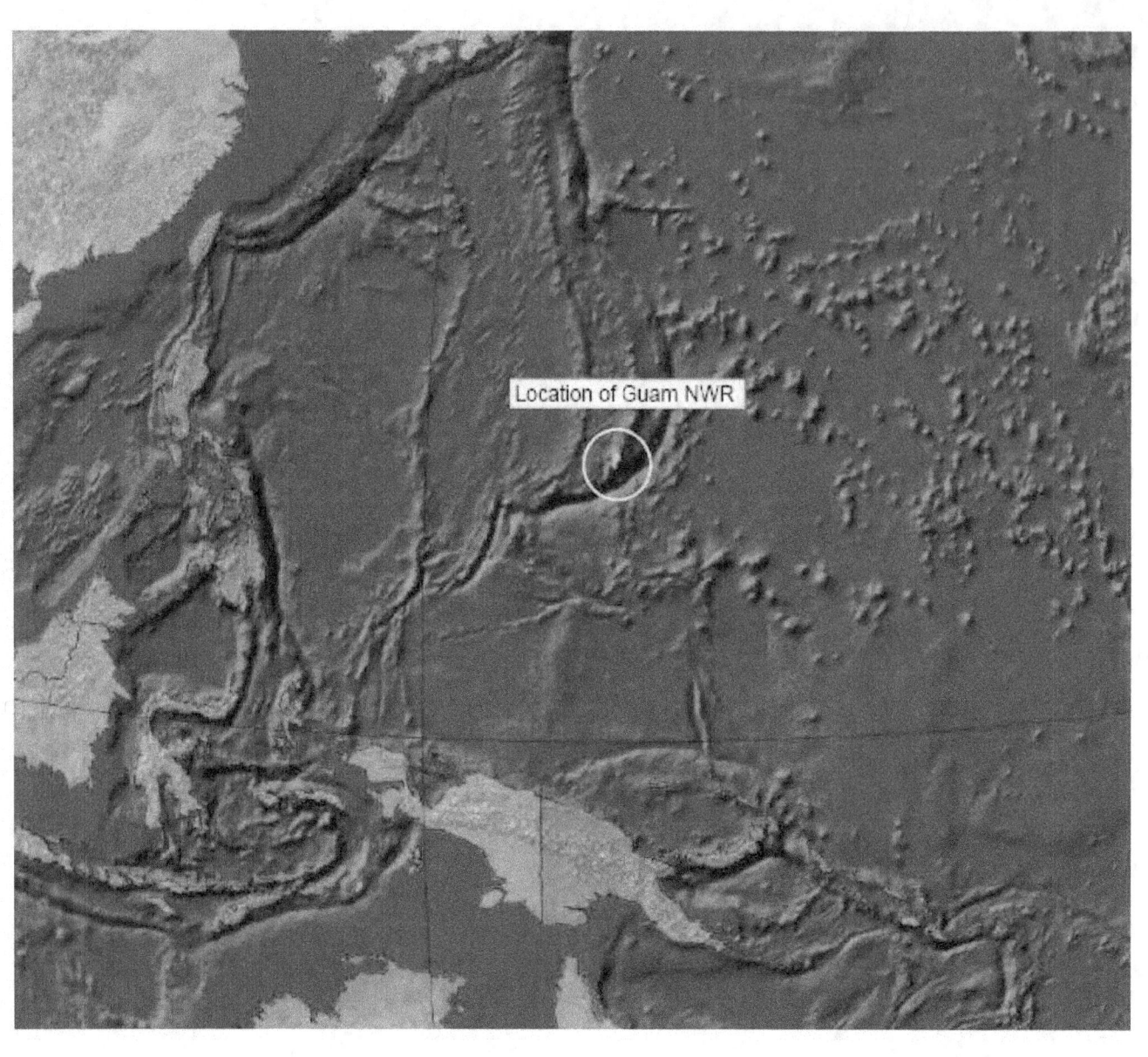

Location of Guam NWR

U.S. Fish & Wildlife Service
Region 1

Appendix J. Integrated Pest Management Program

1.0 Background

Integrated Pest Management (IPM) is an interdisciplinary approach utilizing methods to prevent, eliminate, contain, and/or control pest species in concert with other management activities on refuge lands and waters to achieve wildlife and habitat management goals and objectives. IPM is also a scientifically-based, adaptive management process where available scientific information and best professional judgment of the refuge staff as well as other resource experts are used to identify and implement appropriate management strategies that can be modified and/or changed over time to ensure effective, site-specific management of pest species to achieve desired outcomes. In accordance with 43 CFR 46.145, adaptive management would be particularly relevant where long-term impacts may be uncertain and future monitoring would be needed to make adjustments in subsequent implementation decisions. After a tolerable pest population (threshold) is determined considering achievement of refuge resource objectives and the ecology of pest species, one or more methods, or combinations thereof, would be selected that are feasible, efficacious, and most protective of non-target resources, including native species (fish, wildlife, and plants), and Service personnel, Service authorized agents, volunteers, and the public. Staff time and available funding would be considered when determining feasibility/practicality of various treatments.

IPM techniques to address pests are presented as CCP strategies (see Chapter 2.0 of this CCP/EA) in an adaptive management context to achieve refuge resource objectives. In order to satisfy requirements for IPM planning as identified in the Director's Memo (dated September 9, 2004) entitled *Integrated Pest Management Plans and Pesticide Use Proposals: Updates, Guidance, and an Online Database*, the following elements of an IPM program have been incorporated into this CCP:
- Habitat and/or wildlife objectives that identify pest species and appropriate thresholds to indicate the need for and successful implementation of IPM techniques; and
- Monitoring before and/or after treatment to assess progress toward achieving objectives including pest thresholds.

Where pesticides would be necessary to address pests, this Appendix provides a structured procedure to evaluate potential effects of proposed uses involving ground-based applications to refuge biological resources and environmental quality in accordance with effects analyses presented in Section 4.0 (Environmental Consequences) of this CCP/EA. Only pesticide uses that likely would cause minor, temporary, or localized effects to refuge biological resources and environmental quality with appropriate best management practices (BMPs), where necessary, would be allowed for use on the refuge.

This Appendix does not describe the more detailed process to evaluate potential effects associated with aerial applications of pesticides. Moreover, it does not address effects of mosquito control with pesticides (larvicides, pupacides, or adulticides) based upon identified human health threats and presence of disease-carrying mosquitoes in sufficient numbers from monitoring conducted on Guam Refuge. However, the basic framework to assess potential effects to Refuge biological resources and environmental quality from aerial application of pesticides or use of insecticides for mosquito management would be similar to the process described in this Appendix for ground-based treatments of other pesticides.

2.0 Pest Management Policies

In accordance with Service policy 7 RM 14 (Pest Control), wildlife and plant pests on units of the National Wildlife Refuge System can be controlled to assure balanced wildlife and fish populations in support of refuge-specific wildlife and habitat management objectives. Pest control on federal (refuge) lands and waters is also authorized under the following legal mandates:

- National Wildlife Refuge System Administration Act of 1966, as amended (16 USC 668dd-668ee);
- Plant Protection Act of 2000 (7 USC 7701 et seq.);
- Noxious Weed Control and Eradication Act of 2004 (7 USC 7781-7786, Subtitle E);
- Federal Insecticide, Fungicide, and Rodenticide Act of 1996 (7 USC 136-136y);
- National Invasive Species Act of 1996 (16 USC 4701);
- Nonindigenous Aquatic Nuisance Prevention and Control Act of 1990 (16 USC 4701);
- Food Quality Protection Act of 1996 (7 USC 136);
- Executive Order 13148, Section 601(a);
- Executive Order 13112; and
- Animal Damage Control Act of 1931 (7 USC 426-426c, 46 Stat. 1468).

Pests are defined as "…living organisms that may interfere with the site-specific purposes, operations, or management objectives or that jeopardize human health or safety" from Department policy 517 DM 1 (Integrated Pest Management Policy). Similarly, 7 RM 14 defines pests as "Any terrestrial or aquatic plant or animal which interferes, or threatens to interfere, at an unacceptable level, with the attainment of refuge objectives or which poses a threat to human health." 517 DM 1 also defines an invasive species as "a species that is nonnative to the ecosystem under consideration and whose introduction causes or is likely to cause economic or environmental harm or harm to human health." Throughout the remainder of this CCP/EA, the terms pest and invasive species are used interchangeably because they both can prevent/impede achievement of Guam Refuge's wildlife and habitat objectives and/or degrade environmental quality.

In general, control of pests (vertebrate or invertebrate) on the refuge would conserve and protect the nation's fish, wildlife, and plant resources as well as maintain environmental quality. From 7 RM 14, animal or plant species which are considered pests may be managed if the following criteria are met:

- Threat to human health and well-being or private property, the acceptable level of damage by the pest has been exceeded, or State or local government has designated the pest as noxious;
- Detrimental to resource objectives as specified in a refuge resource management plan (e.g., CCP, HMP), if available; and
- Control would not conflict with attainment of resource objectives or the purposes for which the refuge was established.

From 7 RM 14, the specific justifications for pest management activities on the refuge are the following:

- Protect human health and well being;
- Prevent substantial damage to important to refuge resources;
- Protect newly introduced or re-establish native species;

- Control nonnative (exotic) species in order to support existence for populations of native species;
- Prevent damage to private property; and
- Provide the public with quality, compatible, wildlife-dependent recreational opportunities.

Based upon 50 CFR 31.14 (Official Animal Control Operations), animal species which are surplus or detrimental to the management program of a refuge area may be taken in accordance with federal and state laws and regulations by federal or state personnel or by permit issued to private individuals. In addition, animal species which are damaging or destroying federal property within a refuge area may be taken or destroyed by federal personnel. These conditions are consistent with previously described criteria for pest control activities within 7 RM 14.2.

In accordance with Service policy 620 FW 1 (Habitat Management Plans), there are additional management directives regarding invasive species found on the refuge:

- "We are prohibited by Executive Order, law, and policy from authorizing, funding, or carrying out actions that are likely to cause or promote the introduction or spread of invasive species in the United States or elsewhere."

- "Manage invasive species to improve or stabilize biotic communities to minimize unacceptable change to ecosystem structure and function and prevent new and expanded infestations of invasive species. Conduct refuge habitat management activities to prevent, control, or eradicate invasive species..."

3.0 Strategies

To fully embrace IPM, the following strategies, where applicable, would be carefully considered on Guam Refuge for each pest species:

- **Prevention.** This would be the most effective and least expensive long-term management option for pests. It encompasses methods to prevent new introductions or the spread of the established pests to un-infested areas. It requires identifying potential routes of invasion to reduce the likelihood of infestation. Hazard Analysis and Critical Control Points (HACCP) planning can be used determine if current management activities on a refuge may introduce and/or spread invasive species in order to identify appropriate BMPs for prevention. See http://www.haccp-nrm.org/ for more information about HACCP planning.

  Prevention may include source reduction, using pathogen-free or weed-free seeds or fill and exclusion methods (e.g., barriers) and/or sanitation methods (e.g., wash stations) to prevent re-introductions by various mechanisms including vehicles, personnel, livestock, and horses. Because invasive species are frequently the first to establish in newly disturbed sites, prevention would require a reporting mechanism for early detection of new pest occurrences with quick response to eliminate any new satellite pest populations.

  Prevention would require consideration of the scale and scope of land management activities that may promote pest establishment within un-infested areas or promote the reproduction and spread of existing populations. Along with preventing initial introduction, prevention would involve halting the spread of existing infestations to new sites (Mullin et al. 2000). The primary reason of prevention would be to keep pest-free lands or waters from becoming infested. Executive Order 11312 emphasizes the priority for prevention with respect to managing pests.

The following methods would be used to prevent the introduction and/or spread of pests on Guam Refuge lands:

- Before beginning ground-disturbing activities (e.g., disking, scraping), inventory and prioritize pest infestations in project operating areas and along access routes. Refuge staff would identify pest species on-site or within a reasonably expected potential invasion vicinity. Where possible, the Refuge staff would begin project activities in un-infested areas before working in pest-infested areas.
- Refuge staff would locate and use pest-free project staging areas. They would avoid or minimize travel through pest-infested areas, or restrict to those periods when the spread of seed or propagules of invasive plants would be least likely.
- Refuge staff would determine the need for, and when appropriate, identify sanitation sites where equipment can be cleaned of pests. The Refuge staff would clean equipment before entering lands at on-Refuge approved cleaning site(s). This practice does not pertain to vehicles traveling frequently in and out of the project area that will remain on roadways. Seeds and plant parts of pest plants would need to be collected, where practical. Refuge staff would remove mud, dirt, and plant parts from project equipment before moving it into a project area.
- Refuge staff would clean all equipment before leaving the project site, if operating in areas infested with pests. Staff would determine the need for, and when appropriate, identify sanitation sites where equipment can be cleaned.
- Refuge staff, their authorized agents, and Refuge volunteers would, where possible, inspect, remove, and properly dispose of seed and parts of invasive plants found on their clothing and equipment. Proper disposal means bagging the seeds and plant parts and then properly discarding of them (e.g., incinerating).
- Refuge staff would evaluate options, including closure, to restrict the traffic on sites with on-going restoration of desired vegetation. Refuge staff would revegetate disturbed soil (except travel ways on surfaced projects) to optimize plant establishment for each specific site. Revegetation may include topsoil replacement, planting, seeding, fertilization, liming, and weed-free mulching as necessary. Refuge staff would use native material, where appropriate and feasible. Staff would use certified weed-free or weed-seed-free hay or straw where certified materials are required and/or are reasonably available.
- Refuge staff would provide information, training, and appropriate pest identification materials to permit holders and recreational visitors. Refuge staff would educate them about pest identification, biology, impacts, and effective prevention measures.
- Refuge staff would require grazing permittees to utilize preventative measures for their livestock while on Refuge lands.
- Refuge staff would inspect borrow material for invasive plants prior to use and transport onto and/or within refuge lands.
- Refuge staff would consider invasive plants in planning for road maintenance activities.
- Refuge staff would restrict off-road travel to designated routes.

The following would be methods to prevent the introduction and/or spread of pests into Refuge waters:

- Refuge staff would inspect boats (including air boats), trailers, and other boating equipment. Where possible, the staff would remove any visible plants, animals, or mud before leaving any waters or boat launching facilities. They would drain water from motor, live well, bilge, and transom wells while on land before leaving the site. Staff would wash and dry boats, downriggers, anchors, nets, floors of boats, propellers, axles, trailers, and other boating equipment to kill pests not visible at the boat launch.
- Before transporting to new waters, boats and boating equipment would be rinsed with hot (40°C or 104°F) clean water, sprayed with high-pressure water, or dried for at least 5 days, where possible.
- Refuge staff would maintain a 100-foot buffer of aquatic pest-free clearance around boat launches and docks or quarantine areas when cleaning around culverts, canals, or irrigation sites. Staff would clean equipment before moving to new sites and inspect and clean equipment before moving from one project area to another.

These prevention methods to minimize/eliminate the introduction and spread of pests were taken verbatim or slightly modified from Appendix E of the U.S. Forest Service (2005).

- **Mechanical/Physical Methods.** These methods would remove and destroy, disrupt the growth of, or interfere with the reproduction of pest species. For plants species, these treatments can be accomplished by hand, hand tool (manual), or power tools (mechanical) and include pulling, grubbing, digging, tilling/disking, cutting, swathing, grinding, sheering, girdling, mowing, and mulching of the pest plants. Thermal techniques such as steaming, super-heated water, and hot foam may also be viable treatments.

For animal species, Service employees or their authorized agents could use mechanical/physical methods (including trapping) to control pests as a Refuge management activity. Based upon 50 CFR 31.2, trapping can be used on a refuge to reduce surplus wildlife populations for a "balanced conservation program" in accordance with federal or state laws and regulations. In some cases, non-lethally trapped animals would be relocated to off-refuge sites with prior approval from the state. A pest control proposal (see 7 RM 14.7A-D for required elements) is needed before initiation of trapping activities, except those operations identified in 7 RM 14.7E. In addition, a separate pest control proposal is not necessary if the required information can be incorporated into an EA (or other appropriate NEPA document).

Each of these tools would be efficacious to some degree and applicable to specific situations. In general, mechanical controls can effectively control annual and biennial pest plants. However, to control perennial plants, the root system has to be destroyed or it will resprout and continue to grow and develop. Mechanical controls are typically not capable of destroying a perennial plant's root system. Although some mechanical tools (e.g., disking, plowing) may damage root systems, they may stimulate regrowth producing a denser plant population that may aid in their spread, depending upon the target species (e.g., Canada thistle). In addition, steep terrain and soil conditions would be major factors that can limit the use of many mechanical control methods.

Some mechanical control methods (e.g., mowing), which would be used in combination with herbicides, can be a very effective technique to control perennial species. For example, mowing perennial plants followed sequentially by treating the plant regrowth with a systemic herbicide often would improve the efficacy of the herbicide compared to herbicide treatment only.

- **Cultural Methods.** These methods would involve manipulating habitat to increase pest mortality by reducing its suitability to the pest. Cultural methods would include water-level manipulation, mulching, winter cover crops, changing planting dates to minimize pest impact, prescribed burning (to facilitate revegetation, increase herbicide efficacy, and remove litter to assist in emergence of desirable species), flaming with propane torches, trap crops, crop rotations that would include non-susceptible crops, moisture management, addition of beneficial insect habitat, reducing clutter, vacuuming, proper trash disposal, planting or seeding desirable species to shade or out-compete invasive plants, applying fertilizer to enhance desirable vegetation, prescriptive grazing, and other habitat alterations.

- **Biological Control Agents.** Classical biological control would involve the deliberate introduction and management of natural enemies (parasites, predators, or pathogens) to reduce pest populations. Many of the most ecologically or economically damaging pest species in the United States originated in foreign countries. These newly introduced pests, which are free from natural enemies found in their country or region of origin, may have a competitive advantage over cultivated and native species. This competitive advantage often allows introduced species to flourish, and they may cause widespread economic damage to crops or out compete and displace native vegetation. Once the introduced pest species population reaches a certain level, traditional methods of pest management may be cost prohibitive or impractical. Biological controls typically are used when these pest populations have become so widespread that eradication or effective control would be difficult or no longer practical.

Biological control has advantages as well as disadvantages. Benefits include reducing pesticide usage, host specificity for target pests, long-term self-perpetuating control, low cost per acre, capacity for searching and locating hosts, synchronizing biological control agents to hosts' life cycles, and the unlikelihood that hosts will develop resistance to agents. Disadvantages include the following: limited availability of agents from their native lands, the dependence of control on target species density, slow rate at which control occurs, biotype matching, the difficulty and expense of conflicts over control of the target pest, and host specificity when host populations are low.

A reduction in target species populations from biological controls is typically a slow process, and efficacy can be highly variable. It may not work well in a particular area although it does work well in other areas. Biological control agents would require specific environmental conditions to survive over time. Some of these conditions are understood, whereas, others are only partially understood or not at all.

Biological control agents would not eradicate a target pest. When using biological control agents, residual levels of the target pest typically are expected; the agent population level or survival would be dependent upon the density of its host. After the pest population decreases, the population of the biological control agent would decrease correspondingly. This is a natural cycle. Some pest populations (e.g., invasive plants) would tend to persist for several years after a biological control agent becomes established due to seed reserves in the soil, inefficiencies in the agent's search behavior, and the natural lag in population buildup of the agent.

The full range of pest groups potentially found on Refuge lands and waters include diseases, invertebrates (insects, mollusks), vertebrates and invasive plants (most common group). Often it is assumed that biological control would address many if not most of these pest problems. There are several well-documented success stories of biological control of invasive weed species in the Pacific Northwest, including Mediterranean sage, St. Johnswort (Klamath weed) and tansy ragwort. Emerging success stories include Dalmatian toadflax, diffuse knapweed, leafy spurge, purple loosestrife, and yellow star thistle. However, historically, each new introduction of a biological control agent in the United States has only about a 30% success rate (Coombs et al 2006). Refer to Coombs et. al (2006) for the status of biological control agents for invasive plants in the Pacific Northwest.

Introduced species without desirable close relatives in the United States would generally be selected as biological controls. Natural enemies that are restricted to one or a few closely related plants in their country of origin are targeted as biological controls (Center et al. 1997, Hasan and Ayres 1990).

The Refuge staff would ensure introduced agents are approved by the applicable authorities. Except for a small number of formulated biological control products registered by EPA under FIFRA, most biological control agents are regulated by the US Department of Agriculture (USDA)-Animal Plant Health Inspection Service, Plant Protection and Quarantine (APHIS-PPQ). State departments of agriculture and, in some cases, county agricultural commissioners or weed districts, have additional approval authority.

Federal permits (USDA-APHIS-PPQ Form 526) are required to import biocontrol agents from another state. Form 526 may be obtained by writing:

USDA-APHIS-PPQ
Biological Assessment and Taxonomic Support
4700 River Road, Unit 113
Riverdale, MD 20737
or through the internet at URL address:
http://www.aphis.usda.gov/ppq/permits/bioligical/weedbio.html.

The Service strongly supports the development, and legal and responsible use of appropriate, safe, and effective biological control agents for nuisance and non-indigenous or pest species.

State and county agriculture departments may also be sources for biological control agents or they may have information about where biological control agents may be obtained. Commercial sources should have an Application and Permit to Move Live Plant Pests and Noxious Weeds (USDA-PPQ Form 226 USDA-APHIS-PPQ, Biological Assessment and

Taxonomic Support, 4700 River Road, Unit 113, Riverdale, MD 20737) to release specific biological control agents in a state and/or county. Furthermore, certification regarding the biological control agent's identity (genus, specific epithet, sub-species and variety) and purity (e.g., parasite free, pathogen free, and biotic and abiotic contaminants) should be specified in purchase orders.

Biological control agents are subject to 7 RM 8 (Exotic Species Introduction and Management). In addition, the Refuge staff would follow the International Code of Best Practice for Classical Biological Control of Weeds (http://sric.ucdavis.edu/exotic /exotic.htm) as ratified by delegates to the X International Symposium on Biological Control of Weeds, Bozeman, MT, July 9, 1999. This code identifies the following:

- Release only approved biological control agents,
- Use the most effective agents,
- Document releases, and
- Monitor for impact to the target pest, nontarget species, and the environment.

Biological control agents formulated as pesticide products and registered by the EPA (e.g., *Bti*) are also subject to pesticide use proposals (PUPs) review and approval (see below).

A record of all releases would be maintained with date(s), location(s), and environmental conditions of the release site(s); the identity, quantity, and condition of the biological control agents released; and other relevant data and comments such as weather conditions. Systematic monitoring to determine the establishment and effectiveness of the release is also recommended.

NEPA documents regarding biological and other environmental effects of biological control agents prepared by another federal agency, where the scope is relevant to evaluation of releases on refuge lands, would be reviewed. Possible source agencies for such NEPA documents include the Bureau of Land Management, US Forest Service, National Park Service, US Department of Agriculture-Animal and Plant Health Inspection Service, and the military services. It might be appropriate to incorporate by reference parts or all of existing document(s) from the review. Incorporating by reference (43 CFR 46.135) is a technique used to avoid redundancies in analysis. It also can reduce the bulk of a Service NEPA document, which must only identify the documents that are incorporated by reference. In addition, relevant portions must be summarized in the Service's NEPA document to the extent necessary to provide the decision maker and public with an understanding of the relevance of the referenced material to the current analysis.

- **Pesticides.** The selective use of pesticides would be based upon pest ecology (including mode of reproduction), the size and distribution of its populations; site-specific conditions (e.g., soils, topography); known efficacy under similar site conditions; and the capability to utilize best management practices (BMPs) to reduce/eliminate potential effects to non-target species, sensitive habitats, and the potential to contaminate surface and groundwater. All pesticide usage (pesticide, target species, application rate, and method of application) would comply with the applicable federal (FIFRA) and state regulations pertaining to pesticide use, safety, storage, disposal, and reporting. Before pesticides can be used to eradicate, control, or contain pests on Refuge lands and waters, PUPs would be prepared and approved in accordance with 7 RM 14. PUP records would provide a detailed, time-, site-, and target-specific description of the proposed use of pesticides on the Refuge. All PUPs would be created, approved or disapproved, and stored in the Pesticide Use Proposal System (PUPS), which is a centralized database accessible only on the Service's intranet (https://sds.fws.gov/pups). Only Service employees would be authorized to access PUP records for the Refuge in this database.

Application equipment would be selected to provide site-specific delivery to target pests while minimizing/eliminating direct or indirect (e.g., drift) exposure to non-target areas and degradation of surface and groundwater quality. Where possible, target-specific equipment (e.g., backpack sprayer, wiper) would be used to treat target pests. Other target-specific equipment to apply pesticides would include soaked wicks or paint brushes for wiping vegetation and lances, hatchets, or syringes for direct injection into stems. Granular pesticides may be applied using seeders or other specialized dispensers. In contrast, aerial spraying (e.g., fixed wing or helicopter) would be used only where access is difficult (remoteness) and/or the size/distribution of infestations precludes practical use of ground-based methods.

Because repeated use of one pesticide may allow resistant organisms to survive and reproduce, multiple pesticides with variable modes of action would be considered for treatments on Refuge lands and waters. This is especially important if multiple applications within years and/or over a growing season likely would be necessary for habitat maintenance and restoration activities to achieve resource objectives. Integrated chemical and non-chemical controls also are highly effective, where practical, because pesticide resistant organisms can be removed from the site.

Cost may not be the primary factor in selecting a pesticide for use on the Refuge. If the least expensive pesticide would potentially harm natural resources or people, then a different product would be selected, if available. The most efficacious pesticide available with the least potential to degrade environment quality (soils, surface water, and groundwater) as well as least potential effect to native species and communities of fish, wildlife, plants, and their habitats would be acceptable for use on the Refuge in the context of an IPM approach.

- **Habitat restoration/maintenance.** Restoration and/or proper maintenance of Refuge habitats associated with achieving wildlife and habitat objectives would be essential for long-term prevention, eradication, or control (at or below threshold levels) of pests. Promoting desirable plant communities through the manipulation of species composition, plant density, and growth rate is an essential component of invasive plant management (Masters et al. 1996, Masters and Shelly 2001, Brooks et al. 2004). The following three components of succession could be manipulated through habitat maintenance and restoration: site availability, species availability, and species performance (Cox and Anderson 2004). Although a single method (e.g., herbicide treatment) may eliminate or suppress pest species in the short term, the resulting gaps and bare soil create niches that are conducive to further invasion by the species and/or other invasive plants. On degraded sites where desirable species are absent or in low abundance, revegetation with native/desirable grasses, forbs, and legumes may be necessary to direct and accelerate plant community recovery, and achieve site-specific objectives in a reasonable time frame.

The selection of appropriate species for revegetation would be dependent on a number of factors including resource objectives and site-specific, abiotic factors (e.g., soil texture, precipitation/temperature regimes, and shade conditions). Seed availability and cost, ease of establishment, seed production, and competitive ability also would be important considerations.

4.0 Priorities for Treatments

For many refuges, the magnitude (number, distribution, and sizes of infestations) for pest problems is too extensive and beyond the available capital resources to effectively address during any single field season. To manage pests in the refuge, it would be essential to prioritize treatment of infestations. Highest priority treatments would be focused on early detection and rapid response to eliminate infestations of new pests, if possible. This would be especially important for aggressive pests potentially impacting species, species groups, communities, and/or habitats associated with refuge purpose(s), Refuge System resources of concern (federally listed species, migratory birds, selected marine mammals, and interjurisdictional fish), and native species for maintaining and restoring biological integrity, diversity, and environmental health.

The next priority would be treating established pests that appear in one or more previously un-infested areas. Moody and Mack (1988) demonstrated through modeling that small, new outbreaks of invasive plants eventually will infest an area larger than the established, source population. They also found that control efforts focusing on the large, main infestation rather than the new, small satellites reduced the chances of overall success. The lowest priority would be treating large infestations (sometimes monotypic stands) of well-established pests. In this case, initial efforts would focus upon containment of the perimeter followed by work to control or eradicate the established infested areas. If containment and/or control of a large infestation is not effective, then efforts would focus upon halting pest reproduction or managing source populations. Maxwell et al. (2009) found treating fewer populations that are sources represents an effective long-term strategy to reduce the total number of invasive populations and decrease meta population growth rates.

Although state listed noxious weeds would always be high priority for management, other pest species known to cause substantial ecological impact would also be considered. For example, cheatgrass may not be listed by a state as noxious, but it can greatly alter fire regimes in shrub steppe habitats, resulting in large monotypic stands that displace native bunch grasses, forbs, and shrubs. Pest control would likely require a multi-year commitment from the refuge staff. Essential to the long-term success of pest management would be pre- and post-treatment monitoring, assessment of the successes and failures of treatments, and development of new approaches when proposed methods do not achieve desired outcomes.

5.0 Best Management Practices

Best Management Practices (BMPs) can minimize or eliminate possible effects associated with pesticide usage to non-target species and/or sensitive habitats as well as degradation of water quality from drift, surface runoff, or leaching. Based upon the Department of the Interior Pesticide Use Policy (517 DM 1) and the Service Pest Management Policy and Responsibilities (30 AM 12), the use of applicable BMPs (where feasible) would likely ensure that pesticide uses may not adversely affect federally listed species and/or their critical habitats through determinations made using the process described in 50 CFR part 402.

The following are BMPs pertaining to mixing, handling, and applying pesticides for all ground-based treatments of pesticides which would be considered and utilized where feasible, based upon target- and site-specific factors and time-specific environmental conditions. Although not listed below, the most important BMP to eliminate/reduce potential impacts to non-target resources would be an IPM approach to prevent, control, eradicate, and contain pests.

5.1 Pesticide Handling and Mixing

- As a precaution against spilling, spray tanks would not be left unattended during filling.
- All pesticide containers would be triple rinsed and the rinsate would be used as water in the sprayer tank and applied to treatment areas.
- All pesticide spray equipment would be properly cleaned. Where possible, rinsate would be used as part of the make up water in the sprayer tank and applied to treatment areas.
- Refuge staff would empty and triple rinse pesticide containers that can be recycled at local herbicide container collections.
- All unused pesticides would be properly discarded at a local "safe send" collection.
- Pesticides and pesticide containers would be lawfully stored, handled, and disposed of in accordance with the label and in a manner safeguarding human health, fish, and wildlife and preventing soil and water contaminant.
- Refuge staff would consider the water quality parameters (e.g., pH, hardness) that are important to ensure greatest efficacy where specified on the pesticide label.
- All pesticide spills would be addressed immediately using procedures identified in the Refuge spill response plan.

5.2 Applying Pesticides

- Pesticide treatments would be conducted only by or under the supervision of Service personnel and non-Service applicators with the appropriate state or BLM certification to safely and effectively conduct these activities on Refuge lands and waters.
- Refuge staff would comply with all federal, state, and local pesticide use laws and regulations as well as Departmental, Service, and Refuge System pesticide-related policies. For example, the Refuge staff would use application equipment and apply rates for the specific pest(s) identified on the pesticide label as required under FIFRA.
- Before each treatment season and prior to mixing or applying any product for the first time each season, all applicators would review the labels, material safety data sheets (MSDSs), and PUPs for each pesticide, determining the target pest, appropriate mix rate(s), personal protective equipment (PPE), and other requirements listed on the pesticide label.
- A 1-foot no-spray buffer from the water's edge would be used, where applicable, and would not detrimentally influence effective control of pest species.
- Use low impact herbicide application techniques (e.g., spot treatment, cut stump, oil basal, Thinvert system applications) rather than broadcast foliar applications (e.g., boom sprayer, other larger tank wand applications), where practical.
- Use low volume rather than high volume foliar applications where the low impact methods above are not feasible or practical to maximize herbicide effectiveness and ensure correct and uniform application rates.
- Applicators would use and adjust spray equipment to apply the coarsest droplet size spectrum with optimal coverage of the target species while reducing drift.

- Applicators would use the largest droplet size that results in uniform coverage.
- Applicators would use drift reduction technologies, such as low-drift nozzles, where possible.
- Where possible, spraying would occur during low (average<7mph and preferably 3 to 5 mph) and consistent direction wind conditions with moderate temperatures (typically <85 °F).
- Where possible, applicators would avoid spraying during inversion conditions (often associated with calm and very low wind conditions) that can cause large-scale herbicide drift to non-target areas.
- Equipment would be calibrated regularly to ensure that the proper rate of pesticide is applied to the target area or species.
- Spray applications would be made at the lowest height for uniform coverage of target pests to minimize/eliminate potential drift.
- If windy conditions frequently occur during afternoons, spraying (especially boom treatments) would typically be conducted during early morning hours.
- Spray applications would not be conducted on days with >30% forecast for rain within 6 hours, except for pesticides that are rapidly rain fast (e.g., glyphosate in 1 hour) to minimize/eliminate potential runoff.
- Where possible, applicators would use drift retardant adjuvants during spray applications, especially adjacent to sensitive areas.
- Where possible, applicators would use a non-toxic dye to aid in identifying the target area treated as well as potential over spray or drift. A dye can also aid in detecting equipment leaks. If a leak is discovered, the application would be stopped until repairs can be made to the sprayer.
- For pesticide uses associated with cropland and facilities management, buffers, as appropriate, would be used to protect sensitive habitats, especially wetlands and other aquatic habitats.
- When drift cannot be sufficiently reduced through altering equipment, set up, and application techniques, buffer zones may be identified to protect sensitive areas downwind of applications. The Refuge staff would only apply pesticide adjacent to sensitive areas when the wind is blowing the opposite direction.
- Applicators would utilize scouting for early detection of pests to eliminate unnecessary pesticide applications.
- Refuge staff would consider timing of application so native plants are protected (e.g., senescence) while effectively treating invasive plants.
- Rinsate from cleaning spray equipment after application would be recaptured and reused or applied to an appropriate pest plant infestation.
- Application equipment (e.g., sprayer, ATV, tractor) would be thoroughly cleaned and PPE would be removed/disposed of on-site by applicators after treatments to eliminate the potential spread of pests to un-infested areas.

6.0 Safety

6.1 Personal Protective Equipment

All applicators would wear the specific PPE identified on the pesticide label. The appropriate PPE will be worn at all times during handling, mixing, and applying. PPE can include the following: disposable (e.g., Tyvek) or laundered coveralls; gloves (latex, rubber, or nitrile); rubber boots; and/or an NIOSH-approved respirator. Because exposure to concentrated product is usually greatest during mixing, extra care should be taken while preparing pesticide solutions. Persons mixing these solutions can be best protected if they wear long gloves, an apron, footwear, and a face shield.

Coveralls and other protective clothing used during an application would be laundered separately from other laundry items. Transporting, storing, handling, mixing, and disposing of pesticide containers will be consistent with label requirements, EPA and OSHA requirements, and Service policy.

If a respirator is necessary for a pesticide use, then the following requirements would be met in accordance with Service safety policy: a written Respirator Program, fit testing, physical examination (including pulmonary function and blood work for contaminants), and proper storage of the respirator.

6.2 Notification

The restricted entry interval is the time period required after the application at which point someone may safely enter a treated area without PPE. Refuge staff, authorized management agents of the Service, volunteers, and members of the public who could be in or near a pesticide treated area within the stated re-entry time period on the label would be notified about treatment areas. Posting would occur at any site where individuals might inadvertently become exposed to a pesticide during other activities on the Refuge. Where required by the label and/or state-specific regulations, sites would also be posted on the perimeter and at other likely locations of entry. Refuge staff would also notify appropriate private property owners of an intended application, including any private individuals who have requested notification. Special efforts would be made to contact nearby individuals who are beekeepers or who have expressed chemical sensitivities.

6.3 Medical Surveillance

Medical surveillance may be required for Service personnel who mix, apply, and/or monitor use of pesticides (see 242 FW 7 [Pesiticide Users] and 242 FW 4 [Medical Surveillance]). In accordance with draft Service policy (242 FW 7 [Pesticide Users Safety]), medical monitoring would be necessary for Service personnel and approved volunteers engaged in "frequent pesticide use" that is defined as a "pesticide applicator handling, mixing, and applying pesticides for 8 or more hours in any week or 16 or more hours in any 30 day period." However, Refuge cooperators (e.g., cooperative farmers) and other authorized agents (e.g., state and county employees) would be responsible for their own medical monitoring needs and costs.

Standard examinations (at Refuge expense) of appropriate Refuge staff would be provided by the nearest certified occupational health and safety physician as determined by Federal Occupational Health.

6.4 Certification and Supervision of Pesticide Applicators

Appropriate Refuge staff handling, mixing, and/or applying or supervising others engaged in pesticide use activities would be trained and state or federally (BLM) licensed to apply pesticides to Refuge lands or waters (242 FW 7). Preferably, all Refuge staff participating in pest management activities involving pesticide usage would attend appropriate training. New staff unfamiliar with proper procedures for storing, mixing, handling, applying, and disposing of herbicides and containers would receive orientation and training before handling or using any products. Documentation of training would be kept in the files at the Refuge office.

6.5 Record Keeping

6.5.1 Labels and material safety data sheets

Pesticide labels and MSDSs would be maintained at the Refuge shop and laminated copies in the mixing area. These documents would also be carried by field applicators, where possible. A written reference (e.g., note pad, chalk board, dry erase board) for each tank to be mixed would be kept in the mixing area for quick reference while mixing is in progress. In addition, approved PUPs stored in the PUPS database typically contain website links to pesticide labels and MSDSs.

6.5.2 Pesticide use proposals

A PUP would be prepared for each proposed pesticide use associated with annual pest management on Refuge lands and waters. A PUP would include specific information about the proposed pesticide use including the common and chemical names of the pesticide(s), target pest species, size and location of treatment site(s), application rate(s) and method(s), and federally listed species determinations, where applicable.

In accordance with 30 AM 12 and 7 RM 14, PUPs would be required for the following:

- Uses of pesticides on lands and facilities owned or managed by the Service, including properties managed by Service personnel as a result of the Food Security Act of 1985;
- Service projects by non-Service personnel on Service owned or controlled lands and facilities and other pest management activities that would be conducted by Service personnel; and
- Where the Service would be responsible or provide funds for pest management identified in protective covenants, easements, contracts, or agreements off Service lands.

In accordance with Service guidelines (Director's memo [December 12, 2007]), Refuge staff may receive up to 5-year approvals for Washington Office and field reviewed proposed pesticide uses based upon meeting identified criteria including an approved IPM plan, where necessary (see http://www.fws.gov/contaminants/Issues/IPM.cfm). For a refuge, an IPM plan (requirements described herein) can be completed independently or in association with a CCP or HMP if IPM strategies and potential environmental effects are adequately addressed within appropriate NEPA documentation.

PUPs would be created, approved or disapproved, and stored as records in PUPS, which is a centralized database on the Service's intranet (https://sds.fws.gov/pups). Only Service employees can access PUP records in this database.

6.5.3 Pesticide usage

In accordance with 30 AM 12 and 7 RM 14, the refuge Project Leader would be required to maintain records of all pesticides annually applied on lands or waters under refuge jurisdiction. This would encompass pesticides applied by other federal agencies, state and county governments, non-government applicators including cooperators and their pest management service providers with Service permission. For clarification, pesticide means all insecticides, insect and plant growth regulators, dessicants, herbicides, fungicides, rodenticides, acaricides, nematicides, fumigants, avicides, and piscicides.

The following usage information can be reported for approved PUPs in the PUPS database:
- Pesticide trade name(s)
- Active ingredient(s)
- Total acres treated
- Total amount of pesticides used (lbs or gallons)
- Total amount of active ingredient(s) used (lbs)
- Target pest(s)
- Efficacy (% control)

To determine whether treatments are efficacious (eradicating, controlling, or containing the target pest) and achieving resource objectives, habitat and/or wildlife response would be monitored both pre- and post-treatment, where possible. Considering available annual funding and staffing, appropriate monitoring data regarding characteristics (attributes) of pest infestations (e.g., area, perimeter, degree of infestation-density, percent cover, density) as well as habitat and/or wildlife response to treatments may be collected and stored in a relational database (e.g., Refuge Habitat Management Database), preferably a geo-referenced data management system (e.g., Refuge Lands GIS [RLGIS]) to facilitate data analyses and subsequent reporting. In accordance with adaptive management, data analysis and interpretation would allow treatments to be modified or changed over time, as necessary, to achieve resource objectives considering site-specific conditions in conjunction with habitat and/or wildlife responses. Monitoring could also identify short- and long-term impacts to natural resources and environmental quality associated with IPM treatments in accordance with adaptive management principles identified in 43 CFR 46.145.

7.0 Evaluating Pesticide Use Proposals

Pesticides would be used only on the Refuge for habitat management as well as croplands/facilities maintenance after approval of a PUP. Proposed pesticide uses on the refuge would only be approved where there would likely be minor, temporary, or localized effects to fish and wildlife species as well as minimal potential to degrade environmental quality. Potential effects to listed and non-listed species would be evaluated with quantitative ecological risk assessments. Potential effects to environmental quality would be based upon pesticide characteristics of environmental fate (water solubility, soil mobility, soil persistence, and volatilization) and a quantitative screening tool for potential to move to groundwater. Risk assessments as well as characteristics of environmental fate and potential to degrade water quality for pesticides would be documented in Chemical Profiles (see Section 7.5). These profiles would include threshold values for quantitative measures of ecological risk assessments and screening tools for environmental fate that represent minimal potential effects to species and environmental quality. Only pesticide uses with appropriate BMPs (see Section 4.0) for habitat management and cropland/facilities maintenance on the refuge that would potentially have minor, temporary, or localized effects on refuge biological and environmental quality (threshold values not exceeded) would be approved.

7.1 Overview of Ecological Risk Assessment

An ecological risk assessment process would be used to evaluate potential adverse effects to biological resources as a result of a pesticide(s) proposed for use on the refuge. It is an established quantitative and qualitative methodology for comparing and prioritizing risks of pesticides and conveying an estimate of the potential risk for an adverse effect. The quantitative methodology would be an efficient way to integrate best available scientific information regarding hazard, patterns of use (exposure), and dose-response relationships in a manner that is useful for ecological risk decision-making. It would provide an effective way to evaluate potential effects where there is missing or unavailable scientific information (data gaps) to address reasonable, foreseeable adverse effects as required under 40 CFR Part 1502.22. Protocols for ecological risk assessment of pesticide uses on the refuge were developed through research and established by the EPA (2004). Assumptions for these risk assessments are presented in Section 6.2.3.

The toxicological data used in ecological risk assessments are typically results of standardized laboratory studies provided by pesticide registrants to the EPA to meet regulatory requirements under the FIFRA. These studies assess the acute (lethality) and chronic (reproductive) effects associated with short- and long-term exposure to pesticides on representative species of birds, mammals, freshwater fish, aquatic invertebrates, and terrestrial and aquatic plants, respectively (Table 1). Other effects data publicly available would also be utilized for risk assessment protocols described herein. Toxicity endpoint and environmental fate data are available from a variety of resources. Some of the more useful resources can be found in Section 7.5.

Table 1. Ecotoxicity tests used to evaluate potential effects to birds, fish, and mammals to establish toxicity endpoints for risk quotient calculations.

Species Group	Exposure	Measurement endpoint
Bird	Acute	Median Lethal Concentration (LC$_{50}$)
	Chronic	No Observed Effect Concentration (NOEC) or No Observed Adverse Effect Concentration (NOAEC)[1]
Fish	Acute	Median Lethal Concentration (LC$_{50}$)
	Chronic	No Observed Effect Concentration (NOEC) or No Observed Adverse Effect Concentration (NOAEC)[2]
Mammal	Acute	Oral Lethal Dose (LD$_{50}$)
	Chronic	No Observed Effect Concentration (NOEC) or No Observed Adverse Effect Concentration (NOAEC)[3]

[1]Measurement endpoints typically include a variety of reproductive parameters (e.g., number of eggs, number of offspring, eggshell thickness, and number of cracked eggs).
[2]Measurement endpoints for early life stage/life cycle typically include embryo hatch rates, time to hatch, growth, and time to swim-up.
[3]Measurement endpoints include maternal toxicity, teratogenic effects or developmental anomalies, evidence of mutagenicity or genotoxicity, and interference with cellular mechanisms such as DNA synthesis and DNA repair.

7.2 Determining Ecological Risk to Fish and Wildlife

The potential for pesticides used on the Refuge to cause direct adverse effects to fish and wildlife would be evaluated using EPA's Ecological Risk Assessment Process (US Environmental Protection Agency 2004). This deterministic approach, which is based upon a two-phase process involving estimation of environmental concentrations and then characterization of risk, would be used for ecological risk assessments. This method integrates exposure estimates (estimated environmental concentration [EEC] and toxicological endpoints [e.g., LC$_{50}$ and oral LD$_{50}$]) to evaluate the potential for adverse effects to species groups (birds, mammals, and fish) representative of legal mandates for managing units of the Refuge System. This integration is achieved through risk quotients (RQs) calculated by dividing the EEC by acute and chronic toxicity values selected from standardized toxicological endpoints or published effect (Table 1).

$$RQ = EEC/Toxicological\ Endpoint$$

The level of risk associated with direct effects of pesticide use would be characterized by comparing calculated RQs to the appropriate Level of Concern (LOC) established by the EPA (1998 [Table 2]). The LOC represents a quantitative threshold value for screening potential adverse effects to fish and wildlife resources associated with pesticide use. The following are four exposure-species group scenarios that would be examined to characterize ecological risk to fish and wildlife on the Refuge: acute-listed species, acute-nonlisted species, chronic-listed species, and chronic-nonlisted species.

Acute risk would indicate the potential for mortality associated with short-term dietary exposure to pesticides immediately after an application. For characterization of acute risks, median values from LC$_{50}$ and LD$_{50}$ tests would be used as toxicological endpoints for RQ calculations. In contrast, chronic risks would indicate the potential for adverse effects associated with long-term dietary exposure to pesticides from a single application or multiple applications over time (within a season and over years).

For characterization of chronic risks, the no observed concentration (NOAEC) or no observed effect concentration (NOEC) for reproduction would be used as toxicological endpoints for RQ calculations. Where available, the NOAEC would be preferred over a NOEC value. Listed species are those federally designated as threatened, endangered, or proposed in accordance with the ESA (16 USC 1531-1544, 87 Stat. 884, as amended-Public Law 93-205). For listed species, potential adverse effects would be assessed at the individual level because loss of individuals from a population could detrimentally impact a species. In contrast, risks to nonlisted species would be considered at the population level. An RQ<LOC for a taxonomic group would indicate the proposed pesticide use "may affect, not likely to adversely effect" individuals (listed species) or populations (non-listed species) of the taxonomic group (Table 2). In contrast, an RQ>LOC would indicate unacceptable ecological risk considering the potential for adverse effects.

Table 2. Presumption of unacceptable risk for birds, fish, and mammals (US Environmental Protection Agency 1998).

Risk Presumption		Level of Concern	
		Listed Species	Non-listed Species
Acute	Birds	0.1	0.5
	Fish	0.05	0.5
	Mammals	0.1	0.5
Chronic	Birds	1.0	1.0
	Fish	1.0	1.0
	Mammals	1.0	1.0

7.2.1 Environmental exposure

Following release into the environment through application, pesticides would experience several different routes of environmental fate. Pesticides which would be sprayed can move through the air (e.g., particle or vapor drift) and may eventually end up in other parts of the environment such as non-target vegetation, soil, or water. Pesticides applied directly to the soil may be washed off the soil into nearby bodies of surface water (e.g., surface runoff) or may percolate through the soil to lower soil layers and groundwater (e.g., leaching) (Baker and Miller 1999, Pope et. al. 1999, Buttler et. al. 1998, Ramsay et. al. 1995, EXTOXNET 1993a). Pesticides which would be injected into the soil may also be subject to the latter two fates.

The aforementioned possibilities are by no means complete, but it does indicate movement of pesticides in the environment is complex with transfers occurring continually among different environmental compartments. In some cases, these exchanges occur not only between areas that are close together, but it also may involve transportation of pesticides over long distances (Barry 2004; Woods 2004).

7.2.1.1 Terrestrial exposure

The ECC for exposure to terrestrial wildlife would be quantified using an EPA screening-level approach (US Environmental Protection Agency 2004). This screening-level approach is not affected by product formulation because it evaluates pesticide active ingredient(s). This approach would vary depending upon the proposed pesticide application method: spray or granular.

7.2.1.1.1 Terrestrial-spray application

For spray applications, exposure would be determined using the Kanaga nomogram method (US Environmental Protection Agency 2005*a*, US Environmental Protection Agency 2004, Pfleeger et al. 1996) through the EPA's Terrestrial Residue Exposure model (T-REX) version 1.2.3 (US Environmental Protection Agency 2005*b*). To estimate the maximum (initial) pesticide residue on short grass (<20 cm tall) as a general food item category for terrestrial vertebrate species, T-REX input variables would include the following from the pesticide label: maximum pesticide application rate (pounds active ingredient [acid equivalent] per acre) and pesticide half-life (days) in soil. Although there are other food item categories (tall grasses; broadleaf plants and small insects; and fruits, pods, seeds and large insects), short grass was selected because it would yield maximum EECs (240 ppm per lb ai [active ingredient] per acre) for worst-case risk assessments. Short grass is not representative of forage for carnivorous species (e.g., raptors), but it would characterize the maximum potential exposure through the diet of avian and mammalian prey items. Consequently, this approach would provide a conservative screening tool for pesticides that do not biomagnify.

For RQ calculations in T-REX, the model would require the weight of surrogate species and Mineau scaling factors (Mineau et. al. 1996). Body weights of bobwhite quail and mallard are included in T-REX by default, but body weights of other organisms (Table 3) would be entered manually. The Mineau scaling factor accounts for small-bodied bird species that may be more sensitive to pesticide exposure than would be predicted only by body weight. Mineau scaling factors would be entered manually with values ranging from 1 to 1.55 that are unique to a particular pesticide or group of pesticides. If specific information to select a scaling factor is not available, then a value of 1.15 would be used as a default. Alternatively, zero would be entered if it is known that body weight does not influence toxicity of the pesticide(s) being assessed. The upper bound estimate output from the T-REX Kanaga nomogram would be used as an EEC for calculation of RQs. This approach would yield a conservative estimate of ecological risk.

Table 3. Average body weight of selected terrestrial wildlife species frequently used in research to establish toxicological endpoints (Dunning 1984).

Species	Body Weight (kg)
Mammal (15 g)	0.015
House sparrow	0.0277
Mammal (35 g)	0.035
Starling	0.0823
Red-winged blackbird	0.0526
Common grackle	0.114
Japanese quail	0.178
Bobwhite quail	0.178
Rat	0.200
Rock dove (aka pigeon)	0.542
Mammal (1000 g)	1.000
Mallard	1.082
Ring-necked pheasant	1.135

7.2.1.1.2 Terrestrial – granular application

Granular pesticide formulations and pesticide-treated seed would pose a unique route of exposure for avian and mammalian species. The pesticide is applied in discrete units which birds or mammals might ingest accidentally with food items or intentionally, as in the case of some bird species actively seeking and picking up gravel or grit to aid digestion or seed as a food source. Granules may also be consumed by wildlife foraging on earthworms, slugs or other soft-bodied soil organisms to which the granules may adhere.

Terrestrial wildlife RQs for granular formulations or seed treatments would be calculated by dividing the maximum milligrams of ai exposed (e.g., EEC) on the surface of an area equal to 1 square foot by the appropriate LD_{50} value multiplied by the surrogate's body weight (Table 3). An adjustment to surface area calculations would be made for broadcast, banded, and in-furrow applications. An adjustment would also be made for applications with and without incorporation of the granules. Without incorporation, it would be assumed that 100% of the granules remain on the soil surface available to foraging birds and mammals. Press wheels push granules flat with the soil surface, but they are not incorporated into the soil. If granules are incorporated in the soil during band or T-band applications or after broadcast applications, it would be assumed only 15% of the applied granules would remain available to wildlife. It would be assumed that only 1% of the granules are available on the soil surface following in-furrow applications.

EECs for pesticides applied in granular form and as seed treatments would be determined considering potential ingestion rates of avian or mammalian species (e.g., 10-30% body weight per day). This would provide an estimate of maximum exposure that may occur as a result of granule or seed treatment spills such as those that commonly occur at end rows during application and planting. The availability of granules and seed treatments to terrestrial vertebrates would also be considered by calculating the loading per unit area (LD_{50}/ft^2) for comparison to EPA Level of Concerns (US Environmental Protection Agency 1998). The T-REX version 1.2.3 (US Environmental Protection Agency 2005b) contains a submodel which automates Kanaga exposure calculations for granular pesticides and treated seed.

The following formulas will be used to calculate EECs depending upon the type of granular pesticide application:

- In-furrow applications assume a typical value of 1% granules, bait, or seed remain unincorporated.

$$mg\ a.i./ft^2 = [(lbs.\ product/acre)(\%\ a.i.)(453,580\ mg/lbs)(1\%\ exposed))] / \{[(43,560\ ft^2/acre)/(row\ spacing\ (ft.))] / (row\ spacing\ (ft.)\}$$
$$or$$
$$mg\ a.i./ft^2 = [(lbs\ product/1000\ ft.\ row)(\%\ a.i.)(1000\ ft\ row)(453,580\ mg/lb.)(1\%\ exposed)$$

$$EEC = [(mg\ a.i./ft^2)(\%\ of\ pesticide\ biologically\ available)]$$

- Incorporated banded treatments assume that 15% of granules, bait, or seeds are unincorporated.

$$mg\ a.i./ft.^2 = [(lbs.\ product/1000\ row\ ft.)(\%\ a.i.)(453,580\ mg/lb.)(1-\%\ incorporated)]\ /$$
$$(1,000\ ft.)(band\ width\ (ft.))$$
$$EEC = [(mg\ a.i./ft.^2)(\%\ of\ pesticide\ biologically\ available)]$$

- Broadcast treatment without incorporation assumes 100% of granules, bait, or seeds are unincorporated.

$$mg\ a.i./ft.^2 = [(lbs.\ product/acre)(\%\ a.i.)(453,590\ mg/lb.)]\ /\ (43,560\ ft.^2/acre)$$
$$EEC = [(mg\ a.i./ft.^2)(\%\ of\ pesticide\ biologically\ available)]$$

Where:

- *% of pesticide biologically available = 100% without species specific ingestion rates*

- *Conversion for calculating mg a.i./ft.^{2} using ounces: 453,580 mg/lb. /16 = 28,349 mg/oz.*

The following equation would used to calculate an RQ based on the EEC calculated by one of the above equations. The EEC would be divided by the surrogate LD_{50} toxicological endpoint multiplied by the body weight (Table 3) of the surrogate.

$$RQ = EEC\ /\ [LD_{50}\ (mg/kg)\ *\ body\ weight\ (kg)]$$

As with other risk assessments, an RQ>LOC would be a presumption of unacceptable ecological risk. An RQ<LOC would be a presumption of acceptable risk with only minor, temporary, or localized effects to species.

7.2.1.2 Aquatic exposure

Exposures to aquatic habitats (e.g., wetlands, meadows, ephemeral pools, water delivery ditches) would be evaluated separately for ground-based pesticide treatments of habitats managed for fish and wildlife compared with cropland/facilities maintenance. The primary exposure pathway for aquatic organisms from any ground-based treatments would likely be particle drift during the pesticide application. However, different exposure scenarios would be necessary as a result of contrasting application equipment and techniques as well as pesticides used to control pests on agricultural lands (especially those cultivated by cooperative farmers for economic return from crop yields) and facilities maintenance (e.g., roadsides, parking lots, trails) compared with other managed habitats on the Refuge. In addition, pesticide applications may be done <25 feet of the high water mark of aquatic habitats for habitat management treatments; whereas, no-spray buffers (≥25 feet) would be used for croplands/facilities maintenance treatments.

7.2.1.2.1 Habitat treatments

For the worst-case exposure scenario to non-target aquatic habitats, EECs (Table 4) would be derived from Urban and Cook (1986) which assumes an intentional overspray to an entire, non-target water body (1-foot depth) from a treatment <25 feet from the high water mark using the maximum application rate (acid basis [see above]). However, use of BMPs for applying pesticides (see Section 4.2) would likely minimize/eliminate potential drift to non-target aquatic habitats during actual treatments. If there would be unacceptable (acute or chronic) risk to fish and wildlife with the simulated 100% overspray (RQ>LOC), then the proposed pesticide use may be disapproved or the PUP would be approved at a lower application rate to minimize/eliminate unacceptable risk to aquatic organisms (RQ=LOC).

Table 4. Estimated Environmental Concentrations (ppb) of pesticides in aquatic habitats (1 foot depth) immediately after direct application (Urban and Cook 1986).

Lbs/acre	EEC (ppb)
0.10	36.7
0.20	73.5
0.25	91.9
0.30	110.2
0.40	147.0
0.50	183.7
0.75	275.6
1.00	367.5
1.25	459.7
1.50	551.6
1.75	643.5
2.00	735.7
2.25	827.6
2.50	919.4
3.00	1103.5
4.00	1471.4
5.00	1839
6.00	2207
7.00	2575
8.00	2943
9.00	3311
10.00	3678

7.2.1.2.2 Cropland/facilities maintenance treatments

Field drift studies conducted by the Spray Drift Task Force, which is a joint project of several agricultural chemical businesses, were used to develop a generic spray drift database. From this database, the AgDRIFT computer model was created to satisfy EPA pesticide registration spray drift data requirements and as a scientific basis to evaluate off-target movement of pesticides from particle drift and assess potential effects of exposure to wildlife. Several versions of the computer model have been developed (i.e., v2.01 through v2.10). The Spray Drift Task Force AgDRIFT® model version 2.01 (SDTF 2003, AgDRIFT 2001) would be used to derive EECs resulting from drift of pesticides to Refuge aquatic resources from ground-based pesticide applications >25 feet from the high water mark. The Spray Drift Task Force AgDRIFT model is publicly available at http://www.agdrift.com. At this website, click "AgDRIFT 2.0" and then click "Download Now" and follow the instructions to obtain the computer model.

The AgDRIFT model is composed of submodels called tiers. Tier I Ground submodel would be used to assess ground-based applications of pesticides. Tier outputs (EECs) would be calculated with AgDRIFT using the following input variables: maximum application rate (acid basis [see above]), low boom (20 inches), fine to medium droplet size, EPA-defined wetland, and a ≥25-foot distance (buffer) from treated area to water.

7.2.2 Use of information on effects of biological control agents, pesticides, degradates, and adjuvants

NEPA documents regarding biological and other environmental effects of biological control agents, pesticides, degradates, and adjuvants prepared by another federal agency, where the scope would be relevant to evaluation of effects from pesticide uses on Refuge lands, would be reviewed. Possible source agencies for such NEPA documents would include the BLM, US Forest Service, NPS, USDA-Animal and Plant Health Inspection Service, and the military services. It might be appropriate to incorporate by reference parts or all of existing document(s). Incorporating by reference (40 CFR 1502.21) is a technique used to avoid redundancies in analysis. It also would reduce the bulk of a Service NEPA document, which would only identify the documents that are incorporated by reference. In addition, relevant portions would be summarized in the Service's NEPA document to the extent necessary to provide the decision maker and public with an understanding of relevance of the referenced material to the current analysis.

In accordance with the requirements set forth in 43 CFR 46.135, the Service would specifically incorporate through reference ecological risk assessments prepared by the US Forest Service (http://www.fs.fed.us/r6/invasiveplant-eis/Risk-Assessments/Herbicides-Analyzed-InvPlant-EIS.htm) and BLM (http://www.blm.gov/wo/st/en/prog/more/veg _eis.html). These risk assessments and associated documentation also are available in total with the administrative record for the Final Environmental Impact Statement entitled *Pacific Northwest Region Invasive Plant Program – Preventing and Managing Invasive Plants* (US Forest Service 2005) and *Vegetation Treatments Using Herbicides on Bureau of Land Management Lands in 17 Western States Programmatic EIS (PEIS)* (Bureau of Land Management 2007). In accordance with 43 CRF 46.120(d), use of existing NEPA documents by supplementing, tiering to, incorporating by reference, or adopting previous NEPA environmental analyses would avoid redundancy and unnecessary paperwork.

As a basis for completing "Chemical Profiles" for approving or disapproving Refuge PUPs, ecological risk assessments for the following herbicide and adjuvant uses prepared by the US Forest Service would be incorporated by reference:
- 2,4-D
- Chlorosulfuron
- Clopyralid
- Dicamba
- Glyphosate
- Imazapic
- Imazapyr
- Metsulfuron methyl
- Picloram
- Sethoxydim

- Sulfometuron methyl
- Triclopyr
- Nonylphenol polyethylate (NPE) based surfactants

As a basis for completing "Chemical Profiles" for approving or disapproving refuge PUPs, ecological risk assessments for the following herbicide uses as well as evaluation of risks associated with pesticide degradates and adjuvants prepared by BLM would be incorporated by reference:

- Bromacil
- Chlorsulfuron
- Diflufenzopyr
- Diquat
- Diuron
- Fluridone
- Imazapic
- Overdrive (diflufenzopyr and dicamba)
- Sulfometuron methyl
- Tebuthiuron
- Pesticide degradates and adjuvants (*Appendix D – Evaluation of risks from degradates, polyoxyethylene-amine (POEA) and R-11, and endocrine disrupting chemicals*)

7.2.3 Assumptions for ecological risk assessments

There are a number of assumptions involved with the ecological risk assessment process for terrestrial and aquatic organisms associated with utilization of the US EPA (2004) process. These assumptions may be risk neutral or may lead to an over- or under-estimation of risk from pesticide exposure depending upon site-specific conditions. The following describes these assumptions, their application to the conditions typically encountered, and whether or not they may lead to recommendations that are risk neutral, underestimate, or overestimate ecological risk from potential pesticide exposure.

- Indirect effects would not be evaluated by ecological risk assessments. These effects include the mechanisms of indirect exposure to pesticides: consuming prey items (fish, birds, or small mammals), reductions in the availability of prey items, and disturbance associated with pesticide application activities.
- Exposure to a pesticide product can be assessed based upon the active ingredient. However, exposure to a chemical mixture (pesticide formulation) may result in effects that are similar or substantially different compared to only the active ingredient. Non-target organisms may be exposed directly to the pesticide formulation or only various constituents of the formulation as they dissipate and partition in the environment. If toxicological information for both the active ingredient and formulated product are available, then data representing the greatest potential toxicity would be selected for use in the risk assessment process (US Environmental Protection Agency 2004). As a result, this conservative approach may lead to an overestimation of risk characterization from pesticide exposure.
- Because toxicity tests with listed or candidate species or closely related species are not available, data for surrogate species would most often be used for risk assessments. Specifically, bobwhite quail and mallard duck are the most frequently used surrogates for

evaluating potential toxicity to federally listed avian species. Bluegill sunfish, rainbow trout, and fathead minnow are the most common surrogates for evaluating toxicity for freshwater fishes. However, sheep's head minnow can be an appropriate surrogate marine species for coastal environments. Rats and mice are the most common surrogates for evaluating toxicity for mammals. Interspecies sensitivity is a major source of uncertainty in pesticide assessments. As a result of this uncertainty, data is selected for the most sensitive species tested within a taxonomic group (birds, fish, and mammals) given the quality of the data is acceptable. If additional toxicity data for more species of organisms in a particular group are available, the selected data will not be limited to the species previously listed as common surrogates.

- The Kanaga nomogram outputs maximum EEC values that may be used to calculate an average daily concentration over a specified interval of time, which is referred to as a time-weighted-average (TWA). The maximum EEC would be selected as the exposure input for both acute and chronic risk assessments in the screening-level evaluations. The initial or maximum EEC derived from the Kanaga nomogram represents the maximum expected instantaneous or acute exposure to a pesticide. Acute toxicity endpoints are determined using a single exposure to a known pesticide concentration, typically for 48 to 96 hours. This value is assumed to represent ecological risk from acute exposure to a pesticide. On the other hand, chronic risk to pesticide exposure is a function of pesticide concentration and duration of exposure to the pesticide. An organism's response to chronic pesticide exposure may result from either the concentration of the pesticide, length of exposure, or some combination of both factors. Standardized tests for chronic toxicity typically involve exposing an organism to several different pesticide concentrations for a specified length of time (days, weeks, months, years or generations). For example, avian reproduction tests include a 10-week exposure phase. Because a single length of time is used in the test, time response data is usually not available for inclusion into risk assessments. Without time response data it is difficult to determine the concentration which elicited a toxicological response.

- Using maximum EECs for chronic risk estimates may result in an overestimate of risk, particularly for compounds that dissipate rapidly. Conversely, using TWAs for chronic risk estimates may underestimate risk if it is the concentration rather than the duration of exposure that is primarily responsible for the observed adverse effect. The maximum EEC would be used for chronic risk assessments, although it may result in an overestimate of risk. TWAs may be used for chronic risk assessments, but they will be applied judiciously considering the potential for an underestimate or overestimate of risk. For example, the number of days' exposure exceeding a LOC may influence the suitability of a pesticide use. The greater the number of days the EEC exceeds the LOC translates into a greater ecological risk. This is a qualitative assessment, and is subject to the reviewer's expertise in ecological risk assessment and tolerance for risk.

- The length of time used to calculate the TWA can have a substantial effect on the exposure estimates and there is no standard method for determining the appropriate duration for this estimate. The T-REX model assumes a 21-week exposure period, which is equivalent to avian reproductive studies designed to establish a steady-state concentration for bioaccumulative compounds. However, this does not necessarily define the true exposure duration needed to elicit a toxicological response. Pesticides, which do not bioaccumulate, may achieve a steady-state concentration earlier than 21 weeks. The duration of time for calculating TWAs will require justification and it will not exceed the duration of exposure in the chronic toxicity test (approximately 70 days for the standard avian reproduction study). An alternative to using the duration of the chronic toxicity study is to base the TWA on the application interval. In this case, increasing the application interval would suppress both the estimated peak pesticide concentration and the TWA. Another alternative to using TWAs would be to consider the number of days that a chemical is predicted to exceed the LOC.

- Pesticide dissipation is assumed to be first-order in the absence of data suggesting alternative dissipation patterns such as bi-phasic. Field dissipation data would generally be the most pertinent for assessing exposure in terrestrial species that forage on vegetation. However, this data is often not available and it can be misleading, particularly if the compound is prone to "wash-off". Soil half-life is the most common degradation data available. Dissipation or degradation data that would reflect the environmental conditions typical of Refuge lands would be utilized, if available.

- For species found in the water column, it would be assumed that the greatest bioavailable fraction of the pesticide active ingredient in surface waters is freely dissolved in the water column.

- Actual habitat requirements of any particular terrestrial species are not considered, and it is assumed that species exclusively and permanently occupy the treated area, or adjacent areas receiving pesticide at rates commensurate with the treatment rate. This assumption would produce a maximum estimate of exposure for risk characterization. This assumption would likely lead to an overestimation of exposure for species that do not permanently and exclusively occupy the treated area (US Environmental Protection Agency 2004).

- Exposure through incidental ingestion of pesticide contaminated soil is not considered in the EPA risk assessment protocols. Research suggests <15% of the diet can consist of incidentally ingested soil depending upon species and feeding strategy (Beyer et al. 1994). An assessment of pesticide concentrations in soil compared to food item categories in the Kanaga nomogram indicates incidental soil ingestion will not likely increase dietary exposure to pesticides. Inclusion of soil into the diet would effectively reduce the overall dietary concentration compared to the present assumption that the entire diet consists of a contaminated food source (Fletcher et al. 1994). An exception to this may be soil-applied pesticides in which exposure from incidental ingestion of soil may increase. Potential for pesticide exposure under this assumption may be underestimated for soil-applied pesticides and overestimated for foliar-applied pesticides. The concentration of a pesticide in soil would likely be less than predicted on food items.

- Exposure through inhalation of pesticides is not considered in the EPA risk assessment protocols. Such exposure may occur through three potential sources: spray material in droplet form at time of application, vapor phase with the pesticide volatilizing from treated surfaces, and airborne particulates (soil, vegetative matter, and pesticide dusts). The EPA (1990) reported exposure from inhaling spray droplets at the time of application is not an appreciable route of exposure for birds. According to research on mallards and bobwhite quail, respirable particle size (particles reaching the lung) in birds is limited to maximum diameter of 2 to 5 microns. The spray droplet spectra covering the majority of pesticide application scenarios indicate that less than 1% of the applied material is within the respirable particle size. This route of exposure is further limited because the permissible spray drop size distribution for ground pesticide applications is restricted to ASAE medium or coarser drop size distribution.

- Inhalation of a pesticide in the vapor phase may be another source of exposure for some pesticides under certain conditions. This mechanism of exposure to pesticides occurs post application and it would pertain to those pesticides with a high vapor pressure. The EPA is currently evaluating protocols for modeling inhalation exposure from pesticides including near-field and near-ground air concentrations based upon equilibrium and kinetics-based models. Risk characterization for exposure with this mechanism is unavailable.

- The effect from exposure to dusts contaminated with the pesticide cannot be assessed generically as partitioning issues related to application site soils and chemical properties of the applied pesticides render the exposure potential from this route highly situation specific.

- Dermal exposure may occur through three potential sources: direct application of spray to terrestrial wildlife in the treated area or within the drift footprint, incidental contact with contaminated vegetation, or contact with contaminated water or soil. Interception of spray and incidental contact with treated substrates may pose risk to avian wildlife (Driver et al. 1991). However, available research related to wildlife dermal contact with pesticides is extremely limited, except dermal toxicity values are common for some mammals used as human surrogates (rats and mice). The EPA is currently evaluating protocols for modeling dermal exposure. Risk characterization may be underestimated for this route of exposure, particularly with high risk pesticides such as some organophosphates or carbamate insecticides. If protocols are established by the EPA for assessing dermal exposure to pesticides, they will be considered for incorporation into pesticide assessment protocols.

- Exposure to a pesticide may occur from consuming surface water, dew, or other water on treated surfaces. Water soluble pesticides that have potential to dissolve in surface runoff and puddles in a treated area may contain pesticide residues. Similarly, pesticides with lower organic carbon partitioning characteristics and higher solubility in water have a greater potential to dissolve in dew and other water associated with plant surfaces. Estimating the extent to which such pesticide loadings to drinking water occurs is complex and would depend upon the partitioning characteristics of the active ingredient, soils types in the treatment area, and the meteorology of the treatment area. In addition, the use of various water sources by wildlife is highly species-specific. Currently, risk characterization for this exposure mechanism is not available. The EPA is actively developing protocols to quantify drinking water exposures from puddles and dew. If and when protocols are formally established by the EPA for assessing exposure to pesticides through drinking water, these protocols will be incorporated into pesticide risk assessment protocols.

- Risk assessments are based upon the assumption that the entire treatment area would be subject to pesticide application at the rates specified on the label. In most cases, there is potential for uneven application of pesticides through such plausible incidents such as changes in calibration of application equipment, spillage, and localized releases at specific areas in or near the treated field that are associated with mixing and handling and application equipment as well as applicator skill. Inappropriate use of pesticides and the occurrence of spills represent a potential underestimate of risk. It is likely not an important factor for risk characterization. All pesticide applicators are required to be certified by the state in which they apply pesticides. Certification training includes the safe storage, transport, handling, and mixing of pesticides, equipment calibration, and proper application with annual continuing education.

- The EPA relies on Fletcher (1994) for setting the assumed pesticide residues in wildlife dietary items. The EPA (2004) "believes that these residue assumptions reflect a realistic upper-bound residue estimate, although the degree to which this assumption reflects a specific percentile estimate is difficult to quantify". Fletcher's (1994) research suggests that the pesticide active ingredient residue assumptions used by the EPA represent a 95th percentile estimate. However, research conducted by Pfleeger et al. (1996) indicates EPA residue assumptions for short grass were not exceeded. Behr and Habig (2000) compared EPA residue assumptions with distributions of measured pesticide residues for the EPA's UTAB database. Overall residue selection level will tend to overestimate risk characterization. This is particularly evident when wildlife individuals are likely to have selected a variety of food items acquired from multiple locations. Some food items may be contaminated with pesticide residues whereas others are not contaminated. However, it is important to recognize differences in species feeding behavior. Some species may consume whole above-ground plant material, but others will preferentially select different plant structures. Also, species may preferentially select a food item although multiple food items may be present. Without species-specific knowledge regarding foraging behavior, characterizing ecological risk other than in general terms is not possible.

- Acute and chronic risk assessments rely on comparisons of wildlife dietary residues with LC_{50} or NOEC values expressed as concentrations of pesticides in laboratory feed. These comparisons assume that ingestion of food items in the field occurs at rates commensurate with those in the laboratory. Although the screening assessment process adjusts dry-weight estimates of food intake to reflect the increased mass in fresh-weight wildlife food intake estimates, it does not allow for gross energy and assimilative efficiency differences between wildlife food items and laboratory feed. Differences in assimilative efficiency between laboratory and wild diets suggest that current screening assessment methods are not accounting for a potentially important aspect of food requirements.

- There are several other assumptions that can affect non-target species not considered in the risk assessment process. These include possible additive or synergistic effects from applying two or more pesticides or additives in a single application, co-location of pesticides in the environment, cumulative effects from pesticides with the same mode of action, effects of multiple stressors (e.g., combination of pesticide exposure, adverse abiotic and biotic factors) and behavioral changes induced by exposure to a pesticide. These factors may exist at some level contributing to adverse affects to non-target species, but they are usually characterized in the published literature in only a general manner limiting their value in the risk assessment process.

- It is assumed that aquatic species exclusively and permanently occupy the water body being assessed. Actual habitat requirements of aquatic species are not considered. With the possible exception of scenarios where pesticides are directly applied to water, it is assumed that no habitat use considerations specific for any species would place the organisms in closer proximity to pesticide use sites. This assumption produces a maximum estimate of exposure or risk characterization. It would likely be realistic for many aquatic species that may be found in aquatic habitats within or in close proximity to treated terrestrial habitats. However, the spatial distribution of wildlife is usually not random because wildlife distributions are often related to habitat requirements of species. Clumped distributions of wildlife may result in an under- or over-estimation of risk depending upon where the initial pesticide concentration occurs relative to the species or species habitat.

- For species found in the water column, it would be assumed that the greatest bioavailable fraction of the pesticide active ingredient in surface waters is freely dissolved in the water column. Additional chemical exposure from materials associated with suspended solids or food items is not considered because partitioning onto sediments likely is minimal.

Adsorption and bioconcentration occur at lower levels for many newer pesticides compared with older more persistent bioaccumulative compounds. For pesticides with RQs close to the listed species level of concern, the potential for additional exposure from these routes may be a limitation of risk assessments, where potential pesticide exposure or risk may be underestimated.

- Mass transport losses of pesticide from a water body (except for losses by volatilization, degradation and sediment partitioning) would not be considered for ecological risk assessment. The water body would be assumed to capture all pesticide active ingredients entering as runoff, drift, and adsorbed to eroded soil particles. It would also be assumed that the pesticide active ingredient is not lost from the water body by overtopping or flow-through, nor is concentration reduced by dilution. In total, these assumptions would lead to a near maximum possible water-borne concentration. However, this assumption would not account for potential to concentrate pesticide through the evaporative loss. This limitation may have the greatest impact on water bodies with high surface-to-volume ratios such as ephemeral wetlands, where evaporative losses are accentuated and applied pesticides have low rates of degradation and volatilization.

- For acute risk assessments, there would be no averaging time for exposure. An instantaneous peak concentration would be assumed, where instantaneous exposure is sufficient in duration to elicit acute effects comparable to those observed over more protracted exposure periods (typically 48 to 96 hours) tested in the laboratory. In the absence of data regarding time-to-toxic event analyses and latent responses to instantaneous exposure, risk would likely be overestimated.

- For chronic exposure risk assessments, the averaging times considered for exposure are commensurate with the duration of invertebrate life-cycle or fish-early life stage tests (e.g., 21-28 days and 56-60 days, respectively). Response profiles (time to effect and latency of effect) to pesticides likely vary widely with mode of action and species and should be evaluated on a case-by-case basis as available data allow. Nevertheless, because the EPA relies on chronic exposure toxicity endpoints based on a finding of no observed effect, the potential for any latent toxicity effects or averaging time assumptions to alter the results of an acceptable chronic risk assessment prediction is limited. The extent to which duration of exposure from water-borne concentrations overestimate or underestimate actual exposure depends on several factors. These include the following: localized meteorological conditions, runoff characteristics of the watershed (e.g., soils, topography), the hydrological characteristics of receiving waters, environmental fate of the pesticide active ingredient, and the method of pesticide application. It should also be understood that chronic effects studies are performed using a method that holds water concentration in a steady state. This method is not likely to reflect conditions associated with pesticide runoff. Pesticide concentrations in the field increase and decrease in surface water on a cycle influenced by rainfall, pesticide use patterns, and degradation rates. As a result of the dependency of this assumption on several undefined variables, risk associated with chronic exposure may in some situations underestimate risk and overestimate risk in others.

- There are several other factors that can affect non-target species not considered in the risk assessment process. These would include the following: possible additive or synergistic effects from applying two or more pesticides or additives in a single application, co-location of pesticides in the environment, cumulative effects from pesticides with the same mode of action, effects of multiple stressors (e.g., combination of pesticide exposure, adverse abiotic [not pesticides] and biotic factors), and sub-lethal effects such as behavioral changes induced by exposure to a pesticide. These factors may exist at some level contributing to adverse affects to non-target species, but they are not routinely assessed by regulatory agencies. Therefore, information on the factors is not extensive, limiting their value for the risk assessment process. As this type of information becomes available, it would be included, either quantitatively or qualitatively, in this risk assessment process.

- EPA is required by the Food Quality Protection Act to assess the cumulative risks of pesticides that share common mechanisms of toxicity, or act the same within an organism. Currently, EPA has identified four groups of pesticides that have a common mechanism of toxicity requiring cumulative risk assessments. These four groups are the organophosphate insecticides, N-methyl carbamate insecticides, triazine herbicides, and chloroacetanilide herbicides.

7.3 Pesticide Mixtures and Degradates

Pesticide products are usually a formulation of several components generally categorized as active ingredients and inert or other ingredients. The term active ingredient is defined by the FIFRA as preventing, destroying, repelling, or mitigating the effects of a pest, or it is a plant regulator, defoliant, desiccant, or nitrogen stabilizer. In accordance with FIFRA, the active ingredient(s) must be identified by name(s) on the pesticide label along with its relative composition expressed in percentage(s) by weight. In contrast, inert ingredient(s) are not intended to affect a target pest. Their role in the pesticide formulation is to act as a solvent (keep the active ingredient in a liquid phase), an emulsifying or suspending agent (keep the active ingredient from separating out of solution), or a carrier such as clay in which the active ingredient is impregnated on the clay particle in dry formulations. For example, if isopropyl alcohol would be used as a solvent in a pesticide formulation, then it would be considered an inert ingredient. FIFRA only requires that inert ingredients identified as hazardous and associated percent composition, and the total percentage of all inert ingredients must be declared on a product label. Inert ingredients that are not classified as hazardous are not required to be identified.

The EPA (September 1997) issued Pesticide Regulation Notice 97-6 which encouraged manufacturers, formulators, producers, and registrants of pesticide products to voluntarily substitute the term "other ingredients" for "inert ingredients" in the ingredient statement. This change recognized that all components in a pesticide formulation potentially could elicit or contribute to an adverse effect on non-target organisms and, therefore, are not necessarily inert. Whether referred to as "inerts" or "other ingredients," these constituents within a pesticide product have the potential to affect species or environmental quality. The EPA categorizes regulated inert ingredients into the following four lists (http://www.epa.gov/opprd001/inerts/index.html):
- List 1 – Inert Ingredients of Toxicological Concern
- List 2 – Potentially Toxic Inert Ingredients
- List 3 – Inerts of Unknown Toxicity
- List 4 – Inerts of Minimal Toxicity

Several of the List 4 compounds are naturally-occurring earthen materials (e.g., clay materials, simple salts) that would not elicit toxicological response at applied concentrations. However, some of the inerts (particularly the List 3 compounds and unlisted compounds) may have moderate to high potential toxicity to aquatic species based on MSDSs or published data.

Comprehensively assessing potential effects to non-target fish, wildlife, plants, and/or their habitats from pesticide use is a complex task. It would be preferable to assess the cumulative effects from exposure to the active ingredient, its degradates, and inert ingredients as well as other active ingredients in the spray mixture. However, it would only be feasible to conduct deterministic risk assessments for each component in the spray mixture singly. Limited scientific information is available regarding ecological effects (additive or synergistic) from chemical mixtures that typically rely upon broadly encompassing assumptions. For example, the US Forest Service (2005) found that mixtures of pesticides used in land (forest) management likely would not cause additive or synergistic effects to non-target species based upon a review of scientific literature regarding toxicological effects and interactions of agricultural chemicals (ATSDR 2004, US EPA-ORD 2000). Moreover, information on inert ingredients, adjuvants, and degradates is often limited by the availability of and access to reliable toxicological data for these constituents.

Toxicological information regarding "other ingredients" may be available from sources such as the following:
- TOMES (a proprietary toxicological database including EPA's IRIS, the Hazardous Substance Data Bank, the Registry of Toxic Effects of Chemical Substances [RTECS]).
- EPA's ECOTOX database, which includes AQUIRE (a database containing scientific papers published on the toxic effects of chemicals to aquatic organisms).
- TOXLINE (a literature searching tool).
- Material Safety Data Sheets (MSDSs) from pesticide suppliers.
- Other sources such as the Farm Chemicals Handbook.

Because there is a lack of specific inert toxicological data, inert(s) in a pesticide may cause adverse ecological effects. However, inert ingredients typically represent only a small percentage of the pesticide spray mixture; it would be assumed that negligible effects would be expected to result from inert ingredient(s).

Although the potential effects of degradates should be considered when selecting a pesticide, it is beyond the scope of this assessment process to consider all possible breakdown chemicals of the various product formulations containing an active ingredient. Degradates may be more or less mobile and more or less hazardous in the environment than their parent pesticides (Battaglin et al. 2003). Differences in environmental behavior (e.g., mobility) and toxicity between parent pesticides and degradates would make assessing potential degradate effects extremely difficult. For example, a less toxic and more mobile, bioaccumulative, or persistent degradate may have potentially greater effects on species and/or degrade environmental quality. The lack of data on the toxicity of degradates for many pesticides would represent a source of uncertainty for assessing risk.

An EPA-approved label specifies whether a product can be mixed with one or more pesticides. Without product-specific toxicological data, it would not possible to quantify the potential effects of these mixtures. In addition, a quantitative analysis could only be conducted if reliable scientific information allowed a determination of whether the joint action of a mixture would be additive, synergistic, or antagonistic. Such information would not likely exist unless the mode of action would be common among the chemicals and receptors. Moreover, the composition of and exposure to mixtures would be highly site- and/or time-specific and, therefore, it would be nearly impossible to assess potential effects to species and environmental quality.

To minimize or eliminate potential negative effects associated with applying two or more pesticides as a mixture, the use would be conducted in accordance with the labeling requirements. Labels for two or more pesticides applied as a mixture should be completely reviewed, where products with the least potential for negative effects would be selected for use on the Refuge. This is especially relevant when a mixture would be applied in a manner that may already have the potential for an effect(s) associated with an individual pesticide (e.g., runoff to ponds in sandy watersheds). Use of a tank mix under these conditions would increase the level of uncertainty in terms of risk to species or potential to degrade environmental quality.

Adjuvants generally function to enhance or prolong the activity of pesticide. For terrestrial herbicides, adjuvants aid in the absorption into plant tissue. Adjuvant is a broad term that generally applies to surfactants, selected oils, anti-foaming agents, buffering compounds, drift control agents, compatibility agents, stickers, and spreaders. Adjuvants are not under the same registration requirements as pesticides and the EPA does not register or approve the labeling of spray adjuvants. Individual pesticide labels identify types of adjuvants approved for use with it. In general, adjuvants compose a relatively small portion of the volume of pesticides applied. Selection of adjuvants with limited toxicity and low volumes would be recommended to reduce the potential for the adjuvant to influence the toxicity of the pesticide.

7.4 Determining Effects to Soil and Water Quality

The approval process for pesticide uses would consider potential to degrade water quality on and off the Refuge. A pesticide can only affect water quality through movement away from the treatment site. After application, pesticide mobilization can be characterized by one or more of the following (Kerle et al. 1996):
- Attach (sorb) to soil, vegetation, or other surfaces and remain at or near the treated area;
- Attach to soil and move off-site through erosion from run-off or wind;
- Dissolve in water that can be subjected to run-off or leaching.

As an initial screening tool selected chemical characteristics and rating criteria for a pesticide can be evaluated to assess potential to enter ground and/or surface waters. These would include: persistence, sorption coefficient (K_{oc}), groundwater ubiquity score (GUS), and solubility.

Persistence, which is expressed as half-life ($t_{1/2}$), represents the length of time required for 50% of the deposited pesticide to degrade (completely or partially). Persistence in the soil can be categorized as the following: non-persistent <30 days; moderately persistent = 30 to 100 days; and persistent >100 days (Kerle et. al. 1996). Half-life data is usually available for aquatic and terrestrial environments.

Another measure of pesticide persistence is dissipation time (DT_{50}). It represents the time required for 50% of the deposited pesticide to degrade and move from a treated site; whereas, half-life describes the rate for degradation only. As for half-life, units of dissipation time are usually expressed in days. Field or foliar dissipation time is the preferred data to use for estimating pesticide concentrations in the environment. However, soil half-life is the most common persistence data cited in published literature. If field or foliar dissipation data is not available, soil half-life data may be used. The average or representative half-life value of most important degradation mechanisms will be selected for quantitative analysis for both terrestrial and aquatic environments.

Mobility of a pesticide is a function of how strongly it is adsorbed to soil particles and organic matter, its solubility in water, and its persistence in the environment. Pesticides strongly adsorbed to soil particles, relatively insoluble in water, and not environmentally persistent would be less likely to move across the soil surface into surface waters or to leach through the soil profile and contaminate groundwater. Conversely, pesticides that are not strongly adsorbed to soil particles, are highly water soluble, and are persistent in the environment would have greater potential to move from the application site (off-site movement).

The degree of pesticide adsorption to soil particles and organic matter (Kerle et. al. 1996) is expressed as the soil adsorption coefficient (Koc). The soil adsorption coefficient is measured as micrograms of pesticide per gram of soil (µg/g) that can range from near zero to the thousands. Pesticides with higher Koc values are strongly sorbed to soil and, therefore, would be less subject to movement.

Water solubility describes the amount of pesticide that will dissolve in a known quantity of water. The water solubility of a pesticide is expressed as milligrams of pesticide dissolved in a liter of water (mg/l or ppm). Pesticides with solubility <0.1 ppm are virtually insoluble in water, 100-1000 ppm are moderately soluble, and >10,000 ppm highly soluble (US Geological Survey 2000). As pesticide solubility increases, there would be greater potential for off-site movement.

The Groundwater Ubiquity Score (GUS) is a quantitative screening tool to estimate a pesticide's potential to move in the environment. It utilizes soil persistence and adsorption coefficients in the following formula.

$$GUS = \log 10 \, (t_{1/2}) \times [4 - \log 10 \, (K_{oc})]$$

The potential pesticide movement rating would be based upon its GUS value. Pesticides with a GUS <0.1 would be considered to have an extremely low potential to move toward groundwater. Values of 1.0-2.0 would be low, 2.0-3.0 would be moderate, 3.0-4.0 would be high, and >4.0 would have a very high potential to move toward groundwater.

Water solubility describes the amount of pesticide dissolving in a specific quantity of water, where it is usually measured as mg/l or parts per million (ppm). Solubility is useful as a comparative measure because pesticides with higher values are more likely to move by run-off or leaching. GUS, water solubility, $t_{1/2}$, and K_{oc} values are available for selected pesticides from the OSU Extension Pesticide Properties Database at http://npic.orst.edu/ppdmove.htm. Many of the values in this database were derived from the SCS/ARS/CES Pesticide Properties Database for Environmental Decision Making (Wauchope et al. 1992).

Soil properties influence the fate of pesticides in the environment. The following six properties are mostly likely to affect pesticide degradation and the potential for pesticides to move off-site by leaching (vertical movement through the soil) or runoff (lateral movement across the soil surface).

- Permeability is the rate of water movement vertically through the soil. It is affected by soil texture and structure. Coarse textured soils (e.g., high sand content) have a larger pore size and they are generally more permeable than fine textured soils (i.e., high clay content). The more permeable soils would have a greater potential for pesticides to move vertically down through the soil profile. Soil permeability rates (inches/hour) are usually available in county soil survey reports.

- Soil texture describes the relative percentage of sand, silt, and clay. In general, greater clay content with smaller pore size would lower the likelihood and rate of water that would move through the soil profile. Clay also serves to adsorb (bind) pesticides to soil particles. Soils with high clay content would adsorb more pesticide than soils with relatively low clay content. In contrast, sandy soils with coarser texture and lower water holding capacity would have a greater potential for water to leach through them.
- Soil structure describes soil aggregation. Soils with a well developed soil structure have looser, more aggregated structure that would be less likely to be compacted. Both characteristics would allow for less restricted flow of water through the soil profile resulting in greater infiltration.
- Organic matter would be the single most important factor affecting pesticide adsorption in soils. Many pesticides are adsorbed to organic matter which would reduce their rate of downward movement through the soil profile. Also, soils high in organic matter would tend to hold more water, which may make less water available for leaching.
- Soil moisture affects how fast water would move through the soil. If soils are already wet or saturated before rainfall or irrigation, excess moisture would runoff rather than infiltrate into the soil profile. Soil moisture also would influence microbial and chemical activity in soil, which effects pesticide degradation.
- Soil pH would influence chemical reactions that occur in the soil, which in turn determine whether or not a pesticide will degrade, rate of degradation, and, in some instances, which degradation products are produced.

Based upon the aforementioned properties, soils most vulnerable to groundwater contamination would be sandy soils with low organic matter. In contrast, the least vulnerable soils would be well-drained clayey soils with high organic matter. Consequently, pesticides with the lowest potential for movement in conjunction with appropriate best management practices (see below) would be used in an IPM framework to treat pests while minimizing effects to non-target biota and protecting environmental quality.

Along with soil properties, the potential for a pesticide to affect water quality through run-off and leaching would consider site-specific environmental and abiotic conditions including rainfall, water table conditions, and topography (Huddleston 1996).

- Water is necessary to separate pesticides from soil. This can occur in two basic ways. Pesticides that are soluble move easily with runoff water. Pesticide-laden soil particles can be dislodged and transported from the application site in runoff. The concentration of pesticides in the surface runoff would be greatest for the first runoff event following treatment. The rainfall intensity and route of water infiltration into soil, to a large extent, determine pesticide concentrations and losses in surface runoff. The timing of the rainfall after application also would have an effect. Rainfall interacts with pesticides at a shallow soil depth (¼ to ½ inch), which is called the mixing zone (Baker and Miller 1999). The pesticide/water mixture in the mixing zone would tend to leach down into the soil or runoff depending upon how quickly the soil surface becomes saturated and how rapidly water can infiltrate into the soil. Leaching would decrease the amount of pesticide available near the soil surface (mixing zone) to runoff during the initial rainfall event following application and subsequent rainfall events.
- Terrain slope would affect the potential for surface runoff and the intensity of runoff. Steeper slopes would have greater potential for runoff following a rainfall event. In contrast, soils that are relatively flat would have little potential for runoff, except during intense rainfall events.

In addition, soils in lower areas would be more susceptible to leaching as a result of receiving excessive water from surrounding higher elevations.

- Depth to groundwater would be an important factor affecting the potential for pesticides to leach into groundwater. If the distance from the soil surface to the top of the water table is shallow, pesticides would have less distance to travel to reach groundwater. Shallower water tables that persist for longer periods would be more likely to experience groundwater contamination. Soil survey reports are available for individual counties. These reports provide data in tabular format regarding the water table depths and the months during which it persists. In some situations, a hard pan exists above the water table that would prevent pesticide contamination from leaching.

7.5 Determining Effects to Air Quality

Pesticides may volatilize from soil and plant surfaces and move from the treated area into the atmosphere. The potential for a pesticide to volatilize is determined by the pesticide's vapor pressure which would be affected by temperature, sorption, soil moisture, and the pesticide's water solubility. Vapor pressure is often expressed in mm Hg. To make these numbers easier to compare, vapor pressure may be expressed in exponent form ($I \times 10^{-7}$), where I represents a vapor pressure index. In general, pesticides with $I < 10$ would have a low potential to volatilize; whereas, pesticides with $I > 1,000$ would have a high potential to volatilize (Oregon State University 1996). Vapor pressure values for pesticides are usually available in the pesticide product MSDS or the USDA Agricultural Research Service (ARS) pesticide database.

7.6 Preparing a Chemical Profile

The following instructions would be used by Service personnel to complete Chemical Profiles for pesticides. Specifically, profiles would be prepared for pesticide active ingredients (e.g., glyphosate, imazapic) that would be contained in one or more trade name products that are registered and labeled with EPA. All information fields under each category (e.g., Toxicological Endpoints, Environmental Fate) would be completed for a Chemical Profile. If no information is available for a specific field, then "No data is available in references" would be recorded in the profile. Available scientific information would be used to complete Chemical Profiles. Each entry of scientific information would be shown with applicable references.

Completed Chemical Profiles would provide a structured decision-making process utilizing quantitative assessment/screening tools with threshold values (where appropriate) that would be used to evaluate potential biological and other environmental effects to Refuge resources. For ecological risk assessments presented in these profiles, the "worst-case scenario" would be evaluated to determine whether a pesticide could be approved for use considering the maximum single application rate specified on pesticide labels for habitat management and croplands/facilities maintenance treatments pertaining to the Refuge. Where the "worst-case scenario" likely would only result in minor, temporary, and localized effects to listed and non-listed species with appropriate BMPs (see Section 5.0), the proposed pesticide's use in a PUP would have a scientific basis for approval under any application rate specified on the label that is at or below rates evaluated in a Chemical Profile. In some cases, the Chemical Profile would include a lower application rate than the maximum labeled rate in order to protect Refuge resources. As necessary, Chemical Profiles would be periodically updated with new scientific information or as pesticides with the same active ingredient are proposed for Refuge use in PUPs.

Throughout this section, threshold values (to prevent or minimize potential biological and environmental effects) would be clearly identified for specific information presented in a completed Chemical Profile. Comparison with these threshold values provides an explicit scientific basis to approve or disapprove PUPs for habitat management and cropland/facilities maintenance on the Refuge. In general, PUPs would be approved for pesticides with Chemical Profiles where there would be no exceedances of threshold values. However, BMPs are identified for some screening tools that would minimize/eliminate potential effects (exceedance of the threshold value) as a basis for approving PUPs.

Date: Service personnel would record the date when the Chemical Profile is completed or updated. Chemical Profiles (e.g., currently approved pesticide use patterns) would be periodically reviewed and updated, as necessary. The most recent review date would be recorded on a profile to document when it was last updated.

Trade Name(s): Service personnel would accurately and completely record the trade name(s) from the pesticide label, which includes a suffix that describes the formulation (e.g., WP, DG, EC, L, SP, I, II or 64). The suffix often distinguishes a specific product among several pesticides with the same active ingredient. Service personnel would record a trade name for each pesticide product with the same active ingredient.

Common chemical name(s): Service personnel would record the common name(s) listed on the pesticide label MSDS for an active ingredient. The common name of a pesticide is listed as the active ingredient on the title page of the product label immediately following the trade name, and the MSDS, Section 2: Composition/ Information on Ingredients. A Chemical Profile is completed for each active ingredient.

Pesticide Type: Service personnel would record the type of pesticide for an active ingredient as one of the following: herbicide, dessicant, fungicide, fumigant, growth regulator, insecticide, pisicide, or rodenticide.

EPA Registration Number(s): This number (EPA Reg. No.) appears on the title page of the label and MSDS, Section 1: Chemical Product and Company Description. It is not the EPA Establishment Number that is usually located near it. Service personnel would record the EPA Reg. No. for each trade name product with an active ingredient based upon PUPs.

Pesticide Class: Service personnel would list the general chemical class for the pesticide (active ingredient). For example, malathion is an organophosphate and carbaryl is a carbamate.

CAS (Chemical Abstract Service) Number: This number is often located in the second section (Composition/Information on Ingredients) of the MSDS. The MSDS table listing components usually contains this number immediately prior to or following the % composition.

Other Ingredients: From the most recent MSDS for the proposed pesticide product(s), Service personnel would include any chemicals in the pesticide formulation not listed as an active ingredient that are described as toxic or hazardous, or regulated under the Superfund Amendments and Reauthorization Act (SARA), Comprehensive Environmental Response, Compensation, and Liability Act (CERCLA), Toxic Substances Control Act (TSCA), Occupational Safety and Health Administration (OSHA), State Right-to-Know, or other listed authorities.

These are usually found in MSDS sections titled "Hazardous Identifications", "Exposure Control/Personal Protection", and "Regulatory Information". If concentrations of other ingredients are available for any compounds identified as toxic or hazardous, then Service personnel would record this information in the Chemical Profile by trade name. MSDS(s) may be obtained from the manufacturer, manufacturer's website or from an on-line database maintained by Crop Data Management Systems, Inc. (see list below).

Toxicological Endpoints

Toxicological endpoint data would be collected for acute and chronic tests with mammals, birds, and fish. Data would be recorded for species available in the scientific literature. If no data are found for a particular taxonomic group, then "No data is available in references" would be recorded as the data entry. Throughout the Chemical Profile, references (including toxicological endpoint data) would be cited using parentheses (#) following the recorded data.

Mammalian LD_{50}: For test species in the scientific literature, Service personnel would record available data for oral lethal dose (LD_{50}) in mg/kg-bw (body weight) or ppm-bw. The most common test species in scientific literature are the rat and mouse. The lowest LD_{50} value found for a rat would be used as a toxicological endpoint for dose-based RQ calculations to assess acute risk to mammals (see Table 1 in Section 7.1).

Mammalian LC_{50}: For test species in the scientific literature, Service personnel would record available data for dietary lethal concentration (LC_{50}) as reported (e.g., mg/kg-diet or ppm-diet). The most common test species in scientific literature are the rat and mouse. The lowest LC_{50} value found for a rat would be used as a toxicological endpoint for diet-based RQ calculations to assess acute risk (see Table 1 in Section 7.1).

Mammalian Reproduction: For test species listed in the scientific literature, Service personnel would record the test results (e.g., Lowest Observed Effect Concentration [LOEC], Lowest Observed Effect Level [LOEL], No Observed Adverse Effect Level [NOAEL], No Observed Adverse Effect Concentration [NOAEC]) in mg/kg-bw or mg/kg-diet for reproductive test procedure(s) (e.g., generational studies [preferred], fertility, new born weight). The most common test species available in scientific literature are rats and mice. The lowest NOEC, NOAEC, NOEL, or NOAEL test results found for a rat would be used as a toxicological endpoint for RQ calculations to assess chronic risk (see Table 1 in Section 7.1).

Avian LD_{50}: For test species available in the scientific literature, Service personnel would record values for oral lethal dose (LD_{50}) in mg/kg-bw or ppm-bw. The most common test species available in scientific literature are the bobwhite quail and mallard. The lowest LD_{50} value found for an avian species would be used as a toxicological endpoint for dose-based RQ calculations to assess acute risk (see Table 1 in Section 7.1).

Avian LC_{50}: For test species available in the scientific literature, Service personnel would record values for dietary lethal concentration (LC_{50}) as reported (e.g., mg/kg-diet or ppm-diet). The most common test species available in scientific literature are the bobwhite quail and mallard. The lowest LC_{50} value found for an avian species would be used as a toxicological endpoint for dietary-based RQ calculations to assess acute risk (see Table 1 in Section 7.1).

Avian Reproduction: For test species available in the scientific literature, Service personnel would record test results (e.g., LOEC, LOEL, NOAEC, NOAEL) in mg/kg-bw or mg/kg-diet consumed for reproductive test procedure(s) (e.g., early life cycle, reproductive). The most common test species available in scientific literature are the bobwhite quail and mallard. The lowest NOEC, NOAEC, NOEL, or NOAEL test results found for an avian species would be used as a toxicological endpoint for RQ calculations to assess chronic risk (see Table 1 in Section 7.1).

Fish LC$_{50}$: For test freshwater or marine species listed in the scientific literature, Service personnel would record a LC$_{50}$ in ppm or mg/L. The most common test species available in the scientific literature are the bluegill, rainbow trout, and fathead minnow (marine). Test results for many game species may also be available. The lowest LC$_{50}$ value found for a freshwater fish species would be used as a toxicological endpoint for RQ calculations to assess acute risk (see Table 1 in Section 7.1).

Fish Early Life Stage (ELS)/Life Cycle: For test freshwater or marine species available in the scientific literature, Service personnel would record test results (e.g., LOEC, NOAEL, NOAEC, LOAEC) in ppm for test procedure(s) (e.g., early life cycle, life cycle). The most common test species available in the scientific literature are bluegill, rainbow trout, and fathead minnow. Test results for other game species may also be available. The lowest test value found for a fish species (preferably freshwater) would be used as a toxicological endpoint for RQ calculations to assess chronic risk (see Table 1 in Section 7.1).

Other: For test invertebrate as well as non-vascular and vascular plant species available in the scientific literature, Service personnel would record LC$_{50}$, LD$_{50}$, LOEC, LOEL, NOAEC, NOAEL, or EC$_{50}$ (environmental concentration) values in ppm or mg/L. The most common test invertebrate species available in scientific literature are the honey bee and the water flea (*Daphnia magna*). Green algae (*Selenastrum capricornutum*) and pondweed (*Lemna minor*) are frequently available test species for aquatic non-vascular and vascular plants, respectively.

Ecological Incident Reports: After a site has been treated with pesticide(s), wildlife may be exposed to these chemical(s). When exposure is high relative to the toxicity of the pesticides, wildlife may be killed or visibly harmed (incapacitated). Such events are called ecological incidents. The EPA maintains a database (Ecological Incident Information System) of ecological incidents. This database stores information extracted from incident reports submitted by various federal and state agencies and non-government organizations. Information included in an incident report is date and location of the incident, type and magnitude of effects observed in various species, use(s) of pesticides known or suspected of contributing to the incident, and results of any chemical residue and cholinesterase activity analyses conducted during the investigation.

Incident reports can play an important role in evaluating the effects of pesticides by supplementing quantitative risk assessments. All incident reports for pesticide(s) with the active ingredient and associated information would be recorded.

Environmental Fate

Water Solubility: Service personnel would record values for water solubility (Sw), which describes the amount of pesticide that dissolves in a known quantity of water. Sw is expressed as mg/L (ppm). Pesticide Sw values would be categorized as one of the following: insoluble <0.1

ppm, moderately soluble = 100 to 1000 ppm, highly soluble >10,000 ppm (US Geological Survey 2000). As pesticide Sw increases, there would be greater potential to degrade water quality through run-off and leaching.

Sw would be used to evaluate potential for bioaccumulation in aquatic species [see **Octanol-Water Partition Coefficient (Kow)** below].

Soil Mobility: Service personnel would record available values for soil adsorption coefficient (Koc [μg/g]). It provides a measure of a chemical's mobility and leaching potential in soil. Koc values are directly proportional to organic content, clay content, and surface area of the soil. Koc data for a pesticide may be available for a variety of soil types (e.g., clay, loam, sand).

Koc values would be used in evaluating the potential to degrade groundwater by leaching (see **Potential to Move to Groundwater** below).

Soil Persistence: Service personnel would record values for soil half-life ($t_{1/2}$), which represents the length of time (days) required for 50% of the deposited pesticide to degrade (completely or partially) in the soil. Based upon the $t_{1/2}$ value, soil persistence would be categorized as one of the following: non-persistent <30 days, moderately persistent = 30 to 100 days, and persistent >100 days (Kerle et. al. 1996).

Threshold for Approving PUPs:

If soil $t_{1/2}$ ≤100 days, then a PUP would be approved without additional BMPs to protect water quality.
If soil $t_{1/2}$ >100 days, then a PUP would only be approved with additional BMPs specifically to protect water quality. One or more BMPs such as the following would be included in the **Specific Best Management Practices (BMPs) section** *to minimize potential surface run-off and leaching that can degrade water quality:*
- *Do not exceed one application per site per year.*
- *Do not use on coarse-textured soils where the ground water table is <10 feet and average annual precipitation >12 inches.*
- *Do not use on steep slopes if substantial rainfall is expected within 24 hours or ground is saturated.*

Along with Koc, soil $t_{1/2}$ values would be used in evaluating the potential to degrade groundwater by leaching (see **Potential to Move to Groundwater** below).

Soil Dissipation: Dissipation time (DT_{50}) represents the time required for 50% of the deposited pesticide to degrade and move from a treated site; whereas, soil $t_{1/2}$ describes the rate for degradation only. As for $t_{1/2}$, units of dissipation time are usually expressed in days. Field dissipation time would be the preferred data for use to estimate pesticide concentrations in the environment because it is based upon field studies compared to soil $t_{1/2}$, which is derived in a laboratory. However, soil $t_{1/2}$ is the most common persistence data available in the published literature. If field dissipation data is not available, soil half-life data would be used in a Chemical Profile. The average or representative half-life value of most important degradation mechanism would be selected for quantitative analysis for both terrestrial and aquatic environments.

Based upon the DT_{50} value, environmental persistence in the soil also would be categorized as one of the following: non-persistent <30 days, moderately persistent = 30 to 100 days, and persistent >100 days.

Threshold for Approving PUPs:

If soil DT_{50} **≤100 days, then a PUP would be approved without additional BMPs to protect water** *quality.*
If soil DT_{50} >100 days, then a PUP would only be approved with additional BMPs specifically to protect water quality. One or more BMPs such as the following would be included in the **Specific Best Management Practices (BMPs) section** *to minimize potential surface run-off and leaching that can degrade water quality:*
- *Do not exceed one application per site per year.*
- *Do not use on coarse-textured soils where the ground water table is <10 feet and average annual precipitation >12 inches.*
- *Do not use on steep slopes if substantial rainfall is expected within 24 hours or ground is saturated.*

Along with Koc, soil DT_{50} values (preferred over soil $t_{1/2}$) would be used in evaluating the potential to degrade groundwater by leaching (see **Potential to Move to Groundwater** below), if available.

Aquatic Persistence: Service personnel would record values for aquatic $t_{1/2}$, which represents the length of time required for 50% of the deposited pesticide to degrade (completely or partially) in water. Based upon the $t_{1/2}$ value, aquatic persistence would be categorized as one of the following: non-persistent <30 days, moderately persistent = 30 to 100 days, and persistent >100 days (Kerle et. al. 1996).

Threshold for Approving PUPs:

If aquatic $t_{1/2}$ **≤100 days, then a PUP would be approved without additional BMPs to protect water** *quality.*
If aquatic $t_{1/2}$ >100 days, then a PUP would only be approved with additional BMPs specifically to protect water quality. One or more BMPs such as the following would be included in the **Specific Best Management Practices (BMPs) section** *to minimize potential surface run-off and leaching that can degrade water quality:*
- *Do not exceed one application per site per year.*
- *Do not use on coarse-textured soils where the ground water table is <10 feet and average annual precipitation >12 inches.*
- *Do not use on steep slopes if substantial rainfall is expected within 24 hours or ground is saturated.*

Aquatic Dissipation: Dissipation time (DT_{50}) represents the time required for 50% of the deposited pesticide to degrade or move (dissipate); whereas, aquatic $t_{1/2}$ describes the rate for degradation only. As for $t_{1/2}$, units of dissipation time are usually expressed in days. Based upon the DT_{50} value, environmental persistence in aquatic habitats also would be categorized as one of the following: non-persistent <30 days, moderately persistent = 30 to 100 days, and persistent >100 days.

Threshold for Approving PUPs:

If aquatic DT$_{50}$ **≤100 days, then a PUP would be approved without additional BMPs to protect** *water quality.*
If aquatic DT$_{50}$ >100 days, then a PUP would only be approved with additional BMPs specifically to protect water quality. One or more BMPs such as the following would be included in the **Specific Best Management Practices (BMPs) section** *to minimize potential surface run-off and leaching that can degrade water quality:*

- *Do not exceed one application per site per year.*
- *Do not use on coarse-textured soils where the ground water table is <10 feet and average annual precipitation >12 inches.*
- *Do not use on steep slopes if substantial rainfall is expected within 24 hours or ground is saturated.*

Potential to Move to Groundwater: Groundwater Ubiquity Score (GUS) = $\log_{10}$(soil t$_{1/2}$) x [4 – $\log_{10}(K_{oc})$]. If a DT$_{50}$ value is available, it would be used rather than a t$_{1/2}$ value to calculate a GUS score. Based upon the GUS value, the potential to move toward groundwater would be recorded as one of the following categories: extremely low potential <1.0, low - 1.0 to 2.0, moderate - 2.0 to 3.0, high - 3.0 to 4.0, or very high >4.0.

Threshold for Approving PUPs:

If GUS **≤4.0, then a PUP would be approved without additional BMPs to protect water quality.**
If GUS >4.0, then a PUP would only be approved with additional BMPs specifically to protect water quality. One or more BMPs such as the following would be included in the **Specific Best Management Practices (BMPs) section** *to minimize potential surface run-off and leaching that can degrade water quality:*

- *Do not exceed one application per site per year.*
- *Do not use on coarse-textured soils where the ground water table is <10 feet and average annual precipitation >12 inches.*
- *Do not use on steep slopes if substantial rainfall is expected within 24 hours or ground is saturated.*

Volatilization: Pesticides may volatilize (evaporate) from soil and plant surfaces and move off-target into the atmosphere. The potential for a pesticide to volatilize is a function of its vapor pressure that is affected by temperature, sorption, soil moisture, and the pesticide's water solubility. Vapor pressure is often expressed in mm Hg. To make these values easier to compare, vapor pressure would be recorded by Service personnel in exponential form (I x 10^{-7}), where I represents a vapor pressure index. In general, pesticides with I <10 would have low potential to volatilize; whereas, pesticides with I >1,000 would have a high potential to volatilize (Oregon State University 1996). Vapor pressure values for pesticides are usually available in the pesticide product MSDS or the USDA Agricultural Research Service (ARS) pesticide database (see **References**).

Threshold for Approving PUPs:

If I **≤1000, then a PUP would be approved without additional BMPs to minimize drift and** *protect air quality.*

If I >1000, then a PUP would only be approved with additional BMPs specifically to minimize drift and protect air quality. One or more BMPs such as the following would be included in the **Specific Best Management Practices (BMPs) section** *to reduce volatilization and potential to drift and degrade air quality:*

- *Do not treat when wind velocities are <2 or >10 mph with existing or potential inversion conditions.*
- *Apply the large-diameter droplets possible for spray treatments.*
- *Avoid spraying when air temperatures >85°F.*
- *Use the lowest spray height possible above target canopy.*

Octanol-Water Partition Coefficient (Kow): The octanol-water partition coefficient (Kow) is the concentration of a pesticide in octanol and water at equilibrium at a specific temperature. Because octanol is an organic solvent, it is considered a surrogate for natural organic matter. Therefore, Kow would be used to assess potential for a pesticide to bioaccumulate in tissues of aquatic species (e.g., fish). If Kow>1000 or Sw<1 mg/L AND soil $t_{1/2}$ >30 days, then there would be high potential for a pesticide to bioaccumulate in aquatic species such as fish (US Geological Survey 2000).

Threshold for Approving PUPs:

If there is not a high potential for a pesticide to bioaccumulate in aquatic species, then the PUP would be approved.
If there is a high potential to bioaccumulate in aquatic species (Kow>1000 or Sw<1 mg/L AND soil $t_{1/2}$>30 days), then the PUP would not be approved, except under unusual circumstances where approval would only be granted by the Washington Office.

Bioaccumulation/Bioconcentration: The physiological process where pesticide concentrations in tissue would increase in biota because they are taken and stored at a faster rate than they are metabolized or excreted. The potential for bioaccumulation would be evaluated through bioaccumulation factors (BAFs) or bioconcentration factors (BCFs). Based upon BAF or BCF values, the potential to bioaccumulate would be recorded as one of the following: low – 0 to 300, moderate – 300 to 1000, or high >1000 (Calabrese and Baldwin 1993).

Threshold for Approving PUPs:

If BAF or BCF ≤1000, then a PUP would be approved without additional BMPs.
If BAF or BCF >1000, then a PUP would not be approved, except under unusual circumstances where approval would only be granted by the Washington Office.

Worst-Case Ecological Risk Assessment

Max Application Rates (acid equivalent): Service personnel would record the highest application rate of an active ingredient (ae basis) for habitat management and cropland/facilities maintenance treatments in this data field of a Chemical Profile. These rates can be found in Table CP.1 under the column heading "Max Product Rate – Single Application (lbs/acre – AI on acid equiv basis)." This table would be prepared for a chemical profile from information specified in labels for trade name products identified in PUPs. If these data are not available in pesticide labels, then write "NS" for "not specified on label" in this table.

EECs: An estimated environmental concentration (ECC) represents potential exposure to fish and wildlife (birds and mammals) from using a pesticide. EECs would be derived by Service personnel using an EPA screening-level approach (US Environmental Protection Agency 2004). For each max application rate [see description under **Max Application Rates (acid equivalent)**], Service personnel would record 2 EEC values in a Chemical Profile; these would represent the worst-case terrestrial and aquatic exposures for habitat management and croplands/facilities maintenance treatments. For terrestrial and aquatic EEC calculations, see description for data entry under **Presumption of Unacceptable Risk/Risk Quotients,** which is the next field for a Chemical Profile.

Presumption of Unacceptable Risk/Risk Quotients: Service personnel would calculate and record acute and chronic risk quotients (RQs) for birds, mammals, and fish using the provided tabular formats for habitat management and/or cropland/facilities maintenance treatments. RQs recorded in a Chemical Profile would represent the worst-case assessment for ecological risk. See Section 7.2 for discussion regarding the calculations of RQs.

For aquatic assessments associated with habitat management treatments, RQ calculations would be based upon selected acute and chronic toxicological endpoints for fish and the EEC would be derived from Urban and Cook (1986) assuming 100% overspray to an entire 1-foot deep water body using the max application rate (ae basis [see above]).

For aquatic assessments associated with cropland/facilities maintenance treatments, RQ calculations would be done by Service personnel based upon selected acute and chronic toxicological endpoints for fish and an EEC would be derived from the aquatic assessment in AgDRIFT® model version 2.01 under Tier I ground-based application with the following input variables: max application rate (acid basis [see above]), low boom (20 inches), fine to medium/coarse droplet size, 20 swaths, EPA-defined wetland, and 25-foot distance (buffer) from treated area to water.

See Section 7.2.1.2 for more details regarding the calculation of EECs for aquatic habitats for habitat management and cropland/facilities maintenance treatments.

For terrestrial avian and mammalian assessments, RQ calculations would be done by Service personnel based upon dietary exposure, where the "short grass" food item category would represent the worst-case scenario. For terrestrial spray applications associated with habitat management and cropland/facilities maintenance treatments, exposure (EECs and RQs) would be determined using the Kanaga nomogram method through the EPA's Terrestrial Residue Exposure model (T-REX) version 1.2.3. T-REX input variables would include the following: max application rate (acid basis [see above]) and pesticide half-life (days) in soil to estimate the initial, maximum pesticide residue concentration on general food items for terrestrial vertebrate species in short (<20 cm tall) grass.

For granular pesticide formulations and pesticide-treated seed with a unique route of exposure for terrestrial avian and mammalian wildlife, see Section 7.2.1.1.2 for the procedure that would be used to calculate RQs.

All calculated RQs in both tables would be compared with Levels of Concern (LOCs) established by EPA (see Table 2 in Section 7.2). If a calculated RQ exceeds an established LOC value (in brackets inside the table), then there would be a potential for an acute or chronic effect (unacceptable risk) to federally listed (T and E) species and nonlisted species. See Section 7.2 for detailed descriptions of acute and chronic RQ calculations and comparison to LOCs to assess risk.

Threshold for approving PUPs:

If RQs≤LOCs, then a PUP would be approved without additional BMPs.
If RQs>LOCs, then a PUP would only be approved with additional BMPs specifically to minimize exposure (ecological risk) to bird, mammal, and/or fish species. One or more BMPs such as the following would be included in the **Specific Best Management Practices (BMPs)** **section** *to reduce potential risk to non-listed or listed species:*

- *Lower application rate and/or fewer number of applications so RQs≤LOCs*
- *For aquatic assessments (fish) associated with cropland/facilities maintenance, increase the buffer distance beyond 25 feet so RQs≤LOCs.*

Justification for Use: Service personnel would describe the reason for using the pesticide-based control of specific pests or groups of pests. In most cases, the pesticide label will provide the appropriate information regarding control of pests to describe in the section.

Specific Best Management Practices (BMPs): Service personnel would record specific BMPs necessary to minimize or eliminate potential effects to non-target species and/or degradation of water quality from drift, surface runoff, or leaching. These BMPs would be based upon scientific information documented in previous data fields of a Chemical Profile. Where necessary and feasible, these specific practices would be included in PUPs as a basis for approval.

If there are no specific BMPs that are appropriate, Service personnel would describe why the potential effects to Refuge resources and/or degradation of environmental quality is outweighed by the overall resource benefit(s) from the proposed pesticide use in the BMP section of the PUP. See Section 4.0 of this document for a complete list of BMPs associated with mixing and applying pesticides appropriate for all PUPs with ground-based treatments that would be additive to any necessary, chemical-specific BMPs.

References: Service personnel would record scientific resources used to provide data/information for a chemical profile. Use the number sequence to uniquely reference data in a chemical profile.

The following on-line data resources are readily available for toxicological endpoint and environmental fate data for pesticides:

1. California Product/Label Database. Department of Pesticide Regulation, California Environmental Protection Agency. (http://www.cdpr.ca.gov/docs/label/labelque.htm#regprods)

2. ECOTOX database. Office of Pesticide Programs, US Environmental Protection Agency, Washington, DC. (http://cfpub.epa.gov/ecotox/)

3. Extension Toxicology Network (EXTOXNET) Pesticide Information Profiles. Cooperative effort of University of California-Davis, Oregon State University, Michigan State University,

Cornell University and University of Idaho through Oregon State University, Corvallis, Oregon. (http://extoxnet.orst.edu/pips/ghindex.html)

4. FAO specifications and evaluations for plant protection products. Pesticide Management Unit, Plant Protection Services, Food and Agriculture Organization, United Nations. (http://www.fao.org/WAICENT/FAOINFO/AGRICULT/AGP/AGPP/Pesticid/)

5. Human health and ecological risk assessments. Pesticide Management and Coordination, Forest Health Protection, US Department of Agriculture, US Forest Service. (http://www.fs.fed.us/foresthealth/pesticide/risk.htm)

6. Pesticide Chemical Fact Sheets. Clemson University Pesticide Information Center. (http://entweb.clemson.edu/pesticid/Document/Labels/factshee.htm)

7. Pesticide Fact Sheets. Published by Information Ventures, Inc. for Bureau of Land Management, Dept. of Interior; Bonneville Power Administration, U.S. Dept. of Energy; and Forest Service, US Department of Agriculture. (http://infoventures.com/e-hlth/pesticide/pest-fac.html)

8. Pesticide Fact Sheets. National Pesticide Information Center. (http://npic.orst.edu/npicfact.htm)

9. Pesticide Fate Database. US Environmental Protection Agency, Washington, DC. (http://cfpub.epa.gov/pfate/home.cfm).

10. Pesticide product labels and material safety data sheets. Crop Data Management Systems, Inc. (CDMS) (http://www.cdms.net/pfa/LUpdateMsg.asp) or multiple websites maintained by agrichemical companies.

11. Registered Pesticide Products (Oregon database). Oregon Department of Agriculture. (http://www.oda.state.or.us/dbs/pest_products/search.lasso)

12. Regulatory notes. Pest Management Regulatory Agency, Health Canada, Ontario, Canada. (http://www.hc-sc.gc.ca/pmra-arla/)

13. Reptile and Amphibian Toxicology Literature. Canadian Wildlife Service, Environment Canada, Ontario, Canada. (http://www.cws-scf.ec.gc.ca/nwrc-cnrf/ratl/index_e.cfm)

14. Specific Chemical Fact Sheet – New Active Ingredients, Biopesticide Fact Sheet and Registration Fact Sheet. U.S Environmental Protection Agency, Washington, DC. (http://www.epa.gov/pestidides/factsheets/chemical_fs.htm)

15. Weed Control Methods Handbook: Tools and Techniques for Use in Natural Areas. The Invasive Species Initiative. The Nature Conservancy. (http://tnsweeds.ucdavis.edu/handbook.html)

16. Wildlife Contaminants Online. US Geological Survey, Department of Interior, Washington, D.C. (http://www.pwrc.usgs.gov/contaminants-online/)

17. One-liner database. 2000. US Environmental Protection Agency, Office of Pesticide Programs, Washington, D.C.

Chemical Profile

Date:			
Trade Name(s):		Common Chemical Name(s):	
Pesticide Type:		EPA Registration Number:	
Pesticide Class:		CAS Number:	
Other Ingredients:			

Toxicological Endpoints

Mammalian LD_{50}:	
Mammalian LC_{50}:	
Mammalian Reproduction:	
Avian LD_{50}:	
Avian LC_{50}:	
Avian Reproduction:	
Fish LC_{50}:	
Fish ELS/Life Cycle:	
Other:	

Ecological Incident Reports

Environmental Fate

Water solubility (S_w):	
Soil Mobility (K_{oc}):	
Soil Persistence ($t_{1/2}$):	
Soil Dissipation (DT_{50}):	
Aquatic Persistence ($t_{1/2}$):	
Aquatic Dissipation (DT_{50}):	
Potential to Move to Groundwater (GUS score):	
Volatilization (mm Hg):	
Octanol-Water Partition Coefficient (K_{ow}):	
Bioaccumulation/Biocentration:	BAF:` BCF:

Worst Case Ecological Risk Assessment

Max Application Rate (ai lbs/acre – ae basis)	Habitat Management: Croplands/Facilities Maintenance:
EECs	Terrestrial (Habitat Management): Terrestrial (Croplands/Facilities Maintenance): Aquatic (Habitat Management): Aquatic (Croplands/Facilities Maintenance):

Habitat Management Treatments:

Presumption of Unacceptable Risk		Risk Quotient (RQ)	
		Listed (TandE) Species	Nonlisted Species
Acute	Birds	[0.1]	[0.5]
	Mammals	[0.1]	[0.5]
	Fish	[0.05]	[0.5]
Chronic	Birds	[1]	[1]
	Mammals	[1]	[1]
	Fish	[1]	[1]

Cropland/Facilities Maintenance Treatments:

Presumption of Unacceptable Risk		Risk Quotient (RQ)	
		Listed (T&E) Species	Nonlisted Species
Acute	Birds	[0.1]	[0.5]
	Mammals	[0.1]	[0.5]
	Fish	[0.05]	[0.5]
Chronic	Birds	[1]	[1]
	Mammals	[1]	[1]
	Fish	[1]	[1]

Justification for Use: Specific Best Management Practices (BMPs): References:	

Table CP.1 Pesticide NameTrade Name[a]	Treatment Type[b]	Max Product Rate – Single Application (lbs/acre or gal/acre)	Max Product Rate -Single Application (lbs/acre - AI on acid equiv basis)	Max Number of Applications Per Season	Max Product Rate Per Season (lbs/acre/season or gal/acre/season)	Minimum Time Between Applications (Days)

[a]From each label for a pesticide identified in pesticide use proposals (PUPs), Service personnel would record application information associated with possible/known uses on Service lands.

[b]Treatment type: H – habitat management or CF – cropland/facilities maintenance. If a pesticide is labeled for both types of treatments (uses), then record separate data for H and CF applications.

7.0 References AgDrift 2001. A user's guide for AgDrift 2.04: a tiered approach for the assessment of spray drift of pesticides. Spray Drift Task Force, PO Box 509, Macon, Missouri.

ATSDR (Agency for Toxic Substances and Disease Registry) US Department of Health and Human Services. 2004. Guidance Manual for the Assessment of Joint Toxic Action of Chemical Mixtures. US Department of Health and Human Services, Public Health Service, ATSDR, Division of Toxicology. 62 plus Appendices.

Barry, T. 2004. Characterization of propanil prune foliage residues as related to propanil use patterns in the Sacramento Valley, CA. Proceedings of the International Conference on Pesticide Application for Drift Management. Waikoloa, Hawaii. 15 pages.

Baker, J. and G. Miller. 1999. Understanding and reducing pesticide losses. Extension Publication PM 1495, Iowa State University Extension, Ames, Iowa. 6 pages.

Battaglin, W.A., E.M. Thurman, S.J. Kalkhoff, and S.D. Porter. 2003. Herbicides and Transformation Products in Surface Waters of the Midwestern United States. Journal of the American Water Resources Association (JAWRA) 39(4):743-756.

Brooks, M.L., D'Antonio, C.M., Richardson, D.M., Grace, J.B., Keeley, J.E. and others. 2004. Effects of invasive alien plants on fire regimes. BioScience 54:77-88.

Bureau of Land Management. 2007. Vegetation treatments using herbicides on Bureau of Land Management Lands in 17 western states Programmatic EIS (PEIS). Washington Office, Bureau of Land Management.

Butler, T., W. Martinkovic, and O.N. Nesheim. 1998. Factors influencing pesticide movement to ground water. Extension Publication PI-2, University of Florida, Cooperative Extension Service, Gainesville, FL. 4 pages.

Calabrese, E.J. and L.A. Baldwin. 1993. Performing Ecological Risk Assessments. Lewis Publishers, Chelsea, MI.

Center, T.D., Frank, J.H., and Dray Jr., F.A. 1997. Biological Control. Strangers in Paradise: Impact and Management of Nonindigenous Species in Florida. P.245-263.

Cox, R.D., and V.J. Anderson. 2004. Increasing native diversity of cheatgrass-dominated rangeland through assisted succession. Journal of Range Management 57:203-210.

Dunning, J.B. 1984. Body weights of 686 species of North American birds. Western Bird Banding Association. Monograph No. 1.

EXTOXNET. 1993a. Movement of pesticides in the environment. Pesticide Information Project of Cooperative Extension Offices of Cornell University, Oregon State University, University of Idaho, University of California – Davis, and the Institute for Environmental Toxicology, Michigan State University. 4 pages.

Hasan, S. and P.G. Ayres. 1990. The control of weeds through fungi: principles and prospects. Tansley Review 23:201-222.

Huddleston, J.H. 1996. How soil properties affect groundwater vulnerability to pesticide contamination. EM 8559. Oregon State University Extension Service. 4 pages.

Kerle, E.A., J.J. Jenkins, P.A. Vogue. 1996. Understanding pesticide persistence and mobility for groundwater and surface water protection. EM 8561. Oregon State University Extension Service. 8 pages.

Masters, R.A, and R.L. Sheley. 2001. Invited synthesis paper: principles and practices for managing rangeland invasive plants. Journal of Range Manage 54:502-517.

Masters, R.A., S.J. Nissen, R.E. Gaussoin, D.D. Beran, and R.N. Stougaard. 1996. Imidazolinone herbicides improve restoration of Great Plains grasslands. Weed Technology 10:392-403.

Maxwell, B.D., E. Lehnhoff, L.J. Rew. 2009. The rationale for monitoring invasive plant populations as a crucial step for management. Invasive Plant Science and Management 2:1-9.

Mineau, P., B.T. Collins, and A. Baril. 1996. On the use of scaling factors to improve interspecies extrapolation to acute toxicity in birds. Regulatory Toxicology and Pharmacology 24:24-29.

Moody, M.E., and R.N. Mack. 1988. Controlling the spread of plant invasions: the importance of nascent foci. Journal of Applied Ecology 25:1009-1021.

Morse, L.E., J.M. Randall, N. Benton, R. Hiebert, and S. Lu. 2004. An Invasive Species Assessment Protocol: NatureServe.

Mullin, B.H., L.W. Anderson, J.M. DiTomaso, R.E. Eplee, and K.D. Getsinger. 2000. Invasive Plant Species. Issue Paper (13):1-18.

Oregon State University. 1996. EXTOXNET-Extension Toxicology Network, Pesticide Information Profiles. Oregon State University, Corvallis, Oregon.

Pfleeger, T.G., A. Fong, R. Hayes, H. Ratsch, C. Wickliff. 1996. Field evaluation of the EPA (Kanaga) nomogram, a method for estimating wildlife exposure to pesticide residues on plants. Environmental Toxicology and Chemistry 15:535-543.

Pope, R., J. DeWitt, and J. Ellerhoff. 1999. Pesticide movement: what farmers need to know. Extension Publication PAT 36, Iowa State University Extension, Ames, Iowa and Iowa Department of Agriculture and Land Stewardship, Des Moines, Iowa. 6 pages.

Ramsay, C.A., G.C. Craig, and C.B. McConnell. 1995. Clean water for Washington – protecting groundwater from pesticide contamination. Extension Publication EB1644, Washington State University Extension, Pullman, Washington. 12 pages.

SDTF 2003 Spray Drift Task Force. 2003. A summary of chemigation application studies. Spray Drift Task Force, Macon, Missouri.

Teske, M.E., S.L. Bird, D.M. Esterly, S.L. Ray, S.G. and Perry. 1997. A User's Guide for AgDRIFT™ 1.0: A Tiered Approach for the Assessment of Spray Drift of Pesticides, Technical Note No. 95-10, CDI, Princeton, New Jersey.

Teske, M.E., S.L. Bird, D.M. Esterly, T.B. Curbishley, S.L. Ray, and S.G. Perry. 2002. AgDRIFT®: a model for estimating near-field spray drift from aerial applications. Environmental Toxicology and Chemistry 21: 659-671.

Urban, D.J and N.J. Cook. 1986. Hazard evaluation division standard, standard evaluation procedure, ecological risk assessment. Office of Pesticide Programs, US Environmental Protection Agency, Washington DC. 101 pages.

US Environmental Protection Agency. 1998. A Comparative Analysis of Ecological Risks from Pesticides and Their Uses: Background, Methodology & Case Study. Environmental Fate & Effects Division, Office of Pesticide Programs, U.S. Environmental Protection Agency, Washington, D.C. 105 pages.

US Environmental Protection Agency. 2004. Overview of the ecological risk assessment process in the Office of Pesticide Programs, US Environmental Protection Agency: endangered and threatened species effects determinations, Office of Pesticide Programs, Washington, DC. 101 pages.

US Environmental Protection Agency. 2005a. Technical overview of ecological risk assessment risk characterization; Approaches for evaluating exposure; Granular, bait, and treated seed applications. US Environmental Protection Agency, Office of Pesticide Programs, Washington, DC. http://www.epa.gov/oppefed1/ecorisk_ders/toera_analysis_exp.htm.

US Environmental Protection Agency. 2005b. User's Guide TREX v1.2.3. US Environmental Protection Agency, Office of Pesticide Programs, Washington, DC. 22 pages. http://www.epa.gov/oppefed1/models/terrestrial/trex_usersguide.htm.

US Forest Service. 2005. Pacific Northwest Region Invasive Plant Program Preventing and Managing Invasive Plants Final Environmental Impact Statement. 359 pages.

US Geological Survey. 2000. Pesticides in stream sediment and aquatic biota – current understanding of distribution and major influences. USGS Fact Sheet 092-00, US Geological Survey, Sacramento, California. 4 pages.

Wauchope, R.D., T.M. Buttler, A.G. Hornsby, P.M. Augustijn-Beckers, and J.P. Burt. 1992. The SCS/ARS/CES pesticide properties database for environmental decision making. Reviews of Environmental Contamination and Toxicology 123:1-155.

Woods, N. 2004. Australian developments in spray drift management. Proceedings of the International Conference on Pesticide Application for Drift Management, Waikoloa, Hawaii. 8 pages.

Appendix K. Draft Brown Tree Snake Control Plan

Draft Brown Treesnake Control Plan

April 2009

Prepared by:

The Brown Treesnake Technical Working Group

Abbreviations List

AAFB – Andersen Air Force Base
ANSTF - Aquatic Nuisance Species Task Force
APHIS – Animal and Plant Health Inspection Service
BRD – Biological Resources Discipline
BTS – Brown Treesnake
CBP – Customs and Border Protection
CGAPS – Coordinating Group on Alien Pest Species
CNMI – Commonwealth of the Northern Mariana Islands
CNMI DFW – CNMI Division of Fish and Wildlife
CNMI DLNR – CNMI Department of Land and Natural Resources
DAWR – Guam Division of Aquatic and Wildlife Resources
DOD – Department of Defense
DOI – Department of the Interior
ESA – Endangered Species Act
FORT – Fort Collins Service Center
FAS – Freely Associated States
FSM – Federated States of Micronesia
GPA – Guam Power Authority
GSA – General Services Agency
HDLNR – Hawai'i Department of Land and Natural Resources
HDOA – Hawai'i Department of Agriculture
HISC – Hawai'i Invasive Species Council
IPM – Integrated Pest Management
ISCs – Invasive Species Committees
JGPO – Navy/Joint Guam Program Office
MOA – Memorandum of Agreement
MSA – Munitions Storage Area, Andersen Air Force Base
NABTSCT – North American Brown Tree Snake Control Team
NANPCA – Non-indigenous Aquatic Nuisance Prevention and Control Act
NEPA – National Environmental Policy Act
NGO – Non-Governmental Organization
NISC - National Invasive Species Council
NWR – National Wildlife Refuge
NWRC – National Wildlife Research Center
OIA – Office of Insular Affairs
OMB – Office of Management and Budget
PAG – Port Authority of Guam
PIFWO- Pacific Islands Fish and Wildlife Office
PPQ – Plant Protection and Quarantine
RISC- Regional Invasive Species Council
RRT – Rapid Response Team
SVL – Snout-Vent Length
USDA – U.S. Department of Agriculture
USFWS – U.S. Fish and Wildlife Service
USGS – U.S. Geological Survey
WS – Wildlife Services

Note: Because the Brown Tree Snake Control and Eradication Act of 2004 was titled using "Tree Snake" as two words, this document will continue this convention when referring to the Act itself. However, the more scientifically accepted single word "treesnake" will be used throughout the plan to refer to the Technical Working Group, the current Control Plan, and the reptile.

2009 Draft Brown Treesnake Control Plan
EXECUTIVE SUMMARY

The Draft Brown Treesnake Control Plan, April 2009 presents the actions, activities and contributions made by a multitude of federal agencies and local governments to prevent transport from Guam, and to control this harmful invasive species on Guam. The brown treesnake (BTS) has received international attention due to its extermination of native bird species on Guam, disruption of electrical-power distribution, human health issues arising from snake bites, and increased cargo inspection efforts. The response to these impacts has been the development and implementation of control tools and techniques, legislative action, and preparation of a control plan. This plan describes activities required to prevent snake dispersal to other islands and options to manage the economic and ecological impacts to Guam. It also provides an outline of budgets and future efforts for the prevention, control, and potential eradication of the BTS outside its native range.

The snake's historic range includes portions of Papua New Guinea, the Solomon Islands, Australia, and Indonesia. The high density of BTS on Guam, combined with the island's importance as a transport hub, make its spread from Guam a high-risk threat to other Pacific Islands such as Hawai'i, the Commonwealth of the Northern Mariana Islands (CNMI), Federated States of Micronesia (FSM), Republic of Palau, and Republic of the Marshall Islands. Diego Garcia in the Indian Ocean, other Pacific Island nations, and climatically favorable regions of the U.S. mainland are also at risk. It is critical to prevent the transport of BTS from Guam to other areas as well as to develop capacity to respond to incipient populations in the region. At least 76 credible sightings of BTS (based upon the conditions at the time of sighting and the experience of the people reporting them) have occurred in the CNMI. Eleven snakes have been recovered from these sightings.

The BTS Control Plan includes five main goals: 1) Preventing the Spread of BTS; 2) Early Detection and Rapid Response (EDRR); 3) Control and Management; 4) Restoration of Extirpated Species; and 5) Eradication of BTS on Guam and Saipan. To achieve these goals, control will be implemented using hand capture, traps, canine detection, oral toxicants, physical barriers, and public education. Many of these control efforts have been tested or are in place on Guam, and future efforts are planned to continue testing, improving, and implementing these methods in other areas.

In 2006, the Office of Management and Budget (OMB) requested the U.S. Department of Agriculture (USDA), the U.S. Department of the Interior (DOI), and the National Invasive Species Council to provide a long-term budget plan for BTS inspection, control, and eradication efforts with the ultimate goal of eradicating BTS from Guam. A joint report was prepared by the aforementioned agencies that proposed options ranging from maintaining current funding levels for BTS control to increasing funding to implement full interdiction on Guam and Saipan. The six strategic funding options are presented in Appendix F.

For the purpose of this document, the six funding options have been revised and consolidated into three funding scenarios. The scenarios, titled "A", "B", and "C", are based on and contain components of options 3, 5, and 6 presented in Appendix F. A brief explanation of Scenarios A, B, and C follows:

Scenario A – 100% Interdiction on Guam, Severe Snake Suppression
      Research and Early Detection Research:
100% inspection coverage of cargo departing Guam and funding research for <u>Bait and Lure Development</u> and <u>Bait Delivery Development</u> (Option 3). Research components of <u>Full Interdiction Coverage</u> and <u>Severe BTS Population Suppression on Guam</u> (Option 5) include a <u>Design Control Plan</u> to develop strategies for the spatial application of snake-eradication operations and, <u>Control Plan and Evaluation</u> to monitor efficacy of rodent and/or snake eradication using GIS and spatial analysis.

Research components of a BTS Eradication Program on Saipan and/or elsewhere in the CNMI (Option 6) would include:

- Barrier development (testing of less expensive designs as a component of mid-scale eradication strategies).
- Determine density thresholds for prey control for species which compromise control techniques; develop tools to measure relevant parameters.
- Determine optimal combinations of control techniques for different situations.
- Increase capacity of the Rapid Response Team for extensive snake detection efforts.

Scenario B - 100% Interdiction from Guam, Severe Snake Suppression
      Implementation on Guam, and Early Detection Research:
This scenario builds upon Scenario A by adding operational aspects of severe snake suppression on Guam. This would include such approaches as eradication inside exclusion barriers and suppression of snake populations on a landscape level.

Scenario C - 100% Interdiction from Guam, Severe Snake Suppression on Guam,
      and Early Detection Implementation and Supporting Research in the CNMI:
This scenario builds upon Scenario B by adding the immediate implementation of detection and eradication efforts on Saipan. This scenario will require funding USDA Wildlife Services (USDA/WS), USGS Fort Collins Service Center (USGS FORT), and USGS FORT Rapid Response Team (RRT). USDA/WS Operations would assist with snake inspection of cargo that is outbound from Saipan and assist with trapping/toxicant use in sites of snake reports and sites of concern for potential snake populations. USGS FORT RRT Program would assist with night-time visual searches for snakes and snake searches with dogs. This scenario includes a budget for initiating snake control on Saipan and/or elsewhere in the CNMI.

Multi-year, stable funding to support 100% interdiction efforts on all cargo and vehicles departing Guam, operational facilities, and the necessary research to meet the demand for effective BTS control tools is imperative to prevent BTS transport from Guam and to control incipient populations on neighboring Pacific islands. In this plan we recommend that funding and priorities follow Scenario B for 2-3 years, until adequate tools and procedures are developed to begin eradication efforts on Saipan, following Scenario C.

The recommendations of the *Review of Brown Treesnake Problems and Control Programs* (Colvin et al. 2005) need to be reviewed on a regular basis by the Working Group to assure that progress is being made in addressing the issues discussed in the document.

TABLE OF CONTENTS

LIST OF FIGURES

LIST OF TABLES

1.0 VISION, GOALS, AND OBJECTIVES

The Draft Brown Treesnake Control Plan, March 2009, presents the actions, activities and contributions made by a multitude of federal agencies and local governments to prevent transport from Guam and to control this harmful nonnative invasive species on Guam. The BTS has received international attention due to its extermination of native bird species on Guam, disruption of electrical-power distributions, human health issues arising from snake bites, and increased cargo inspection efforts. The response to these impacts has been the development and implementation of control tools and techniques, legislative action, and preparation of a control plan. This plan describes activities required to prevent snake dispersal to other islands, options to manage the economic and ecological impacts to Guam, and provides an outline of budgets and future efforts for the prevention, control, and potential eradication of BTS outside its native range.

The vision of the BTS Technical Working Group is to eliminate the adverse impacts of the BTS. It is the policy of the working group to control and eradicate snakes on Guam and Saipan and to prevent the BTS spread. As identified by the BTS Technical Working Group, the goals and objectives of the BTS Control Plan are to:

Goal 1: Prevent the Spread of BTS
      Objective A) 100% outbound interdiction on Guam
      Objective B) 100% inbound interdiction on U.S. sites other than Guam
      Objective C) 100% outbound interdiction on Saipan and other areas where incipient populations may be evident in the future
      Objective D) Develop tools to improve interdiction

Goal 2: Early Detection and Rapid Response (EDRR)
      Objective A) Implement EDRR programs
- Saipan
- Tinian
- Rota
- Hawai'i

      Objective B) Develop tools to improve EDRR

Goal 3: Control and Management
      Objective A) Protect human health, safety and quality of life
      Objective B) Protect power and infrastructure
      Objective C) Protect agriculture and pets
      Objective D) Develop tools for control and management
      Objective E) Reduce snake populations to support interdiction
      Objective F) Protect extant native wildlife

Goal 4: Restoration
      Objective A) Create snake-reduced habitat for reintroduction of native wildlife
      Objective B) Improve BTS control tools for reintroduction of native wildlife

Goal 5: Eradication on Guam and Saipan
      Objective A) Improve tools for landscape-scale eradication
      Objective B) Develop long range strategic plan for BTS eradication

2.0 BACKGROUND AND OVERVIEW

2.1 Introduction

The BTS was unintentionally introduced to the island of Guam, most likely as a stowaway shortly after World War II (Rodda et al.1992). As snake populations increased, native vertebrates including birds, lizards and bats were severely depredated. The rapid decline of birds was especially dramatic since the snake was virtually unseen and not suspected to be the culprit until the mid- to late- 1980s. BTS have impacted shipping and transportation due to increased biosecurity needs, electrical infrastructure due to power outages, and human health due to snake bites. These factors have necessitated regulatory action and extensive management of BTS by a large number of agencies.

2.2 Impacts to Vertebrates on Guam

As a result of the BTS's introduction and establishment, populations of reptiles, birds, and the native Mariana fruit bat (*Pteropus mariannus mariannus*) have been directly impacted. Following the snake's introduction, nearly all of the native forest birds disappeared from southern and central Guam by the 1960's (Savidge 1987). By 1986, nine of 12 native forest bird species were extinct or extirpated from Guam, and populations of several other native non-forest birds were severely diminished (Engbring and Fritts 1988). Captive breeding and hand-rearing are used to maintain extant populations of Guam rails (*Gallirallus owstoni*) and Guam Micronesian kingfishers (*Halcyon cinnamomina cinnamomina*). Native and introduced birds remaining in the wild on Guam are summarized in Table 1.

Table 1. Remaining Native and Introduced Birds on Guam

Common Name	Scientific Name	Native (N) or Introduced (I)	Status on Guam
Yellow bittern	*Ixobrychus sinensis*	N	Rare
Micronesian starling	*Aplonis opaca guami*	N	Rare
Brown noddy	*Anous stolidus*	N	Uncommon
White tern	*Gygis alba*	N	Rare
Pacific reef heron	*Egretta sacra*	N	Uncommon
Mariana crow	*Corvus kubaryi*	N	Rare (2 indiv.)
Mariana swiftlet	*Aerodramus bartschi*	N	Rare (1 colony)
Mariana common moorhen	*Gallinula chloropus guami*	N	Uncommon
Black drongo	*Dicrurus macrocercus*	I	Common
Eurasian tree sparrow	*Passer montanus saturatus*	I	Common
Philippine turtle dove	*Streptopelia bitorquata*	I	Common
Black francolin	*Francolinus francolinus*	I	Common

The native Mariana fruit bat on Guam has declined from a relatively stable colony in the north of about 300 individuals in the 1990's to less than 50 as of August 2008 (USFWS 2006, SWCA 2008). Lack of juvenile recruitment in the mid-1980s was attributed to BTS and continues to be a significant concern for survival of bats on Guam (Wiles 1987a).

Snakes have also depredated Guam's populations of native lizards. Populations of the snake-eye skink (*Cryptoblepharus poecilopleurus*), Slevin's skink (*Emoia slevini*), azure-tailed skink (*Emoia cyanura*), moth skink (*Lipinia noctua*), mangrove skink (*Emoia atrocostata),* and

Micronesian gecko (*Perochirus ateles*) are no longer found on Guam, or are reduced to very low numbers (Rodda and Fritts 1992, Rodda et al. 1997, M. Christy, SWCA, unpublished data).

The disappearance of most of Guam's native vertebrates may have caused a number of indirect effects that warrant investigation for long-term ecosystem management. For instance, bat species such as fruit bats (*Pteropus* spp.) are important for pollination (Fujita and Tuttle 1991) and seed dispersal of forest plants (Cox et al. 1991). The Mariana fruit bat is responsible for the dispersal of about 40% of tree species on Guam (Wiles 1987b). Some Guam flora, such as *Erythrina variegata* and *Bruguiera gymnorrhiza*, are dependent on birds or fruit bats for seed dispersal and pollination and have declined due to lack of these animals (Muniappan 1988, Mortensen et al. 2008, Rogers 2008). In addition, the loss of most insectivorous birds and many species of lizard may leave Guam vulnerable to a variety of insect pests. For example, extensive defoliation of the introduced tangantangan tree (*Leucaena leucocephala)* is caused by a number of insects, one imported from Hawai'i, that also reduce locally grown fruit and vegetable production (USGS 2005). Without predators, insects arriving to Guam via ships or airplanes could pose a higher threat to agricultural crops, public health and the island ecosystems.

2.3 Socioeconomic and Human Health Impacts

Guam has suffered more than ecological consequences. The abundance of snakes in close proximity to people in Guam affects the quality of life on the island. They may invade homes, hotels, commercial buildings and other urban habitats in search of food and refuge.

BTS routinely climb human-made structures, including guy wires leading to power poles supporting transformers, distribution lines, and high-voltage transmission lines. When they simultaneously touch live and grounded conductors, they create faults, short circuits, and electrical damage. This has resulted in frequent losses of electrical generation to Guam, from partial to island-wide blackouts. More than 1,600 power outages in the nineteen-year period from 1978 to 1997 and almost 200 in 2002 were attributed to BTS (Fritts 2002). Between March 2003 and March 2004, Guam Power Authority recorded 195 snake-caused power outages (1 outage every 1.8 days), and during 2007 Naval Public Works reported 42 power outages caused by snakes (1 outage every 8.8 days) (Shwiff et al. 2009). The incidence of snake-caused outages increased fivefold from 1978 to 1982, a period of rapid snake population growth (Fritts and Chiszar 1999). Such power failures, brownouts, and electrical surges damage electrical appliances and interrupt all activities dependent on electrical power, including commerce, banking, air transportation, and medical services. A single island-wide outage is estimated to cost over $3 million in lost productivity, an estimate that does not account for repair costs, damage to electrical equipment, and lost revenues (Fritts 2002). Estimates place annual costs of snake-caused outages at around $4.5 million, not including personal equipment failures, shorter equipment life span, or increased costs due to purchasing personal electrical generators (Fritts 2002).

The U.S. Navy and Guam Power Authority (GPA) operate 23 major power-distribution circuits on Guam; this compartmentalization of the electrical system reduces the chances of outages affecting large regions or the entire island. In 1998, the GPA instituted a program with the U.S. Department of Agriculture, Wildlife Services (USDA/WS) to reduce the number of snakes around seven GPA substations. Program efforts include a combination of snake trapping, night-time spotlight searches, and elimination or lowering of guy wires and/or installing flanges to prevent snake access. The program has expanded to include 17 substations. Since the program's inception USDA/WS has removed more than 5,000 snakes from the targeted substations, and snake-related power faults have been substantially reduced as a result of this effort (USDA/WS 2006).

Many smaller Pacific islands have very few power-generating facilities and distribution lines. If the snake becomes abundant on these islands, damages to the electrical systems are likely to affect an entire island or large municipal areas.

By extrapolation from Guam's experience, establishment of the BTS in Hawai'i would have severe consequences. Estimates of potential losses range widely due to uncertainty surrounding the snake's potential arrival and establishment patterns. Burnett (2007) concluded that if an infestation were recognized immediately and efficient levels of interdiction and control measures were adopted (best case scenario), the State of Hawai'i could expect to bear $4.5 to $7 million annual losses on Oahu alone. On the other hand, if current funding levels are maintained and BTS reach their estimated carrying capacity of 7.5 million individuals, economic losses due to power outages, medical costs and, endangered-species protection efforts would increase to $917 million annually.

In a recent study Shwiff et al. (2009) estimated the potential annual cost to Hawai'i using medical expenses, power outages, and tourism rates would range from $593 million to $2.14 billion. The authors projected the annual medical cost for treating 665 to 1,330 people at a cost of $191,520 and $303,040. They also projected that Oahu would experience total power outages of 1,209 hours annually. This equates to a range of $456 million to $761 million per year. In high damage estimate scenarios, declining tourism was expected to contribute 64% of total projected costs. As a result of visitor survey analysis, they estimated between one and 10% decline in tourist days spent in Hawai'i due to the presence of BTS. This equates to economic losses between $138 million and $1.38 billion per year for direct, indirect and induced impacts to tourism alone.

Less obvious is the BTS impact on the agricultural industry, both directly by predation on poultry (Fritts and McCoid 1991) and indirectly by predation on insectivores that cause insect numbers to increase and in turn damage crops. Since the BTS preferentially prey on birds and eggs, it is difficult to raise poultry for commercial production in the presence of the snake.

BTS are mildly venomous and constrict resisting prey. Although its bite generally does not require medical attention for adults, the snake preponderantly attacks sleeping infants and small children on Guam, who are more vulnerable to envenomation. An average of 170 patients per year reported snakebites at medical facilities on Guam from 1998 to 2004 (Shwiff et al. 2009). A 24-month study, between 1989 and 1991, reported that 60% of all snakebite victims treated at medical facilities on Guam were less than six years old. All of the children under the age of five were sleeping in their homes at the time of the encounter (Fritts et al. 1994b).

Studies have also shown that symptoms and magnitude of reactions vary depending on age, weight, health, and body chemistry (Fritts et al. 1990, 1994b). Children exhibit more serious symptoms due to their small size. Potentially serious respiratory distress and neurological disorders in infants did not become apparent until one to six hours after the bite (Fritts et al. 1994b).

2.4 Impact on Military Missions and Readiness
An additional socioeconomic impact is the effect on military readiness. The costs of training and operations are increased due to inspection, quarantine and snake control requirements. Additional planning and logistical considerations necessitated by these requirements can delay

the initiation of training exercises, prolong exercises, or render them impractical to conduct if the inspection process is incompatible with the exercise logistics and mission. Day-to-day operations such as transporting personnel, equipment, and cargo from Guam require additional time and expense to conduct inspections.

2.5 Regulatory Actions Taken

Over the past two decades, considerable effort has been expended by federal, state, and local agencies on BTS control, interdiction and research. Between 1992 and 1996, the Departments of Agriculture, Commerce, Defense, and Interior; the CNMI, Territory of Guam, and State of Hawai'i signed a five-year Memorandum of Agreement (MOA) that established a policy framework and working relationship related to the BTS issue. In 1999, the MOA was renewed with an additional agency, the Department of Transportation (Appendix A).

In 1993, the BTS Technical Working Group (formerly the Brown Tree Snake Control Committee) was established by Aquatic Nuisance Species Task Force, in response to the 1990 Nonindigenous Aquatic Nuisance Prevention and Control Act. This committee was comprised of the aforementioned signatories of the 1992 MOA.

In May 1993, the BTS Control Committee met to review the status of control efforts and establish an integrated pest-management approach to interdiction. An outcome of that meeting was the production of a draft BTS Control Plan that provided a coordinated basis for control and interdiction throughout the Pacific. In April 1995, the draft plan was released for public review and comment. A final plan was made available in April 1996 and approved by the Aquatic Nuisance Species Task Force in June 1996.

From 1991 to 2004, Congress passed four amendments and/or laws intended to help prevent the accidental and intentional introduction of BTS from Guam to other areas. In 1991, Congress authorized the Secretary of Defense to take action to prevent introduction to other areas of the U.S. from Guam via aircraft or cargo as part of the National Defense Authorization Act for fiscal years 1992 and 1993. In 1998, 7 U.S.C., Section 426 authorized the Secretary of Agriculture to take actions necessary to prevent the inadvertent introduction of BTS to other areas of the U. S. from Guam. During the same year the Lacey Act (18 U.S.C. 42) of 1900, was amended, prohibiting the purposeful importation or shipment of "injurious species" into the United States, its territories, and or possessions; the USFWS is charged with listing injurious species and enforcement of these provisions. In 2004, Congress passed the Brown Tree Snake Control and Eradication Act, acknowledging the need for improved and better-coordinated control, interdiction, research, and eradication of the BTS on the part of the U. S. The Act authorized $10,600,000 in annual appropriations from 2006-2010 for the Secretaries of the participating agencies to implement their respective control, research, and interdiction activities. In FY2007 and FY2008, DOI received $2.9M each year, DOD received $2.9M and $3.1M, and USDA received $358K and $565K respectively. This Act, pending funding, authorized the establishment of federal pre-departure quarantine protocols for cargo and other items shipped from Guam and authorized funding for quarantine enforcement by states and territories. The Act also requires the BTS Technical Working Group to ensure that federal, state, territorial and local agency efforts are coordinated, complementary, technically effective, and cost-effective.

Also in 2004, a review of BTS programs was initiated by the DOI, Office of Insular Affairs (OIA). An independent panel was assembled to evaluate research and control by federal, state, and local programs relating to the BTS. The panel consisted of four individuals from the private and public sectors recognized as international experts in applied ecology and public policy, specializing in environmental management, applied herpetology, invasive-species biology, plant and animal quarantine, and vertebrate pest control. The panel was charged with assessing progress in achieving objectives outlined in the 1996 *Brown Tree Snake Control Plan* and developing recommendations to improve the effectiveness of federal, state and local BTS research and control programs. The *Review of Brown Treesnake Problems and Control Programs: Report of Observations and Recommendations* was published in March 2005 (Appendix B). The panel's findings assisted the Committee in updating this plan, and are summarized on Section 6. Federal, state, territorial and commonwealth acts and authorities pertaining to BTS control and interdiction are summarized in Appendix C.

It is intended upon this revision of the plan to have the following agencies as signatories:
- U.S. Department of the Interior
- U.S. Department of Agriculture
- U.S. Department of Defense
- Guam Department of Agriculture
- CNMI Department of Land and Natural Resources
- Hawai'i Department of Agriculture
- Hawai'i Department of Land and Natural Resources

3.0 BROWN TREESNAKE BIOLOGY

3.1 Species Description and Historic Range

Like other members of its genus, BTS is an arboreal, nocturnal, slender snake with grooved venom-conducting teeth at the rear of the upper jaw. The species can attain relatively large size, facilitating predation of a broad range of vertebrates. On Guam, the maximum body size (snout-vent length [SVL]) for females is 1.6 meters (m), and 2.1 m for males (total lengths 2.0 and 3.1 m respectively), with an average total length of 1.2 m for both sexes. The largest snakes on Guam are substantially larger than those in the native Australian range, where the maximum length is reported as 1.8 m (Rodda and Savidge 2007). The largest recorded snake on Guam measured approximately 3.1 m. Except for the difference in size, the sexes are similar in appearance.

The BTS natural distribution extends from Sulawesi in Indonesia east through New Guinea to the Solomon Islands and south along the northern and eastern rims of Australia (Figure 1). Color pattern and scalation are variable across the snake's range, but are relatively uniform at any locality (Fritts 1988).

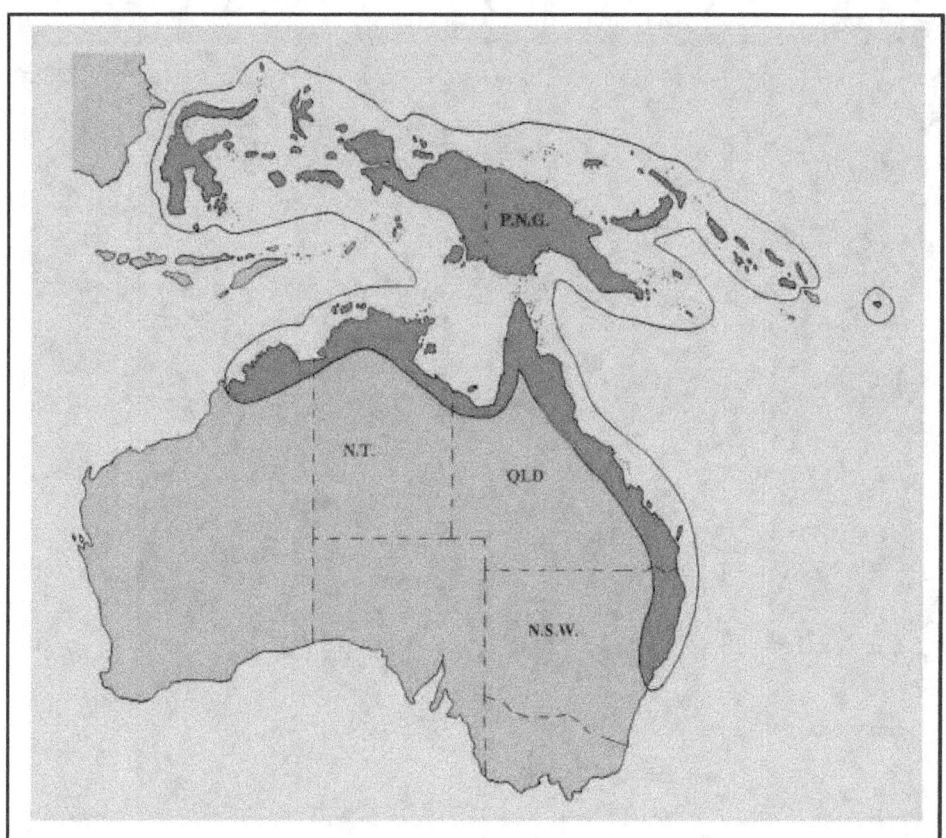

Figure 1. Brown Treesnake Native Range Shown in Red. P.N.G. = Papua New Guinea, N.T. = Northern Territory, QLD = Queensland, N.S.W. = New South Wales. N.T., QLD and N.S.W. are part of Australia.
Source: http://www.fort.usgs.gov/resources/education/bts/resources/bts_rangemap.asp

3.2 Current Nonnative Range and Extra-limital Sightings

To date, BTS has been reported from 11 islands to which it is not native (Fritts 1988, McCoid and Stinson 1991), as well as in southern Texas, Oklahoma, Alaska, and New Zealand (Fritts et al.1994a, Gill et al. 2001, Fritts et al. 2005). Histories and incidents are briefly described here.

The BTS has been established on Guam, the southernmost island in the Mariana Islands (Figure 2), since the late 1940's or early 1950's. Populations on Guam have been estimated by visual and trap surveys, removal, and mark-recapture sampling since 1985, but no data are available prior to 1985 (Fritts and Chiszar 1999) as its presence raised limited concern. The population reached peak densities of 50-100 snakes per hectare at different times, depending upon an area's colonization history (Rodda et al. 1992). While native vertebrate populations have dwindled or disappeared, introduced prey populations (primarily rodents, shrews, geckos and skinks) continue to support large populations of snakes. Recent estimates of treesnake

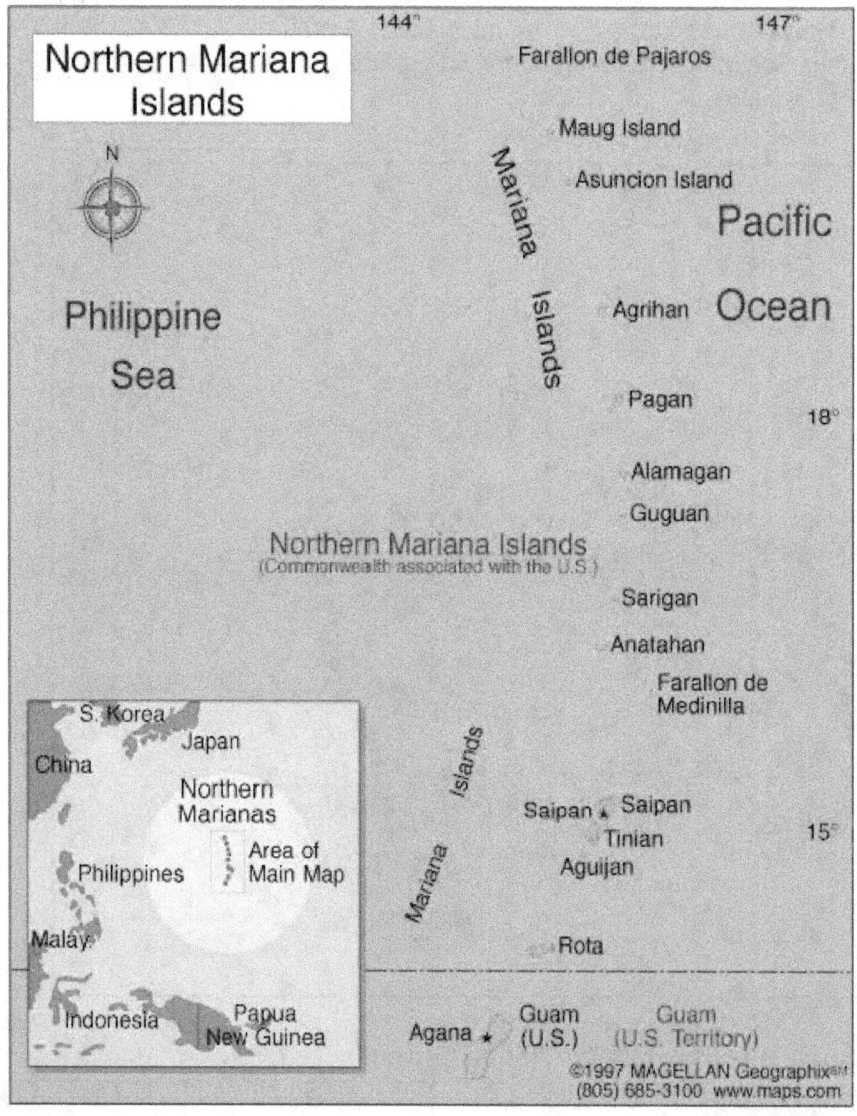

Figure 2. Guam and the Commonwealth of the Northern Mariana Islands (CNMI).

densities are 10-25 individuals per hectare, although population levels appear to be highly variable depending upon prey availability (Rodda et al. 1998a).

Snake sightings in the CNMI have increased alarmingly in recent years. Since 1986, roughly 76 snake sightings on Saipan have been considered credible based upon conditions and the observer's familiarity with snakes. Eleven snakes were recovered from these sightings (N. Hawley, USFWS, personal communication). Several Saipan snake sightings were clustered near the commercial airport or the seaport; the remaining were scattered across the island (Figure 3). The frequency of sightings suggests that a BTS population is established on Saipan, although there have been no confirmed reports of reproduction. In addition to the snake sightings on Saipan, nine sightings have been reported on Tinian, and two dead snakes have been recovered in cargo arriving on Rota (N. Hawley, USFWS, personal communication). Currently, 90% of all cargo and vessels originating in Guam are inspected upon arrival in the CNMI (N. Hawley, USFWS, personal communication) utilizing detector dog teams (Engeman et al. 2002). However, once a snake has dispersed from the point of initial introduction, the chances of capture are reduced. Therefore, it is crucial that inspections continue and that snakes be captured at the point of initial introduction.

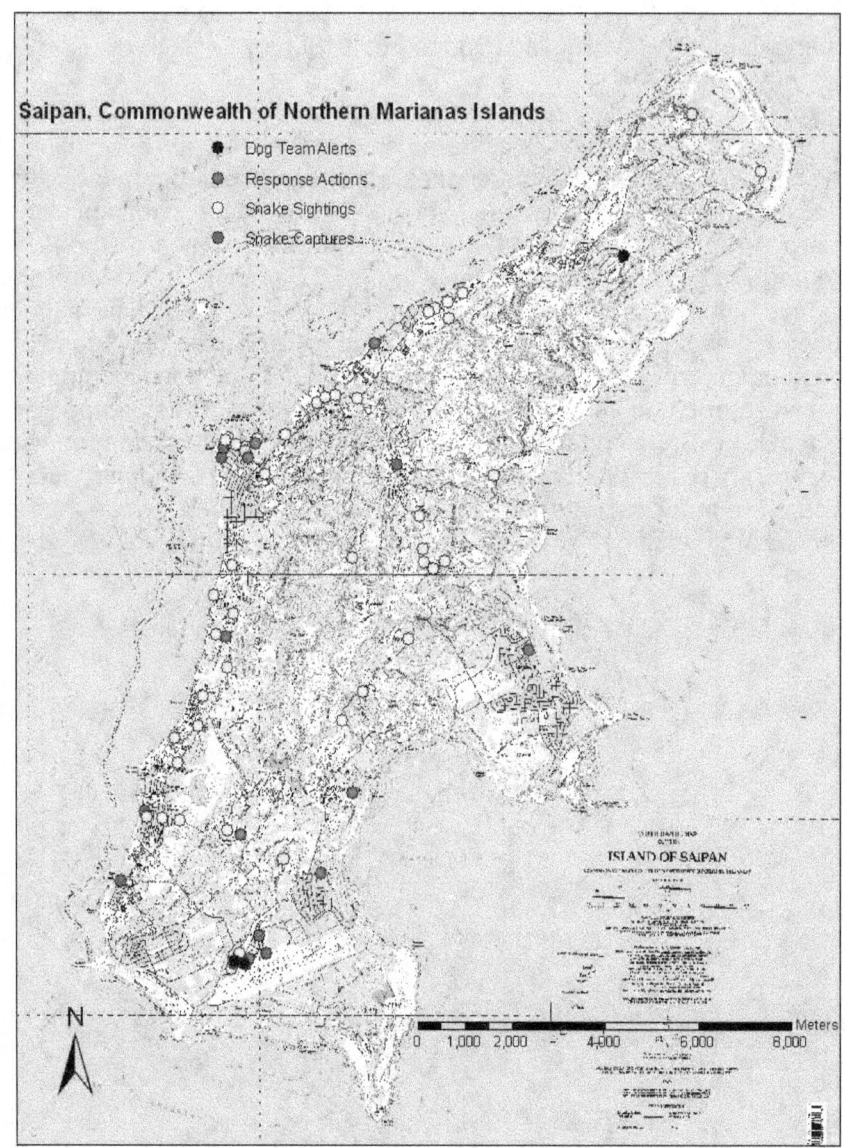

Figure 3. Brown treesnake reports on Saipan, Commonwealth of Northern Mariana Islands 1982 - 2008. Source: Stanford, 2008.

Several BTS have been discovered on other islands of the Pacific and Indian Oceans. On November 3, 1994, one was discovered in the seaport at Kolonia in Pohnpei in the Federated States of Micronesia (FSM) in association with containerized cargo. Previous snake sightings on Pohnpei, Chuuk, and Kosrae have been received and investigated, but none could be confirmed as BTS (Brown Tree Snake Control Committee 1996). Two dead BTS were found on military C-141 aircraft in the Republic of the Marshall Islands, one in 1997 and one in 1998. In addition, a single live BTS was found on the landing gear of a military C-141 in 2000 and was subsequently killed by a moving fuel truck. All three BTS were found on Kwajalein Atoll (M. Nicholson, Kwajalein Army Base, personal communication). In June 1986, a BTS was discovered on the island of Diego Garcia in the Indian Ocean, a ship carrying naval cargo from

Guam was the likely source. A dead BTS was found in February 2008 aboard a cargo ship berthed in Chuuk en route from Guam.

BTS have been repeatedly found in the Hawaiian Islands. Since 1981, eight are known to have arrived on the island of Oahu through commercial and military aircraft from Guam. Six were caught at the Honolulu International Airport and Hickam Air Force Base, one near an aircraft hangar at Barbers Point Naval Air Station, and one in an U.S. Army Schofield Barracks warehouse. All these captures occurred prior to the establishment of the federal interdiction program on Guam in 1995. The last confirmed sighting was a BTS found dead in a compartment adjacent to the wheel well of a Continental Airlines aircraft being serviced in Honolulu in 1998. The carcass was extremely desiccated. Airline officials stated that the aircraft had been "cycled" over a period between Guam and Houston return via Honolulu so the length of time the BTS was in the compartment was unknown (D. Cravalho Jr., HDOA, personal communication). A recent, but unconfirmed, sighting on Oahu was at Marine Corps Base Hawai'i in Kaneohe, April 2008.

The first documented BTS intercepted on the mainland U.S. was discovered in a crate of household goods en route from Guam in May of 1993. Delivered to Ingleside Naval Station on the north side of Corpus Christi Bay in Texas, the snake had survived 7 months in the crate since leaving Guam. It was subsequently killed. A dead BTS was found in the wheel well of a military C-5 transport plane at Elmendorf AFB in Alaska in August 2002. The transport plane had flown from Andersen AFB in Guam via Japan. The most recently discovered BTS was at McAlester Ammunition Plant in Oklahoma in September of 2005. The snake had survived in a shipment of military supplies for 3 months, and was also killed upon discovery.

A live BTS was found in Auckland, New Zealand (date not indicated) in a shipment of lumber from the Solomon Islands (Gill et al. 2001). Note that this snake originated from its native range rather than Guam as in the above cases.

3.3 Life History
The BTS is highly adaptable and not limited to specific habitats, forest strata, or seasons. However extreme dryness, bright sunlight, high daytime temperatures, or freezing conditions will reduce its activity and the occurrence of frost may limit its range (Rodda and Savidge 2007). The diet of BTS is opportunistic, including active and inactive prey (e.g., geckos and eggs), carrion and almost all live terrestrial vertebrates (amphibians, reptiles, birds, and mammals) of a suitable size. In the wild, BTS has been observed consuming meals approximately 70% of its body mass (Rodda et al. 1999a). Food availability also appears to be an important factor limiting survival and reproductive output of newly mature females on Guam.
Little is known about the reproductive habits of the BTS, as gravid females and eggs are infrequently found, and mating has never been observed on Guam (Rodda and Savidge 2007, Savidge et al. 2007). In Australia, reproduction is highly seasonal, whereas on Guam reproduction can occur year-round. This lack of seasonal reproduction may be due to Guam's annual variation in temperature of only 1.4°C and/or that the Guam population may be derived from a reproductively aseasonal population in the Admiralty Islands. Two other species of *Boiga* and other colubrid species have been shown to reproduce after long periods (up to 6 years) of isolation, suggesting either long-term sperm storage or asexual reproduction. However neither sperm storage nor asexual reproduction has been confirmed on Guam (Savidge et al. 2007).

Additional life history characteristics are summarized in Table 2.

Appendix K provides a history of key events from the time of BTS introduction on Guam in the 1940s until completion of this plan update.

Table 2. Brown Treesnake Life History on Guam
(Source: R. Reed and G. Rodda, USGS FORT)

Family	Colubridae
Scientific name	*Boiga irregularis*
Native range	Eastern Indonesia, Papua New Guinea, Solomon Islands, northern and eastern Australia
Nonnative range	Guam and Saipan
Diet	Birds and their eggs, lizards, frogs, small mammals
Maximum total length	2.0 m (female); 3.1 m (male)
Mature SVL	952 mm (female); 962 mm (male)
Hatchling SVL	375 mm
Mature weight	89 g (female); 113 g (male)
Maximum weight	542 g (female), 2600 g (male)
Hatchling weight	5-10 g
Reproductive strategy	Oviparous (egg-laying)
Reproductive timing	Capable of breeding year-round, mostly in spring and summer
Average Clutch size	4.3 eggs (range = 2-11)
Population density	10-25 snakes/ha
Life span in captivity	>15 years
Home range	Up to 100 ha
Population limiting factors	Food availability

4.0 BROWN TREESNAKE CONTROL METHODS

BTS control activities on Guam have two fundamental goals: 1) prevent dispersal to other land masses (interdiction), and 2) resource protection, including power resources, endangered native wildlife, and human health and safety. To achieve these objectives, BTS control has utilized visual searches, traps, hand captures, canine detection, oral toxicants, physical barriers, and public education (Rodda et al. 1998b, Campbell et al 1999, Vice and Pitzler 2002). Efforts to prevent the spread of snakes focus on Guam's military and commercial sea and air-ports of exit, with secondary containment activities conducted in Saipan, Tinian, Rota, and Hawai'i. A Rapid Response Team (RRT), with approximately 70 trainees available, can be deployed to snake sighting locations to find and capture snakes that have eluded interdiction (Stanford and Rodda 2007).

On Guam, BTS-caused power outages have been reduced through trapping and hand capture at key production and distribution points around the island. A program, initiated in 1998 between the Guam Power Authority and USDA/WS, has reduced outages at selected substations (see Section 2.3 of this plan).

Risk to human health and safety has been reduced in residential areas on DOD installations through intensive trapping and hand capture by USDA/WS, coupled with public awareness education.

Some protection from BTS predation is afforded Guam's endangered forest birds through intensive trapping, barriers on nest trees, and intermittent use of oral toxicants. Trapping with live mice as lures in modified minnow-type traps has been used extensively (Rodda et al. 1999b). Although labor-intensive, the traps are effective at removing snakes larger than 900 mm body length (Rodda et al. 2007, Tyrrell et al. 2009). Effectiveness of capture decreases when availability of snake prey in the environment increases (Gragg et al. 2007). Electrified wire barriers are also labor-intensive but have been successful in protecting individual nest trees (Aguon et al. 1999). These barriers have been primarily utilized for the protection of Mariana crows. The method relies on the ability to find individual nests, and may require the removal of surrounding trees to prevent snakes from bridging onto the nest tree. Oral toxicants (acetaminophen tablets) have been effective at killing BTS and show great promise for large area snake removal (Savarie et al. 2001). At present, the toxicants are individually placed in a neonatal mouse which is time consuming. However, the development of an effective bait delivery system will greatly improve efficacy. Current work to find an effective delivery system is also focused on finding a solution to reduce the probability of unintentional consumption by non-target animals. Research into the use of bait tubes to prevent birds, rats and crabs from accessing the toxic bait, and aerial delivery systems that will permit broad area application of baited toxicants are examples of major breakthroughs anticipated in the near future. Aerial broadcasting also allows toxicant baits to hang in trees, out of reach of many non-targets. Less expensive and mass-producible bait alternatives such as beef/dead mouse combinations are being examined by the USDA National Wildlife Research Center (USDA-NWRC) with promising initial results.

Localized suppression of BTS populations on Guam is executed using traps and toxicants, although full scale eradication is not feasible at present with existing techniques. Current suppression efforts are primarily used to reduce snake populations around high risk areas such as cargo holding and transfer areas, airports, power substations and, to a lesser degree, residential areas (Vice and Pitzler 2002). Emerging technologies such as aerial delivery of oral toxicants, permanent barriers, and dog detection in non-cargo situations are being developed.

Population control in large tracts of contiguous forest has been limited by constant BTS immigration and the need for continuous trap and toxicant bait-station maintenance. A large-scale trapping effort (1200 acres) at the Munitions Storage Area (MSA) at Andersen AFB has succeeded in lowering BTS populations. If the area was surrounded by an effective barrier to block snake immigration, control in the area would be more effective. New barrier technology has opened the possibility of severely reducing, or even exterminating, populations within an exclosure. Detailed information on proposed research and management needs are provided in Appendix E.

Despite tremendous advances in the timeliness of public reporting of potential sightings in Saipan, no live, free-roaming BTS have been captured (Stanford and Rodda 2007). The abundance of prey appears to limit the effectiveness of food-based capture techniques. Intuitively, there is a low probability of visually detecting a cryptic snake in extremely low densities, particularly if the need to forage is diminished as a result of the surrounding prey-rich environment. Improved early detection and response techniques are clearly needed for successful eradication of new infestations. Research and development of forest-based canine detection techniques by USGS is showing promise for such an application. So too is current research by USDA-NWRC into the use of pheromones and lures as attractants.

5.0 LEADERSHIP, COMMUNICATION, AND COORDINATION

This section provides an overview of the leadership, communication, and coordinating roles among partners involved in BTS control. Inter-agency commitment to communication and coordination is addressed in Colvin et al. (2005), Appendix B. The following is a description of roles and responsibilities for providing control and interdiction support through funding, operations, and research.

5.1 U.S. Department of the Interior (DOI)
Several agencies in the Department of the Interior are integral to the effort to control BTS. In general, the Office of Insular Affairs (OIA) is the funding arm of DOI for this effort; the U.S. Fish and Wildlife Service (USFWS) provides coordination of the multi-agency effort and some funding. The U.S Geological Survey (USGS) provides research, method development and rapid response capabilities.

5.1.1 Office of Insular Affairs (OIA)
The OIA carries out the Secretary's responsibilities for U.S.-affiliated islands. These include the territories of Guam, American Samoa, the U.S. Virgin Islands, and the CNMI, as well as the three Freely Associated States (FAS): FSM, the Republic of the Marshall Islands, and the Republic of Palau. The OIA's primary role in assisting the BTS program is to fund interdiction efforts to prevent the snake from dispersing to other islands. It also places a high priority on providing a stable funding source for research related to interdiction and control efforts.

5.1.2 U.S. Department of the Interior, Fish and Wildlife Service (USFWS)
U.S. Fish and Wildlife Service is the regulatory and management arm of the DOI for fish and wildlife resources. Its primary mission is to conserve, protect, and recover populations of fish, wildlife, and plants for the continuing benefit of the public. Regulatory authorities include the National Environmental Policy Act, Endangered Species Act, Sikes Act, Migratory Bird Treaty Act, the Fish and Wildlife Coordination Act, and other legislation specifically related to the interdiction of invasive species such as Executive Order 13112, the Brown Tree Snake Control and Eradication Act of 2004, the National Invasive Species Act of 1996, and the Nonindigenous Aquatic Nuisance Prevention and Control Act of 1990.

USFWS Pacific Islands Fish and Wildlife Office (PIFWO) provide technical assistance and coordination support to the BTS Technical Working Group and, through the regulatory process, works to prevent the spread of the snake to other Pacific islands. Through recovery planning for federally listed endangered species, the PIFWO works closely with federal and territorial agencies to develop interdiction and control strategies on Guam and the CNMI. In addition, PIFWO administers grants to Guam and the CNMI for local BTS programs to help restore ecosystems and wildlife populations impacted by BTS. These grants originate from Aquatic Nuisance Species funds and, when available, Endangered Species Act Section 6 funds.

The USFWS Guam National Wildlife Refuge (Guam NWR) supports BTS research efforts by providing office and lab space for USGS Guam-based scientists and other visiting researchers. The Guam NWR provides a field site for the USGS BTS Rapid Response Team to train individuals from throughout the Pacific in snake searching and handling techniques. The Guam NWR also works to increase public awareness on invasive species issues through education and outreach.

5.1.3 U.S. Department of the Interior, Geological Survey (USGS)

The U.S. Geological Survey is the scientific and research arm of the DOI. The primary role of USGS in BTS management include: 1) quantifying its effects on utilities, wildlife, human health and agriculture; 2) devising and evaluating new tools for control; and 3) quantifying snake and snake-prey populations. Research and development activities by USGS have been key to devising many of the control methods described in Chapter 4.

In 2002, at the request of OIA, USGS created a team of expert snake searchers, called the Rapid Response Team (RRT). The RRT was designed to detect and delineate possible incipient BTS populations in the American-associated islands of the Pacific. The RRT also provides training opportunities and snake-control supplies to Emergency Snake Control Teams in Hawai'i and the CNMI. The RRT coordinator supports the Dogs in the Woods Project, initiated in fiscal year 2004 to use dogs to locate BTS in forest and other wildland areas. It is envisioned that when the program becomes operational, it will come under USDA/WS.

5.2 U.S. Department of Agriculture, Animal and Plant Health Inspection Service, Wildlife Services (USDA/WS)

The U.S. Department of Agriculture, Animal and Plant Health Inspection Service, Wildlife Services is mandated to provide federal leadership to manage human and wildlife conflicts. USDA/WS is responsible for interdiction and area-based control of the BTS on Guam. USDA/WS works cooperatively with federal and local agencies and private industry to reduce snake-caused damage at a variety of locations around the island, and to detect and remove snakes from outbound aircraft and cargo on Guam. USDA/WS interdiction program has been very successful at intercepting snakes in cargo and keeping recipient locales snake-free.

5.2.1 National Wildlife Research Center (NWRC)

The National Wildlife Research Center is the research arm of USDA/WS, providing scientific information and developing methods for wildlife damage management. The NWRC has been involved in developing BTS control tools since 1991, using funding from the DOD, DOI, USDA and other agencies. Research has focused on chemical control methods.

5.3 U.S. Department of Defense (DOD)

The U.S. Department of Defense's major goals related to BTS are to prevent spread of the species via the military transportation system. DOD also supports research on methods of widespread BTS control. The DOD BTS Control Program was initiated in 1988 in cooperation with the USFWS and DAWR to provide technical training of military personnel to reduce the risks of snakes leaving Guam in military traffic.

Since 1993, the DOD has contracted with the USDA/WS, a unit of the Animal and Plant Health Inspection Service (APHIS) within USDA to prevent export of BTS from Guam. DOD currently provides $4.3 million annually for this purpose, which serves as a model interdiction program that has potential for emulation by other governments. The Air Force and Navy have control and interdiction plans to prevent the spread of BTS through routine cargo and transportation activities, and military training exercises operating between Guam and neighboring islands. COMNAVMAR Instruction 5090.10A, and 36 Wing Instruction 32-7004 operating instructions are attached (Appendix D).

The overall goals of an integrated control program are to:
- prevent the dispersal of BTS via military material, aircraft, and vessels to other Pacific islands and the U.S. mainland by interdiction operations implemented at DOD and DOD/civilian joint-use transportation sites on Guam; and

- provide personnel upon request to monitor DOD training sites on Saipan and Tinian during military exercises.

Routine inspections are conducted by USDA/WS on outbound military material, including luggage, personal property (e.g., household goods, privately owned vehicles, and unaccompanied baggage), DOD-owned and leased ships, aircraft, and DOD cargo shipped from or transiting through Guam. USDA/WS also provides material and training assistance to the Hawai'i Department of Agriculture and the Hawai'i Department of Land and Natural Resources to implement a BTS contingency plan on and adjacent to military installations in Hawai'i. Both state agencies currently provide BTS detection and control assistance to the military in Hawai'i.

5.4 U.S. Department of Transportation (USDOT)
The U.S. Department of Transportation, through the Federal Aviation Administration (FAA), supports BTS research efforts by providing funding for eligible and allowable airport construction projects to airports in Guam, CNMI, Hawai'i, Republic of the Marshall Islands, FSA, and Republic of Palau. The FAA also assists in the dissemination of information through FAA-sponsored workshops throughout the Pacific and Micronesia, with specific topics on brown treesnake and other alien species.

5.5 Port Authority of Guam (PAG)
The Jose D. Leon Guerrero Commercial Port /Port Authority of Guam is a public corporation and an autonomous instrument of the Government of Guam. Its mission is to provide for the needs of ocean commerce, shipping, recreational and commercial boating, and navigation to the territory of Guam. With awareness training provided by local and federal agencies, the PAG supports efforts to control and prevent BTS introduction to snake-free areas.

5.6 Guam Department of Agriculture, Division of Aquatic and Wildlife Resources (DAWR)
The Guam Department of Agriculture's Division of Aquatic and Wildlife Resources (DAWR) manage "Guam's wildlife resources for the benefit of present and future generations". The goal of DAWR Wildlife Section is to aid in the recovery of endangered animal and plant species, manage sustainable populations of game species, and promote public awareness of natural resources. Similar to a state fish and game office, DAWR receives annual federal appropriations through Pittman-Robertson Wildlife Restoration Fund, Endangered Species Section 6 and State Wildlife Grant Programs.

The DAWR BTS Research and Control Program focuses on BTS control in support of native species recovery through the development of control tools and creation of snake-reduced habitat. The DOI OIA has funded DAWR's BTS project since 1990. Current recovery efforts include snake trapping in support of the reintroduction of endangered species and installing electrical barriers on trees with active nests to increase reproductive potential.

5.7 Commonwealth of the Northern Mariana Islands (CNMI), Department of Lands and Natural Resources (DLNR), Division of Fish and Wildlife (DFW)
The CNMI Department of Lands and Natural Resources is mandated under the Commonwealth Public Law No.2-51 (codified under code 2653) to protect and augment wildlife resources. The CNMI DLNR BTS Program receives operational funding from OIA and USFWS to support trapping, snake detection dogs, containment barriers, outreach, rapid response and response training. The program's goal is to prevent further introductions of BTS into CNMI and to eradicate any that may be present. Specific program objectives include: (1) inspection of all high-risk inbound cargo from Guam; (2) eradication or containment of incipient BTS populations;

(3) protection of native wildlife from snake predation; and (4) development and implementation of effective awareness and outreach programs that increase snake sighting rapid response.

5.8 Hawai'i Department of Agriculture (HDOA), Plant Quarantine Branch (PQB)

Hawai'i Department of Agriculture, Plant Quarantine Branch, protects Hawai'i's agricultural and horticultural industries, public health, and natural resources through the interdiction and exclusion of invasive species, which includes harmful non-domestic animals, plants, and microorganisms. The PQB's BTS Inspection Program has been funded by the U.S. Department of the Interior's OIA, USDA/WS, and the State of Hawai'i. The program uses trained canine teams to inspect incoming military and civilian aircraft and ships carrying cargo arriving from Guam. HDOA developed a response protocol that provides graphic information assigning responsibilities to agencies and contact numbers in the event of a snake sighting within Hawai'i. Hawai'i has also been involved in the development of the BTS Rapid Response Team. HDOA's goal is to have a minimum of two PQB inspectors on each of the four main Hawaiian Islands trained in rapid-response techniques.

5.9 Hawai'i Department of Land and Natural Resources (HDLNR), Division of Forestry and Wildlife (DOFAW)

The Hawai'i Department of Land and Natural Resources, Division of Forestry and Wildlife is mandated to protect the natural resources of the State of Hawai'i. In this capacity DOFAW staff have worked to ensure that both state and federal regulations and programs to prevent the introduction and establishment of BTS in Hawai'i are fully funded and implemented. Through the Hawai'i Invasive Species Council, created in 2003 to provide leadership on invasive species issues at the cabinet level, DOFAW has promoted the development of control regulations and projects, including funding a pilot cargo-certification program with USDA/WS on Guam. Through a Memorandum of Understanding with the Hawai'i Department of Agriculture, DLNR participates in local snake-sighting response efforts. DOFAW and Invasive Species Committee staffs have participated in training on Guam to improve local rapid-response to snake sightings, with support from OIA.

5.10 Hawai'i Invasive Species Council (HISC)

The Hawai'i Invasive Species Council was established to provide policy level direction, coordination, and planning among state departments, federal agencies, and international and local initiatives for the control and eradication of harmful invasive species infestations throughout the State, and for preventing the introduction of other invasive species that may be potentially harmful. HISC aims to maintain a comprehensive overview of issues and implement state-wide invasive species prevention, early detection and control program for terrestrial and aquatic invaders. The focus is on programmatic and capacity shortfalls not currently addressed by state agencies. HISC supports local capacity (e.g. ISCs), and interagency coordination at the state level to respond to BTS, and is an additional forum for promotion of any BTS issues. HISC's research grant program has given money for BTS control method development.

5.11 Coordinating Group on Alien Pest Species (CGAPS)

The Hawai'i Coordinating Group on Alien Pest Species is a voluntary partnership formed in 1995, aimed at facilitating interagency and NGO communication and cooperation on invasive species issues. It also promotes awareness of the problems, concerns as well as the changes that are necessary for protecting Hawai'i. CGAPS has played an active role in supporting agencies involved in containing and controlling BTS, primarily via public outreach and media assistance. CGAPS will continue to focus on BTS issues as one of its top ten most important actions, as it has since its inception.

5.12 National Invasive Species Council (NISC)

The National Invasive Species Council is an inter-Departmental council that helps to coordinate and ensure complementary, cost-efficient and effective Federal activities regarding invasive species. NISC was established February 3, 1999 by Executive Order 13112. NISC members include three co-chairs: the secretaries of Agriculture, Commerce, and Interior, as well as the secretaries of State, Defense, Homeland Security, Treasury, Transportation, Health and Human Services, and the Administrators of the Environmental Protection Agency, the U.S. Agency for International Development, the U.S Trade Representative, and the National Aeronautics and Space Administration. NISC staff work with NISC members to implement Council goals. NISC staff are active participants in many BTS efforts, such as the preparation of reports to OMB and Congress, and the reauthorization of the BTS MOA.

5.13 Regional Invasive Species Council (RISC)

The Micronesia Regional Invasive Species Council is an inter-jurisdictional, regional council established by the Chief Executives of Micronesia to coordinate and promote collaborative efforts to address the serious invasive species issues facing Micronesia. RISC capitalizes on the close cultural, economic and political ties in the region to develop joint policy initiatives, combine limited resources, and promote efficiency by sharing and capitalizing on members' strengths and capabilities. RISC members provide invasive species policy and management recommendations directly to the Chief Executives Micronesia and work with public, non-profit and private sector partners to promote public awareness and outreach. RISC has been instrumental in encouraging the Chief Executives of Micronesia to become directly involved in various BTS policy issues and funding efforts.

5.14 Aquatic Nuisance Species Task Force (ANSTF)

The Aquatic Nuisance Species Task Force is an intergovernmental organization dedicated to preventing and controlling aquatic nuisance species, and implementing the Nonindigenous Aquatic Nuisance Prevention and Control Act (NANPCA) of 1990. The various NANPCA mandates were expanded later with the passage of the National Invasive Species Act (NISA) in 1996. The Task Force consists of 10 Federal agency representatives and 12 Ex-officio members, and is co-chaired by the U.S. Fish and Wildlife Service and National Oceanic and Atmospheric Administration. The Task Force coordinates governmental efforts dealing with ANS in the U.S. with those of the private sector and other North American interests via regional panels and issue-specific committees and work groups. The BTS Technical Working Group drafts the BTS Control Plan for review and approval by the Task Force.

5.15 North American Brown Tree Snake Control Team (NABTSCT)

The North America Brown Tree Snake Control Team is a collaborative effort between federal agencies, state agencies, and private organizations to prevent the Brown Tree Snake from entering the continental United States. Pathways of entry by Brown Tree Snakes into the continental United States have been identified and through education and awareness programs and NABTSCT is establishing blockades to such pathways. If Brown Tree Snakes are sighted in the continental United States, a rapid response assessment will be conducted by NABTSCT stakeholders.

6.0 INTERAGENCY PANEL RECOMMENDATIONS

Concerned with the perpetual risk of BTS transport outside of the United States, OIA convened an expert panel in January 2004 to assess the BTS control program and its progress in achieving the objectives outlined in the 1996 Brown Tree Snake Control Plan. The panel conducted a review of the multi-agency and local government activities and reported the findings in the Review of the BTS Problems and Control Programs, Report of Observations and Recommendation, dated March 2005 (Colvin et al. 2005). The two overarching goals and ten overarching themes of the report are presented below, as originally written; the full report is provided in Appendix B. A section has been added indicating how these recommendation have been addressed, and what remains to be done.

6.1 Two Overarching Goals

1. Prevention of BTS dispersal to other islands, thereby preventing additional and widespread regional impacts and damage.
2. Control and eradication of BTS island-wide or on significant portions of Guam, thereby reducing or eliminating impacts and damage there.

6.2 Ten Overarching Themes

1. Leadership
Considerable leadership and potential for leadership exist at the implementation level, among field and research staff. However, stronger leadership and involvement at the policy and senior management levels are essential to ensure long-term sustainability of BTS control efforts; this should be a priority. Many program elements seem to be managed from the bottom up, based on the personal dedication of a few individuals. An effective program requires strong, diverse, and committed leadership at all levels of the organizations involved, from government to private industry. Immediate action is required; there is too much at risk from both an economic and scientific perspective. Although the interagency committee approach to planning is important and valuable, this committee does not represent senior-level decision makers or funders. Ultimately clear commitment to the problem and accountability must be established at the senior level among the agencies involved.

2. Goal Setting and Planning
Long-term vision defined objectives and goals, and the establishment of milestones (interim goals and objectives) that are scheduled and tracked should replace cyclic, short-term planning. Planning must be integrated among agencies to maximize the accomplishment of shared (defined) objectives and to assure understanding and recognition of critical-path tasks (i.e., essential actions and priorities for moving forward). The BTS Technical Working Group (BTS Control Committee) has been established for the purpose of integrative planning and appears to have made much progress on inter-agency cooperation in recent years. Planning must be realistic, practical, and flexible for the magnitude of the spreading problem. Planning should include risk and alternatives assessment and a process for continuous improvement and periodic review. Appropriate input should be sought from a wide range of stakeholders.

3. Communication and Coordination

Communication is occurring vertically and laterally within the organizations involved in BTS research and control. Some communication paths are working well and others can and must be enhanced. Success ultimately is predicated upon open communication and, most importantly, cooperation among numerous entities. Communication includes various government agencies, but also must include the general public and private industry (e.g., transportation, construction). Impressively, the BTS Technical Working Group (BTS Control Committee) has helped pull agencies together for planning and information sharing. Whether for BTS or other invasive species, the public and policy makers must be made aware of the risks and impacts. Education of stakeholders should be accomplished through diverse methods and broad participation; the public is an important part of front-line monitoring and reporting. Establishment of a permanent outreach and coordinator position for the committee may be valuable and should be considered.

4. Funding and Resource Allocation

Overall funding is distinctly inadequate relative to the magnitude of the existing problem, and to the emerging problems and associated risks for other islands. Short-term funding cycles are hampering necessary research and interdiction activities and are restricting the forward momentum needed for an effective program to control invasive species. Because BTS efforts are underfunded, the risk of much higher costs looms in the future to resolve expanding threats not addressed now. The cost-sharing among agencies and the transportation industry has improved greatly, but there is still room for more improvement. OIA is carrying much of the funding responsibility at present, and, inappropriately, the perceived ownership of the problem. Greater and sustainable investment by the military agencies is warranted as part of their doing business in high-risk areas for invasive species dispersal and their overall stewardship of natural resources on their lands.

5. Interdisciplinary Activities

The BTS program must be recognized as interdisciplinary, requiring practical and flexible integration of multiple program elements and skills. Research is a central theme in BTS control, and especially important are the closed population studies and bait and delivery system development. Regional issues, coordination, capacity building, rapid response, outreach, and interdiction are all inter-related and, as such, must be appropriately funded and closely integrated for a holistic approach to control/eradication and ultimately restoration. A shared work plan with commonly accepted milestones is the best way to assure integration and cooperation among participants. The interagency approach used now for the BTS program serves as a model for invasive species management and control.

6. Research

Excellent research has been conducted on many aspects of BTS biology and control measures. Additional ecological research is needed to facilitate control and interdiction, including studies of population dynamics and reproductive biology. Research and development of control measures need much greater support, particularly in the area of baits and attractants, practical methods for delivery, application of control agents, and logistics associated with control and interdiction. Pursuing these critical research topics is central to the resolution of BTS issues. Further exploratory research may be needed as proven technology for vertebrate control continues to evolve. Research by all parties should be closely coordinated and integrated to maximize efficient use of funds and execution in the field.

7. Program Execution

The program accomplishments to date are impressive. However, a general shift from a reactive effort to a proactive, sustainable program is needed. For example, this shift might include tailoring local integrated pest management (IPM) programs to incorporate BTS interdiction. However, a critical shift is needed away from interdiction focused on BTS capture (under the 1996 BTS Control Plan) with short-term funding. A plan for program execution is needed that defines the process for implementing long-term priorities (e.g., improved control measures and emergency response capabilities, attempts at full-scale eradication), defining milestones, and monitoring results. Such a plan also should articulate the policy, funding, research, and regulatory support necessary to accomplish its stated goals and objectives.

8. Restoration

The goals of BTS control can be described as (1) restoration of extirpated species on Guam and (2) protecting fauna and other resources in the region from extirpation or damage by BTS. Restoration activities and planning need to be coordinated with the development and implementation of BTS control technology. Restoration projects must consider the multiple invasive species present (in addition to BTS) that may impede reintroduction efforts and the development of self-sustaining populations. Habitat loss appears to be a significant issue that also must be addressed as part of restoration planning. Restoration could be coordinated with a control/eradication project, with distinct planning linkages between them. Separate funding mechanisms for restoration efforts are required.

9. Regional Perspective

BTS is not just a Guam problem; it is a growing regional issue, and a serious risk in terms of potential economic and natural resource losses. The threat to islands other than Guam, particularly Saipan, is a serious concern requiring immediate attention. A synergistic, regional perspective is required when developing strategies, mobilizing resources, and executing a management and control program. The efforts underway on BTS control and interdiction provide an excellent model for management of any invasive species using a regional, cooperative, and holistic perspective. Various regional organizations, policy makers, and government officials need to be actively tracking and supporting BTS efforts.

10. Management and Accountability

The efforts of numerous people involved with BTS have been admirable, especially given the many organizations involved and limited funding available. However, it now is essential to move forward to the next level of program implementation with clear priorities, accountability, institutionalized procedures and processes to achieve necessary goals. A diversity of skills and personnel resources are needed to assure sustainability and efficient program execution. Skills in biological sciences must be complemented with skills in project management, scheduling, budgeting, policy development, and stakeholder outreach. The critical nature of the BTS problem and the associated risks warrant dedicated resources for program management and coordination. However, achieving program goals and dedicating resources will require agencies to affirm their policies and priorities, and to assume greater responsibility for the problem.

6.3 Progress Made in Addressing Recommendations

Since the 2005 Report, progress has been made on a number of the Panel's recommendations, while some areas are still in need of improvement. There has been increased participation of higher-level officials from DOI, and particularly DOD, with the working group and with other planning efforts. The latter is due in part to the heightened profile of the BTS issue in relation to the military build-up on Guam, and has resulted in better communication and coordination, and commitment to stable annual funding for interdiction on Guam.

Much progress has been made in researching BTS control methods. Lack of trapping success for smaller snakes has been explained by prey selectivity, so new attractants are being developed in response. The effects of prey abundance on trapping success have been quantified, so the need to control prey in areas that are to be trapped is better understood. Delivery methods for toxicants have been developed; bait tubes have been shown to be highly effective at excluding non-targets, and aerial delivery systems and alternatives to prenatal mice baits are being developed. Improvements in manual capture techniques in wildland situations include determining the optimal headlamp beam width and bulb type, and successes with dog searching.

Efforts are being expanded from reactive capture on Guam (Theme 7 above) to area-wide control, and proactive monitoring efforts on Saipan. The construction of a snake-proof barrier on Andersen Air Force Base has been contracted, and larger plans for area wide control on the Guam National Wildlife Refuge Overlay are being developed with the goal of restoring native fauna. Rat control on Cocos Island will provide the opportunity to determine if BTS are present, if so eradicate them, and restore native fauna there as well.

Regional efforts toward awareness and involvement in BTS issues include the formation of the Regional Invasive Species Council, and efforts to conduct meetings in Micronesia, facilitating attendance by representatives from at-risk areas. A regional biosecurity plan is being developed in response to increased military traffic in the region.

In addition to the multi-agency effort toward updating this plan, the OMB budget exercise outlining the costs of alternatives for long-term area-wide control has expanded efforts in BTS management beyond short-term single-agency cyclical planning. Annual reporting to OIA, and efforts of NISC to coordinate the budgeting process across all agencies are steps toward a system of accountability to assure that milestones are being achieved, but a unified system of accounting and milestones common to all cooperating agencies still needs to be developed.

7.0 CURRENT FUNDING AND ALLOCATIONS

During fiscal year 2008, the BTS program had a total operating budget of $8,311,148. Funding contributions and expenditures are shown in Tables 3 and 4:

Table 3. BTS Funding Sources - Fiscal Year 2008

AGENCY	AMOUNT
Department of Interior	$3,341,112*
Department of Defense	$4,316,646*
U.S. Department of Agriculture	$565,000*
Guam Power Authority	$88,000
Total	$8,310,758

* DOD, DOI and USDA provide in-kind services such as office space, fuel, and limited salary in addition to funds indicated above.

Table 4. BTS Program Funding Allocation - Fiscal Year 2008

AGENCY	AMOUNT
USDA – APHIS – Wildlife Services (WS)	$5,217,500
Government of Guam	$290,000
USGS – BRD	$1,175,000
CNMI- DFW	$317,336
Hawai'I - DOA	$238,246
USFWS	$221,159
USDA – APHIS – WS – National Wildlife Research Center	$60,000
Andersen Air Force Base (HMU)	$748,646
NISC	$25,000
Smaller grants and coordination	$17,871
Total	$8,310,758

8.0 PROPOSED SNAKE INTERDICTION, CONTROL AND FUNDING NEEDS

Territorial, state, and federal agencies have been addressing BTS control, interdiction and research needs since the 1980s. In 1988, the first report documenting regional programmatic strategies for this pest was published (Fritts 1988). Interdiction, control, and research strategies for control of BTS have remained fairly consistent during programmatic and budgetary planning changes.

The first BTS Control Plan prepared for the Aquatic Nuisance Species Task Force by the BTS Control Committee was completed in November 1996. An update and revision of this plan started in 2004, and provides an opportunity to reflect and respond to the recommendations of the Interagency Panel (Section 6.0).

In a November 2005 a joint report prepared by the USDA, DOI, and NISC at the request of the Office of Management and Budget (OMB), six strategic budgetary options were proposed (BTS Budget Exercise, Appendix F). Each budget option provided costs and performance measures to cover a full range of potential levels of control ranging from a slow decline in interdiction capabilities to aggressive population reduction on Guam and eradication on Saipan. A detailed description of each budget option, an overview of the 2006 budget, expenditure spreadsheets for each option, and performance measures over a 10-year period are presented in Appendix F.

8.1 Future Funding Needs: Three Scenarios
For the purpose of this document the six funding options discussed in Appendix F have been revised and consolidated into three funding scenarios. The scenarios are based on, and contain, components of options 3, 5, and 6 of the BTS Budget Exercise. Options 1 and 2 did not meet the objectives of this plan, and elements of Option 4 are contained in Options 3 and 6. A brief explanation of Scenarios A, B, and C follow:

Scenario A – 100% Interdiction on Guam with Severe Snake Suppression
    Research and Early Detection Research, to include:

1) 100% inspection coverage of high-risk cargo departing Guam and funding research for <u>Bait and Lure Development</u> and <u>Bait Delivery Development</u> (Option 3). Research components include testing alternatives to the expensive and time-consuming use of neonatal mice to deliver acetaminophen toxicants, alternatives to live mice in traps, and ways to efficiently assemble and deliver baited toxicants to snakes over a large area while avoiding consumption by non-target species.

2) Research components of Full Interdiction Coverage and Severe BTS Population Suppression on Guam (Option 5) include a <u>Design Control Plan</u> to develop strategies for the spatial application of snake-eradication operations and, <u>Control Plan and Evaluation</u> to monitor efficacy of rodent and/or snake-eradication using GIS and spatial analysis.

3) Research components of a BTS Eradication Program on Saipan and/or elsewhere in the CNMI (Option 6) would include:
   - Barrier development (testing of designs that show more cost-effective promise as a component of mid-scale eradication strategies).
   - Determine appropriate density thresholds to control prey species whose densities compromise control techniques, and develop tools to measure relevant parameters.

- Determine optimal combinations of control techniques for different situations.
- Ramping up the Rapid Response Team for extensive snake detection efforts.

Scenario B - 100% Interdiction from Guam, Severe Snake Suppression on Guam, Implementation and Research and Early Detection Research

This scenario builds upon Scenario A by adding operational aspects of severe snake suppression on Guam. This would include such approaches as eradication inside exclusion barriers, and suppression of snake populations on a landscape level.

Scenario C - 100% Interdiction from Guam, Severe Snake Suppression on Guam, Implementation and Research, and Early Detection Implementation in the CNMI and Supporting Research

This scenario builds upon Scenario B by adding the immediate implementation of detection and eradication efforts on Saipan. This scenario will require funding to USDA WS, USGS FORT RRT, and USGS FORT. USDA WS Operations would assist with snake inspection of cargo that is outbound from Saipan and assist with trapping/toxicant use in sites of snake reports and sites of concern for potential snake populations. USGS FORT RRT Program would assist with night-time visual searches for snakes and snake searches with dogs. This scenario includes a budget for initiating snake control on Saipan and/or elsewhere in the CNMI. Since there are limited tools available to deal with this situation, actual costs of program implementation would be refined as tools are developed.

8.2 Budget Scenarios Comparison to 2007 Funding

Table 5 describes the three different budget scenarios and compares them to the FY 2007 BTS budget. Funding needed would be the difference between current funding levels and each option.

Currently, either Scenario B or Scenario C would address the five goals outlined in Section 1.0 of this plan. The objectives under Goal 5 are to develop the tools and long-range strategies to eradicate BTS from Saipan, and from significant landscapes on Guam. While these components are not presently achievable, we expect that given high priority and adequate and appropriate funding, they will be ready for implementation well within this planning cycle. Therefore, we recommend that Scenario B be used as the funding goal for the first several years of the cycle, until the consensus of the Working Group is that the tools and long-term strategy are in place to justify and pursue the program and funding outlined in Scenario C.

8.3 Conclusions

The draft BTS Control Plan provides a summary of past efforts and next steps to be taken. Past efforts by many agencies and organizations have been considerably successful in containing BTS on Guam. These efforts are coordinated through the guidance provided by The BTS Technical Working Group, and in previous versions the BTS Control Plan. The BTS Technical Working Group should collaborate on endeavors recommended in the Review of the BTS Problems and Control Programs, Report of Observations and Recommendation, dated March 2005 (Colvin et al. 2005).

Table 5. Budget Scenarios Comparison to 2007 Budget

	FY07 Funding	SCENARIO A. 100% Interdiction on Guam / Severe Snake Suppression on Guam Research / Early Detection Research / FY08 Dollars	Difference between FY07 funding and SCENARIO A.	SCENARIO B. 100% Interdiction on Guam / Severe Snake Suppression on Guam Implementation & Research/ Early Detection Research / FY08 Dollars	Difference between FYO7 funding and SCENARIO B.	SCENARIO C. 100% Interdiction on Guam / Severe Snake Suppression on Guam Implementation & Research/ Early Detection Implementation in the CNMI & Supporting Research / FY08 Dollars	Difference between FYO7 funding and SCENARIO C.
	dollars in thousands	dollars in thousands	dollars in thousands	dollars in thousands	dollars in thousands	dollars in thousands	dollars in thousands
USDA APHIS WS OPS	$3,512	$5,762	+$2,250	$10,597	+$7,085	$12,108	+$8,596
USDA APHIS WS NWRC	$442	$4,124	+$3,682	$4,124	+$3,682	$4,124	+$3,682
USGS BRD FORT	$867	$2,230	+$1,363	$2,230	+$1,363	$2,230	+$1,363
USGS RRT	$418	$386	-$32	$386	-$32	$1,105	+$687
GovGuam	$260	$338	+$78	$338	+$78	$338	+$78
CNMI - DFW / USFWS (CNMI related)	$401	$522	+$121	$522	+$121	$1,468	+$1,067
USFWS	$53	$150	+$97	$150	+$97	$150	+$97
HAWAI'I	$210	$468	+$258	$468	+$258	$468	$258
Other	$96	$0	-$96	$0	-$96	$0	-$96
All Agencies	$6,259	$13,979	$7,720	$18,815	$12,748	$21,991	$15,732

9.0 REFERENCES

Aguon, C. F., R. E. Beck, Jr., and M. W. Ritter. 1999. A method for protecting nests of the Mariana Crow from Brown Treesnake predation, p. 460-467. *In* G. H. Rodda, Y. Sawai, D. Chiszar, and H. Tanaka [eds.], Problem snake management: the Habu and the Brown Treesnake. Cornell Univ. Press, Ithaca, New York.

Brown Tree Snake Control Committee. 1996. Brown tree snake control plan. Approved by Aquatic Nuisance Species Task Force. .

Burnett, K. 2007. Optimal prevention and control of invasive species: The case of the brown treesnake. Ph.D. Dissertation, University of Hawai'i at Manoa, HI.

Campbell, E. W., III, G. H. Rodda, T. H. Fritts, and R. L. Bruggers. 1999. An integrated management plan for the Brown Treesnake (*Boiga irregularis*) on Pacific islands, p. 423-435. *In* G. H. Rodda, Y. Sawai, D. Chiszar, and H. Tanaka [eds.], Problem snake management: the Habu and the Brown Treesnake. Cornell Univ. Press, Ithaca, New York.

Colvin, B.A., M.W. Fall, L.A. Fitzgerald, and L.L. Loope. 2005. Review of brown treesnake problems and control programs: report of observations and recommendations. Prepared for U.S. Department of Interior, Office of Insular Affairs. .

Cox, P.A., T. Elmqvist, E.D. Pierson, and W.E. Rainby. 1991. Flying foxes as strong interactors in south pacific island ecosystems: a conservation hypothesis. Conservation Biology 5: 448-454.

Cravahlo Jr., Domingo. Inspection and Compliance Section Chief, Hawai'i Department of Agriculture, Plant Quarantine Branch. Personal communication, May 2007.

Engbring, J. and T.H. Fritts. 1988. Demise of an insular avifauna: The brown tree snake on Guam. Transactions Western Section of the Wildlife Society 24:31-37.

Engeman, R.M., D.S. Vice, D. York, and K.S. Gruver. 2002. Sustained evaluation of the effectiveness of detector dogs for locating brown tree snakes in cargo outbound from Guam. International Biodeterioration & Biodegradation. 49:101-106.

Fritts, T.H. 1988. The Brown Tree Snake, *Boiga irregularis*, A threat to Pacific Islands. Biological Report 88:31

Fritts, T.H. 2002. Economic costs of electrical system instability and power outages caused by snakes on the Island of Guam. Int. Biodeterioriation and Biodegradation 49:93-100.

Fritts, T.H. and D. Chiszar. 1999. Snakes on electrical transmission lines: patterns, causes, and strategies for reducing electrical outages due to snakes. Pp. 89-103. In G.H. Rodda, Y. Sawai, D. Chiszar, and H. Tanaka, eds. Problem snake management: the habu and the brown treesnake. Cornell University Press. Ithaca, NY:

Fritts, T.H. and M.J. McCoid. 1991. Predation by the brown tree snake (*Boiga irregularis*) on poultry and other domesticated animals in Guam. Snake 23:75-80.

Fritts, T.H., M.J. McCoid, and E.W Campbell III. 1994a. A brown tree snake (Colubridae: *Boiga irregularis*) sighting in Texas. Texas Journal of Science 46:365-368.

Fritts, T.H., M.J. McCoid, and R.L. Haddock. 1990. Risks to infants on Guam from bites of the Brown Tree Snake (*Boiga irregularis*). American Journal of Tropical Medicine and Hygiene 42:607-611.

Fritts, T.H., M.J. McCoid, and R.L. Haddock. 1994b. Symptoms and circumstances associated with bites by the brown tree snake (Colubridae: *Boiga irregularis*) on Guam. Journal of Herpetology 28:27-33.

Fritts, T.H., D.L. Tanner, J. Stanford, and T. Kman. 2005. Brown treesnake (*Boiga irregularis*): fact sheet for Pacific Island residents and travelers. Fort Collins, CO: U.S. Geological Survey, Fort Collins Science Center. Fact Sheet 2005-3109.

Fujita, M.S. and M.D. Tuttle. 1991. Flying Foxes (Chiroptera: Pteropodidae): Threatened animals of key ecological and economic importance. Conservation Biology 5:455-463.

Gill, B.J., D. Bejakovich, and A.H. Whitaker. 2001. Records of foreign reptiles and amphibians accidentally imported to New Zealand. New Zealand Journal of Zoology. 28: 351-359.

Gragg, J.E., G.H. Rodda, J.A. Savidge, G.C. White, K. Dean-Bradley, and A.R. Ellingson. 2007. Response of brown treesnakes to reduction of their rodent prey. Journal of Wildlife Management 71:2311–2317.

Hawley, N. USFWS Biologist/CNMI DFW Herpetologist, Commonwealth of the Northern Mariana Islands Division of Fish and Wildlife, Department of Land and Nature Resources. Personal communication, May 2007.

McCoid, M.J. and D.W. Stinson. 1991. Recent snake sightings in the Marianas Islands. 'Elepaio. 51:36-37.

Mortensen, H.S., Y.L. Dupont, and J.M. Olsesen. 2008. A snake in paradise: disturbance of plant reproduction following extirpation of flower-visitors on Guam. Biological Conservation. 141:2146-2154.

Muniappan, R. 1988. Biological control of the weed, *Lantana camara* in Guam. Journal of Plant Protection in the Tropics 5:99–101.

Nicholson, Michael. Installation Pest Management Supervisor, Kwajalein Atoll, Republic of the Marshall Islands. Personal communication, May 2007.

Reed, R. and G. Rodda, U.S. Geological Survey, Fort Collins Science Center, Personal communication. Dec. 2008, March 2009.

Rodda, G.H. and J.A. Savidge. 2007. Biology and Impacts of Pacific Island Invasive Species. 2. *Boiga irregularis*, the Brown Tree Snake (Reptilia: Colubridae). Pacific Science 61: 307-324.

Rodda, G.H. and T.H. Fritts. 1992. The impact of the introduction of the colubrid snake *Boiga irregularis* on Guam's lizards. Journal of Herpetology 26:166-174.

Rodda, G.H., E.W Campbell III, and T.H. Fritts. 1998a. Sampling techniques for snakes and their prey. Brown Treesnake Research Symposium, Hawai'i Secretariat for Conservation Biology, Honolulu, H!.

Rodda, G.H., T.H. Fritts, and D. Chiszar. 1997. The disappearance of Guam's wildlife: new insights for herpetology, evolutionary ecology, and conservation. BioScience 47:565-574.

Rodda, G. H., T. H. Fritts, C. S. Clark, S. W. Gotte, and D. Chiszar. 1999b. A state-of-the-art trap for the Brown Treesnake, p. 268-305. In G. H. Rodda, Y. Sawai, D. Chiszar, and H. Tanaka [eds.], Problem snake management: the Habu and the Brown Treesnake. Cornell Univ. Press, Ithaca, New York.

Rodda, G.H., T.H. Fritts, and P.J. Conry. 1992. Origin and population growth of the brown tree snake, *Boiga irregularis*, on Guam. Pacific Science 46:26-57.

Rodda, G.H., T.H. Fritts, M.J. McCoid, and E.W Campbell III. 1999a. An Overview of the Biology of the Brown Treesnake (*Boiga irregularis*), a Costly Introduced Pest on Pacific Islands. Pp. 44-80. In G.H. Rodda, Y. Sawai, D. Chiszar, and H. Tanaka, eds. Problem Snake Management: the Habu and the Brown Treesnake. Cornell University Press Ithaca, NY.

Rodda, G. H., T. H. Fritts, G. Perry, and E. W. Campbell, III. 1998b. Managing island biotas: can indigenous species be protected from introduced predators such as the Brown Treesnake?, p. 95-108. In K. G. Wadsworth [ed.], Trans. 63rd No. Amer. Wildl. Natur. Resour. Conf. Wildlife Mgmt. Inst., Washington, DC.

Rodda, G. H., J. A. Savidge, C. L. Tyrrell, M. T. Christy, and A. R. Ellingson. 2007. Size bias in visual searching and trapping of Brown Treesnakes on Guam. Journal of Wildlife Management 71:656-661.

Rogers, H. 2008. Brown Tree Snake could mean Guam will lose more than its birds. http://www.sciencedaily.com/releases/2008/08/080808090313.htm

Savarie, P. J., J. A. Shivik, G. C. White, J. C. Hurley, and L. Clark. 2001. Use of acetaminophen for large scale control of Brown Treesnakes. Journal of Wildlife Management 65:356-365.

Savidge, J.A. 1987. Extinction of an island forest avifauna by an introduced snake. Ecology 68:660-668.

Savidge, J.A., F.J Qualls, and G.H Rodda. 2007. Reproductive biology of the brown tree snake *Boiga irregularis* (Reptilia: Colubridae), during colonization of Guam and comparison with that in their native range. Pacific Science 61:191-199.

Shwiff, S.A., K.N. Kirkpatrick and K. Gebhardt. 2009. The Potential Economic Damage of the Introduction of the Brown Treesnake, *Boiga irregularis* (Reptilia: Colubridae) to the Islands of Hawai'i. In review.

Stanford, J. W., and G. H. Rodda. 2007. The Brown Treesnake Rapid Response Team, p. 175-217. In G. W. Witmer, W. C. Pitt, and K. A. Fagerstone [eds.], Managing Vertebrate Invasive Species: Proceedings of an international symposium. USDA-APHIS Wildlife Services National Wildlife Research Center, Fort Collins, CO.

Stanford, J. 2009. U.S. Geological Survey, Rapid Response Team.
SWCA. 2008. The effects of flight operations on endangered Mariana fruit bats and Mariana crows: A monitoring program for Andersen AFB, Guam. Air Force Center for Engineering and the Environment Brooks City-Base, TX.

Tyrrell, C. L., M. T. Christy, G. H. Rodda, A. A. Yackel Adams, A. R. Ellingson, J. A. Savidge, K. Dean-Bradley, and R. Bischof. 2009. Evaluation of trap capture in a geographically closed population of Brown Treesnakes on Guam. Journal of Applied Ecology 46:128-135.

U.S. Department of Agriculture, Wildlife Services (USDA/WS). 2006. Brown treesnake control, annual progress report for Guam Power Authority, Fiscal Year 2005.

USFWS. 2006. Biological Opinion. Letter to Lt. Col Marvin W. Smith, Jr., Andersen AFB from Mr. Patrick Leonard, Field Supervisor, Pacific Islands Fish and Wildlife Office, USFWS, 03 Oct 2006. Subject: Biological Opinion on the Establishment and Operation of and Intelligence, Surveillance, Reconnaissance, and Strike Capability Project on Andersen AFB, GU.

U.S. Geological Survey (USGS). 2005. Ecological Perturbations and Consequences. Available at: http://www.fort.usgs.gov/resources/education/bts/impacts/eco_perturb.asp.

Vice, D. S., and M. E. Pitzler. 2002. Brown Treesnake control: economy of scales, p. 127-131. In L. Clark, J. Hone, J. A. Shivik, R. A. Watkins, K. C. Vercauteren, and J.K. Yoder [eds.], Human conflicts with wildlife: economic considerations. Proc. Third NWRC Spec. Symp., Nat. Wildl. Res. Center, Fort Collins CO.

Wiles, G.J. 1987a. The status of fruit bats on Guam. Pacific Science 41:148-157.

Wiles, G.J. 1987b. Current research and future management of Marianas fruit bats (Chiroptera: Pteropodidae) on Guam. Australian Mammalogy. 10:93-95.

Appendix L. Species Lists

List of selected nonnative species known on Guam. Data compiled from: http://www.invasivespecies.net/database/species/search.asp?sts=sss&st=sss&fr=1&sn=&rn=guam&hci=-1&ei=-1&x=33&y=10, and http://www.guaminsects.net/uogces/kbwiki/index.php?title=Oryctes_rhinoceros, and Christy et al. 2007.

Species Name	Chamorro Name	Common Name	Species Type
PLANT			
Abelmoschus moschatus	Kå'mang tasi	`aute toga	herb, shrub
Acacia confuse	Boiffuring (CNMI)	small Philippine acacia	shrub, tree
Acacia farnesiana	Kandaroma	ıcia jaune	shrub, tree
Adenanthera pavonina	Kulales	bead tree	Tree
Antigonon leptopus	Kadena de amor (Spanish)	chain-of-love	Vine
Arundo donax	Karisu	bamboo reed	Grass
Asparagus densiflorus		asparagus fern	Fern
Canna indica	Mongos hålom tåno	canna lily	Herb
Chromolaena odorata	Masigsig	bitter bush	Herb
Coccinia grandis		ivy gourd	Vine
Cryptostegia grandiflora		rubber vine	Vine
Eichhornia crassipes		water hyacinth	aquatic plant
Elaeis guineensis		African oil palm	Palm
Gracilaria salicornia		red algae	Algae
Hedychium flavescens		yellow ginger	Herb
Hydrilla verticillata		water weed	aquatic plant
Ipomoea aquatica		aquatic morning glory	Vine
Lantana camara		lantana	Shrub
Leucaena leucocephala	Tangantangan	tangantangan	Tree
Ligustrum sinense		Chinese ligustrum	shrub/tree
Melia azedarach		umbrella tree	shrub/tree
Mikania micrantha		mile-a-minute weed	Vine
Mimosa diplotricha		giant sensitive plant	Shrub
Mimosa pudica		sensitive plant	Shrub
Passiflora foetida	Kinahulu' atdåo	passionflower	Vine
Pennisetum polystachyon	Dadalak Katu	feathery pennisetum	Grass

Species Name	Chamorro Name	Common Name	Species Type
Pennisetum setaceum		fountain grass	Grass
Pistia stratiotes		water lettuce	aquatic plant
Pittosporum undulatum		sweet pittosporum	Shrub
Psidium guajava		guava	shrub/tree
Ricinus communis		castor-oil-plant	shrub/tree
Schinus terebinthifolius		Brazilian pepper tree	Tree
Sorghum halepense		Johnson grass	Grass
Spathodea campanulata		African tulip tree	Tree
Sphagneticola trilobata		trailing daisy	Herb
Syzygium cumini		black plum	Tree
Tabebuia heterophylla		white cedar	Tree
Tradescantia spathacea		boat lily	Herb
Urochloa maxima		Guinea grass	Grass
Ziziphus mauritiana		Chinese apple	shrub/tree

VERTEBRATE

Species Name	Chamorro Name	Common Name	Species Type
Bufo marinus	Rana' tupu	cane toad	Amphibian
Eleutherodactylus planirostris	Råna'	greenhouse frog	Amphibian
Fejervarya cancrivora	Råna'	crab-eating frog	Amphibian
Fejervarya cf. *limnocharis*	Råna'	Indian rice frog	Amphibian
Litoria fallax	Råna'	eastern dwarf treefrog	Amphibian
Polypedates megacephalus	Råna'	Hong Kong whipping frog	Amphibian
Rana guentheri	Råna'	Gunther's amoy frog	Amphibian
Anolis carolinensis		green anole	Reptile
Boiga irregularis	Kulepbla	brown treesnake	Reptile
Carlia ailanpalai		curious skink	Reptile
Norops sagrei		brown anole	Reptile
Pelodiscus sinensis	Haggan chino	Chinese softshell turtle	Reptile
Trachemys scripta elegans		red-eared slider	Reptile

Species Name	Chamorro Name	Common Name	Species Type
Varanus indicus		mangrove monitor	Reptile
Dicrurus macrocercus		black drongo	Bird
Francolinus francolinus		black francolin	Bird
Gallus gallus	Mannok machalek	feral chicken	Bird
Passer montanus		Eurasian house sparrow	Bird
Streptopelia bitorquata	Paluman mansu	Philippine turtle dove	Bird
Canis lupus	Ga'lagu	domestic dog	Mammal
Cervus mariannus	Binadu	Philippine deer	Mammal
Felis catus	Katu	house cat	Mammal
Mus musculus	Chakan guma'	house mouse	Mammal
Rattus exulans	Cha'kan Pasifiko	Pacific rat	Mammal
Rattus norvegicus	Cha'kan Norway	Norway rat	Mammal
Rattus rattus	Cha'kan atilong	black rat	Mammal
Suncus murinus		shrew	Mammal
Sus scrofa	Babuin halom tano'	feral pig	Mammal
Cichla ocellaris		eyespot cichlid	Fish
Clarias batrachus		walking catfish	Fish
Cyprinus carpio		common carp	Fish
Gambusia affinis		mosquito fish	Fish
Micropterus salmoides		large-mouth bass	Fish
Oreochromis mossambicus		Tilapia	Fish
Poecilia reticulata		guppy	Fish

INVERTEBRATE

Species Name	Chamorro Name	Common Name	Species Type
Achatina fulica	Akaleha' dangkulo	giant African land snail	Snail
Aedes albopictus		Asian tiger mosquito	Mosquito
Anoplolepis gracilipes	Otdot amariyo	yellow crazy ant	Ant
Aulacaspis yasumatsui		Asian cycad scale	Scale
Chthamalus proteus		Atlantic barnacle	Crustacean
Coptotermes formosanus		formosa termite	Termite

Species Name	Chamorro Name	Common Name	Species Type
Culex quinquefasciatus		southern house mosquito	Mosquito
Euglandina rosea		rosy wolf snail	Snail
Oryctes rhinoceros		coconut rhinoceros beetle	Beetle
Pheidole megacephala		lion ant	And
Platydemus manokwari		flatworm	Flatworm
Pomacea canaliculata		apple snail	Snail
Pison, Sceliphron, Chalybion	Gonggong	mud daubers (3 species)	Wasp
Quadrastichus erythrinae		gall wasp	Wasp
Solenopsis geminata	Otdot agaga'	tropical fire ant	Ant
Technomyrmex albipes	Otdot	white-footed ant	Ant
Pheidole megacephala	Otdot	big-headed ant	Ant

Coral species reported from the Reef Flat and Fore Reef sites at the Ritidian Unit of the Guam NWR. Derived from Donaldson and Rongo (2006).

Scientific Name	Chamorro Name	Common Name	Site(s) Found
MICRO-ORGANISM			
Banana bunchy top virus		BBTV	Virus
HELIOPORIDAE	Cho'Cho'		
Heliopora coerulea		Blue coral	REEF FLAT
POCILLOPORIDAE			
Pocillopora damicornis		Lace coral	REEF FLAT
Pocillopora eydouxi			FORE REEF
Pocillopora setchelli			REEF FLAT
Stylophora mordax			REEF FLAT
ACROPORIDAE		*Table, plate, and Rice Corals*	
Acropora abrotanoides			REEF FLAT
Acropora digitifera			REEF FLAT
Acropora palifera			REEF FLAT
Acropora spp.			FORE REEF

Scientific Name	Chamorro Name	Common Name	Site(s) Found
MICRO-ORGANISM			
Astreopora randalli			REEF FLAT
PORITIDAE		*Poritid Corals*	
Porites lichen		Lichen or Yellow Finger coral	REEF FLAT
Porites lobata		Lobe or Lobed Porous coral	REEF FLAT
Porites lutea		Mound coral	REEF FLAT
Porites vaughani			REEF FLAT
AGARICIIDAE		*Cactus, Elephant Skin, Plate, Lettuce Corals*	
Pavona varians		Corrugated or Frilly coral	REEF FLAT
FAVIIDAE		Honeycomb and Brain Corals	
Cyphastrea chalcidicum			REEF FLAT
Favia favus			REEF FLAT
Favia mathaii			REEF FLAT
Favia pallida			REEF FLAT
Goniastrea edwardsi			REEF FLAT
Goniastrea retiformis			REEF FLAT
Leptastrea purpurea			REEF FLAT
Platygyra daedalea			REEF FLAT
Platygyra pini			REEF FLAT
SIDERASTREIDAE			
Psammocora stellata			REEF FLAT

Fish species observed at the Ritidian Unit of the Guam NWR by Donaldson and Rongo (2006).

Scientific Name	Chamorro Name	Common Name
CARCHARHINIDAE		*Requiem Sharks*
Carcharhinus melanopterus		Reef blacktip shark
SYNODONTIDAE		*Lizardfish*
Synodus dermatogenys		
HOLOCENTRIDAE		*Squirrelfishes*
Myripristis amaena		
Myripristis berndti		Bigscale soldierfish
Myripristis murdjan		
Neoniphon sammara		
Sargocentron diadema		Crown squirrelfish
Sargocentrum spiniferum		
FISTULARIDAE		*No common name*

Scientific Name	Chamorro Name	Common Name
Fistularis commersoni		
SERRANIDAE		*Groupers and Sea Basses*
Cephalopholis argus		Peacock grouper
Epinephelus merra		Honeycomb merra
Epinephelus tauvina		Greasy grouper
CIRRHITIDAE		*No common name*
Cirrhitus pinnulatus		
Paracirrhites forsteri		
APOGONIDAE		*Cardinalfishes*
Apogon novemfasciatus		
CARANGIDAE		*Jacks*
Caranx melampygus		Bluefin trevally
LETHRINIDAE		*Emperors*
Gnathodentex aureolineatus		Yellowspot emperor
Monotaxis grandoculis		Bigeye emperor
NEMIPTERIDAE		*No common name*
Scolopis bilineata		
MULLIDAE		*Goatfishes*
Mulloidichthys flavolineatus		
Mulloidichthys vanicolensis		
Parupeneus crassilabris		
Parupeneus cyclostomus		Yellowsaddle goatfish
Parupeneus multifasciatus		Multibarred goatfish
PEMPHERIDAE		*Sweepers*
Pempheris oualensis		Bronze sweeper
CHAETODONTIDAE		*Butterflyfishes*
Chaetodon auriga		Threadfin butterflyfish
Chaetodon bennetti		
Chaetodon citrinellus		Speckled butterflyfish
Chaetodon ephippium		
Chaetodon lunula		Racoon butterflyfish
Chaetodon melanotus		
Chaedodon ornatissimus		Ornate butterflyfish
Chaetodon reticulatus		Reticulated butterflyfish
Chaetodon trifascialis		Chevroned butterflyfish
Chaetodon ulietensis		
Forcipiger flavissimus		Long-nosed butterflyfish
Heniochus chrysostomus		
POMACANTHIDAE		*Angelfishes*
Pomacanthus imperator		Emporer angelfish
Pygoplites diacanthus		Regal angelfish
POMACENTRIDAE		*Damselfishes*
Abudefduf sexfasciatus		Banded sergeant

Scientific Name	Chamorro Name	Common Name
Abudefduf sordidus		Black-spot sergeant
Abudefduf septemfasciatus		
Abudefduf vaigiensis		
Chrysiptera biocellata		
Chrysiptera brownriggi		
Chrysiptera glauca		Gray demoiselle
Chrysiptera traceyi		
Plectroglyphidodon dickii		Dick's damsel
Plectroglyphidodon johnstonianus		Johnston Island damsel
Plectroglyphidodon lacrymatus		Jewel damsel
Plectroglyphidodon leucozonus		White-band damsel
Plectroglyphidodon phoenixensis		Phoenix Islands damsel
Pomacentrus vaiuli		
Stegastes albifasciolatus		White-bar gregory
Stegastes fasciolatus		Pacific gregory
Stegastes lividus		
Stegastes nigricans		Dusky farmerfish
LABRIDAE		*Wrasses*
Anampses caeruleopunctatus		Blue-spotted wrasse
Anampses meleagrides		Yellowtail wrasse
Cheilinus trilobatus		Tripletail wrasse
Cheilinus undulates		Humphead wrasse, Napoleonfish
Coris aygula		Clown coris
Coris gaimard		Yellowtail coris
Epibulus insidiator		
Gomphosus varius		Bird wrasse
Halichoeres hortulanus		Checkerboard wrasse
Halichoeres margaritaceus		Weedy surge wrasse
Halichoeres ornatissinus		Ornate wrasse fish
Halichoeres richmondi		
Halichoeres trimaculatus		Three-spot wrasse
Hemigymnus fasciatus		Barred thicklip wrasse
Hemigymnus melapterus		
Labroides dimidiatus		Bluestreak cleaner wrasse
Novaculichtyhs taeniourus		Dragon wrasse, Rockmover wrasse
Oxycheilinus unifasciatus		
Stethojulis bandanensis		Red-shoulder wrasse
Stethojulis strigiventer		
Thalassoma		Twotone wrasse

Scientific Name	Chamorro Name	Common Name
amblycephalum		
Thalassoma hardwicke		
Thalassoma lutescens		Sunset wrasse
Thalassoma purpureum		Surge wrasse
Thalassoma quinquevittatum		Five-stripe surge wrasse
SCARIDAE		*Parrotfishes*
Calatomus carolinus		Bucktooth parrotfish, Stareye parrotfish
Chlorurus microrhinus		
Chlorurus sordidus		
Scarus niger		Black parrotfish
Scarus psittacus		
PINGUIPEDIDAE		*No common name*
Parapercis clathrata		
Parapercis millipunctata		
BLENNIIDAE		*Blennies*
Cirripectes variolosus		Red-speckled blenny
Ecsenius bicolor		
Exallias brevis		
Plagiotremus tapeinosoma		Piano blenny, Scale-eating blenny
Salarias fasciatus		
GOBIIDAE		*Gobies*
Valenciennea strigata		
ZANCLIDAE		*No common name*
Zanclus cornutus		
SIGANIDAE		*Rabbit fish*
Siganus spinus		
ACANTHURIDAE		*Surgeonfishes and Unicornfishes*
Acanthurus guttatus		Spotted surgeonfish
Acanthurus lineatus		
Acanthurus nigoris		
Acanthurus nigricans		
Acanthurus nigrofuscus		Brown surgeonfish
Acanthurus triostegus		
Ctenochaetus binotatus		
Ctenochaetus striatus		Striped bristletooth
Naso annulatus		
Naso lituratus		Liturate surgeonfish
Zebrasoma flavescens		
Zebrasoma scopas		Brown tang
BALISTIDAE		*Triggerfishes*
Balistapus undulatus		Orangestriped triggerfish
Pseudobalistes		Yellowmargin

Scientific Name	Chamorro Name	Common Name
flavimarginatus		triggerfish
Rhinecanthus aculeatus		
Rhinecanthus rectangulus		Wedge picassofish, Humuhumu
Sufflamen chrysoptera		
MONACANTHIDAE		*Filefishes*
Amanses scopas		Broom filefish
Oxymonacanthus longirostris		
OSTRACIIDAE		*Trunkfishes*
Ostracion cubicus		
TETRAODONTIDAE		*Puffers*
Canthigaster janthinoptera		
Canthigaster solandri		Spotted sharpnose puffer

Appendix M. References

Amori, G. and M. Clout. 2003. Rodents on islands: a conservation challenge. Pages 63-68 *in* Singleton, G.R., Hinds, L.A., Krebs, C.J. and Spratt, D.M. (editors): Rats, mice and people: rodent biology and management. ACIAR Monograph No. 96.

April, V. 2006. Talagi pictograph cave, Guam. Micronesian 5: 53-69.

Asami, R., T. Yamada, Y. Iryu, C.P.Meyer, T.M. Quinn, and G. Paulay. 2004. Carbon and oxygen isotopic composition of a Guam coral and their relationship to environmental variables in the western Pacific. Palaeography, Palaeoclimatology, Paleoecology 212: 1-22.

ATSDR (Agency for Toxic Substances and Disease Registry). 2002. Public health asssessment. Division of Health Assessment and Consultation, Federal Facilities Assessment Branch. Andersen Air Force Base, Yigo, GU. [online] http://www.atsdr.cdc.gov/HAC/pha/anderson/and_toc.html.

Baker, R.H. 1946. Some effects of the war on the wildlife of Micronesia. Transcripts of the North American Wildlife Conference 11: 207-13.

Baker, R.H. 1951. The avifauna of Micronesia, its origin, evolution, and distribution. University of Kansas Publication 3:1–359.

Baker, J.D., C.L. Littnan, D.W. Johnston. 2006. Potential effects of sea level rise on the terrestrial habitats of endangered and endemic megafauna in the Northwestern Hawaiian Islands. Endangered Species Research 2: 21-30.

Bennett, D. 1995. A little book of monitor lizards. Viper Press, Aberdeen, UK.

Best, B. R., and C. E. Davidson. 1981. Inventory and atlas of the inland aquatic ecosystems of the Marianas Archipelago, University of Guam. Technical Report No. 75.

Birkeland, C. 1997. Life and death of coral reefs. Chapman and Hall, NY.

Bjorndal, K.A. 1997. Foraging ecology and nutrition of sea turtles. Pages 199-231 *in* Lutz, P.L. and J.A. Musick (editors). The biology of sea turtles. CRC Press, Boca Raton, FL.

Bowen, B.W. 1995. Molecular genetic studies of marine turtles. Pages. 585-588 *in* K. Bjorndal (editor). Biology and conservation of sea turtles, Second Edition, Smithsonian Institution Press, Washington, D.C.

Broderick, D., C. Moritz, J.D. Miller, M. Guinea, R.I.T. Prince and C.J. Limpus. 1995. Genetic studies of the hawksbill turtle *Eretmochelys imbricata*: evidence for multiple stocks in Australian waters. Pacific Conservation Biology. 1:123-132.

Buddemeier, R.W., J.A. Kleypas, and R.B. Aronson. 2004. Coral reefs and global climate change: Potential contributions of climate change to stresses on coral reef ecosystems. Pew Centre for Global Climate Change: Arlington, VA.

Burdick, D. 2005. Guam Coastal Atlas. University of Guam Marine Laboratory Multimedia Publication No. 4, University of Guam Marine Laboratory, GU.

Burdick, D. 2006. Guam Coastal Atlas. Providing benthic habitat data and other coastal information for the nearshore waters of Guam. University of Guam Marine Laboratory Technical Report No.114, University of Guam Marine Laboratory, Mangilao, GU.

Burns, W. 2002. Pacific Island developing country water resources and climate change. Pages 113-133 *in* P. Gleich (editor). The world's aater 2002-2003: The Biennial Report on Freshwater Resources. Island Press, Washington, DC.

Carr, A., M. H. Carr, and A. B. Meylan. 1978. The ecology and migrations of sea turtles, 7. The West Caribbean green turtle colony. Bulletin of American Museum of Natural History 162: 1-46.

Carter, L.M., E.Shea, M.Hamnett, C.Anderson, G. Dolcemascolo, C.Guard, M. Taylor,T. Barnston,Y. He, M. Larsen, L. Loope, L. Malone, G. Meehl. 2001. Potential Consequences of Climate Variability and Change for the U.S.-Affiliated Islands of the Pacific and Caribbean. Pp. 315-349. in Climate Change Impacts on the United States: The Potential Consequences of Climate Variability and Change. National Assessment Synthesis Team, US Global Change Research Program. Cambridge University Press: Cambridge, UK.

Carver, E. and J. Caudill. 2007. Banking on Nature 2006: The Economic Benefits to Local Communities of National Wildlife Refuge Visitation. Division of Economics, U.S. Fish and Wildlife. Washington, DC. 382 pp.

Caudill, J. and E. Henderson. 2005. Banking on Nature 2004: The Economic Benefits to Local Communities of National Wildlife Refuge Visitation. Division of Economics, U.S. Fish and Wildlife. Washington, DC. 435 pp.

Chaloupka, M.Y. and C.J. Limpus. 1997. Robust statistical modeling of hawksbill sea-turtle growth rates (Southern Great Barrier Reef). Marine Ecology Progress Series. 146:1-8.

Chaloupka, M., and C. Limpus. 2005. Estimates of sex- and age-class-specific survival probabilities for a southern Great Barrier Reef green sea turtle population. Marine Biology 146: 1251-1261.

Chaloupka, M., C. Limpus and J. Miller, 2004. Green turtle somatic growth dynamics in a spatially disjunct Great Barrier Reef metapopulation. Coral Reefs 23: 325 – 335.

Chantler, P. and G. Driessens. 2000. Swifts: A guide to the swifts and treeswifts of the world. Second edition. Pica Press, UK.

Chester, R.H. 1969. Destruction of Pacific corals by the sea star *Acanthaster planci*. Science 165: 280-283.

Chiroptera Specialist Group 1996. *Pteropus tokudae*. IUCN 2007. 2007 IUCN Red List of Threatened Species. [online] www.iucnredlist.org.

Chiroptera Specialist Group 2000. *Emballonura semicaudata*. IUCN 2007. 2007 IUCN Red List of Threatened Species. [online] www.iucnredlist.org.

Christy, M.T., C.S. Clark, D.E. Gee, D. Vice, D.S. Vice, M.P. Warner, C,L. Tyrrell, G.H. Rodda, and J.A. Savidge. 2007. Recent records of alien anurans on the Pacific Island of Guam. Pacific Science 61: 469-584.

Cobb, K.M., C.D. Charles, H. Cheng, and L. Edwards. 2003. El Nino/Southern Oscillation and tropical Pacific climate during the last millennium. Nature 424(6946). 5 pp.

Colgan, M. 1987. Coral reef recovery on Guam (Micronesia) after catastrophic predation by *Acanthaster planci*. Ecology 68:1592-1605.

Conry, P.J. 1988. Management of feral and exotic game species on Guam. Transcript of Western Section of the Wildlife Society 24: 26-30.

COMNAVMAR 2001. INRMP for Navy Lands, Guam.

Cowie, R.H. 1992. Evolution and extinction of Partulidae, endemic Pacific island land snails. Philosophical Transcripts of the Royal Society of London B 335: 167-191.

Cox, P.A. and T. Elmqvist. 2000. Pollinator extinction in the Pacific Islands. Conservation Biology 14: 1237-1239.

Cox, P.A., T. Elmqvist, E.D. Pierson, and W.D. Rainey. 1991. Flying foxes as strong interactors in South Pacific island ecosystems: a conservation hypothesis. Conservation Biology 5: 448-54.

Craig, R.J. 1992. Ecological characteristics of a native limestone forest on Saipan, Mariana Islands. *Micronesica* 25(1):85-97.

Crossland, M.R. 2000. Direct and indirect effects of the introduced toad *Bufo marinus* (Anura: Bufonidae) on populations of native anuran larvae in Australia. Ecography 23: 283-290.

Cruz, J., L.Arriola, N. Johnson, and G. Beauprez. 2000. Wildlife and vegetation surveys Aguiguan 2000. Technical Report No 2 Commonwealth of the Northern Maraina Islands-Department Fish and Wildlife, Saipan, CNMI.

Cruz, J., L.Arriola, N. Johnson, and G. Beauprez. 2000. Wildlife and vegetation surveys Alamagan 2000. Technical Report No 4 Technical Report No 2 Commonwealth of the Northern Maraina Islands-Department Fish and Wildlife, Saipan, CNMI.

Cummings, V. 2002. Sea turtle conservation in Guam. Pages 37-38 *in* Kinan, I. (editor). Proceedings of the Western Pacific sea turtle cooperative research and management workshop. Western Pacific Regional Fishery Management Council, Honolulu, HI.

DeMattia, E. A., L. M. Curran, and B. J. Rathcke. 2004. Effects of small rodents and large mammals on Neotropical seeds. Ecology 85: 2161–2170.

Dickman, C.R. 1996. Impact of exotic generalist predators on the native fauna of Australia. Wildlife Biology 2:185-195.

Dickinson, E. C. (editor). 2003. The Howard and Moore complete checklist of the birds of the world. Third edition. Princeton University Press, Princeton, NJ.

Donaldson, T.J. and Y. Sadovy. 2001. Threatened fishes of the world: *Cheilinus undulatus* Ruppell, 1835 (Labridae). Environmental Biology of Fishes 62:428.

Donaldson, T.J. and T. Rongo. 2006. Coral reef investigations at the Guam National Wildlife Refuge, Ritidian Unit. University of Guam Marine Laboratory. Technical Report No. 117.

Donnegan, J.A., S.L. Butler, W. Grabowiecki, B.A. Hiserote, and D. Limtiaco. 2004. Guam's forest resources, 2002. Resource Bulletin PNW-RB-243. Portland, OR: U.S. Department of Agriculture, Forest Service, Pacific Northwest Research Station.

Dougherty, M., and M. Falanruw. 1993. Fruit bats key link in Pacific island forest ecosystems. Progress Reports to Cooperators on selected activities. Institute of Pacific Islands Forestry 17-18.

Drahos, N. 2006. Who really killed the birds of Guam? Self-published. Aurora, NY.

Ehleringer, J.R., T.E. Cerling, and M.D. Dearing. 2002. Atmospheric CO_2 as a global change driver influencing plant-animal interactions. Integrated and Comparative Biology 42:424–430.

Ehrhart, L.M., 1982. A review of sea turtle reproduction. Pages 29-38. *in* Bjorndal, K.A. (editor). Biology and conservation of sea turtles. Smithsonian Institution Press, Washington, DC.

Eldredge, L.G. 1983. Summary of environmental and fishing information on Guam and the Commonwealth of the Northern Mariana Islands: Historical background, description of the islands, and review of the climate, oceanography, and submarine topography. NOAA Technical Memorandum NOAA-TM-NMFS-SWFC-40. .

Eldredge, L. 2003. The marine reptiles and mammals of Guam. Micronesica 35-36: 653-660.

Engbring, J. and F.L. Ramsey. 1984. Distribution and abundance of the forest birds of Guam: results of a 1981 survey. U.S. Fish and Wildlife Service. FWS/OBS-84/20.

Esselstyn, J.A., G.J. Wiles, and A. Amar. 2004. Habitat use of the Pacific Sheath-tailed Bat (*Emballonura semicaudata*) on Aguiguan, Mariana Islands. Acta Chiropterologica 6: 303-308.

Federal Register. 2007a. Notice of intent to prepare a comprehensive conservation plan; announcement of public meeting and open house; and request for comments. Vol. 72(129): 37037-37039.

First Hawaiian Bank. 2006. Guam Outlook Brighter than in Several Years. Economic Forecast 2007-2008 Edition. Available at: https://www.fhb.com/pdf/EconForecastGuam06.pdf.

Fish, M.R., I.M. Côté, J.A. Gill, A.P. Jones, S. Renshoff, A.R. Watkinson. 2005. Predicting the impact of sea level rise on Caribbean sea turtle nesting habitat. Conservation Biology 19: 482–491.

Fosberg, F.R. 1960. The vegetation of Micronesia. Bulletin of the American Museum of Natural History 119: 1-75.

Fritts, T. H. 1988. The brown tree snake, *Boiga irregularis*, a threat to Pacific Islands. U.S. Fish and Wildlife Service Biological Report No. 88 (31).

Fritts, T.H. and G.H. Rodda. 1998. Alien snake threatens Pacific islands. Endangered Species Bulletin 23: 10-11.

Fritts, T.H., and G.H. Rodda. 1998. The role of introduced species in the degradation of island ecosystems: a case history of Guam. Annual Review of Ecology and Systematics 29: 113-1.

Fritts, T.H. 2002. Economic costs of electrical system instability and power outages caused by snakes on the Island of Guam. International Biodeterioration & Biodegradation 49(2-3): 93-100.

Geering, W.A., A. Forman, and M.J. Nunn. 1995. Exotic diseases of animals: a field guide for Australian veterinarians. Australian Government Publication Service, Canberra, ACT.

Gingerich, S.B. 2003. Hydrologic resources of Guam. U.S. Geological Investigations Report No 03-4126.

Godley, B.J., S. Richardson, A.C. Broderick, M.S. Coyne, F. Glen, and G.C. Hays. 2002. Long-term satellite telemetry of the movements and habitat utilisation by green turtles in the Mediterranean. Ecography 25: 352 – 362.

Grimsditch, G.D. and R.V. Salm. 2005. Coral reef resilience and resistance to bleaching. The World Conservation Union. Gland, CH.

Guam Bureau of Statistics and Plans. 2006. 2005 Guam statistical yearbook. Office of Governor Felix P. Camacho. Hagåtña, GU.

GDAWR (Guam Division of Aquatic and Wildlife Resources), Department of Agriculture. 2006a. Guam comprehensive wildlife conservation strategy. Mangilao, GU.

GDAWR (Guam Division of Aquatic and Wildlife Resources). 2006b. Endangered species recovery report for the Aga, *Corvus kubaryi*, on Guam, Subpermit TE-032209-8 activities; 2005-2006 breeding season; reporting period: September 2005 to June 2006. Division of Aquatic and Wildlife Resources, Department of Agriculture, Mangilao, Guam.

GEPA (Guam Environmental Protection Agency) 1998. Clean water action plan for Guam - unified watershed assessment. CWAP Working Group, Guam.

GEPA (Guam Environmental Protection Agency) 2007. Guam 2006 Integrated Water Quality Monitoring and Assessment Report. Barrigada, Guam.

Guard, C., A.N.L. Chiu, and M.A. Lander. 2003. NOAA/NWS meteorological assessment for Typhoon Pongsona in: Pohnpei State, FSM; Chuuk State, FSM; Guam; and Rota, CNMI. NOAA/NWS. Tiyan, GU.

GVB (Guam Visitor's Bureau) 2006. Guam Visitors Bureau Guam Factsheet Number 4. Tumon Bay, GU.

GVB (Guam Visitor's Bureau) 2007. Guam Statistic Report – January 2007. Tumon Bay, GU.

Hatase, H., K. Sato, M. Yamaguchi, K. Takahashi, and K. Tsukamoto. 2006. Individual variation in feeding habitat use by adult female green sea turtles (*Chelonia mydas*): are they obligately neritic herbivores? Oecologia 149: 52-64.

Hays, G., A. Broderick, F. Glen, and B. Godley. 2003. Climate change and sea turtles: a 150-year reconstruction of incubation temperatures at a major marine turtle rookery. Global Change Biology 9: 642-646.

Hiles, G.A. 2007. March 2007 Current Employment Report. Department of Labor, Government of Guam.

Hinkley, A. D. 1962. Diet of the giant toad, *Bufo marinus* (L.), in Fiji. Herpetologica 18: 253–259.

Hirth, H. F. 1997. Synopsis of the biological data on the green turtle *Chelonia mydas* (Linnaeus 1758). U.S. Fish and Wildlife Service Biological Report No. 97.

Hopper, D.R., and Smith B.D. 1992. Status of tree snails (Gastropoda: Partulidae) on Guam, with a resurvey of sites studied by H. E. Crampton in 1920. Pacific Science 46: 77–85.

Horvitz, C.C., J.B. Pascarella, S. McMann, A. Freedman, and R.H. Hofstetter. 1998. Functional roles of invasive non-indigenous plants in hurricane-affected subtropical hardwood Forests. Ecological Applications 8: 947-974.

Howard F.W., A. Hamon, M. McLaughlin, and T. Weissling. 1999. *Aulacaspis yasumatsui* (Homoptera: Sternorrhyncha: Diaspididae), a scale insect pest of cycads recently introduced into Florida. Florida Entomologist 82: 14–27.

Hughes. L. 2000. Biological consequences of global warming: Is the signal already apparent? Trends in Ecology and Evolution 15:56–61.

IPCC (Intergovernmental Panel on Climate Change). 2007. Working group II to the third assessment report, Climate Hhange 2007: Impacts, adaptation, and vulnerability. Cambridge University Press, UK.

IPCC (Intergovernmental Panel on Climate Change). 2001. Working group II to the third assessment report, climate change 2001: Impacts, adaptation, and vulnerability. Cambridge University Press, UK.

Janeke, D.S. 2006. Nocturnal movements and habitat use of the flying fox, *Pteropus mariannus mariannus,* on Guam. MSc Thesis, University of Guam, GU.

Jenkins, J.M. 1979. Natural history of the Koko (Guam rail). Condor 81: 404-408.
Jenkins, J.M. 1983. The native forest birds of Guam. Ornithological Monographs No. 311-61
American Ornithologists' Union, Washington, DC.

Jocson, J.M.U., J.W. Jenson, and D.N. Contractor. 2002, Recharge and aquifer response:
Northern Guam Lens Aquifer, Guam, Mariana Islands. Journal of Hydrology 260:231-254.

Johnson, N.C. 2001. A survey of Mariana fruit bats in the Mariana Islands, including recent
minimum population estimates, July 2001. Pages 49–90 in Annual report FY
2001, Division of Fish and Wildlife, Saipan, CNMI.

Jones, R.S., R.H. Randall, and R.D. Strong. 1976. Biological impact caused by changes on a
tropical reef. Univ. Guam Marine Laboratory Technical Report No. 28.

Kayanne, H., T. Ishii, E. Matsumoto, and N. Yonekura. 1993. Late Holocene sea-level change on
Rota and Guam, Mariana Islands, and its constraint on geophysical predictions. Quaternary
Research 40:189-200.

Kelty, R. and J. Kuartei. 2004. Status of the coral Reefs in Micronesia and American Samoa.
Pages 381- 409. *In* Status of the Coral Reefs of the World: 2004. Australian Institute of Marine
Science, Townsville, QLD.

Khosrowpanah, S. and J.M.U. Jocson. 2005. Environmental assessment for non-point sources of
pollution for UGUM watershed. Water and Environmental Research Institute Technical Report
No. 109.

King, B. 1962. Guam field notes. Elepaio 23: 29-31.

Knutson, K. and S. Vogt 2002. Philippine deer (*Cervus mariannus*) and feral pig
(*Sus scrofa*) population sampling in the secondary limestone forests of northern Guam. Report for
Andersen Air Force Base, U.S. Fish and Wildlife Service, Environmental Office, Andersen Air
Force Base, Guam and Guam National Wildlife Refuge.

Kolinski, S. P., R. K. Hoeke, S. R. Holzwarth, and P. S. Vroom. 2005. Sea turtle abundance at
isolated reefs of the Mariana Archipelago. Micronesica 37: 287–296.

Kurashina, H., J.A. Simons, J.A. Toenjes, J. Allen, S.S. Amesbury, G.M. Heathcote, R.H. Randall,
B.D. Smith, R.A. Stephenson, and E.F. Wells. 1990. Archaeological investigations at the Naval
Facility (NAVFAC), Ritidian Point, Guam, Mariana Islands. Department of the Navy, Naval
Facilities Engineering Command Contracts, Marianas, GU.

Lander, Mark A. and Charles P. Guard. 2003. Creation of a 50-year rainfall database, annual
rainfall climatology, and annual rainfall distribution map for Guam. University of Guam, Water
and Environmental Research Institute of the Western Pacific. Technical Report No. 102.

Lawrence, J. H. and M. Dougherty. 1993. Storms, drought, loss of seed dispersers, and development imperil Guam's native limestone forests. Progress report to cooperators on selected activities. Institute of Pacific Islands Forestry. 1993: 16-17.
Lee, M.A.B. 1974. Distribution of native and invader plant species on the island of Guam. Biotropica 6:158-164.

Lemke, T.O. 1986. Distribution and status of the Sheath-tailed Bat (*Emballonura semicaudata*) in the Mariana Islands. Journal of Mammalogy 67: 743-746.

Limpus, C.J. 1992. The hawksbill turtle, *Eretmochelys imbricata*, in Queensland: population structure within a southern Great Barrier Reef feeding ground. Wildlife Research. 19: 489-506.

Limpus, C.J. 1995. Global overview of the status of marine turtles: a 1995 viewpoint. Pages 605-609 *in* Bjorndal, K.A. (editor). Biology and conservation of Sea Turtles. Revised Edition. Smithsonian Institution Press. Washington, DC.

Limpus, C. and M. Chaloupka. 1997. Nonparametric regression modeling of green sea turtle growth rates (southern Great Barrier Reef). Marine Ecology Progress Series 149: 23-34.

Limpus, C. J. and J. D. Miller. 2000. Final report for Australian hawksbill turtle population dynamics project. Japanese Bekko Association and the Queensland Parks and Wildlife Service, Queensland Parks and Wildlife Service, Brisbane, QLD.

Lobban, C. S. and M. Schefter. 1997. Tropical Pacific island environments. University of Guam Press, Mangilao, GU.

Lounibos, L.P. 2002. Invasions by insect vectors of human disease. Annual Review of Entomology 47: 233-266.

Makowski, C., J.A. Seminoff, and M. Salmon. 2006. Home range and habitat use of juvenile Atlantic green turtles (*Chelonia mydas* L.) on shallow reef habitats in Palm Beach, Florida, USA. Marine Biology 148: 1167-1179.

Marler, T.E., and J.H. Lawrence. 2004. Chemical limitations of yoga root growth in an acid soil. Micronesica 37: 157-161.

Marshall, J. T., Jr. 1949. The endemic avifauna of Saipan, Tinian, Guam, and Palau. Condor 51: 200-221.

Marshall, S.D. 1989. Nest sites of the Micronesian Kingfisher on Guam. Wilson Bulletin 101: 472-477.

McCoid, M.J. 1993. The "new" herpetofauna of Guam, Mariana Islands. Herpetological Review 24:16-17.

McCoid, M.J. 1999. Established exotic reptiles and amphibians of the Mariana Islands. Pages 453-459 *in* Rodda, G.H., Y. Sawai, D. Chiszar, and H. Tanaka, (editors). Problem snake management: The habu and the brown treesnake. Cornell University Press, Ithaca, NY.

Merrill, E.D. 1919. Additions to the flora of Guam. Philippine Journal of Science 15:539-544.

Meylan, A.B., B.W. Bowen, and J.C. Avise. 1990. A genetic rest of the natal homing versus social facilitation models for green turtle migration. Science 248: 724-727.

Meylan, A. B., and M. Donnelly. 1999. Status justification for listing the hawksbill turtle (*Eretmochelys imbricate*) as critically endangered on the 1996 IUCN Red List of Threatened Animals. Chelonian Conservation and Biology 3: 200-204.

Michael, G.A. 1987. Notes on the breeding biology and ecology of the Mariana or Guam Crow. Aviculture Magazine 93: 73-82.

Michener, W.K., E.R. Blood, K.L. Bildstein, M.M. Brinson, and L.R. Gardner. 1997. Climate Change, Hurricanes and Tropical Storms, and Rising Sea Level in Coastal Wetlands. Ecological Applications Vol. 7(3):770-801.

Morton, J.M., S. Plentovich, and T. Sharp. 1999. Reproduction and juvenile dispersal of Mariana Crows (Corvus kubaryi) on Rota (1996-1999). Unpublished report submitted to the U.S. Fish and Wildlife Service, Honolulu, HI.

Morton, J. M., F. A. Amidon, and L. R. Quinata. 2000. Structure of a limestone forest on northern Guam. Micronesica 32: 229-244.

Moore, A., I. Iriarta, and R. Quitugua. 2005. Asian cycad scale *Aulacaspis yasumatsui* Takagi (Homoptera: Diaspididae). Cooperative Extension Service, Agriculture and Natural Resource Division, University of Guam, Pest Sheet 2005-01.

Mortimer, J.A. and R. Bresson, 1999. Temporal distribution and periodicity in hawksbill turtles (*Eretmochelys imbricata*) nesting at Cousin Island, Republic of Seychelles, 1971-1997. Chelonian Conservation and Biology 3: 318-325.

Morton, J.M., F.A. Amidon, and L.R. Quinata. 2000. Structure of a limestone forest on northern Guam. Micronesica 32:229-244.

Mrosovsky N 1994. Sex ratio of sea turtles. Journal of Experimental Zoology 270: 16–27.

Muniappan, R. 2005. Foreign exploration for natural enemies of the cycad scale, *Aulacaspis yasumatsui* (Homoptera: Diaspididae). University of Guam, GU.

Musick, J.A. and C.J. Limpus. 1997. Habitat utilization and migration in juvenile sea turtles. Pages 137-163 *in* Lutz, P.L. and J.A. Musick (editors). The biology of sea turtles, Volume 2 CRC Press, Boca Raton, FL.

Myers, R.F. 1999. Micronesian reef fishes. Third edition. Coral Graphics, Barrigada, GU.

Mylroie, J.E., J.W. Jenson, J.M.U. Jocson, and M.A. Lander. 1999. Karst geology and hydrology of Guam: A preliminary report. Water and Environmental Research Institute Technical Report No. 98.

Mylroie, J.E., J.W. Jenson, D. Taborosi, J.M.U. Jocson, D.T. Vann, and C. Wexel. 1991. Karst features of Guam in terms of a general model of carbonate island karst. Journal of Cave and Karst Studies 63: 9-22.

National Audubon Society.1989–2006. The Christmas Bird Count Historical and Current Year's Results. [online] http://www.audubon.org/bird/cbc.

Naumann, I. D. and J. A. L. Watson. 1987. Wasps and bees (Hymenoptera) on rock faces at Koolburra. Rock Art Research 4: 26-7.

Neill, C. and J. Rea. 2004. Territory of Guam fire assessment. U.S. Forest Service, Pacific Southwest Region Fire Management. Vallejo, CA.

Nicholls, R.J., P.P. Wong, V.R. Burkett, J.O. Codignotto, J.E. Hay, R.F. McLean, S. Ragoonaden, and C.D. Woodroffe. 2007. Coastal systems and low-lying areas. Climate change 2007: impacts, adaptation and vulnerability. Pages 315-356 *in* Parry, M.L., O.F. Canziani, J.P. Palutikof, P.J. van der Linden and C.E. Hanson (editors). Contribution of working group II to the fourth assessment report of the intergovernmental panel on climate change. Cambridge University Press, Cambridge, UK.

NMFS-USFWS (National Marine Fisheries Service and U.S. Fish and Wildlife Service). 2007a. Green sea turtle (*Chelonia mydas*) 5 – year review: summary and evaluation. National Marine Fisheries Service - U. S. Fish and Wildlife Service, Silver Spring, MD.

NMFS-USFWS (National Marine Fisheries Service and U.S. Fish and Wildlife Service 2007b. Hawksbill sea turtle (*Eretmochelys imbricata*) 5 – year review: summary and evaluation. National Marine Fisheries Service - U. S. Fish and Wildlife Service, Silver Spring, MD.

NMFS-USFWS (National Marine Fisheries Service and U.S. Fish and Wildlife Service 2007c. Leatherback sea turtle (*Dermochelys coriacea*) 5 – year review: summary and evaluation. National Marine Fisheries Service - U. S. Fish and Wildlife Service, Silver Spring, MD.

NMFS-USFWS (National Marine Fisheries Service and U.S. Fish and Wildlife Service 1998a. Recovery plan for U.S. Pacific populations of the green turtle (*Chelonia mydas*). National Marine Fisheries Service - U. S. Fish and Wildlife Service, Silver Spring, MD.

NMFS-USFWS (National Marine Fisheries Service and U.S. Fish and Wildlife Service 1998b. Recovery plan for U.S. Pacific populations of the hawksbill turtle (*Eretmochelys imbricata*). National Marine Fisheries Service - U. S. Fish and Wildlife Service, Silver Spring, MD.

NOAA (National Oceanic and Atmospheric Administration). 2004. Pacific Islands Fisheries Science Center. Bathymetry data download. http://www.pifsc.noaa.gov/cred/hmapping/datadownload.php

NOAA Species of concern: proactive Conservation Program. 2006. National Marine Fisheries Service. [online] http://www.fpir.noaa.gov/Library/PRD/SOC/PIR%20SOC%20fact%20sheet%20PDF.pdf

NOAA. 2007. Species of Concern Program 2007 Report. Available at http://www.nmfs.noaa.gov/pr/pdfs/species/concern_report2007.pdf.

ODUSD[I&E] (Office of the Deputy Under Secretary of Defense, Installations and Environment). 2006. Defense environmental programs fiscal year 2006 annual report to congress. [online] https://www.denix.osd.mil/denix/Public/News/OSD/DEP2006/deparc2006.html.bak.

Overseas Private Investment Corporation. 2000. Climate change: assessing our actions. Agency of the United States Government. Washington, DC.

Pacific Islands Fisheries Science Center, NOAA. 2004. Gridded bathymetry of northeastern Guam, including Pati Point Marine Preserve. [online] http://www.pifsc.noaa.gov/cred/hmapping/hmap_data.php.
Paulay, G. 2003. Marine biodiversity of Guam and the Marianas: overview. Micronesica 35-36: 3-25.

Paulay, G. and Y. Benayahu. 1999. Patterns and consequences of coral bleaching in Micronesia (Majuro and Guam) in 1992-1994. Micronesica 32: 109-124.

Pelletier, D., D. Roos, and S. Ciccione. 2003. Oceanic survival and movements of wild and captive-reared immature green turtles (Chelonia mydas) in the Indian Ocean. Aquatic Living Resources 16: 35-41.

Peterson, G.D. Jr. 1956. Suncus murinus, a recent introduction to Guam. Journal of Mammalogy 37: 278-279.

Plotkin, P. 2003. Adult migrations and habitat use. Pages 225-242 in Lutz, P., J. Musick, and J. Wyneken (editors). The biology of sea turtles, volume 2. CRC Press, Boca Raton FL.

Porter, V., T. Leberer, M. Gawel, J. Gutierrez, D. Burdick, V. Torres, and E. Lujan. 2005. The state of coral reef ecosystems of Guam. Pages.442- 487 in The state of coral reef ecosystems of the United States and Pacific freely associated states: 2005. National Oceanic and Atmospheric Administration (NOAA).

Prasad, U.K. and H.I. Manner. 1994. Climate change and sea level rise issues in Guam. Report on a preliminary mission. Apia, Western Samoa: South Pacific Regional Environmental Programme. SPREP Reports and Studies Series No. 82.

Pratt, H. D., P. L. Bruner, and D. G. Berrett. 1987. The birds of Hawaii and the tropical Pacific. Princeton University Press, Princeton, NJ.

Priddel, D. and N. Carlile. 1998. Conservation of the endangered Gould's petrel Pterodroma leucoptera leucoptera. Pacific Conservation Biology 3: 322–329.

Pritchard, P. C. H. 1982. Marine turtles of Micronesia. Pages 263–272 *in* K. A. Bjorndal (editor) Biology and conservation of sea turtles. Proceedings of the world conference on sea turtles. Smithsonian Institution Press, Washington, DC.

Puglise, K.A. and R. Kelty. 2007. NOAA coral reef ecosystem research plan for fiscal years 2007 to 2011. NOAA Coral Reef Conservation Program. NOAA Technical Memorandum CRCP 1: 91-95.

Pultz, S., D. O'Daniel, S. Krueger, H. McSharry, and G. Balazs. 1999. Marine turtle survey on Tinian, Mariana Islands. Micronesica 32: 85–94.

Quinata, L.R. 1994 Vegetation baseline survey - Andersen Air Force Base, Guam. U.S. Fish and Wildlife Service, Dededo, GU.

Randall, J.E. 1972. Chemical pollution in the sea and the crown-of-thorns starfish (*Acanthaster planci*). Biotropica 4: 132-144.

Randall, R. H. 2000. Telecom communication with Dr. Randall, former University of Guam, Professor at Guam Marine Laboratory. Misc. note on file.

Randall, R.H. 1979. Geological features within the Guam seashore study area. University of Guam Marine Laboratory. Technical Report No. 55.

Randall, R. H. and R. F. Myers. 1983. The Corals. guide to the coastal resources of Guam. Volume 2. University of Guam Press, Mangilao, GU.

Raulerson, L. and A. Rinehart. 1991. Trees and shrubs of the Northern Mariana Islands. Commonwealth of the Northern Mariana Islands Coastal Resources Management, Saipan.

Read, J. and K. Moseby. 2006. Vertebrates of Tetepare Island, Solomon Islands. Pacific Science 60: 69–79.

Reichel, J.D., G.J. Wiles, and P.O. Glass. 1992. Island extinctions: the case of the endangered Nightingale reed-warbler. Wilson Bulletin 104: 44-54.

Richardson, J. I., R. Bell, and T. H. Richardson. 1999. Population ecology and demographic implications drawn from an 11-year study of nesting hawksbill turtles, *Eretmochelys imbricata*, at Jumby Bay, Long Island, Antigua, West Indies. Chelonian Conservation and Biology 3: 244-250.

Ritter, M.W., and C.M. Naugle. 1999. Population characteristics, germination and proposed management of *Elaeocarpus joga* Merr. on Guam: a regionally endemic tree. Micronesica 31: 275-281.

Rodda G.H., and T.H. Fritts. 1992. The impact of the introduction of the colubrid snake, *Boiga irregularis* on Guam's lizards. Journal of Herpetology 26: 166-174.

Rodda, G.H., Y. Sawai, D. Chiszar, and H. Tanaka. 1999 Problem snake management: the habu and the brown treesnake. Cornell University Press, Ithaca, NY.

Royal Society. 2005. Ocean acidification due to increasing atmospheric carbon dioxide. The Royal Society, London, UK.

Rudd, M.A. and M.H. Tupper. 2002. The impact of Nassau grouper size and abundance on scuba diver site selection and MPA economics. Coastal Management 30:133-151.

Ruddiman, W.F.R. 2001. Earth's climate: past and future. WH Freeman, NY.

Savidge, J.A. 1987. Extinction of an island forest avifauna by an introduced snake. Ecology 68: 660-668.

Schreiner, I.H. 1997. Demography and recruitment of selected trees in limestone forest of Guam in relation to introduced ungulates. Micronesica 30: 169–181.

Schreiner, I. and D. Nafus. 1991. Survey of the insect pests of *Serianthes nelsonii* in Guam and Rota. University of Guam, Mangilao, GU.
Schreiner, I.H. and D.M. Nafus. 1997. Butterflies of Micronesia. University of Guam, Mangilao, GU.

Seminoff, J.A. 2004. MSTG global assessment of green turtles. IUCN Marine Turtle Specialist Group Review.

Solomon, S., D., Qin, M. Manning, Z. Chen, M. Marquis, K.B. Averyt, M. Tignor and H.L. Miller (editors). 2007. Climate change 2007: The physical science basis. Contribution of working group I to the fourth assessment report of the intergovernmental panel on climate change. Fourth assessment report of the intergovernmental panel on climate change. Cambridge University Press: Cambridge, UK.

Stephens, Sonia. 2007. Pacific island network vital signs monitoring plan, Appendix E: tropical working group report – freshwater biology. National Park Service, US Department of Interior. [online] http://science.nature.nps.gov/im/units/pacn/monitoring/plan/PACN_MP_ AppendixE_FreshwaterBio.pdf.

Stinson, D.W. 1994. Birds and mammals recorded from the Mariana Islands. Natural History Research Special Issue 1: 333-344.

Stojkovich, J.O. 1977. Survey and species inventory of representative pristine marine communities on Guam. University of Guam Marine Laboratory Technical Report No. 40. Sea Grant Publication UGSG-77-12: 1-183.

Stone, B. C. 1970. The flora of Guam. Micronesica 6: 1-659.

Stophlet, J.J. 1946. Birds of Guam. Auk 63: 534-540.

SWCA and Tom Nance Water Resource Engineering. 2007. Proposed Supplemental Water Supply for the Fena Reservoir System, Naval Magazine, Guam. Prepared for SAIC, Fort Monmouth and US Navy Region Marianas.

Taboroši D. 2004. Field guide to caves and karst of Guam. Bess Press, Honolulu, HI.

Takano, L.L. and S.M. Haig. 2004a. Distribution and abundance of the Mariana subspecies of the Common Moorhen. Waterbirds 27: 245-250.

Takano, L.L. and S.M. Haig. 2004b. Seasonal movement and home range of the Mariana Common Moorhen. The Condor 106: 652-663.

Torikai, J.D. 1997. Rainfall, ground-water, and ocean tide data, Guam, 1996. U.S. Geological Survey Open File Report No. 97-239.

Tracey, J.I., S.O. Schlanger, J.T. Stark, D.B. Doan, and H.G. May. 1964. General geology of Guam. U.S. Geological Survey Professional Paper 403-A.

Tubb, J.A. 1966. Notes on birds of Guam. The Natural History Bulletin of the Siam Society 21: 135-138.

Unipingo 2005. All of the listed information is available at the following Guam Portal website: http://www.guamportal.com/guam_attractions.html

USAF (United States Department of the Air Force). 2006. Final environmental impact statement; establishment and operation of an intelligence, surveillance, reconnaissance, and strike capability, Andersen Air Force Base, Guam. Department of the Air Force, Pacific Air Forces, Hickam Air Force Base, HI.

U.S. Congress. 2006. H. Con. Res. 398. Washington, D.C.

U.S. Department of the Interior. 2001. Secretarial Order No. 3226. Washington, D.C.

USEPA (U.S. Environmental Protection Agency). 2000. Endangered and threatened wildlife and plants; proposed endangered status for three plants from the Mariana islands and Guam. Federal Register 65, No 106.

U.S. Fish and Wildlife Service. 1982. Refuge Manual. Washington, D.C.

USFWS (U.S. Fish and Wildlife Service). 1984. Endangered and threatened wildlife and plants: determination of endangered status for seven birds and two bats on Guam and the Northern Mariana Islands. 50 CFR Part 17. Federal Register 49:33,881–33,885.

USFWS (U.S. Fish and Wildlife Service). 1990a. Guam Mariana fruit bat and little Mariana fruit bat recovery plan. Portland, OR.

USFWS (U.S. Fish and Wildlife Service). 1991a. Recovery Plan for the Mariana Common Moorhen (Gallinule), *Gallinula chloropus guami*. U.S. Fish and Wildlife Service, Portland, OR.

USFWS (U.S. Fish and Wildlife Service). 1991b. Recovery Plan for the Mariana Islands population of the Vanikoro Swiftlet, *Aerodramus vanikorensis bartschi*. U.S. Fish and Wildlife Service, Portland, Oregon.

USFWS (U.S. Fish and Wildlife Service). 1990b. Native forest birds of Guam and Rota, Commonwealth of the Northern Mariana Islands Recovery Plan. U.S. Fish and Wildlife Service, Portland, OR.

USFWS (U.S. Fish and Wildlife Service). 1992. Draft environmental assessment, proposed Guam National Wildlife Refuge, Territory of Guam. Region 1, Portland, OR.

USFWS (U.S. Fish and Wildlife Service). 1993. Final environmental assessment for the proposed Guam National Wildlife Refuge, Territory of Guam. Region 1, Portland, OR.

USFWS (U.S. Fish and Wildlife Service). 1994a. Wildland fire management plan. Guam National Wildlife Refuge. Dededo, GU.

USFWS (U.S. Fish and Wildlife Service). 1994b. Recovery plan for *Serianthes nelsonii.* Region 1, Portland, OR

USFWS (U.S. Fish and Wildlife Service). 1994c. Draft environmental assessment for the proposed Ritidian Point Territorial Park, Territory of Guam. Region 1, Portland, OR.

USFWS (U.S. Fish and Wildlife Service). 1998a. Recovery Plan for the Micronesian Megapode (*Megapodius laperouse laperouse*). U.S. Fish and Wildlife Service, Portland, OR.
USFWS (U.S. Fish and Wildlife Service). 1998b Recovery Plan for the Nightingale Reed-warbler, *Acrocephalus luscinia.* Portland, OR.

USFWS (U.S. Fish and Wildlife Service) and U.S. Air Force. 2001. Draft integrated natural resources management plan for Andersen Air Force Base, Guam, Mariana Islands. Volume I. Prepared for 36 CEV Environmental Office, Andersen Air Force Base, GU.

USFWS (U.S. Fish and Wildlife Service). 2004. Draft Revised Recovery Plan for the Sihek or Guam Micronesian Kingfisher (*Halcyon cinnamomina cinnamomina*). Portland, OR.

USFWS (U.S. Fish and Wildlife Service). 2005a. Washington slands National Wildlife Refuges. Draft comprehensive conservation plan and environmental Assessment. WA.

USFWS (U.S. Fish and Wildlife Service). 2005b. Draft Revised Recovery Plan for the Aga or Mariana Crow, *Corvus kubaryi.* Portland, OR.

USFWS (U.S. Fish and Wildlife Service). 2005c. Endangered and threatened wildlife and plants; Mariana Fruit Bat (*Pteropus mariannus mariannus*): reclassification from endangered to threatened in the Territory of Guam and listing as threatened in the Commonwealth of the Northern Mariana Islands. 50 CFR Part 17. Federal Register 70: 1,190-1,210.

USFWS (U.S. Fish and Wildlife Service). 2005d. Pacific Islands (excluding Hawaii) plants and animals: Updated August 29, 2005 Listed, Proposed or Candidate species, as designated under the U.S. Endangered Species Act. [online]
http://www.fws.gov/pacificislands/wesa/pacificislandslisting.pdf.

USFWS (U.S. Fish and Wildlife Service). 2006. Draft Recovery Plan for Nosa Luta or Rota Bridled White-eye (*Zosterops rotensis*). Portland, OR.

USFWS (U.S. Fish and Wildlife Service). 2007a. Guam NWR planning update 1, July 2007. Portland, OR.

USFWS (U.S. Fish and Wildlife Service). 2007b. Threatened and endangered species of the Hawaiian and Pacific islands: Green Sea Turtle *Chelonia mydas*. [online] http://www.fws.gov/pacificislands/wesa/grnturtindex.html).

USFWS (U.S. Fish and Wildlife Service). 2007c. Threatened and endangered species of the Hawaiian and Pacific islands: Hawksbill Sea Turtle *Eretmochelys imbricate*. [online] http://www.fws.gov/pacificislands/wesa/hawksturtindex.html).

USFWS (U.S. Fish and Wildlife Service). 2007d. Guam National Wildlife Refuge Scoping Report CCP/EA, Guam.

Van Beukering P., W. Haider, M. Longland, H. Cesar, J. Sablan, S. Shjegstad, B. Beardmore, Y. Liu, and G.O. Garces. 2007. The economic value of guam's coral reefs. University of Guam Marine Laboratory Technical Report No. 116.

Vitousek, Peter M. 1994. Beyond Global Warming: Ecology and Global Change. Ecology 75(7):1861–1876.

Vogt, S. R. and L. L. Williams. 2004. Common flora and fauna of the Mariana Islands. Published by Laura L. Williams and Scott R. Vogt, Saipan, CNMI.

Walther G.R., E. Post, P. Convey P, A. Menzel, C. Parmesank, T.J.C. Beebee, J. Fromentin, O. Hoegh-GuldbergI, and F. Bairlein. 2002. Ecological responses to recent climate change. Nature 416: 389–395.

Wanless, R.M., A. Angel, R.J. Cuthbert, G.M. Hilton, P.G. Ryan. 2007. Can predation by invasive mice drive seabird extinctions? Biology Letters 3: 241-244.

Ward, R.A. 1984. Mosquito fauna of Guam: case history of an introduced fauna. Pages 143–162 *in* Laird M, (editor). Commerce and the spread of pests and disease vectors. Praeger, NY.

Watson, R.J. 1946. Bird notes from Guam. The Raven 17: 40-42.

Wetterer, J. K. 2007. Biology and impacts of Pacific islands invasive species. 3. The African big-headed ant, *Pheidole megacephala* (Hymenoptera: Formicidae). Pacific Science 61: 437-456.

Wheeler, M.E. 1979. The biology of the Guam deer. Technical Report 3, Division of Aquatic and Wildlife Resources, Mangilao, GU.

Wiles, G.J. 1987. The status of fruit bats on Guam. Pacific Science 41: 148-157.

Wiles, G. J. 1998a. Current status, distribution, and natural history of Mariana Fruit Bats. Job Progress Report (1 October 1997 to 30 September 1998). Division of Aquatic and Wildlife Resources, Manigalo, GU.

Wiles, G.J. 1998b. Records of communal roosting in Mariana Crows. Wilson Bulletin 110: 126-128.

Wiles, G. J. 1999. Current status, distribution, and natural history of Mariana Fruit Bats. Job Progress Report (1 October 1998 to 30 September 1999). Division of Aquatic and Wildlife Resources, Manigalo, GU.

Wiles, G.J. 2005. A checklist of the birds and mammals of Micronesia. Micronesica 38: 141-189.

Wiles, G. J., C. F. Aguon, G. W. Davis, and D. J. Grout. 1995. The status and distribution of endangered animals and plants in northern Guam. Micronesica 28: 31-49.

Wiles, G.J., J. Bart, R.E. Beck, Jr., C.F. Aguon. 2003. Impacts of the Brown Tree Snake: Patterns of decline and species persistence in Guam's avifauna. Conservation Biology 17: 1350-1360.

Wiles, G.J., D.W., Buden, and D.J. Worthington, 1999. History of introduction, population status, and management of Philippine deer (*Cervus mariannus*) on Micronesian Islands. Mammalia 63: 193-215.

Wiles, G. J., T.O. Lemke, and N.H. Payne. 1989. Population estimates of fruit bats (*Pteropus mariannus*) in the Mariana Islands. Conservation Biology 3: 66-76.

Wiles, G. J., G. H. Rodda, R. H. Fritts, and E. M. Taisacan. 1990. Abundance and habitat use of reptiles on Rota, Mariana Islands. Micronesica 23:153–166.

Wiles, G.J., I.H. Schreiner, D. Nafus, L.K. Jurgensen, and J.C. Manglona. 1996. The status, biology, and conservation of *Serianthes nelsonii* (Fabaceae), an endangered Micronesian tree. Biological Conservation 76: 229-239.

Wiles, G. J. and D. H. Woodside. 1999. History and population status of Guam Swiftlets on Oʻahu, Hawaiʻi. ʻElepaio 59:57–61.

Wiles, G.J. and D.J. Worthington. 2002. A population assessment of Pacific Sheath-tailed Bats (*Emballonura semicaudata*) on Aguiguan, Mariana Islands. U.S. Fish and Wildlife Service Reprot, HI.

Witzell, W.N. 1983. Synopsis of biological data on the hawksbill turtle *Eretmochelys imbricata* (Linnaeus, 1766). FAO Fisheries Synopsis No 137.

Wolanski, E., R.H. Richmond, G. Davis, E. Deleersnijder, and R.R. Leben. 2003. Eddies around Guam, an island in the Mariana Islands group. Australian Institute of Marine Science. [online] http://www.aims.gov.au/ibm/pages/news/eddies-around-guam.html.

WPRFMC (Western Pacific Regional Fishery Management Council). 2005. Fishery Ecosystem Plan for the Marianas Archipelago. Honolulu, HI.

Writing Refuge Management Goals and Objectives (USFWS 20XX), Preplanning Guidance for Comprehensive Conservation Plans: A Handbook (USFWS 2006), and Identifying Refuge Resources of Concern and Management Priorities: A Handbook (USFWS 2007).

Young, F.J. 1988. Soil survey of Territory of Guam. U.S. Department of Agriculture, Soil Conservation Service.